UNSETTLED LABORS

RACHEL H. BROWN

Unsettled Labors

Migrant Care Work in Palestine/Israel

DUKE UNIVERSITY PRESS
Durham and London
2024

Project Editor: Michael Trudeau
Designed by A. Mattson Gallagher
Typeset in Untitled Serif by Westchester Publishing Services

Library of Congress Cataloging-in-Publication Data
Names: Brown, Rachel H., [date], author.
Title: Unsettled labors : migrant care work in Palestine/Israel /
Rachel H. Brown.
Description: Durham : Duke University Press, 2024. | Includes
bibliographical references and index.
Identifiers: LCCN 2023046387 (print)
LCCN 2023046388 (ebook)
ISBN 9781478030591 (paperback)
ISBN 9781478026358 (hardcover)
ISBN 9781478059585 (ebook)
Subjects: LCSH: Older people—Home care—Israel. | Live-in
household employees—Israel. | Caregivers—Israel. | Palestinian
Arabs—Employment—Israel. | Foreign workers—Legal status,
laws, etc.—Israel. | Settler colonialism—Israel. | Palestine—
Colonization. | Israel—Ethnic relations. | BISAC: SOCIAL
SCIENCE / Ethnic Studies / Middle Eastern Studies | POLITICAL
SCIENCE / History & Theory
Classification: LCC HV1484.I82 B77 2024 (print) | LCC HV1484.I82
(ebook) | DDC 362.61/2095694—DC23/ENG/20240412
LC record available at https://lccn.loc.gov/2023046387
LC ebook record available at https://lccn.loc.gov/2023046388

CONTENTS

ACKNOWLEDGMENTS

Since this book went into production, the Israeli government has been committing genocide in Gaza with the backing of the United States. The American liberal news media would seem to suggest that Israel's latest bombardment began after October 7, 2023, following Hamas's killing of 1,200 Jewish Israelis. But as countless Palestinians, anti-Zionist Jews, and the majority of the international community have long maintained, the latest assault on Gaza is part of a long history of settler colonial violence preceding and leading up to Israeli statehood. This "founding" Israeli moment (also known as the Nakba, or "catastrophe," to indigenous Palestinians) led to the expulsion and forced flight of 750,000 Palestinians, land theft, massacre, and—in tried-and-true settler colonial fashion—the designation of Palestinians as "infiltrators" on their own land. Since October 2023, Israel has killed over 35,000 Gazans. It has starved Palestinians, denying them access to humanitarian aid, and has targeted hospitals, health-care workers, universities, schools, churches, mosques, journalists, and residential neighborhoods. I hope that when this book is read, there is a ceasefire and a reckoning with the long history of Israeli settler colonial violence in all its forms.

I am first and foremost indebted to the many people who worked or are still working as caregivers and community organizers who spoke with and invited me into their community spaces. I am grateful for their time and generosity.

I could not have started this project without the guidance and support of my mentors at the CUNY Graduate Center. Rosalind Petchesky has, from the beginning, encouraged me to pursue this research and write this book. Her friendship, mentorship, and example have deeply shaped who I wish to be as a person and scholar. Carol Gould has been incredibly generous throughout and beyond graduate school, and my interest in many of the topics the book covers began in her class. Joe Rollins encouraged me to tell the less told stories and to trust my analytic instinct. Susan Buck-Morss helped me develop ideas that are central to the project and think about issues of labor and solidarity in a broader context. Linda Alcoff listened as I talked through ideas about resistance and the state and provided tremendous encouragement in each of our conversations. While at CUNY, I was fortunate to have received awards that helped fund my research and writing time: the Braham Dissertation Fellowship, Enhanced Chancellor's Fellowship, Women's Studies Certificate Program Koonja Mitchell Award, and the Advanced Research Collaborative Fellowship.

I would have finished neither graduate school nor this book without my CUNY comrades. At the time, I somehow took for granted that having friends, political allies, cothinkers baked into one's everyday life was completely normal, and as time has passed, I realize how special having them in my everyday life was and is. John McMahon, Amy Schiller, Emily Crandall, Sumru Atuk, B Lee Altman, Jon Keller, Joanna Tice, Erika Iverson, Julie Hollar, Elena Cohen, and Abigail Kolker were central to this experience. A special thank you to both Johns for helping me land on my feet. And a big shout-out goes to the *Always Already Podcast* crew's James Padilioni. The *AAP* crew has been a source of fun and excitement over the last six years that keeps me going.

I am incredibly lucky to have such supportive colleagues in the Women, Gender, and Sexuality Studies Program (WGSS) at Washington University in Saint Louis. Rebecca Wanzo has been a wonderful chair and mentor, talking me through multiple revisions and the publication process. I am indebted to my department colleagues for their encouragement and feedback, including Mary Ann Dzuback, Andrea Friedman, Shefali Chandra, Marlon Bailey, Barbara Baumgartner, Heather Berg, René Esparza, Trevor Sangrey, Cynthia Barounis, Amy Cislo, Ivan Bujan, Bahia Munem, Amber Musser, Jeffrey McCune, Linda Nicholson, Allison Reed, Tamsin Kimoto, Donna Kepley, and Crystal Odelle.

Outside of WGSS, Clarissa Hayward has been a truly wonderful mentor, generously helping me navigate the publishing world and the profession. I am deeply grateful for others at Washu who have encouraged me with their feedback and general presence as I shepherded the book along; in particular, Fannie Bialek, Dana Lloyd, Jennifer Hudson, Anika Walke, and Eman Ghanayem. I was lucky to have received a First Book Fellowship from the Center for the Humanities, where, through my book manuscript workshop, I received invaluable feedback from Jasbir Puar and Rhacel Salazar Parreñas. Their comments and suggestions shaped the book as it is today. Feedback from Adrienne Davis, Ignacio Infante, Christina Ramos, Jessica Rosenfeld, Samantha Pergadia, Dorothy Pokua, and Joy Sales, as well as from my WGSS colleagues, helped tremendously in sharpening my introduction.

Working with Courtney Berger at Duke University Press has been a wonderful experience as a first-time author. I greatly appreciate her patience, kindness, and guidance as I navigate the academic publishing world. I am also grateful to Laura Jaramillo for helping with the review process and to both anonymous reviewers for their constructive, generative, and incisive feedback. Their suggestions have expanded the framing of the book and deepened my analysis. The editorial genius of Megan Milks at Ideas on Fire helped me shape the conceptual arc of my book and sharpen my arguments.

I have also benefitted from the incredible mentorship of Banu Subramaniam through the Five College Women's Studies Research Center Associateship, which provided a space to develop my writing in community. I also thank Suzanna Walters for her support through the Visiting Scholar program in the WGSS Program at Northeastern University. Over the years, I have received beneficial feedback on the project in its various iterations— and on the book-writing process more generally—from conference buddies, workshop coattendees, mentors, visiting speakers, and others I have been lucky enough to meet through our shared work. A special thanks is due to Caryl Nuñez, Ajay Parasram, Ethel Tungohan, Liora Halperin, Jake Beckert, Lori Marso, Frances Hasso, Phyllis Palmer, and Karen Starr.

Getting to spend a summer with the Alternative Information Center in Jerusalem and Beit Sahour fifteen years ago was a huge part of my political education. I am endlessly grateful to Connie Hackbarth for welcoming me into the space, and to Sergio Yani, Shir Hever, and Reuven Abergel for allowing me to learn from their inspirational work.

In Saint Louis, I have been blessed to have the camaraderie, love, and support of friends and community without whom I would neither have emerged from the pandemic nor found the rejuvenating space necessary to finish a book. Much gratitude goes to Tila Neguse, Arif Haque, Sandra Tamari, Steve Tamari, Clara Wilkins, Juan Pablo Argente Rodríguez, James

Meinert, Mary Densmore, Chris Singer, Molly Metzger, Johnny Wu Gabbert, Michael Berg, Heather Berg, Kit Smemo, Mykael Ornbaun, Kaveh Razani, Vanity Gee, Brett Maricque, Anna Piller, Alix Gerber, Maddie Kronfeld, Sunny Lin, Mamie Noble, Chelsea Viteri, Jim Lochhead, and the inspiring Saint Louis Palestine Solidarity Committee family.

Many other friendships have sustained and inspired me over the last several years of book writing. Diana Sierra Becerra and Kevin Young were hands down the best thing to come of living in Northampton, and their camaraderie is a source of love and joy. Rachel Riskind has been a pillar of support, reality, hilarity, and connection since birth. Getting to navigate the feudal absurdity of academia, the turns and twists of adulthood, and the beauty of writing with Courtney Cook has been a blessing. Nick Micinski and Khameer Kidia have been the most beautiful and fun comrades with whom to be in and think through the world. Verónica Zebadúa-Yáñez has been a supreme comrade and friend over the last several years of wading through the academic world. I remain indebted to the enduring friendships of Danielle Chu, Ricky Perry, Kevin Anderle, Corey Solinger, Ming-Ming Lee, Sheila Desai, David Leskowitz, Emily Luhrs, Jacqui Vainik, Yael Shy, Max Cohen, Tsipe Angelson, Lisa Kronberg, Wendy Kohn, Tiferet Zimmern-Kahan, and Hania Bekdash, who have celebrated and supported me through life's twists and turns.

I would have none of the opportunities afforded to me without my family. My aunts, Ruth Beilin and Bets Brown, have cheered me on across the finish line. My in-laws, Ajay Issar, Shridhar Issar, Vinay Issar, and Shashi Sang, have supported and encouraged me. My mother and father, Elaine Beilin and Bob Brown, and my sister, Hannah Brown, have unconditionally cheered me on, and I am grateful for their presence, love, and curiosity. A special thanks also goes to Aaron, Jacob, and Hugh for their humor and support. Lastly, I could not have completed this book without my partner, Siddhant Issar. He has given extensive feedback on the project over the better part of a decade, helped remind me what the book is about during the lows, taken on the majority of reproductive labor during the final push, and shared humor, love, and support. And boundless gratitude goes to Kavi and Amaya, who bring joy, wisdom, and complete delight to each day.

Introduction

[My employers] keep on asking me, "Are you a nurse?!" And I say, "I don't have to be a nurse! I will be with her twenty-four hours a day, don't you know that?!" I have to be aware what will happen to her, we have to be aware, we want to stay more years! So we have to look after them very good! We have the law here that it's only four years and three months [we can stay], and I'm already here for nine years now.

Alice

Alice, an assistant pharmacist from the Philippines, works as a caregiver outside Afula, a small city in the northern district of Palestine/Israel.[1] Taken from the name for the Palestinian village 'al-Fuleh, Afula was established in 1925 by the American Zion Commonwealth (AMZIC), a land-purchasing colonial corporation committed to Jewish settlement in Palestine.[2] According-ing to the purchasing agreement, indigenous Palestinians were required to buy portions of their own land or leave within four years.[3] Alice cares for and lives around the clock with Sarah, an elderly Jewish Israeli woman living with dementia who is largely immobile and spends most of her day in bed. She describes anticipating Sarah's every need, from the reorienting Sarah requires during hallucinations, to the life-saving medications that sustain her. Like 78 percent of elderly Jewish Israelis, Sarah was not born in Palestine/Israel, having left Morocco in the 1950s.[4] Though neither she nor Alice are indigenous, Sarah, as a settler-citizen, is socially constructed as an a priori inheritor of the land, while Alice is associated with foreignness, mobility, and impermanence. While Alice wishes to "stretch" time so she can earn money and be with her boyfriend, she holds neither hopes nor desires for making her relation to the land permanent, a territorial and temporal entitlement reserved for Jews and their descendants.[5]

Despite—and because of—her alienation, Alice knows how to care for Sarah better than anyone in Sarah's home, including Sarah's children and grandchildren. Alice notes her employers' regular surprise at the depth of her medical knowledge and the meticulous care she provides. Proving oneself indispensable to elderly settler-citizens also allows migrant caregivers to strategically ingratiate themselves into employers' families, a burden extending from Israel's strict deportation, migration, and citizenship policies. Scrupulous attention to Alice's employer is also a risk mitigation strategy, helping her minimize financial indebtedness, increase her bargaining power, finance her children's education, and build a second home for her family in Manila. While Alice expresses joy and fulfillment in aspects of her job—she explains, "I'm kind of loving to give my service to people"—she also says that "work is always work," and the job is only as good as the employer.

Alice has been in Palestine/Israel beyond the four years and three months allotted by her visa and must either work without documentation when Sarah dies, or seek a rarely granted "special visa."[6] Under the Israeli Law of Return, which privileges Jewish settlement over the Palestinian right of return, migrant caregivers can only remain inside the state as long as they are working for an elderly or disabled citizen.[7] They cannot enter with immediate family, nor can they marry other migrants, and until it was ruled unconstitutional by the High Court, they could not remain in the country with newborn babies beyond three months.[8] In practice, this pregnancy policy still often holds.[9] Each month after their visa expires, migrant caregivers must pay an increasing percent of their monthly salary to a deposit fund that they cannot collect until they leave the country.[10] As a disincentive for overstaying, after six months, this money disappears.[11] Further, Israel's effective "binding" policy, which ties workers' legal status to their employment, prevents migrant caregivers from switching employers more than twice in two years, even under abusive circumstances.[12] It also restricts employment to the nursing sector and requires that they work exclusively in one of three geographical areas.[13] Were Sarah to become ill or injured during Alice's rest hours or days off, Alice could face accusations of patient neglect, deportation, or job loss. These regulations apply regardless of a caregiver's financial status and whether they have paid off the high-interest loans required to migrate. These constraints permeate Alice's relationship with her employer and inform the many ways she gains control over the work process. They also constitute a form of "settler common sense," taking as given employers' temporal fixity as inheritors of the land, naturalizing migrant caregivers as mobile and transient subjects, and erasing Palestinian dispossession and resistance.[14]

Alice, like many migrant caregivers, is both central to the functioning of Sarah's family and yet continually under their surveillance. She is expected to learn aspects of Jewish Israeli culture and perform familial closeness. Yet, she cares for Sarah from outside the Jewish collectivity. With past employers, Alice faced accusations of violence and theft, and was threatened with calls to immigration police while she was undocumented. The legal topography Alice navigates is bound up with the physical health of Sarah's body. Alice's story invites the question of how multigenerational imaginaries of aging and care are tied to migrant precarity and resistance and to the quotidian normalization of settler emplacement and indigenous dispossession.

This book argues that migrant eldercare is a critical yet overlooked component of the economic, cultural, biological, and discursive reproduction of settler colonialism in Palestine/Israel. It is also a site of labor that at times unsettles the givenness of settler emplacement and the temporal boundaries exclusively positioning Jews as the unquestioned inheritors of the land. The home, as a topography of risk that is contiguous with the nation, is a site where migrant caregivers do the "unsettled labors" of eldercare that render them neither wholly incorporable into the nation nor existentially alienable to the extent that Palestinians are made to be. As I discuss in the following pages, I choose the phrase "unsettled labors" to highlight both my methodological approach—situating migrant eldercare, as one form of reproductive labor, within the larger project of denaturalizing the colonial state—and the liminal positioning of migrant caregivers as workers whose "labour[s] of care" disrupt the constitution of the Jewish Israeli home and nation as the exclusive realm of Jews, even as their labors ensure its reproduction.[15] Through this lens, I suggest how migrant caregivers' various subject positions unfold in relation to indigeneity, the purchasing power of the "citizen-consumer," and the colonial processes of racialization and anti-Blackness.[16] The home, as the locus of eldercare, is more than a site where bosses and workers dialectically emerge. It is also where Jewish Israelis reinforce their own emplacement and disavow collective violence against Palestinians as the condition of possibility for the family and national home.

I treat the home as a topography of risk that is contiguous with and inseparable from the nation. This topography is shaped by Israel's jus sanguinis citizenship regime, demographic preoccupations with maintaining the "Jewish character" of the state, invocation of a perpetual state of emergency, and particular features of neoliberal flexibilization in Palestine/Israel.[17] The concept of a topography departs from the binary notion of a "frontier" where the "domestic" and "foreign" meet, demarcating distinctive sites of indigenous and settler sovereignty. It asks how intimacies attributed to a so-called private sphere are a product of past and ongoing histories of imperialism— whether land dispossession or neoliberal precaritization—that are the conditions of possibility for private property and the family.[18] I center the messy space of simultaneous closeness, criminalization, resistance, and collective care beyond a settler-native binary where migrants negotiate settler colonial capitalism, forging community and creatively improving their working conditions.[19]

Migrant eldercare is not the only form of labor reproducing the home and unsettling a rigid indigenous-settler binary. Indeed, though not the focus of my project, in far smaller numbers migrant caregivers also tend to disabled Israeli citizens, many of whom are not part of the elderly population.[20] Rather, eldercare is a crucial but overlooked site that brings into sharp relief the gendered dynamics of intergenerational care provision under neoliberal capitalism. It is a prism through which the comparative racialization and positioning of settler, migrant, and native populations unfold. As one form of care work, eldercare is a focal part of what I call the coloniality of Israel's reproductive regime, the nexus of policies, laws, and social discourses that materially and discursively reproduce Israeli settler colonialism, even as migrant caregivers resist the worst effects of this regime on a daily basis.[21] Israel's reproductive regime governs not only the differential sustenance of

individuals' daily existence but also the promotion of biological reproduction and the (re)generation of narratives around aging, racial and colonial
longevity, and Jewish national vulnerability. Pronatalist policies for Jewish
Israelis, disinvestment in the Palestinian family, killing of Palestinians by the
Israeli military and West Bank settlers, and regulation of Palestinian sexuality, reproduction, and birth are as much a part of this regime as reproductive labors such as eldercare.[22] As Frances Hasso illustrates, the biopolitical
logic of Israel's regime is an extension of British and Zionist control over
aspects of social reproduction since early Zionist settlement.[23] This logic is
also evident in what Jewish National Fund head Joseph Mahmani called the
"judaization" of the land.[24] In the present, medicalization of child birth,
laws of conversion, policies on migration and the Law of Return, a history
of sterilization of Ethiopian women and placement of Yemenite children in
Ashkenazi homes, statistical counting of Palestinians, demolition of Palestinian homes and farms, mass killing and bombing of Palestinians, and
separation of Palestinian families naturalize the eugenic investment in settler life and the disinvestment in non-Jewish elderly life.[25] Orientalist tropes
representing Israel as a small country besieged by its Arab neighbors depict
Israel as a vulnerable "[family] in arms" facing the permanent and existential threat of annihilation.[26] As I draw out through each chapter, it is within
this regime that I locate the state provisioning of care—and eldercare in
particular, as a form of labor at once conjuring the image of the elderly Jewish Israeli—and the state's rhetorical claims to fragility.[27]

Unsettled Labors

The concept of "unsettled labors" highlights several important aspects of
migrant reproductive work and migrant caregivers' positioning within the
Zionist state.[28] By reproductive labors, I refer not only to care and domestic work but, more capaciously, also to the physical and ideological labor
of making indigenous land into a "familiar" (and familial) national home,
whether through the violent practice of "making the desert bloom" or
through the dissemination of Zionist ideologies to future settler-citizens.[29]
The term "unsettled labors" highlights my methodological approach: drawing on decolonial critiques of the state to situate migrant labor as a matter
of racialization *and* colonization. For decolonial scholars and organizers,
"unsettling" has been described as a praxis whose aim is to unravel the

making of the nation-state and the concomitant calls for indigenous recognition and sovereignty with the goal of giving land back to indigenous communities.[30] Michelle Murphy situates "unsettling" as "not confined to indigenous people, but a project that also responsibilizes settlers to histories, entanglements, and complications that come from the historical and current structural violence of colonialism."[31] The ongoing nature of dispossession and indigenous resistance reminds us that what Kēhaulani Kauanui calls "enduring indigeneity" underwrites labor relations, even where indigeneity may not be directly invoked.[32] As Palestinian scholars and organizers have long shown, framing the occupied West Bank and Gaza Strip as the only sites of occupation normalizes the 1948 boundaries of the state (indeed, as Jamil Hilal argues, the term "Palestinian occupied territories" has come to denote only the West Bank and Gaza).[33] Important critiques have also pointed to the everyday violence of "normalcy" under settler colonialism, the relegation of the violence of expulsion to an Israeli past, and the prevailing assumption that Israel is "the only guard against Palestinian violence."[34] By unsettling migrant care work, I aim to link feminist calls for the valuation of reproductive labor to these broader critiques. I thus deploy the term in reference to both the labors of live-in eldercare done by migrants and their positioning within Palestine/Israel.

Important Israel studies scholarship discusses the racial exclusions and exploitation migrant workers face, but this body of work largely leaves untouched Israel's status as a settler colonial state hinging upon land annexation. Racial exclusions of migrant laborers are not solely aimed at preserving a racially "pure" body politic but rather at doing so to justify territorial control. Migrant care work, like other migrant labors, is "constitutive of the inner logics of settler political economy."[35] In this way, the concept of "unsettling" also destabilizes a rigid settler-native binary that sees migrant populations as exogenous to settler colonial capitalism. (Im)migrants in settler colonies and their respective social positions have variously been conceptualized through the terms "arrivant,"[36] "subordinate settler,"[37] "settlers of color,"[38] "working-class settlers,"[39] and the "refugee settler condition,"[40] as well as part of the condition of "immigrant settlerhood."[41] Like Palestinians, migrant workers are treated as outside of "settler time," from Zionist narratives writing settler-citizens onto the history of the land, to settler claims to modernity situating Israel as a "high-tech," developed, "start-up nation."[42] Yet, unlike Palestinians, they cause settler society demographic anxiety without threatening Israel's founding mythology through claims to territorial belonging. As Sarah Willen powerfully articulates, Palestinians are the "'Real' Others" posing an existential and material threat to Jewish Israeli hegemony, while migrant laborers are the "'Other' Others" who become threatening when they cease to be individual workers and take collective action.[43] Eritrean and Sudanese asylum seekers, in contrast, interrupt Zionist calls for demographic purity through their appeal to permanency on the basis of international human rights law.[44]

The term "unsettled" also resituates labor itself as a capacious set of colonial relations that exceeds the production of commodities and provisioning of services. In the arena of eldercare, the bathing, feeding, dressing, calming, and reorienting of one's employer comprise not only interactions between employer and employee but also affective exchanges where subjects embody and resist racial, gender, and class hierarchies that have been shaped by and through colonial encounters. "Unsettling" as a method also draws aspirational connections between Marxist feminist commitments to denaturalization and demystification (of housework as "not really work," for example) and decolonial approaches, such that "housework" is also seen as a territorial project of accumulation.[45] This dual demystification is especially important in light of political and theoretical discussions about gendered labor and transnational migration in the wake of neoliberal restructuring. Ample literature shows how structural adjustment reforms have led to the outsourcing of reproductive labors, largely, though not exclusively, to women from the Global South. I ask how labors of homemaking (in the house and nation) shed light on the ways that land and labor—as the two constitutive categories framing the settler colonial paradigm—are shaped by gendered and sexual norms and subject positions.[46] Focusing on the "uneven times of neoliberalism" unearths the ambiguities and inconsistencies of settler colonialism as a productive social force and reveals the limitations of a universalizing neoliberal framework that occludes the disparate manifestations of retrenchment, outsourcing, value-creation, and privatization in localized and historical contexts.[47]

"Unsettled labors" also highlights the ways migrant caregivers contest Israel's temporal boundaries by "stretching" the time allotted by their visa. In the Israeli context, legal exclusions are conditioned by Zionist mythology around a Jewish "birthright" to land. This "birthright" is both a territorial and a temporal claim, conjuring a "mythical past and redemptive future" that can only be achieved through a Jewish nation-state.[48] Compared to other migrant-receiving countries, Israel has one of the shortest visa lengths, a policy shaped by the desire to safeguard a Jewish majority as justification for territorial control.[49] In contrast to Palestine/Israel, in the United Arab Emirates (UAE), for example, temporality becomes a technology of state power where "waiting" for a change in legal status is itself a disciplinary tactic.[50] Migrant caregivers' experiences in Palestine/Israel are not as readily captured by the framework of waiting, as they generally do not expect a shift in legal status to begin with.[51] In contrast to Kuwait, where noncitizens outnumber citizens, and where naturalization was once possible, migrant workers form a distinct minority in the Zionist state and have always been temporary.[52] Further, caregivers often understand their own temporal presence as bounded. Even as migrants strategically position themselves as explicitly temporary, they challenge these temporal boundaries on a daily basis, finding creative ways to lengthen their stays through building relationships, choosing employers who are more likely to help them secure visa extensions, and finding ways to collectively protect each other from deportation.[53]

To this end, I also draw on the concept of "unsettling" to highlight the ways migrant care work both reproduces and interrupts the exclusively Jewish constitution of the home and nation. This disruption stems from caregivers' intimate and foreign positioning in the household and nation as non-Jewish others.[54] Migrant caregivers describe relationships of physical closeness, affective distance, assimilation, and alienation unfolding in employment relationships and in Israel more broadly. Their marginalization constitutes a form of unbending alienation and exclusion from citizenship, residency, and the Jewish Israeli family, despite, paradoxically, their centrality to the functioning of the home and the Jewish Israeli popular imagination of aging.[55] Paradoxically, their indispensability to elderly survival—and their very presence as non-Jewish others in the Jewish Israeli home space— interrupts Zionist notions of the home itself as the most important site of Jewish continuity and reproduction, as the anchoring unit of the nation. Against the risks and exclusions they face in the home, caregivers navigate shifting power relations, making the home a place that more readily incorporates their needs.

Finally, "unsettling" highlights how caregivers forge a living and build community beyond a settler-native binary. Because caregivers are unable to write themselves or be written into a Zionist past and future, the state has "denied recognition" of migrant caregivers as "legitimate political actor[s]," making the field of political contestation negligible.[56] The strategies of risk mitigation and resistance caregivers adopt stem, in part, from the fact of this limited political terrain. As Attiya Ahmad shows, temporal bound-edness does not preclude the forging of deep ties and affinities.[57] Despite state efforts to stymie the collective life of non-Jewish migrants, caregiv-ers establish communal spaces of care and mutual aid beyond the nuclear family, unsettling the state's racist instrumentalizing of non-Jewish work-ers. Since arriving in large numbers in the mid-1990s, migrants have built extensive community networks on the basis of religion, cultural affiliation, and hometown region. Caregivers refuse their peripheral positioning, creat-ing belonging through claims to their own Christian faith, love for particular aspects of Jewish Israeli culture, deep attachments to the families for whom they work, or gratitude for Israel's migration regime when compared to par-ticular other countries.[58] For others, conveying "national love" or solidarity with various settler subjectivities allows migrants excluded from the "ideal form" of the nation to contingently "pass into the community," at least on a momentary basis.[59]

Situating Palestine/Israel

The workings of neoliberal capitalism in settler colonial states requires we understand how tactics of managing racial and indigenous difference shift under changing modes of political economy. Homemaking, as a central goal of settler projects, takes on a heightened significance in the Israeli context that is not simply interchangeable with other states that outsource care.[60] This outsourcing is inextricably tied to the historical role reproductive labor has played in constituting colonies, farms, and houses as self-justificatory evidence of land ownership. As a society whose raison d'être is Jewish con-trol over territory, the ideological and material reproduction of the Jewish population is central to the demographic peopling of land as "facts on the ground."[61] Still, Israel's labor outsourcing regime is not wholly exceptional among high-income "migrant-receiving" states, nor among other settler co-lonial states such as Canada, Australia, and the United States. Arguably like all states, Israel produces legal exclusions as a way of fortifying an "imagined community."[62] Denmark, Singapore, Malaysia, the UAE, and Taiwan also require that migrants remain permanently temporary.[63] Singapore and Saudi Arabia place restrictions on migrant pregnancies, and Canada pre-vents migrants from initially migrating with family.[64] Whereas pregnancy is not explicitly prohibited, the sexual rights and health of migrant women are closely monitored in Malaysia, South Korea, Singapore, Taiwan, and Gulf Cooperation Council (GCC) states.[65] As in Israel, these policies serve as a form of discipline stemming from racist fears of migrant sexuality and reproductivity.[66] Similar "binding" policies exist in Taiwan and GCC countries, closely tying workers' employment mobility and residency rights to employment status.[67] The Israeli government, in this respect, is more restrictive than Canada, and less so than the UAE and Singapore, where workers require an employer's permission to switch jobs.[68] As in the UAE, Denmark, Hong Kong, Singapore, and Taiwan, where the right to remain inside the state is linked to employment status, migrant caregivers navigate daily the impacts of debt bondage.[69]

Many countries also bar migrant caregivers from permanent residency while restricting caregivers from leaving employers. While Israel and Taiwan are among the strictest with respect to residency caps, Taiwan's temporal allotment of twelve years is significantly longer than that of Israel.[70] In the Palestinian/Israeli context, the formality of exclusion often demands that non-Jewish workers prove they pose no threat to demographic control over land. As tactics of territorial control, the jus sanguinis nature of citizenship law and demographic management also profoundly impacts reproductive policies for migrant women.[71] Rather than claiming singularity, I am interested in the social meaning of migrant eldercare in Israel as it emerges through Israel's self-fashioning as an exceptional "start-up" nation[72] that commonly styles itself the "only democracy in the Middle East."[73] Not only is Israel the sole settler state in the Middle East region; it also has the highest percentage of elderly receiving long-term care from temporary migrants. This is true even as the proportion of migrants to citizens contrasts with GCC states such as Kuwait and Qatar, where the former significantly outnumber the latter.[74] Among Organisation for Economic Co-operation and Development (OECD) countries, Israel ranks thirtieth out of thirty-five countries for percentage of gross domestic product (GDP) spent on long-term care.[75] A notable 55 percent of long-term care workers are migrants (who, unlike citizens, are required to live with their employers), and at least 30 percent of frail elderly—those over sixty-five with attenuated disabilities—are cared for by migrants, while 41 percent of the general over-sixty-five population are granted permits for migrant caregivers.[76]

In contrast, the majority of elderly in surrounding states are cared for by family in multigenerational households. While surrounding states such as

Lebanon, Jordan, and those of the GCC grant permits to migrants for a range of domestic services, the Israeli state only does so for eldercare and care for the disabled.[77] The percentage of citizens over sixty-five is also significantly higher in Israel at 12.2 percent, a number that is expected to increase, as compared to 5.7 percent regionally.[78] According to the Central Bureau of Statistics, between 2015 and 2035, the percentage of Israeli elderly is expected to increase by 77 percent.[79] By some estimates, there will be one migrant caregiver for every fifth elderly Israeli by 2025.[80] This reality raises crucial questions about why migrant women are allowed into particular facets of Jewish Israeli family life and society but not others, a discussion to which I turn in the subsequent pages.

Israel also holds unique features among settler states. Whereas in civic settler states like the United States and Canada, racial hierarchy belies the formally declared values of equality, in Palestine/Israel, an ethno-racial settler state, not all citizens can be nationals, and exclusionary particularism is overtly expressed in the Declaration of Independence and the Basic Laws that function as Israel's de facto constitution.[81] In the United States and Canada, temporary migrants may tactically appeal to universal liberal tropes characterizing the state as a "nation of immigrants" to advocate for status change or belonging, yet such universalism does not exist in Palestine/Israel, leaving racialized migrant laborers in a distinctive discursive terrain.[82] Over sixty discriminatory laws against Palestinians also profoundly impact social discourses naturalizing and justifying caregivers' right to legal protection and collective identity.[83] At the time of writing, the formal nature of exclusion has most recently been made plain through the 2018 Nation-State Bill defining Israel as the "nation-state of the Jewish People," the ongoing burning of and attacks against Palestinian property and land in the West Bank (most recently in Hawara), and renewed government commitments to ethnic cleansing.[84]

Further, in contrast to settler states who claim their frontiers "closed" under industrial capitalism, Israel treats its "frontier" as "open" for ongoing colonization, and its ambiguous and unresolved borders conjure, as Iyko Day argues, nineteenth-century North American frontier violence.[85] Israel thus offers a glimpse into the ways neoliberal restructuring can itself be a strategy of settler domination and concomitant neoliberal discourses, a mode of settler self-indigenizing.[86] As Andy Clarno and Leila Farsakh have shown, this relationship is particularly evident in the neoliberal period following the Oslo Peace Accords, when heightened securitization and indirect rule over the West Bank created Palestinian reserves of surplus labor.[87] Since this period, increased closures between Israel and the West Bank, the outsourcing of jobs in West Bank industries, and the influx of migrant workers from Southeast Asia and Eastern Europe have complicated continual reliance on West Bank Palestinian laborers.[88]

Discourses denying Palestinian indigeneity and depicting Palestinians as "infiltrators" also place pressure on non-Jewish temporary migrants to express loyalty to the Zionist project.[89] Zionist anxieties around the loss of a Jewish majority due to the presence of "foreign" workers is heightened by exiled Palestinians' claim to a right of return.[90] As Evyn Lê Espiritu Gandhi shows, these exclusions position Ashkenazi Jews as refugees par excellence deserving of protection.[91] The language of permanent crisis also generates a "temporal frame of emergency" constructing those who oppose aspects of Israeli security policy or Zionist ideology as moral threats to the survival of the Jewish people.[92] This legal exceptionalism manifests in Israel's declared immunity from international law, customs, and covenants that migrant caregivers could otherwise leverage, under the premise that Israel is bound to the Law of Armed Conflict rather than international human rights law.[93] The invocation of a state of exception also enables Israel to evade ratification of other covenants with relevance to migrant caregivers, such as the Convention on the Elimination of All Forms of Discrimination against Women (CEDAW) and the International Labour Organization (ILO) Convention 189. Historically, the government has rejected annual recommendations by the CEDAW Committee to protect Palestinian women in the West Bank and Gaza and to implement General Recommendation 26 on Women Migrant Workers.[94]

As a result, migrants have fewer channels for the effective invocation of human rights norms, and workers must carefully choose when and how to negotiate for their rights. While some caregivers suggest that they actively avoid politics, others spend their rest days learning Israeli labor and migration law, studying Hebrew so they can better understand what their employers say about them, and attending "Know Your Rights" workshops. Some leverage law through direct conversations with employers, while others strategically create relationships of indispensability that mitigate against poor labor protections. In different ways, Israel's logic of emergency thus renders Palestinians, migrant caregivers, and asylum seekers outside the ambit of the law where legal protection is concerned but well within the law when securitization is desired.[95]

In what follows, I detail the framework through which I understand eldercare within a broader discussion about land and labor. I then provide background on Israeli neoliberal restructuring and the transnational organization of migration facilitating this restructuring. Finally, I turn to the methodology and layout of the book.

Eldercare as Reproductive Labor

Reproduction of the Jewish Israeli home-as-nation hinges on the labor of ensuring intergenerational futurity. From a Marxist feminist perspective, central to this project is the reproductive labor of caring for children (future workers), current workers, the elderly (former workers), and the disabled. Unlike childcare, the "product" of eldercare is not future workers who generate wealth for the family or future soldiers who will defend the nation. Eldercare is nevertheless a site of labor extraction while also producing cultural and ethical scripts about the nation's orientation toward some of its vulnerable citizens. The elderly must be kept alive and their (consumptive, emotional, and cognitive) needs met, not because of their earning potential or their military capacities but because of their social value as members of families and societies.[96] For Marx, reproduction is as much about meeting the consumptive needs of the working class as a totality as it is individual workers.[97] Expanding this analysis, migrant eldercare is part of the reproduction of settler capitalist society as a social whole, both because it frees Jewish Israelis—typically women—to join the labor force and take care of working adults and future workers, *and* because it gives capacity to those filling other ideological roles, whether cooking family recipes, hosting Shabbat meals and holidays, ensuring the continuity of religious observance, or tending to children coming home from army duty on the weekends.

Physically and symbolically, migrant eldercare is central to the survival and protection of what is often referred to as Israel's "founding generation"—those citizens who were present during or fought for Israeli statehood, or those who are Holocaust survivors.[98] Significantly, of the thirty-eight thousand elderly Jewish Israelis employing migrant caregivers, more than half are Holocaust survivors.[99] Founding generation narratives around statehood, the Holocaust, and anti-Semitism are lynchpins in Israel's justification for its raison d'être. As a "remembering collective," elderly survivors are central to maintaining an ethos of shared experience through which the establishment of an exclusionary Jewish state in Palestine became a way of "giv(ing) the survivors a voice" and "redeeming [victims'] death."[100] The reproduction of Israeli settler society as a social class depends upon the twin metaphors of the youthful "new Jew"—tellingly named the *sabra*, or strong, masculine Jewish Israeli—and the comparatively "weak" victim of diasporic anti-Semitism, as captured by the image of the elderly Holocaust survivor. The elderly thus need migrant caregivers to sustain their relationship to the nation as heroic and vulnerable victims that keep the Holocaust and the "founding" of Israel alive while becoming symbolic proxies for the vulnerability of the collective Jewish Israeli body.[101]

Beyond the symbolic significance of the "founding generation," the labor of eldercare is also distinctive from childcare due to the importance of matrilineal descent and its politicization in Israel. Since 1949, childcare done by Jewish Israeli "heroine mother[s]" has been thought to culturally and ideologically fortify a Jewish future, while biologically ensuring racial continuity and purity. As demographic bearers of the nation, mothers reinforce the religious emphasis on the need to be "fruitful and multiply."[102] Through pronatalist policies and state rewards for mothering, this cultural and religious imperative morphs into a political one, making the Jewish Israeli home the site of Zionist ideological and Jewish biological continuance. In contrast to the labors of childcare, eldercare requires neither that the caregiver pass down matrilineal identity, nor that they teach Jewish practices, rituals, and Zionist beliefs.

Finally, eldercare is part and parcel of Israel's broader demographic concern with promoting the health and growth of a Jewish majority as self-justification for continued land colonization and a perceived strengthening of the collective body through the early Zionist commitment to scientific and racial "improvement."[103] This demographic reality is bolstered by a burgeoning "Longevity Industry," a nexus of technological, biomedical, corporate, and state entities committed to positioning Israel as a leader in increasing the lifespan of Israel's aging population and in biotechnological innovation more broadly.[104]

To preserve the language used by workers themselves, I use the term "caregiver" when referring to migrants doing live-in eldercare while drawing out the affective valences of eldercare as a specific kind of care work. I treat care as a labor, a relation, a process, and a discourse, and I draw at different points on the terms "eldercare" and "care work." At times, I use the latter term to adopt the language workers use in their own stories, while at other moments, I draw on the former to emphasize the specific labors of tending to the elderly. While I take "care work" to include a multitude of tasks limited neither to eldercare nor to labors taking place inside the home, in my discussions of post-1990 migrant labor, I use the term to denote tasks such as taking charges to doctors' appointments and adult daycare, giving massages, shopping, bathing and dressing charges, navigating hospital and insurance systems, working with charges on cognitive skills, providing emotional support and companionship, helping charges integrate into their own families as their conditions worsen, acting as death doulas, and arranging for peaceful transitions in charges' final days. Migrant caregivers' labors also include the often extracontractual, socially stigmatized "dirty work" of household maintenance, such as cooking, laundry, cleaning excrement, and washing dishes.[105] In these ways, care work is also a form of affective labor, in its connotation both as a labor producing a service rather than a product and as a job requiring workers to convey particular emotional orientations.[106] For Alice, the nexus of migration and employment laws restricting worker mobility demand that she exert herself around the clock, helping her employer walk, shower, use the bathroom, sleep, eat, and relax. Caregivers must often lift the elderly without assistance several times a day, an activity that has caused injury and chronic pain for many.[107] The scrupulous labor Alice provides is as much out of love as it is because she "want[s] to stay more years," a possibility wrapped up in Sarah's bodily integrity.

Thus, for Alice and others, care is "more than a feeling"; it is a set of labors aimed at preserving elderly life.[108] Treating care as a necessarily positive or "innocent" virtue among interdependent individuals, as care ethicists such as Sara Ruddick and Virginia Held do, elides the structural conditions forcing economic and legal dependency through processes of colonialism, imperialism, and nation-building while overlooking the rootedness of care in labor relations.[109] Deracinated from political economy and race, contemporary divisions of reproductive labor become dehistoricized and naturalized. As Black feminist theorists and scholars of race and capitalism have shown, the exploitation and expropriation of Black women's reproductive and productive labors generates economic and symbolic value, reproducing capital for ongoing projects of displacement, dispossession, and extralegal violence.[110] In the settler context of the United States, Black women's labor not only underpinned the wealth of enslavers and the industrial economy but, postemancipation, divisions of labor have manifested in racial exploitation in the domestic work sector.[111] While not suggesting historical uniformity, I draw from this methodological approach to reproductive labor—and from theories of intersectionality (in addition to their longer genealogies)—to situate eldercare, as one form of reproductive labor, within the historical trajectory of settler colonialism, capital accumulation, and racialization.[112] Such an approach invites us to consider care as an effect of imperial intervention and contemporary circuits of capital and as an undergirding resource in the "intersectionality of struggles" against late capitalism across colonial contexts.[113]

Beyond its capture by the state, care can also be a mode of surviving and building alternatives to settler colonial capitalism, even as the state and employers alike may "instrumentalize empathy and care to their own ends."[114] The lives of migrant workers in Palestine/Israel beyond a settler-native binary is marked by what Evyn Lê Espiritu Gandhi calls "archipelagos" of solidarity.[115] Black feminist approaches to care emphasize community, self-care, and "love-politics" as crucial to resisting the exploitation of Black women in the face of capitalism and state violence and to "producing new forms of political communities."[116] As anticolonial, queer of color, and disability justice traditions have long theorized, care is a labor and resource required for community survival and thriving against the forces of white supremacy, slavery, colonialism, ableism, and patriarchy. Among these traditions, Leah Lakshmi Piepzna-Samarasinha, Uma Narayan, Shatema Threadcraft, Kim TallBear, and others have suggested how care can be a site of paternalism and violence *and* a form of, in the oft-quoted words of Audre Lorde, "self-preservation" and "political warfare."[117] Depictions of caregivers as agentless victims without their own supportive networks and modes of surviving the state overlook the multiple reasons for migration, workers' navigation of asymmetrical employment relationships, the strategic use of familial tropes to increase bargaining power or find meaning in work, and the close bonds caregivers form with charges.[118] Care is also not only a resource transferred by a biological caretaker in one country to a dependent in someone else's nuclear family.[119] Though caregivers navigate the pain of family separation, they find inventive ways to balance their duties to family members, friends, and transnational communities, providing for biological family and kinship networks and redefining the meaning of partnership, parenthood, and friendship.[120] Care is laborious and political, used to manage and engineer demographic projects and build resistant networks of solidarity that refuse the strictures of the state.

Centering the messier politics of care is not to deny the complex and contradictory relationships between migrant caregivers and their employers, nor to minimize elderly vulnerability. Alice's relationship with Sarah is one of immense contradictions, involving closeness, trust, strain, isolation, and exploitation. Alice cares deeply for Sarah, whom she calls *eema*, the Hebrew word for mother, and says she enjoys "showing [her] what love is" and "feel[ing] the love" when Sarah expresses gratitude. She explains, "Of course we are here for the money, but for me it's also the service that we're willing to give." The complexity Alice describes necessitates attention to what Joan Tronto calls the "injustice justified by care" as well as to the potentialities in creating alternatives to these injustices through collective care.[121]

Land, Reproductive Labor, and Neoliberal Restructuring

My argument that migrant care work—and eldercare in particular—is an overlooked site of settler colonial reproduction hinges on the situatedness of this work within Israel's reproductive regime. The biopolitical investment in settler life and disinvestment in all other life occurs through the uneven distribution of health, social, and economic resources, each of which is necessary for the social reproduction of communities and families.[122] Under neoliberal restructuring, non-Jewish migrant labor "triangulates" the differential investment in indigenous and settler populations as the state manages the dual need for cheap labor and territorial control.[123] Like other reproductive labors before it, migrant eldercare is one aspect of what Glen Coulthard terms "colonial-capital accumulation." Building on Marx's notion of "primitive accumulation"—the violent process of labor exploitation and land expropriation required to jumpstart capitalism—Coulthard argues that native dispossession is a far more central driving force of settler colonial capitalism than orthodox Marxist analyses allow.[124] Erecting homes, neighborhoods, settlements, and communities through reproductive labor has in the past and present been central to the creation of the familial and national home as an "object of material reconfiguration."[125] Despite the ubiquitous figure in Zionist mythology of the pioneering Ashkenazi mother tilling soil, under British and Zionist control, reproductive labors done by Mizrahi Jewish and Palestinian women, the latter of whom also faced dispossession, were necessary to the maintenance of Zionist settlements.[126] In the early years of colonization, Palestinians were both employed as a source of less costly labor and later excluded from labor markets under the "conquest of labor" period where *avoda ivrit*, or "Hebrew labor," was exclusively employed as a way of ensuring access to land and reserving better jobs for Ashkenazi Jews.

The Zionist imperative to "people" the land by creating literal homes in Palestine is thus an explicitly gendered one intertwined with control of reproductive labor markets.[127] Precisely because the Zionist project has not uniformly relied on indigenous Palestinians as a source of exploitable labor across settlement waves and labor sectors, the "settler colonial mode of production," as Day suggests, relies on racialized "alien labor" that takes place on land belonging to native populations.[128] Exemplifying this reality in the neoliberal era, in 1993 Israeli prime minister Yitzhak Rabin noted that the government "[needed] to bring thousands of foreign workers to reduce the number of Palestinians walking around in our streets."[129] The state thus granted the first visas to workers from Thailand, Romania, Bulgaria, and China to fill in temporary labor gaps in the construction industry.[130] Rabin's comment suggests how methods for maintaining territorial control and repressing resistance shift in response to changing political-economic commitments. In the period of the early 1990s following the Oslo Peace Accords—a time wherein austerity measures were already underway—the state promoted a policy of separation between Israelis and Palestinians in the West Bank and Gaza, increasing the number of checkpoints and work permits required to enter Israel. This shift created a series of "disconnected Palestinian population reserves,"[131] generating a "surplus population" of "redundant" Palestinian workers that the state hoped to "contain" through the military and administrative division of the West Bank.[132] More broadly, under neoliberal restructuring, the processes of protecting a Jewish majority and controlling land have taken the form of targeted austerity and disinvestment in non-Jewish life through privatization; the "bantustanisation" of the West Bank; increased surveillance; deregulation of the nursing, agriculture, and construction sectors; and an impressive rise in inequality and reduced public expenditure.[133]

Thus, neoliberal restructuring in Palestine/Israel was shaped not only by a global turn to economic liberalization but also by the colonial imperative to create a system of "enclosure and indirect rule" to maintain territorial control.[134] While Israeli austerity measures are not new to late capitalism—indeed, they have guided policy throughout British Mandate and Zionist periods—since the 1990s, they involve new global populations that are accompanied by the circulation of updated discourses exceptional-izing Israel as a site of modernity.[135] Importantly, I do not make a simplis-tic causal claim about Palestinian securitization, the decrease in reliance on Palestinian labor, and the presence of migrant caregivers. As Farsakh shows, the entrance of migrant laborers into the Israeli economy did not neatly or uniformly decrease the demand for Palestinian workers.[136] In-deed, the first time non-Jewish temporary migrants were granted visas for caregiving followed the passage of the Long-Term Care Insurance Program (LTCIP) in 1988. Instead of implying linear causation, this post-Oslo shift to migrant labor signifies a "conjuncture," what Stuart Hall describes as "a period when different social, political, economic and ideological contradic-tions that are at work in society and have given it a specific and distinctive shape come together, producing a crisis of some kind."[137] The presence of migrant caregivers, then, emerges at a conjuncture where neoliberal capital-ism and settler colonialism meet—a coming together of austerity policies, economic liberalization, discursive shifts toward the "modern" and finan-cially healthy Jewish Israeli family, and the ongoing demographic demands of an occupying state attempting to justify its control over a sovereign people who continually resist. Chief among the contradictions of this conjuncture is that the Zionist insistence on Jewish demographic supremacy requires for its maintenance the presence and reproductive labors of non-Jews. A nexus of labor, citizenship, and migration laws and policies thus creates a "vulner-able labor force" that meets the need of Israel's eldercare crisis alongside the reality of an exploding elderly population, all the while not altering Jewish control over territory.[138]

Symbolically, the image of the migrant caregiver embedded within the Jewish Israeli nuclear family represents the economic liberalization of Israel and its shift from an upper-middle to a high-income country characterized by privatization and flexibilization. Migrant caregivers signify Israeli "set-tler modernity" and a "Global North" cosmopolitanism.[139] Indeed, some have called the presence of migrant caregivers a "luxury" service, as the number of permits issued to workers in some years exceeds the growth in the aging population. That is, the relative affordability of hiring migrant caregivers allows citizens to employ them in excess of the formal number of elderly qualifying for the in-home care benefit based on need.[140] The avail-ability of permits will likely only increase, given the impressive growth of Israel's elderly population; between 2017 and 2035, the overall size of the elderly population is expected to have expanded by 103 percent.[141] Notably, advertisements by recruitment companies for aging in place regularly feature the Jewish Israeli *saba* (grandfather) and *savta* (grandmother) as the overt and silent referents of eldercare benefits. That Jewish Israelis are the citizens predominantly appropriating this status symbol is evidence of how care can become an effect of the "biopolitics of settler colonialism."[142] Yet this "luxury" is made possible by the increased vulnerability of workers in the social service sector, including those previously benefiting from welfare services, disproportionately Palestinian women citizens of Israel and Mizrahi women.[143]

Because round-the-clock labor is particularly costly for patients, precarious workers have been integral to the transition from a "collectivist welfare" society (for Jewish Israelis) to a neoliberal liberalized economy.[144] As the elderly population expands, the burden on government spending for eldercare increases, making privatization an attractive cost-saving mechanism. Put in starker terms, migrant caregivers can earn the same amount of money for six days of live-in, round-the-clock labor as live-out, citizen caregivers earn for forty-three hours of work.[145] It was during this turn to labor flexibilization—the introduction of outsourcing, private service delivery, temporary employment, zero-hour contracts, benefit cutbacks, and weakened union protections—that the LTCIP was born.[146] Granting vouchers for in-home care to qualified elderly and disabled citizens based on age, dependency, and income, the LTCIP generated a private market for care procurement mediated through private placement agencies. For live-in migrant caregivers, the main effects of flexibilization are temporary contracts that are tied to workers' legal status; "contract substitution," or on-the-job changes to a contract after a worker signs it; and a lack of transparency and accountability in recruitment and enforcement.[147]

In contrast to Jewish Israeli families, employment of migrant caregivers is vastly less common among even wealthy Palestinian citizens, and caregivers are far less often placed in Palestinian families—a reality shaping the focus of my project. First, the total elderly population includes only 8 percent Palestinian citizens of Israel. Further, in 2015, the population of Palestinians living in Israel was composed of only 4 percent elderly citizens, as compared to 13 percent among the total Jewish Israeli population.[148] While from 2015 to 2035 the elderly Jewish Israeli population is projected to increase by 77 percent, among Palestinian citizens of Israel it will increase by 14 percent.[149] Unlike Jewish Israelis, the overwhelming majority of Palestinian citizens of Israel benefitting from the LTCIP use in-kind support to compensate family members, neighbors, and friends for their care labor, and they more often rely upon informal care structures through multigenerational family arrangements.[150] The fewer affordable in-home care options for Palestinian citizens are also due to broader health-care inequalities and related issues of access to health-care institutions, including higher rates of uninsured persons; lack of health-care access; disinvestment in longevity and end-of-life care for Palestinians; spatial segregation; economic strangulation; and criminalization.[151] These disparities have worsened alongside state retrenchment, manifesting in gaps in life expectancy, chronic morbidity, and infant mortality between Jewish Israelis and Palestinians, and between Ashkenazi and Mizrahi Jewish Israelis.[152] It is within this broader economy of apartheid, occupation, ethnic cleansing, and disinvestment that I locate access to live-in, long-term eldercare.[153]

The Transnational Organization of Migration

At the nexus of settler colonialism and neoliberal restructuring, the unsettled labors of migrant care work are also a product of structural adjustment policies, national debt, and colonial histories of labor exploitation. Transnationally, the reproductive labor sector is shaped by civil society groups, informal migrant networks, unions, private recruitment agencies, and human rights organizations. It is also shaped by financial institutions such as the World Bank and International Monetary Fund (IMF), both of which were key engineers of structural adjustment, conditional aid, and welfare retrenchment deeply impacting migrant-sending countries. Coupled with a growth in the aging population, neoliberal restructuring has increased the demand for migrant reproductive labor, creating an "international transfer of caretaking" that capitalizes on racialized and gendered hierarchies and demands that workers provide particular "tradable competences" to middle- and high-income countries.[154]

Under pressure from the IMF and World Bank, many formerly colonized states began implementing labor-export-oriented policies in the 1970s and 1980s. Reflecting this trend, according to the ILO, there are roughly 67 million domestic workers globally, 11.5 million of which are international migrants. Of this total, over 73 percent are women, a phenomenon often labeled the "feminization of labor."[155] Yet care migration from the Philippines is equally rooted in historical and ongoing forms of US and European imperialism. Notably, in the Philippines, the United States' military presence facilitated the "empire of care" that underwrites the ongoing migration of nurses.[156] In the Philippines and other labor-export states, migrant workers contribute sizably to the GDP.[157] Former president of the Philippines Corazon Aquino famously dubbed migrant women "new national heroes and heroines," depicting overseas employment as a form of national service.[158] These histories implicate Israel as a newer "host" country of formerly colonized states enmeshed in debt relations with the Global North.

Since the mid-1990s, in addition to private procurement schemes, labor migration has been facilitated by private employment agencies, the for-profit, market-driven organizations upholding the "migration industry."[159] A mark of the widespread delegation of care to the private sector, agencies operate at the local, regional, and transnational levels, recruiting migrants in their home countries through local agents or subagents, holding predeparture trainings, working with placement agencies in receiving countries to match workers with employers, and acting as intermediaries between employers and workers. Private agencies notoriously charge exorbitant fees for processing visas and work permits, requiring migrants to use property or personal possessions as collateral. Compounded by a lack of social and legal protections, agencies create a transnational rotational system whereby the continual entry of new workers into the market generates continual profit.[160]

These disparities suggest how the racializing and gendering of caregivers is shaped not only by employers' attitudes but also by the private sector, which marketizes sexist and racist stereotypes about which workers constitute "good" caregivers. Suggesting how care work is continually racialized and gendered, agencies "set" prices for visas from different countries. While recruitment agencies have charged Filipinx caregivers on average USD $8,000 to migrate, they charge South Asian migrants upward of USD $10,000.[161] For male caregivers from India, recruitment fees tend to be the highest. Jay, a caregiver from India who formerly worked as a driver in Saudi Arabia, said he has friends who paid as much as USD $17,000. Such disparities also inform how migrants evaluate Israel among other "destination" states. Among migrant-receiving countries, Palestine/Israel is generally thought of as a strong second-tier option that is less desirable than Canada, where there is hope for residency, citizenship, and employment options outside the nursing industry, and more desirable than the UAE, Cyprus, Saudi Arabia, Kuwait, Malaysia, Singapore, and Hong Kong.[162] Many workers described the middling position of Palestine/Israel in comparative terms—while recruitment fees are generally much higher than in GCC states, salaries are also often better.

Operating at the "meso" level of the migration industry are national employment and migration regimes determining visa lengths, workers' legal and social rights, and states' and placement agency's responsibilities.[163] National laws and policies influence demand for workers by providing tax credits and cash in-kind for purchasing care on the market. When bilateral agreements exist, as they now do between Israel and the Philippines, Nepal, Sri Lanka, and Ukraine, they can theoretically influence exploitative price-setting practices though enforcement challenges.[164] This "meso" level is also shaped by transnational legal frameworks and institutions governing labor migration. Following decades of advocacy, the ILO now formally recognizes domestic and household labor, in particular since the passage of the 1996 Home Work Convention (C177) and the 2011 Domestic Workers Convention (C189).[165] Still, the power of the ILO largely lies in its provisioning of technical assistance in the domestication of transnational labor standards.[166] In the Israeli context, the weight of unratified convention C189 is more symbolic than substantive, and its tenets remain a marginal conversation among caregivers.[167] Alongside the International Organization of Migration, the World Bank, the OECD, and the IMF, the leading international, intergovernmental bodies addressing migration regularly position migration as a form of economic development, perpetuating particular "gendered migration narratives" around the trafficked migrant victim in search of economic opportunity.[168] Such approaches ultimately leave intact the racialized and gendered organization of transnational labor markets for care, even as they may formally advocate on behalf of worker protections.[169] The onus of clamping down on exploitative recruitment agencies thus often falls upon governments, who benefit most from the cost-saving spoils of worker precarity.

The transnational organization of migration is also shaped by migrant networks, which share information about available jobs with friends and family; build communities of support and mutual aid in receiving countries; work with embassies, nongovernmental organizations, and sometimes recruitment agencies to negotiate their rights; and organize political campaigns. In the Israeli case, these networks often take the form of mutual aid and service provision, as workers are constricted by the threat of deportation and, as in many countries, an absence of domestic worker trade unions.[170] Migrant networks also push against reductionist notions of migrants as development entrepreneurs. Care migration is not solely determined by economics, but also by class, sexuality, access to health services, religion, personal desire to travel, and love—familial, platonic, and romantic. Ella, an evangelical Christian from the Philippines, came to Palestine/Israel to be close to the places where Jesus once lived. Mayra, a caregiver from Central Province, Sri Lanka, came to escape "personal problems for [her] family" following the conflict between the Tamil minority and Sinhalese majority. Alka, a devout evangelical Christian from Nepal, originally migrated to save money for her son's college tuition. Kyra, a caregiver from India, migrated to support her family, but chose Palestine/Israel so she could be closer to her boyfriend working in Dubai. Workers migrate for myriad reasons shaped but not solely determined by restructuring under late capitalism.

Book Layout and Methods

To draw out the entanglements of care work with economic exploitation, race, colonialism, and resistance, I read worker and employer narratives, court documents, parliamentary proceedings, media discourse, recruitment agency websites, and government statements as texts that comparatively racialize and gender migrant caregivers as differently disposable, vulnerable, flexible, dangerous, and desirable in relation to Palestinian workers, Eritrean and Sudanese asylum seekers, Mizrahi (Middle Eastern) Jewish Israelis, and Ashkenazi (European) Jewish Israelis. As a project of grounded, interdisciplinary political theory, my analysis frames each of these sources, as well as events, meetings, and gatherings I was invited to attend during my fieldwork, as lenses into the social construction of eldercare. As a work of grounded political theory, I draw on this multimodal archive to draw out the intimate "scenes of close connection" between reproductive labor markets, Jewish Israeli homes, globally dispersed recruitment agencies, and the historical building of Jewish colonies.[171] My aim is to adopt what Lisa Wedeen calls a "sense of epistemological reflexivity" toward academic disciplines that otherwise mystify labor relations through a siloed approach.[172] This methodology stems from a commitment within critical political theory to inductive, nonideal theory—the formulation of theory based upon the world that is.[173] Such an approach treats theory as "a recursive process," one continually reshaped and reworked in response to the experiences of those facing social and political violence, with the aim of shifting these conditions in the world as it is, whether through consciousness-raising or solidarity.[174]

Throughout the book, I draw from a range of interdisciplinary secondary literature, including settler colonial studies, migration studies, Palestine studies, Israel studies, and feminist theories of reproduction. Drawing from scholarship across disciplines enables a *longue durée* examination of care work beyond the neoliberal present. In thinking through Israel's reproductive regime and its multiple colonial instantiations, I take my cue from Michel Foucault's concept of biopolitics as the "political ordering of life" that manages, counts, quantifies, and disaggregates at the level of population, where "life" denotes both the biological and the constitution of the ethical.[175] I interrogate how migrant care work unfolds within a broader field of violence exposing Palestinians to surveillance and spatial confinement under a "regime of movement," land dispossession, injury, and death.[176]

I rely on critical discourse and narrative analyses to foreground not only workers' stories, but also my own position as what I call, drawing on Abigail Bakan's work, a "settler-in-waiting" in Palestine/Israel and a white settler living on Osage land.[177] In its attention to "explicit and opaque socially shared sets of rules," discourse analysis is particularly suited to the Israeli case, where dominative subjects conceal the conditions of possibility for their own sense of home and belonging.[178] By contrast, narrative analysis foregrounds how workers understand their own positions in relation to a shifting terrain of risk.

The field work portion of my archive is based upon seventy interviews and time spent with migrant community leaders, caregivers, employers, and Israeli advocacy workers. The bulk of interviews, including follow-ups, were conducted in person between December 2013 and January 2015, with some additional interviews conducted online in 2021. The periodization of this project is thus prepandemic; with the exception of a few interviews in 2021, our discussions focused largely on caregivers' years of employment before March 2020. During my intermittent time spent in Palestine/Israel between December 2013 and January 2015—one of many periods I spent in the region—I was invited to attend religious services and festivals organized within migrant Filipinx and Nepalese communities, as well as birthday parties, group dinners, hangouts in weekend flats, group trips during caregivers' days off from work, beauty pageants, fundraisers, and informal community gatherings in workers' shared apartments. I was also invited to attend a weekly Catholic Mass held for the Filipinx community, events within a Filipinx evangelical community, and events for World Migrant Day held by migrant community clergy. Additionally, I visited the Nepalese, Indian, and Sri Lankan embassies to learn about migrant civil society structures and migration rates.

I was largely introduced to employers through Jewish Israeli friends and their family members. By interviewing both elderly employers and their adult children, I could glean aspects of the caregiver/employer relationship from a multigenerational perspective. Citizen-employers had employed caregivers from the Philippines, Nepal, Sri Lanka, India, Romania, and Colombia. They were born in Israel or came from the United States, Poland, Bulgaria, Russia, Iraq, Morocco, and Egypt, among other places. Some employers paid caregivers' salaries themselves, suggesting relative economic security, while others received government subsidies. Employers' adult children were largely Israeli-born citizens who had served in the army and grown up immersed in Zionist culture. Many had taken on Hebraicized names, a practice that began at the start of the twentieth century as a self-indigenizing shedding of nonindigenous Jewish diasporic identity. I met caregivers through acquaintances involved in migrant worker organizing, and these interlocutors put me in contact with others expressing interest in my project. They had previously worked in Saudi Arabia, UAE, Qatar, Hong Kong, Singapore, and Japan, among other places. Some were nurses, paramedics, teachers, and small business owners in their home countries. Others had worked in factories or for airlines, or had been involved in political activism before they migrated. Almost all had been previously employed in other geographical regions of Israel, from remote towns in the South; to *kibbutzim* (collective settlements); to the larger cities of Haifa (originally composed of fifty-two Palestinian villages), Tel Aviv—built upon the Palestinian villages of Sumail, Shaykh Muwannis, Jammasin al-Gharbi, Irshad, Manshiyya, Salama, Abu Kabir—and Jerusalem/al-Quds; to towns along the border with Gaza.[179] Though I never directly asked, given how easily one's status can change from documented to undocumented, it is likely that several of the experiences caregivers shared with me were shaped by the specter of being undocumented. At some times, workers volunteered their undocumented status.

Conversations I held with caregivers and employers were continually inflected by my position as a white Ashkenazi Jewish American located in the academy. Under the Law of Return, I hold the possibility of claiming settler-citizen status despite my lack of native relation to the land and the absence of a right of return for Palestinians. This is partly what this project is about—the ideologies and laws regularizing a Jewish diasporic "birthright" and framing non-Jewish migrant workers, asylum seekers, and indigenous Palestinians as interlopers. While many Jewish Israelis welcomed me into their home, I was at moments aware of initial skepticism toward my project. One of the first questions some employers asked was whether I was Jewish and why I was so focused on studying Palestine/Israel when care migration is a transnational phenomenon. Inquiries into my status as a Jew were telling of the ways religion, class, race, and settler status influenced what employers assumed about my own political orientations. At other moments, my positionality impacted the elements of stories interviewees chose to share with me and those they did not. Sam, for instance, highlighted his deep love for "the Jewish people" many times during the afternoon we spent together. This could be an effect of my privileged positioning within the state or of his own political and religious beliefs. To this end, I situate myself as a (shifting) proxy for the hegemonic social status of many employers. These tensions underlie my own attempts to weave together these diverse narratives as they abut and converge with media and court archives and the public rhetoric of politicians.

Outside of this project, my knowledge of the broader sociopolitical context is shaped by my time interning at the Alternative Information Center, an anti-Zionist organization based in Jerusalem and Beit-Sahour in the West Bank, and the United Nations Relief and Works Agency (UNRWA) in East Jerusalem, an experience that taught me about the fraught relationship between grassroots resistance and the top-down imposition of international priorities. During this time and other visits between 2008 and 2012, I was able to learn from Palestinian and Jewish Israeli activists and organizers, attending protests in Silwan and Sheikh Jarrah and traveling throughout the West Bank. Outside of this project, my broader contextual knowledge also stems from field work done in 2010 on how Palestinian and Jewish Israeli women have strategically deployed or rejected international legal frameworks through grassroots organizing. Also beyond my role as a researcher I volunteered with claims-processing efforts for asylum seekers in January 2014 and as an English tutor within a Spanish-speaking migrant community in Tel Aviv. My positioning is also informed by many years attending Hebrew School, where we were taught, as many Jewish Americans are, that the modern colonial state of Israel is an unquestionable and exclusive homeland for Jews. It is also shaped by my own familial embroilment with colonization, as I am the granddaughter of a Jewish British soldier stationed in mandate Palestine in the mid-1940s. In his lifetime, my grandfather at once experienced anti-Semitism and accrued the power and privilege of citizen-soldiers serving empire. His positioning encapsulates the tragic ways that European anti-Semitism—as one facet of European racism—became a self-justifying mechanism for the British and Zionist colonization of Palestine while participation in colonization served as entrée into greater Europeanness for many Ashkenazi Jews.

The book proceeds through five chapters. In chapter 1, I situate migrant care work within what I term the "coloniality of Israel's reproductive regime"—the economic, cultural, biological, and discursive reproduction of Israeli settler colonialism and its rootedness in the *longue durée* of imperialism. Here, I take a cue from Jodi Byrd, Nada Elia, and Steven Salaita, who locate settler colonialism as one form of European and US imperialism.[180] Methodologically unsettling care work, I draw on decolonial, Marxist feminist, and Zionist labor history, asking how the systems of meaning attached to care and domestic labor during early colonial encounters undergird "colonial-capital accumulation" in the present.[181] Treating care and reproductive labor as one component of this regime, and as a counterpart to the expropriation of Palestinian land, I examine the *comparative* racialization of Palestinian, Mizrahi, and South and Southeast Asian workers. I suggest how worker and citizen narratives, rulings, government rhetoric, and private recruitment agencies comparatively gender and racialize migrant caregivers. I examine throughout how the treatment of elderly Jewish Israelis as the "ideal image" of vulnerability parallels and stands in for histories of protecting the health of the Jewish collective body.[182]

In chapter 2, I show how migrant caregivers are at once treated as intimate members of the family and "foreign" interlopers excluded from Zionist temporality. While their treatment by the state as "national helpers" reinvigorating the nation and workers performing exceptionally intimate labors enables task expansion, their constitution as a non-Jewish demographic threat justifies surveillance. Their unsettled positioning disrupts the home and nation as an exclusionary Jewish space, even as, paradoxically, live-in eldercare is central to its reproduction. Treating the household and nation as a contiguous terrain of risk, I contend that the dual demands of their positioning as intimate and alien require that they engage in "affective automation," or the repetitive execution of physical and emotional tasks despite their own limits. This continual demand for labor impacts their exposure to injury within a broader "economy of injury" predicated on the disavowal of indigeneity.[183]

Examining the relationship between the migrant caregiver and the citizen-employer from the perspective of Jewish Israeli employers, in chapter 3, I explore how a "settler common sense" is the background against which the labors of eldercare unfold in the home.[184] Drawing on employer narratives, government statements, and recruitment agency websites, I highlight two common tropes among employers. The "kinship trope" portrays migrants as "one of the [racial] family," despite their exclusion from Zionist time, while the "development trope" depicts them as agents of economic empowerment and Israel as a bastion of economic entrepreneurialism and "gender modernity."[185] Both discourses reinforce settler-employers' position as rightful heirs to the land and disavow native dispossession, even as at other times employers also suggest how caregivers' labors unsettle the home as an exclusionary site of Jewish continuity. I highlight how settler-employers expect migrants' contingent cultural assimilation within Jewish Israeli families despite their essentialized treatment as workers from "developing" countries and their permanent exclusion from Jewish cultural and religious practices.

If injury and surveillance characterize care work, so too do resistance, creative defiance, and community organizing. Chapters 4 and 5 focus on migrant caregivers' "frontstage" and "backstage" strategies for unsettling the asymmetrical employment relationship and surveillance within and beyond the home. Drawing on workers' stories, in chapter 4, I focus on "frontstage" strategies caregivers use to navigate exploitation, including creating indispensability, quitting, direct contestation, and strategic deference. I also examine alignments between migrant caregivers and the state, suggesting how resistance to flexibilization does not necessarily result in a disavowal of settler colonialism. Drawing on Sara Ahmed's concept of "national love," I examine how a love of Israel—in the form of Christian Zionism and sometimes Islamophobia—can reinforce settler exceptionalism. In chapter 5, I ask how caregivers unsettle the colonial commitment to a Jewish majority by sustaining collective forms of life, whether through mutual aid, legal defense, service provision, or emotional support networks. I foreground the dangers of being collectively visible and political among migrant workers and Eritrean and Sudanese asylum seekers, whose treatment is heavily shaped by the dialectic of labor exploitation and anti-Blackness.

I conclude by exploring in brief how the COVID-19 pandemic makes plain particular aspects of Israel's reproductive regime. Each chapter suggests how laws, policies, and household exchanges constitute elderly Jewish Israelis as worthy of care while treating migrant precarity as an unfortunate byproduct of late capitalist markets. Rather than providing an exhaustive exploration of "alien," settler, and native labors from the narrative perspectives of each, I ask how the meaning and value of migrant labor shifts from the comparative vantage point of migrants. For Alice and Sarah, as for other workers and employers, household exchanges naturalize poverty, (neo)colonialism, and land expropriation, yet they also contest exploitative tropes about work, race, colonialism, and gender. Migrant caregivers creatively navigate laws designed to ensure the unpaid extraction of their labor and to prevent them from taking root, establishing expansive networks of mutual aid and solidarity, providing for families and kinship networks, and engaging in workplace resistance and horizontal care beyond the bounds of settler colonial and neoliberal extractivism. These networks, and the individual and collective ways they are built, inspire new and creative ways of imagining care beyond its utility to the state.

As a whole, this book reframes migrant eldercare as a site where gendered, racialized, and indigenous difference is reproduced and challenged at a time when Israel publicly affirms and engages in ongoing practices of ethnic cleansing. In doing so, the book confronts certain commonsense notions of an "aging crisis" as solely a question of the distribution of care. Instead, I argue, a politics of care is only as good as governing logics and social ideologies concerning who is worthy of life. Underlying questions about care—for the elderly, families, communities, kinship networks, and land—are fundamental assumptions about who does and does not have a right to a collective future. This reality requires reorienting feminist discussions concerning care, vulnerability, and dependency around the constitutive relationship between global political economy, indigenous and migrant resistance, and gendered labor in the past and present. As legacies of imperialism continue to animate patterns of migration and capital, migrant caregivers' perspectives and experiences navigating labor extraction and creating community networks can inform contemporary struggles against the uneven violences of settler colonial capitalism.

1

The Coloniality of Israel's Reproductive Regime

Jennifer, a caregiver from the Philippines, has cared for Leah, an elderly woman from Bulgaria, for eight years. Leah, a Holocaust survivor and member of Israel's "founding generation," first hired a Jewish Israeli woman of Mizrahi descent to care for her several hours a day.[1] Once Leah became more dependent and needed additional hours of care, she hired Jennifer, who, as a temporary migrant, is required to live with her around the clock. Leah describes her relationship with Jennifer fondly. She details at length the family home Jennifer is building in the Philippines with her salary and Jennifer's willingness to help during her hours off. When I ask Leah why Palestinians do not typically work as live-in caregivers, she notes, "You know, if you have an Arab, you never know what he's going to do. You're afraid. For instance, we have here Arabs that clean the stairs. Sometimes I'm afraid when I see them. They are very polite, they work a lot of times, but they look nice, [and] then they take a knife." Depicting Palestinians as untrustworthy, deceptive, and dangerous, Leah illustrates how migrant caregivers' social constitution as "safe" and proximate workers necessarily forms in relation to the "danger" of Palestinians perceived to infiltrate the intimate family and national home. For Leah, it is more desirable to employ Palestinians in manual labor outside of the domestic arena. Notably, her description of grounds workers as male reveals how gendered racisms cohere to paint Palestinian men as unnatural caregivers. While "Arabs" may "take a knife," South and Southeast Asian migrants, the majority of whom are women, are perceived by many employers, and within popular discourse, as "naturally" caring.[2]

Leah's depiction of Palestinians and migrant caregivers echoes former Israeli prime minister Yitzhak Rabin's call for "bring[ing] thousands of foreign workers to reduce the number of Palestinians walking around in our streets."[3] Beyond an employer-employee dyad, the feminized and racialized meaning of care emerges in relation to disavowed populations who may be physically absent from the site of labor. News and social media stories about Palestinian workers posing a latent security threat reinforce the racialization of South and Southeast Asian caregivers as comparatively benign. A 2016 cleaning company leaflet circulating across Facebook is revealing of the association between Palestinian workers and settler panic. The advertisement, which reads, "Don't want to hire an Arab worker for security reasons? . . . There's a solution," presents prospective Jewish Israeli employers with a hierarchy of fees for hiring differently racialized workers. According to the flier, hiring Black asylum seekers mitigates financial loss for employers, as compared to Eastern Europeans (who are "better workers" and whose wages are higher).[4] In another example, a widely covered story featured Nimer Jamal, a West Bank Palestinian working as a cleaner in Har Adar, a Jewish settlement built on over 1,000 dunams (roughly 250 acres) of land from the Palestinian villages of Biddu, Beit Surik, and Qatanna.[5] Jamal shot and killed three Jewish settlers, becoming a sensationalist tale in the media about the risks of employing Palestinians within familial spaces. Articulating a wider mistrust of Palestinian laborers, Jamal's former employer told the press, "I don't know how to tell my children that for two and a half years a terrorist worked in our house."[6] She also says that "this was a man who we talked with, whom my children gave drinks and food."[7] Through this story, the employer's initial judgment of Jamal as "completely normal" and "good-natured" is proven imprudent.[8] Within the settler imaginary, the dissemination of such stories attaches a sense of untrustworthiness and violence to Palestinian workers who collectively become a proxy for violence against the Jewish home.

Leah's accounting of home, danger, and care suggests how local perceptions of caregivers from South and Southeast Asia are shaped by colonial
notions of a non-European worker in the home and settler anxieties about
native Palestinians. As I suggest in the following pages, this perception of
danger is part and parcel of broader nationalist language positioning Palestinians in particular and non-Jews more broadly as an "insidious virus"
within a collective Jewish body.[9] As Bayan Abusneineh argues, the Zionist
project of settlement in Palestine has, since its early days, been premised
upon creating a "body politic of white Europeans" who will bring strength,
longevity, and health to the nation.[10] Since the late nineteenth century, modern political Zionism has been a "bodily revolution" aimed at "strengthening" the Jewish people and ridding them of the fragmented and fragile, weak
and hypomasculine diaspora Jew who has been "disembodied" by exile.[11]
The "strengthening" of the Jewish people through settlement of land, and
of the land through peopling, is also a project of "regeneration" and "racial
improvement" enabling the realization of Jewish collective survival.[12] This
regeneration revives "the bodies of Jews," positioned by European society
as a "degenerate race."[13] The collective body's survival thus depends on ridding it of exposure to racial weakening, manifest in challenges to the Jewish
demographic makeup of the state, and political challenges to legitimacy,
itself hinging on the vulnerability of diaspora Jews.[14] As Nadia Abu El-Haj
suggests, this preoccupation with strengthening the collective Jewish body
was as much about improving the physical body as it was an invocation of
race science as a way of "building *the nation*" and establishing a racial connection to the land.[15]

A key component of the collective body's health is thus the reproduction
of its constituting bodies, whether workers, soldiers, or "pioneers," *and* the
elderly, whose existence as members of the "founding generation" ensures
the continuity of Israel as a "remembering collective."[16] While seemingly
contradictory, elderly longevity is necessary to the vitality of the Holocaust
as a key originating narrative of the state.[17] Though racialized in markedly
different ways, this narrative extends to Jewish Israeli elderly from the
Middle East and North Africa who are also differentially incorporated into
the mythos of the state's founding and are recently counted as Holocaust survivors through a state-adopted definition centered on "persecution *linked*
to the Nazis."[18] Preserving elderly life is a way of "linking a Jewish past with
an Israeli present" and enlivening a "collectivist 'language of commitment'"
to the national body, whether through renewed calls for military occupation

and violence or ideological conviction.[19] From a Zionist perspective, Jewish Israeli elderly exemplify the latent vulnerability of the collective body to attack in the present and the consequent need to manage its health through biopolitical intervention. Israel's reproductive regime serves this end, preserving and invigorating the collective body through racial management, exclusionary land control, and the accumulation and "depletion" of resources necessary for social reproduction.[20] As I suggest in the introduction, I conceive of Israel's reproductive regime as the nexus of policies, laws, and social discourses that materially and discursively reproduce Israeli settler colonialism. Historically and in the present, this biopolitical logic is evident in the racial and colonial segmentation of labor markets, the differential allocation of health resources under British and Zionist colonization, internal displacement, house demolitions, imprisonment, land confiscation, bombings, and military infliction of injuries and death.[21] The provisioning of care and the designation of some bodies as vulnerable is neither innocent nor apolitical, but rather, part of a broader reproductive regime vested in strengthening the collective Jewish body through this differential provisioning and elimination of resources. From a Zionist nationalist perspective, long-term care for the elderly—a process that can span decades—must be undertaken by workers who will not permanently "infiltrate" or "compromise" the healthy composition of the Jewish collective body.

In this chapter, I draw out the multiple facets of reproductivity entangled with live-in eldercare, from the economic to the territorial, symbolic, and ideological. Through the framework of Israel's reproductive regime, I methodologically "unsettle" migrant eldercare in Israel as the sole effect of racial discrimination under neoliberal restructuring. Instead, I suggest how it is not only a form of labor but also a site where racial, gender, class, and colonial positionings are produced and thwarted. By foregrounding the expropriation of land in the *longue durée* of reproductive labor, I underscore how, as Frances Susan Hasso argues, "the extraction of labor and life are the very grounds of colonialism and imperialism" and key sites of gendering and racialization.[22] Framing migrants' challenges as solely an effect of racial exclusions takes for granted the borders of the nation and the processes of land dispossession required for its consolidation. My analysis hinges on the argument that intergenerational reproduction—that is, reproduction of not only future soldiers and workers, but also members of the "founding generation"—is biopolitical. The project of promoting the collective life of some at the expense of others is necessarily one wherein the provisioning of care for particular bodies—and the social meaning of these bodies—is determined by larger strategies of settlement, expropriation, and collective violence. To be clear, my argument is not that the elderly are at fault for seeking care, nor that workers providing care are willingly engaging in Israel's reproductive regime. Indeed, Holocaust survivors, like all elderly, deserve care, respect, and the resources needed for individual and community reproduction, as do the workers caring for them. My aim instead is to draw out the structural matrixes of accumulation, depletion, protection, and violence through which live-in, long-term care for the elderly—a project exclusively undertaken by migrants—becomes intelligible.

To unsettle migrant carework in Palestine/Israel, I locate live-in eldercare as a site of "colonial-capital accumulation." For Glen Coulthard, "colonial-capital accumulation" denotes the "co-foundational" processes of labor exploitation and land expropriation necessary to sustain settler colonial capitalism in the past and present.[23] Colonial-capital accumulation tracks the amassing of capital *and* the dispossession of land required for the expansion of settler colonialism. Alongside military incursion, media campaigns, and cultural erasure, colonial-capital accumulation is one mechanism through which Israel's reproductive regime sustains itself. I draw on the concept of coloniality—the social classification system of superiority and inferiority beginning under early colonial control and outliving its formal end—to highlight how categories of East and West, European and non-European, and citizen and migrant enable the devaluation of care work and to highlight the subsequent accumulation of wealth and resources in the past and present.[24] As Encarnación Gutiérrez Rodríguez suggests, migrant domestic work is imbued with coloniality because it revitalizes and refigures colonial hierarchies as they become codified in migration and asylum policies throughout nineteenth-century Europe and the Americas and only deepens through privatization, structural adjustment, and the coerced shift to labor-export economies.[25] Live-in, long-term eldercare is shaped by labor hierarchies undergirding the *longue durée* of settler reproduction, whether the work of sustaining homes, communities, plantations, cooperative settlements, cities, farms, or family emplacement.

The lens of "coloniality" thus locates the *contemporary* expropriation of reproductive labor within the legacy and present of the colonization of Palestine and the European imperial project of which it is a part. The term "coloniality" suggests how racialized and gendered expectations of migrant caregivers are part and parcel of the "internationalist character of settler colonialism" and its European racial order in the past and present.[26] Coloniality also contextualizes the contemporary turn to privatization in the field of eldercare by tracking how employer and agency assumptions about caregivers from particular states enable the extraction of value by recruitment companies. My aim is not to delineate a neat, transhistorical theory of reproductive labor or race, nor to provide a comprehensive history of reproductive labors in Palestine. Rather, I seek to frame Israel's turn to migrant care work since the 1990s within the longer history of gendered, non-European labor, emphasizing how it is both a racial and a colonial relation.

To this end, I begin by examining care work as a site of colonial-capital accumulation through which the state amasses the wealth and resources needed to sustain the collective body. Drawing from scholarship on divisions of labor prior to state Zionist colonization, I suggest how reproductive labors aimed at preserving settler homes, farms, and communities have always been infused with the dual imperatives to accumulate resources *and* to protect the collective Jewish body from threats to settler domination. I then examine private, for-profit agencies as contemporary sites of colonial-capital accumulation, showing how they monopolize the coloniality of migrant labor to marketize and sell gendered, sexualized, and racialized stereotypes about caregivers. Finally, I examine how migrant caregivers' positioning rests upon and enables the hierarchical ordering of vulnerabilities at the household and national levels. I also contextualize care for the "founding generation" within broader government and legal discourses that position the elderly citizen as the ideal symbol of the collective body's vulnerability, even as Zionist cultural emphases on youthfulness have at key moments rejected the image of the victimized (and elderly) Jew.

Migrant Eldercare as Colonial-Capital Accumulation

While caregivers from South and Southeast Asia are relatively new to the nursing sector, the social construction of their labor is bound up with a longer genealogy of reproductive labors that rely upon, replicate, and resist racial, gendered, and colonial relations. As state strategies for the biopolitical management of capital, territory, and populations shift, so too do the social meaning and racial coding of these labors. Through a review of continuities and ruptures in reproductive labor as a land *and* labor relation, I suggest how care work has long been a site of colonial-capital accumulation, from early Zionist settlement to the present.[27] The capital relation as an analytic centers labor extraction and proletarianization—the process by which workers lose their mode of subsistence and have only their labor to sell—and the colonial relation foregrounds land theft, encroachment, and the siphoning of natural resources. As Coulthard argues, colonial-capital accumulation centers land as the complement to, and the backdrop against which, proletarianization takes place rather than as merely the means of forcing those dispossessed of their land into the wage relation.[28] Underlying Israel's economy is a logic of capital accumulation for its own sake *as much as* for the purpose of demographic control over territory.[29] Indeed, the decision to settle Ottoman Palestine was not exclusively motivated by economic gain, and during the first two waves of settlement, the dual "conquest of labor" and "conquest of land" evidence both proletarianization and dispossession as core building blocks of the state.[30]

Like other reproductive "alien labors"—those labors done by (im)migrant populations—live-in eldercare generates surplus value for families and the state by virtue of the noncitizen-citizen wage differential.[31] As opposed to childcare, a job done predominantly by Israelis, demands for migrant eldercare generate a market for private placement agencies to profit from the illegal charging of brokerage fees. Rather than emerging anew in the 1990s, contemporary constructions of migrant caregivers as "flexible" and "mobile" are imbricated in the historical devaluation of labor done by "alien" Yemenite Jewish and working-class Palestinian women.[32] In what follows, I review reproductive labors at the start of the twentieth century and in the years before World War I and the Labor Zionist call for the conquest of labor, which they hoped would create an exclusively Jewish work force to the exclusion of Palestinians.[33] Though never a fully completed project, the call for outsourcing was necessary to uphold an imagined Ashkenazi settler vanguard in the first decades of settlement, a dynamic inflecting the contemporary positioning of Ashkenazi Jews—and, in uneven ways, Mizrahi Jews—as "natural" managers of migrant caregivers.

Reproductive Labor, Land, and Resistance

Like other reproductive labors, migrant care work is tethered to the physical and symbolic "conquest of land" aimed at "destroy[ing] to replace."[34] In forging expropriated land into a "domestic" space, Jewish settlers engaged in a form of "self-indigenizing" that has in many ways succeeded in portraying contemporary Jewish Israeli citizen-employers as themselves outside the category of "settler."[35] As Nadera Shalhoub-Kevorkian shows, Jewish homemaking was a site of home destruction for Palestinians at the level of "nation, land, community and family."[36] Indeed, the physical precondition for the making of the Jewish Israeli home was the displacement of over half of the Palestinian population, just as the destruction of at least 418 Palestinian villages is the enabling condition of Zionist collective self-determination.[37] Across distinctive waves of Zionist settlement, homemaking has taken place through the building of agricultural settlements, the procurement of land acquisition grants, the establishment of philanthropic associations, the quest to use archaeological findings as justification for displacement, the extension of military rule into the West Bank and Gaza, the razing of homes and villages, and the takeover of roads, farm land, and natural resources. Revealing how the collective body's survival is premised upon the casting of indigenous populations as foreign, Palestinians who were expelled in 1948 were placed under the legal category of "infiltrator," positioning them as latent threats to settlers' newly acquired land.[38] This categorization constituted Palestinians as latent threats to the Jewish collective body such that "the simple fact of being-at-home" amounts to "an act of terrorism and an incitement to violence."[39]

At the close of the nineteenth century, land expropriation was facilitated by the Zionist view that Palestine was "a land without a people for a people without a land."[40] While initially the term "conquest of labor" largely referenced the self-focused process of taking on agricultural labor, Labor Zionist leaders of the second wave of settlement turned away from hiring indigenous Palestinian workers, a population originally seen as a source of cheap labor, and instead toward replacing Palestinians with Jewish workers.[41] Unlike those who settled before them in the last decades of the nineteenth century—settlers largely funded by private capital who employed Palestinian workers—Labor Zionists called for economic separation and an exclusionary Jewish socialism.[42] While many Yemenite Jews had already settled in Palestine at the end of the previous century, in 1911, Labor Zionist leader Shmuel Yavnieli visited Yemen to recruit Jewish workers that could replace Palestinian manual laborers.[43] Zionists thought this strategy would secure Jewish economic self-sufficiency and access to land and increase the standard of living for European Jewish settlers who feared their wages would be suppressed by Palestinian workers.[44] While the conquest of labor ultimately failed, it was nevertheless important in creating a "racialized vision of labor" in Palestine, a process Labor Zionists hoped would realize their agenda of creating a Jewish settler proletariat.[45] As Jamil Hilal notes, the primary goal of Zionist settlement was not the pure exploitation of indigenous populations but rather their displacement. In creating a "fully-fledged class society of Jewish settlers," Zionist leaders were as much committed to reserving better jobs for Ashkenazi Jewish settlers as they were to expropriating land to present settlement as an irreversible fact.[46]

During the first decades of the twentieth century, these racial/colonial divisions of labor were both material and ideological, building on and reinforcing the coloniality of various reproductive labors. As Gershon Shafir shows, the World Zionist Organization (WZO), the Planters' Society—a Zionist corporation selling plots of land to Jewish settlers—and settlers themselves created a social and economic distinction between Palestinian and Yemenite laborers, portraying the former as threatening to the project of Jewish settlement and the latter as economically beneficial, adding to the overall number of Jewish settlers without requiring bosses to pay more than "Arab wages."[47] In contrast to the depiction of Yemenite Jews as "natural laborers," European Jewish settlers were thought to be "ideological" builders of the nation with the cultural acumen to constitute a "vanguard."[48] Suggesting how Yemeni workers could facilitate both capital and colonial accumulation, Aharon Eisenberg, general director of the Planters' Society, remarked in 1903 that the Yemeni settler was "capable of being a loyal Hebrew worker" while bringing "hope to ridding us of the Arab worker."[49] Likewise, fourth prime minister of Israel Golda Meir asked whether Ashkenazi settlers could help "elevate [Mizrahi Jews] to a suitable level of civilization."[50] Such sentiment echoed "father of modern political Zionism" Theodor Herzl's claim that an exclusionary Jewish state could be a "wall of defense for Europe in Asia, an outpost of civilization against barbarism,"[51] and the Zionist belief that an inflow of capital would better living conditions for Palestinian peasants.[52] Thus, Yemenite workers were welcome as an "alien" labor force who were less likely to threaten the health of the Jewish collective body while still requiring lower wages than European Jews. At the same time, unlike Palestinians, they were included within Zionist temporal claims to Jewish futurity through their manual part in "redeeming" the land. Through their presence, European Jewish settlers could secure higher paying jobs by elevating the social value of their own labor while comparatively devaluing that of non-Europeans and Palestinians. The Zionist engineering of a reproductive Mizrahi workforce, as an outcome of the broader shift away from reliance on Palestinian labor, suggests how the very category "settler" is laden with internal racial and colonial hierarchies that become a buffer between "ideal" settler and indigenous populations.

The coloniality of reproductive labors in particular is evident in Yemenite and Palestinian women's work as domestic servants, cleaners, washerwomen, launderers, and weeders for Ashkenazi families in houses, on farms, and in domestic industries such as textiles.[53] Amid labor market restrictions imposed by the Ashkenazi elite, domestic work was one of the only jobs Yemenite Jewish women could obtain. Indeed, the (re)generation of settlements, home spaces, and families required the undertaking of everyday tasks from laundry service, to domestic care, to field work. As Smadar Lavie's work shows, many Yemenite women, racialized as less feminine than Askhenazi women, also did field work alongside Yemenite Jewish men.[54] In contrast to the image of the pioneering Ashkenazi woman lauded in Labor Zionist mythology, Yemenite women were referred to as *teimonichkas*, a Yiddish diminutive translating to "little Yemeni women."[55] Even young Yemenite girls were employed as "scrubwomen, washerwomen, or in the fields."[56] Yemenite and Palestinian girls also endured poor conditions within *moshavot*—more rural Jewish settlements—sometimes working over twelve hours at a time without breaks.[57] Both Yemenite and Palestinian women were also employed in the homes of European Jews, though the latter more often worked in the homes of wealthy Palestinian families.[58] These divisions of reproductive labor were marked by separate living arrangements, as Yemenite women were forbidden from living inside the Ashkenazi settlements where they worked, and, like Palestinians, were excluded from the Histadrut—the Jewish labor union.[59]

The engineering of racial/colonial divisions of reproductive labor thus functioned as a form of colonial-capital accumulation, such that European settlers could extract surplus value from Palestinian and Yemenite women's labors toward the project of forging a sense of at-homeness in the nation. Yet such activities required the maintenance of not only households and farms but also ideologies situating European Jews as the "true" proletarian political subjects and Mizrahi women as feminized and racialized workers. The ideological construction of work in and around Jewish settlements and homes was gendered first because it was premised upon the notion of a pioneering, proletarian European Jewish settler who was an active "fighting Jew," a form of reactionary masculinity contrasting with the Talmud-studying, "passive" Jew facing European anti-Semitism.[60] Yet this work was also comparatively premised upon the construction of Mizrahi and Palestinian femininity as more indelicate and rugged than that of Ashkenazi women.[61] In a clear example of such ideological orientations, Jessie Sampter, a celebrated Jewish American settler within Zionist historiography, remarked that Yemenite Jews were "a thrifty, sturdy folk, inured to hardship, learned and pious, and speaking a pure Sephardic Hebrew." As Sampter saw it, the role of Western settlers was to teach Yemenite Jews the ways of "education, gender roles, science, medicine, and rational religion."[62] Tellingly, the very historiography of reproductive labors during the first decades of the twentieth century itself reveals the coloniality of reproductive labor. As Nahla Abdo shows, the predominant Israel Studies approach to "women's work" during the prestate years has valorized Ashkenazi women as hard-working pioneers forging the nation and fighting for a place of equality among Ashkenazi men, a narrative celebrated today among Zionist women's organizations such as Hadassah. Such narratives omit how the fight for "equality" among Ashkenazi women settlers relies on the dispossession of Palestinian women's land and the exploitation of both Palestinian and Mizrahi women's labors.[63]

Importantly, the diverse labors Palestinian women have undertaken since the start of the twentieth century suggest how colonial-capital accumulation is neither a complete nor one-directional process, but rather, it is continually resisted through labor and collective action. As one component of Palestinian women's broader political resistance to Israeli occupation, participation in the "resistance economy" has continually unsettled the Zionist drive to build a national home; rural and urban Palestinian women have fought the worst effects of "colonial-capital accumulation" in the agricultural and domestic sectors.[64] Their labor has been both a survival strategy to cope with the loss of land and a form of resistance to Israel's reproductive regime. During the British Mandate period, Palestinian women played a large role in subsistence agriculture and food production during a period of increased landlessness.[65] Palestinian working-class women's labors included domestic work for middle-class Palestinian families and, on fewer occasions, Jewish families; stone moving; infrastructure work under British colonial rule (for example, in the village of al-Birweh); agricultural labor; sewing work; and the management of the household economy in ways that benefitted the whole family.[66] In the poststate period, rural Palestinian women have also resisted "colonial-capital accumulation" through the secret cultivation of lands taken during the Nakba.[67]

To resist the proletarianization of the Palestinian economy that has taken place since 1967, rural women in particular have turned to income-generating activities such as food processing, the marketing of small-scale agriculture, bread-making, and other forms of food production.[68] Particularly for the rural and working class, ongoing land theft since 1967 has been the basis of proletarianization and entrance into additional industries catered to Jewish Israeli consumers, such as food, cleaning, and textiles. At times, loss of land has also forced Palestinians into jobs within Jewish settlements, plantations, and occasionally homes.[69] Creeping Israeli encroachment in the 1970s further facilitated Palestinian women's increased presence in *moshavim* and vegetable and citrus plantations and in seasonal cash crop work, textiles, cleaning, and food processing.[70] The racial/colonial organization of labor markets was also a "strengthening" of the Jewish collective body and a bulwark against the perceived vulnerability of Jewish settlement, one achieved by weeding out those Zionists considered racially weak or inadequately civilized, so as to guard against the "physical degeneration of the people."[71] As Amal Samed shows, Palestinian women's increased presence on Jewish plantations and *moshavim* was an extension of land colonization dating back to the late nineteenth century, one that led to fears of indigenous women laborers on Jewish cooperative farms and settlements, as evidenced by Minister of Agriculture Aharon Uzan's statement that "the domination of Jewish agriculture by Arab workers is a cancer in our body."[72] Urban and rural Palestinian women across class positions have fought against the worst effects of such racism and corresponding processes of proletarianization through the reproductive labors of mutual aid and protection, the boycott of Israeli goods, women's cooperatives, and the cultivation of crops on land threatened by imminent military takeover.[73] Contemporarily, these practices offset the effects of the increase in Palestinian men leaving agriculture to enter the Israeli labor market.[74]

Suggesting how the contemporary economic positioning of settler-citizens relies upon histories of dispossession, the post-1967 proletarianization of the Palestinian economy was accompanied by a general "deproletarianization" of the Jewish population, who increasingly became managers.[75] This transformation is crucial to the present-day positioning of settler-employers as managers of migrant caregivers. Contemporarily, the coloniality of reproductive labors morphs in relation to political economy. As land encroachment continues, working-class Palestinian women are increasingly doing domestic work for Jewish families in West Bank settlements and for wealthy Palestinian families in Gaza.[76] Palestinian domestic workers in Jewish settlements—unlike migrant caregivers—do not live inside their employers' homes, even when they do eldercare.[77] Some also continue to work as seasonal agricultural laborers in West Bank settlements, a job with few safety nets attached.[78] In contrast, Yemeni Jewish women—and Mizrahi women more broadly—would eventually be absorbed into Jewish Israeli society as a "settler working class."[79]

In contrast, once deemed the pioneering vanguard, Ashkenazi Jewish Israelis still benefit from their positioning as "natural" managers. Mizrahim, newly settled Russian Jews, Palestinians, and non-Jewish migrant women are disproportionately represented in the domestic service sector and other devalued, feminized professions, even as the managerial class has marginally expanded to include Mizrahi women.[80] In contrast, Ashkenazi women's labor market participation, itself often predicated upon the reallocation of care and domestic duties to Mizrahi women, is now also dependent upon non-Jewish migrants, as a new gendered population of "alien labor."[81]

Rather than constituting a separate political or ethical field, migrant care work is thus one mode of ongoing colonial-capital accumulation in a longer trajectory of land and labor expropriation and race-making and an economic, discursive, and social element of Israel's broader reproductive regime.[82] As Palestinian, Mizrahi, and non-Jewish migrants' reproductive labors suggest, the transformation of newly expropriated land into a resource for settlers is not merely a function of labors traditionally conceived of as "productive," such as construction, agriculture, and drilling. It equally requires the (re)generation of households, settlements, farms, and families—labors shaped by feminized and racialized constructions of household and agricultural labors. Situated within Israel's reproductive regime, the allocation of caring labors that invest in settlers' health, longevity, and very sense of self unfolds alongside forms of land dispossession that deprive others of similar collective longevity. Alongside acts of "depletion," from home demolitions to the designating of Palestinian land for military use, to the blockading and razing of Gaza, the labors of settlement building generate demographic facts through land capture as an end in itself. The post–Oslo Peace Accords approach of outsourcing labor away from Palestinians and strangulating and segmenting the West Bank Palestinian workforce—strategies that involve labor exploitation and land expropriation—has engineered the arrival of migrant workers, those also deemed less "threatening" to the collective body, both because they are not

Palestinian and also because their temporariness protects this body from permanent racial alteration.

Against the backdrop of this genealogy, to unsettle migrant eldercare is to examine how the act of laboring is always about more than commodity or service produced, or the relation between worker and boss. Intergenerational reproduction is shaped by the overdetermined "ideal image" of the elderly Holocaust survivor as much as the masculine, youthful European Jewish pioneer forging a claim to settlement through labor force participation. As I suggest later, this image functions as a reminder of why—and from whom—the collective body must remain safe.

Neoliberal Restructuring and Contemporary Colonial-Capital Accumulation

Contemporary colonial-capital accumulation is premised upon the increased marketization of gendered labors and the differential valuing of who is worthy of care, collectively and individually. While the gendered racialization of care work has long enabled its devaluation, Israel's turn to private service delivery of eldercare has fortified these differences in new ways. Since the 1990s, Israel's turn to new procurement arrangements in the field of eldercare has implicated employers and private recruiters alike in multiple "precarity chains," or the circuits of migration that transfer debt across networks, families, and geopolitical space.[83] Prior to state retrenchment policies, the Israeli government was a central player in care service delivery. Beginning in the 1980s, eldercare services were increasingly provided through competitive tendering as the government aimed to cut costs and state responsibility in the areas of welfare, health care, and education.[84] Meanwhile, services are increasingly measured according to production rather than quality of services and jobs.[85] Neoliberal restructuring has furthered the deskilling of caring professions in an already highly feminized sector, increasing job insecurity, particularly for Palestinian women workers, and leading to a drop in union protections. Worker precarity has thus become part of Israel's reproductive regime, which facilitates increased vulnerability to debt, deportation, and work-related injuries for some, while mitigating vulnerability for others.[86] The Israeli state further enhances these chains of precarity through its policies of prioritizing Jewish settlement, which by extension prevent migrant workers from coming to Israel with immediate family members, and prohibiting migrants from marrying and becoming pregnant, both policies aimed at ensuring Jewish territorial control.

Neoliberal reforms in Palestine/Israel have equally been a matter of altering tactics of land expropriation. As Andy Clarno shows, neoliberal restructuring created a "surplus" laboring population in the West Bank that rendered Palestinian workers "redundant."[87] Following Oslo, Israeli strategies for land control have relied upon a system of military enclosure that creates a "warehous[ing]" of Palestinian workers as labor is outsourced to surrounding countries and to migrant workers.[88] This post-Oslo system of indirect rule has also engendered the privatization of Israel's security industry, which has allowed a growing number of Israeli technology and security elites to profit from the occupation.[89] Under neoliberal restructuring, the racial/colonial inequalities underwriting colonial-capital accumulation have also expanded, as non-Jewish populations increasingly "subsidize the benefits, salaries, and profits of the dominant Ashkenazi society."[90] The turn to migrant eldercare facilitated by the uneven replacement of Palestinians with migrants is thus part of a broader "market-based strategy of colonization."[91]

Private Agencies

Caregivers' accounts of agency exploitation and unremunerated labor illustrate how racialized and gendered hierarchies become the condition of possibility for colonial-capital accumulation under late capitalism, as devaluation is as much a denigration of workers as it is their labors.[92] Part of the transnational web of companies incurring profit through labor migration, Israeli "manpower" agencies require migrants to pay several thousand dollars to receive their work permits and visas. Keren, a Jewish Israeli migrant advocacy worker, said that despite bilateral agreements between Israel and the Philippines, some caregivers are paying USD $7,000–$18,000. Like households, private recruitment agencies further facilitate the expropriation of care work through the reproduction of European and non-European difference. This reinscription of colonial categories is evident in the *hierarchy* of fees agencies charge, something caregivers frequently discuss. With limited formal pressure from the Israeli government to make their practices transparent, agencies are relatively free to charge different amounts to migrants depending upon their gender and country of origin. According to workers, Filipina women are typically charged the lowest fees, while Indian men are charged the highest. Data collected by migrant advocacy organization Kav LaOved likewise suggest that Filipinx workers pay significantly less than South Asian workers. More broadly, several workers suggested that private agencies present particular caregivers as being more exploitable than others, signaling to employers that the purpose of hiring a migrant caregiver is not to have them help with the various tasks delineated in the work contract, but rather to supplement as large a portion of the household labor as possible. Speaking to this "selling" of caregiver competences, Abigail, a real estate agent and business student from the Philippines who paid USD $7,000 for her visa in 2007, notes, "They give the hardest job to those who just arrive because the new ones don't know anything and have more patience." In contrast, caregivers who have been in Palestine/Israel many years and openly demand their rights have been referred to by employers and recruitment agents alike as "damaged goods," while those who have just arrived are considered to have a *rosh naki* (clear head) and be more amenable to compliance. The amount of time a worker has been in Palestine/Israel thus shapes perceptions about how much unpaid labor they are willing to do and how able they are to refuse unpaid tasks.

Not only do agencies attempt to advertise less experienced caregivers as "good hires," but they also marketize and "sell" the racialized, sexualized, and gendered stereotypes of employers through the setting of migration fees. Abigail further explains:

> At first the government only took workers from the Philippines in Israel . . . we are more aware of what we need to pay [than other caregivers]. In general, Nepalese, they are more eager to come here . . . when they are being offered to pay $10,000 [USD], they are accepting it. They are willing to pay that, while in the Philippines, we have other options. . . . Most of the time it's the agency who dictates, "Oh, we'll give you Indians, they're good at this, blah, blah, blah, they're good at that." They know how to talk the talk. It happened before that some Indians are stuck. No one wants to accept them. They are accepting salaries of $200 a month.

The hierarchical ladder of fees Abigail describes suggests how the coloniality of migrant labor influences the actual cost of migration, the amount of debt workers take on, the salaries they receive, and the value bosses and agencies extract. As Abigail suggests, in promoting various stereotypes, agents play upon the relatively lower economic status of migrants within economic echelons or sending countries that may make them more willing to incur high debt and to retain a job at any cost. Indeed, employers can make requests to agencies about what nationality they prefer a caregiver to be. In financing these exorbitant fees, many migrants sell land or jewelry or take out high-interest loans that can take upward of a year and a half to pay back.[93]

Agencies also accumulate wealth by organizing various schemes that deprive workers of their visas after they have paid thousands of dollars to come to Palestine/Israel. The most well-documented of these scams is that of the "flying visa," a complex scheme workers regularly discuss wherein recruitment agents pay either elderly Israeli citizens or their adult children to file an application with the national insurance administration for permission to hire a migrant caregiver. Under regular circumstances, once the national insurance agency grants this permission, private agencies are allotted one visa by the government for the purpose of "recruiting" a migrant from abroad. It is during this phase of the "matching" process that private agencies charge exorbitant fees to migrants for the "processing" of their visa. Under the flying visa scheme, private agencies encourage Israelis to find a reason to reject the caregiver assigned to them so they can then apply for a "replacement" caregiver, thereby generating more money for the private recruitment agent through the fees they will charge the "replacement" migrant. Typically, the citizen who was given the voucher will receive a cut of the earnings from the agency. Lina explains how the flying visa scheme impacted her sister: "My sister came here on a flying visa. The agency brought her on a blind visa and the Minister [of Interior] did not want to give her a visa . . . she got taken three times to jail and government wouldn't give her a visa, and also she's working. . . . For one year she didn't get a salary. . . . I want my sister to go back to Nepal because it's very difficult work and nobody helps." Though the scheme Lina describes has since been declared illegal, agencies continue to commodify migrant caregivers through highly secretive processes of "price-setting," through which they determine how much money they can charge migrants according to country, gender, age, and workers' degree of economic need. According to Abigail, agencies are deeply secretive about the processes by which they set these prices, which allows them to avoid accountability:

> You're not going to see who you pay your money to because you're going to pay it to one agent then they pay it to another agent—if there's a conflict about this and that, they don't know which agencies

to point to, and then the agencies are not going to accept [responsi-bility]. . . . The agency will just say, "No, we didn't accept any [pay-ment] from you! Why did you pay the money?" . . . Even when I paid, I asked, "Can I have a receipt?" "No, we're not giving any receipt, and you're not going to tell that you paid me like this," because they know it's illegal. . . . Those agencies, they have connections with the Knes-set . . . they're even using dead people's visas.

As a result of these secretive practices, attempts at fighting illegal fees are ad hoc rather than collective and organized, and they depend upon a caregiver's ability to strategically negotiate with individual bosses. The privatized nature of these recruitment practices transfers responsibility for "the legal-normative failures" of Israeli labor policy to private agencies, precluding them from being held accountable.[94] This lack of transparency further entrenches migrant eldercare as a site of colonial-capital accumula-tion through which private actors can amass profit through quasi-legal and extralegal recruitment methods.

Finally, the coloniality of migrant care work is also evident in the differ-ences between migrant and citizen wages and entitlements—a reality agen-cies leverage to their benefit. By virtue of their constitution as noncitizen temporary workers, migrant caregivers are excluded from overtime pay and restricted from social and legal protections, while the cost of employ-ing migrants is three times cheaper than that of citizens. Their own time is thus worth less than that of citizen workers, and their labor more readily extractable. For instance, while caregivers are entitled to take a rest period of twenty-five consecutive hours a week and eight hours a day, many work continuously for at least twelve hours a day and are on call around the clock, even during the night.[95] Up to 30 percent of caregivers do not take their va-cation days and must ask for permission to visit their families at home.[96] Caregivers also take on the labors of care demanded by their charges' family members, despite their terms of contract. In contrast to the daily reality of caregiving, the standard employment contract that Filipinx caregivers re-ceive assigns them only one charge, while prohibiting "domestic chores for other family members," "animal care," and "driving/chauffeur duties."[97] Equally mystifying of the reality of caregiving, agency advertisements paint live-in care work as difficult but financially and personally rewarding. An advertisement by Israeli recruitment agency RavGil, for example, states that caregivers in Palestine/Israel enjoy a "high [monthly] salary," and "full support by social workers," and even "occasional gifts for caregivers."[98] In reality, many caregivers do laundry, cook for, and clean up after multiple members of the family with little support from agencies. Cindy explains, "My agency is useless, and my employer's [family are siblings] with the agency social worker's husband, so there's this connection and I can't even complain [to them]. They even went to a house where I was, over *pesach* (Passover), and it was uncomfortable. I decided after that to keep more distance from my [employer's] family. Social workers only come once a year to collect money from the family and don't care how I'm doing." As Cindy suggests, the privatization of labor arbitration overwhelmingly reinforces the prioritization of the elderly's needs and vulnerabilities over that of caregivers, making eldercare a site of public and private sector accumulation.

Finally, the gendered division of eldercare is also shaped by the "demand side" of the Israeli eldercare market and the system of quotas that agencies set. A 2019 Recruitment Specification Form posted by the Philippines Overseas Employment Administration (POEA), for instance, states that during the process of recruiting five hundred Filipinx caregivers, the Israeli government will select "approximately 90% women and 10% men."[99] Similarly, in their plan to implement a bilateral agreement with Nepal, the Israeli government has said it will aim to recruit 70 percent women and 30 percent male caregivers.[100] Predeparture orientations (PDOs) reinforce gendered expectations of how migrant caregivers "ought" to act, promoting the notion of "ideal migrant subjects" that will fulfill the expectations of Israel's settler-consumers.[101] Rachel Silvey and Rhacel Salazar Parreñas, for instance, offer the example of a three-day predeparture training in the Philippines, at which a trainer explains that "if you are a cell phone, you are an open line. Everything depends on your employer—your work, your rest. . . . You can't tell your madam, 'it is 10 P.M., go to sleep now.'"[102] As Ethel Tungohan shows, PDOs position caregivers as dutiful workers.[103] Brian, a caregiver and community organizer from the Philippines, showed me the manual from his predeparture training, which includes other forms of bodily discipline. Among the instructions in the training manual is the injunction to "have a smile in your voice" when talking to employers and answering the phone and to refrain from wearing nail polish. The imperative to "have a smile," among other instructions migrants receive during predeparture trainings, sheds light on the intimate processes by which gendered and racialized ideologies about care work unfold across transnational spaces, reinscribing colonial categories such as worker and boss, East and

West, and developed and undeveloped. These characterizations, as Nicole Constable suggests, paint migrant domestic workers as "docile social bodies," a form of physical, moral, and emotional discipline that is often reproduced through employers' expectations of caregivers within the home.[104]

Households

An equally salient site of colonial-capital accumulation is the employer's home itself. While agencies may set and reflect gendered and racialized expectations of caregivers, employers articulate these expectations on a daily basis. Among employers, the devaluation of care and domestic labor as "not really work" blurs the line between work and rest, enabling labor extraction.[105] In reality, the informal nature of the home and the coloniality of migrant care work render the many labors of eldercare "low skill." The legally sanctioned blurring of the line between work and rest is precisely the mechanism through which employers accumulate savings in payments they would otherwise be required to pay citizen caregivers.[106] As David explains, "You live in a house, so it's different because even if we have laws like in our contracts, even if we have a ten-hour workday, if you're sleeping and he needs something at night, you're not going to ignore him . . . the time and the work hours are not really strictly observed . . . it's kind of murky." The "murky" legal situation David describes is exacerbated by presumptions of migrant caregivers as being always available to tend to employers' every need.

Stories from workers and employers reveal how individual employers' gendered racisms shape their expectations of how caregivers "ought" to perform their job and whether they can refuse extracontractual labor. Describing her "preference" for hiring Filipina caregivers, Leah casually notes, "I heard from my friends that they [Filipinos] are better." Yet, she later suggests how class status, educational background, and ability to converse in English also shape employers' expectations. While Filipinx migrant caregivers in Israel generally come from lower-middle-class backgrounds, have attended college, and are fluent in English, migrant caregivers from India more often come from working-class backgrounds, have attended college less often, and are less fluent in English. Leah illustrates as much, noting that "there are many caregivers from India also. It seems they know how to serve us. Because they are used to it. They don't have the possibility to go to the university." Leah's insistence that Indian caregivers "know how to serve us" illustrates how the coloniality of migrant care work is shaped by proximity to a middle-class income, higher education, and English. It also suggests how private recruitment agencies exploit degrees of economic precarity when placing workers with employers. The label "unskilled" becomes a tool for extracting more unpaid work hours, challenging workers' ability to contest task expansion, and enhancing employers' power to determine when caregivers "deserve" physical and emotional breaks. As I discuss in chapters 4 and 5, this dynamic requires that workers deploy "tacit skills" to navigate bosses' expectation that they be constantly available.

Several caregivers described employers' "preferences" for Filipina caregivers, whom employers thought of as innately "caring" and "sweet," a colonial coding that consistently arose. Abigail noted that a recruitment agent once told her, "You are so spoiled because you are *choosing* work!" This account suggests the racialized hierarchy of workers—Nepalese and Indian caregivers have more difficulty finding jobs and generally are placed in more difficult or less desirable environments.[107] Employers' stereotypes reveal how racist and sexist expectations about how particular workers "ought" to perform their duties can function as a form of "affective blackmail," such that deviating from or refusing the emotional labor of particular performances can lead to accusations of negligence, laziness, coldness, or even moral opprobrium, each of which hold economic and legal consequences for workers.[108]

Many workers also said their employers preferred women caregivers, whom they described as more agreeable and less likely to draw lines between work and rest. Supporting this assertion, Esther, an employer living in Jerusalem, notes that while men are more forceful, "women aren't like this. . . . They take care of things, are ready to help, to clean, sometimes they cook, they do things without being asked, they're more a part of the family, and they play with the grandchildren." Compounding these gendered dynamics are the sexual politics of the job, which can blur the line between expectations of caregiving and companionship, particularly for migrants, who are required to live with their employers. As James articulates, "The people in Israel, they don't really want a caregiver; they want a housemate too. According to the law, our work is only to take care of certain people . . . but what the employers of Israel expect is that we do work as a housemate; not only taking care of *aba* and *eema*. So they expect that women do that.

So there's lots of visas for women."[109] James suggests how the requisite affectations of eldercare attach to particular spaces. As an often unspoken, commonly extracontractual feature of many service jobs, eldercare demands the display of affectivities catering to the whims and fantasies of bosses, charges, and clients. James adds that women "can do the housekeeping well, they can take care well, they can cook well. The women's nature is to do these things, whereas they consider the men a little unhygienic." Rahul, a caregiver and former steel factory manager from Jaipur, India, relays that employers prefer women caregivers "because when they are old, they like to go to the park and the coffee shop to meet friends and they are happy to be with a young lady . . . if a young girl goes with him, they like it. They think, 'I'll get married.'"

Sam and Rahul also suggest how reproductive labor is shaped by workers' own gendered perceptions about care and domestic work. Sam describes having to bear his family's disapproval of eldercare as a form of "dirty work." He notes, "My brother and sister-in-law said, 'Don't go work as a caregiver in Israel. Do you know what kind of job you need to do there? You need to clean stool and urine and work twenty-four-seven and make enema and give showers and [clean] sputum. It's very dirty and hard work and you can catch diseases. . . . If you catch serious diseases, what will happen? You will spoil your life!'" Relaying a similar stigma, one that is reflective of both gender and class position, Rahul notes, "In my house, sometimes if I wanted to help my mother or sister, if my father saw me, he's kidding with me, 'He's behaving like a woman, he's doing a woman's work.' They don't know what I'm doing here. If they knew, they would call me right now." While women caregivers also expressed ambivalence about being caregivers, these conflicting feelings were more often articulated as disappointment about their own downward social mobility in Palestine/Israel, or intraclass dynamics reflecting a hesitation to do "dirty work" or housecleaning, rather than working in a feminized profession.[110]

Structurally, the gendered and racialized devaluation of workers and their work reinforces the worst effects of labor flexibilization, while reaffirming employers' assumption that migrant caregivers must willingly perform the role of housekeeper. Another near ubiquitous experience is having to take care of a couple, or even a family, despite being contractually responsible for only one person. This form of task expansion often doubles or even triples a caregiver's work. Peter, a caregiver from the Philippines working for an elderly gentleman outside Tel Aviv, explains,

For me, it's not an easy job because I do everything . . . *bituach mashlim* [supplemental insurance], *kupat holim* [HMO insurance], and dialysis now. So it's very difficult. Two, three times a week . . . the wife also is not in good health, so sometimes [my employer] calls me and the woman also calls me so I don't know what I can do, go to my employer or go to the wife? So sometimes I'm shouting with the couple. I will fight with the wife. What can I do? It's my work and I must be workful, so patient.

Like Peter, Serene struggles to manage caring for more than one charge. She explains,

In my previous job—they are the ones who took me from the Philippines—it was written in the contract that I'd be working with four people, and when I start working here, I'm actually working with eight people so it's illegal. So they wrote the wrong information in the contract so I told them it's not fair because I've been working for eight people and not just my employer alone. It's a nineteen-year-old girl and I'm working with her family . . . that's seven more. I don't have any problems with her alone . . . after a month I realized I really can't do this, so I told her straight.

Refusing extracontractual work is risky for workers who have overstayed their visa or switched employers more than twice in two years. Caregivers whose employers are acutely ill or suffering from dementia said they would remain on duty throughout the night because their charges would regularly wake in pain, from a nightmare, or to go to the bathroom. Some caregivers describe sleeping by their employers' beds when they are legally finished with the workday, for fear their charges could hurt themselves. Mayra notes that "I have no free time. [My employer] wakes up in the night, and he wants to go outside. I stay near him—I go near them to sleep on the floor because I don't want him to fall down. If he falls down it's very dangerous . . . it's a twenty-four-hour job. I go out sometimes but not too much because I'm afraid he'll fall down. It's a challenge like this. I don't have a day off." For Mayra, keeping her employer safe from injury requires working during her daily and weekly rest hours. For some caregivers, these expectations contrasted starkly with the way recruitment agents presented the job to them before migration. Rahul explains,

When I came here, I did work like a maid. People are not going according to [the] law. . . . If they follow the law, they have to pay us a lot of money and they can't pay. Before I came here, I looked at the website and I read everything about how many hours I have to do, what I have to do here—they said if we see something we have to clean it, but not like cleaners. Here they say, "here is the dust, clean it!" Like torture! . . . Some people, I think they are crazy. They don't know anything about humanity.

In contrast to these accounts, Rivka, an employer, offers her perception that "[caregivers] don't do anything, they just sit there, just talk and go for walks with their employers, shop occasionally, and just sit in the house." She also explains that she "want[s] a caregiver that is clean [because] I need the house clean and I'm worried about mess." While there are many employers more greatly attuned to the reality of being a caregiver, Rivka's comment highlights the sizable gap between employers' perceptions of the work-rest divide and the reality of live-in eldercare.

The extent to which the gendered racialization of citizen and noncitizen labor has become imbricated in the social fabric of contemporary Israeli society is also evident in Shmuel's story of how his mother hired a caregiver:

[My mother] would go to the *moadon* [daycare for the elderly] and see all her friends with caregivers and say, "Why don't I have one?" And that's how it started. . . . My mother wanted someone to help her with cleaning . . . she felt lonely and wanted somebody . . . the nurse from *betuach leumi* [national insurance] would come in and ask my mother, "I'm very thirsty, can you get me a glass of water?" And my mother would jump! That was enough for the nurse to realize she didn't need one . . . after something like ten or eleven times, [she] qualified. [The elderly] are smarter in this sense and they were able to fool the nurse.

Shmuel reveals the centrality of migrants to Israeli popular perceptions of aging. When his mother first applied for in-home care services, it was not out of medical necessity, but rather because she "would . . . see all her friends with caregivers" and decided she wanted this convenience and companionship. That shared strategies exist for "fool[ing] the nurse" speaks to migrant caregivers' role as status symbols.

The gap between expectations and realities of the job can also lead to profound disappointment. Pamela, a high school science teacher from the Philippines, expresses a similar sense of frustration. She notes, "I had very nice expectations. I thought I'd be wearing a white gown and going to the hospital and then coming home. I didn't know I'd have to stay twenty-four hours with the person in the house." Pamela's conjuring of a white gown represents the impression some caregivers have of the work before they arrive, assuming they will be treated as workers with skills and experiences in nursing, paramedics, teaching, and caregiving, rather than told their work is "unskilled" by virtue of their status as migrants. Indeed, the contract caregivers receive from sending-state employment offices refers to care work as "skilled."[111]

It is expressly the coloniality of migrant care work—its connection to past histories and ongoing realities of racial and gender differentiation—that enable its devaluation. In the Israeli context, this differentiation is a product of past and ongoing histories of land expropriation and the concomitant creation of laboring "buffer" populations. Recruitment agencies and employers naturalizing the effortful nature of care work reinforce this devaluation, extracting greater amounts of unpaid labor while reaffirming the role of settler-consumers as "natural" managers. Reproductive labors are thus a site of hyperprivatized capital-colonial accumulation under neoliberal retrenchment, even as they have long been a form of accumulation enmeshed with exploitation, extractivism, and disinvestment.

Caring for the Elderly Body

Across the *longue durée* of Zionist settlement, reproductive labors are sites of ongoing colonial-capital accumulation whose intended product is the forming of a domestic home on seized land and the "recruiting and control of labor" as a strategy for preserving the racial makeup of the Jewish collective body.[112] Central to this preservation are the labors of intergenerational reproduction that citizens outsource to migrants on a daily basis. Symbolically, the labor of protecting, caring for, and accompanying Israel's "founding generation" at the end of their lives is deeply tied to the regeneration of myths and narratives about the latent fragility and vulnerability of the Jewish collective body. As Idith Zertal argues, Holocaust testimonies are a "precious asset to the nation and the movement," and survivors themselves, a "remembering collective" generating a "shared sense of nationhood" and a common goal of redemption through land settlement.[113] The pinnacle of this goal—realizing the strength of the collective body in the form of an impenetrable Jewish state—becomes a way, in part, of "redeeming [victims'] death," and thus creating an "indissoluble" connection between Israel's enduring existence and the Holocaust.[114] At the same time, whether through national commemorations, Israel Defense Forces (IDF) ceremonies, government speeches, or civil society initiatives, mention of the Holocaust can be a way to invoke the primordial and ongoing vulnerability of the collective body to attack. Significantly, many members of the "founding generation" are both Holocaust survivors and veterans of the fledgling IDF paramilitary that facilitated the Nakba in the years leading up to statehood. Against this complex symbolic terrain, non-Jewish migrants, as caretakers of the elderly, become an intimate part of this narrative, a topic to which I turn in the next chapter.

As the caretakers of the elderly beneficiaries of in-home care, migrant caregivers guard the bodies of elderly Israelis, many of whom are part of this "founding generation." They stay beside them during "rest" hours, help them avoid injury, and ensure that they live the rest of their lives in dignity and safety.[115] On a daily basis they address the traumas of elderly Jewish Israelis who have suffered from anti-Semitism and fascism, bearing witness to their stories and memories of violence. They help their employers process traumas that resurface at the end of their lives and make sense of past experiences. They also regularly hear employers' stories about being separated from their families in Russia and Poland, escaping concentration camps, and being confronted by German or Soviet soldiers. Maria, a caregiver from the Philippines, describes finding ways to calm her employer when she expresses both fear and anger as past memories surface. Maria explains, "She's got Alzheimer's. She would cry so loud. She was a soldier and she's a Holocaust survivor, that's why she's always afraid. After she came [to Palestine] at ten she was a paramilitary. The husband was a general. Now she's for the whole day not leaving the house. Talking, crying so loud . . . in the street, everybody knows us. When she cries and runs in the street I have to follow her. Children visit and you have to tell everything to the children. She can go in the road where there's cars." Maria's daily work as a caregiver involves intimately navigating the past traumas her employer experienced as a Holocaust survivor while also helping the adult children navigate the emergence of these traumas as they resurface. Like Maria,

Cindy deals daily with her employer's traumatic experiences surviving Nazi terror. She explains that her employer, who also has Alzheimer's disease, regularly tells her, "You're killing me! You're trying to kill me, you German! You German, you're trying to kill me! You have no brain!" In trying to make sense of these moments, Cindy explains, "Jews also experience a lot of hurt and that's also why they're insecure."

Not unlike Maria and Cindy, Shmuel recalls how his elderly mother, who came to Palestine from Rabat, Morocco, unintentionally imposes her own past traumas onto her caregiver. His story suggests how Mizrahi settler-employers transfer their own difficult experiences of violence onto caregivers, as another "founding myth" of the nation:[116]

> Each time she goes home my mother becomes more dependent on her [caregiver], and now my mother is completely in a state, she's going on, she's thinking many times that Sarah is her boss, that Sarah is the owner of the place. She will say things to her as if she's the commandante. She has memories of a tough commandante in Marseille. They were in transit camps and wanted to make sure people behaved properly, so they have these commandantes and she thought Sarah was her commandante. I'd tell her this is your house and she works for you! She'd say, "No, no, no, no"—she couldn't accept.

As Maria, Cindy, and Shmuel begin to suggest, caregiving entails ascertaining aspects of their charge's personal history to understand what events trigger traumatic memories, knowing how to calm and reorient charges, reminding them of the names of their family members, dressing them, helping them bathe and use the bathroom, feeding them, and rocking them to sleep when they wake from nightmares. Beyond those elderly identified as Holocaust survivors, many employers are, in Nik's words, "*memash* [really] like a baby," needing assistance, guidance, and direction throughout the day.

When invoked by the state, Holocaust trauma functions as a justification for ongoing violence against Palestinians in the name of defending the collective body.[117] Through speeches and commemorations tying Holocaust remembrance to Israeli independence, the state invokes the need to protect this body through military invasion and depletion of Palestinian resources. This metaphorical transference between elderly bodies and the nation suggests that the Jewish Israeli collective body *is* the victimized European Jew, while, by quiet extension, Palestinians are akin to European oppressors.

Such transference obscures the disproportionate power Israel holds over the resources required for Palestinian social reproduction, the ongoing control Israel exacts over Palestinian movement and life, and the conditions of European imperialism enabling the ongoing impunity of the Israeli state. It also erases the many elderly Jewish Israeli citizens who come from non-European countries, holding different traumas and other diasporic memories, while writing Palestinian trauma and resistance alike out of history. As a Jerusalem Center for Public Affairs report states, "Israel's unique situation—a small and vulnerable country surrounded by many large and hostile neighbors—led to its ambiguous nuclear deterrent policy that has been in place since the 1960s and has received very broad support from all parts of the Israeli political spectrum. The policy has not changed in four decades despite major changes in the government, and can be expected to continue as long as rejection of Israel's legitimacy and threats to national survival continue."[118] Depicting the nation as a vulnerable collectivity surrounded by irrational violence, the institute juxtaposes the "small" size of Israel to its "large and hostile" surroundings.[119] It is in this sense that the Israeli state is not only settler colonial, but also what Ilan Pappé terms "*shtetl* colonial"—that is, "a formidable and fierce *shtetl* state" whose fierceness becomes justified by "the weak and poor *shtetl* of Eastern Europe."[120] Referring to the small Jewish villages throughout Eastern Europe that were subject to violent anti-Semitism, the *shtetl* connotes a state of collective being antithetical to national strength and sovereignty. Whereas *shtetl* life recalls the impossibility of assimilation and equal belonging, Jewish life under modern political Zionism evokes liberation through national sovereignty, strength, and a loss of collective fragility and dependency. When decontextualized and instrumentalized by the state, the image of the *shtetl* and the vulnerability of Eastern European Jews to genocide, exclusion, and violent pogroms can be temporally transferred by settler-citizens onto the Jewish Israeli collective body writ large, ignoring practices of ethnic cleansing against Palestinians.[121]

Commemorative speeches regularly illustrate this linkage. In particular, Holocaust Remembrance Day speeches by Israeli officials draw close linkages between the Holocaust and the need for a "strengthening" of "the Jewish people" in the land of Palestine. In his 2005 speech in Birkenau, Poland, Prime Minister Ariel Sharon exemplifies this transference. He states, "And so Holocaust survivors stand here among us today—again, on this cursed land, surrounded by people in uniform. But this time, these are not German

SS soldiers lusting to murder, but the grandchildren of the survivors—soldiers in the Israel Defense Forces, the army of the free and sovereign Jewish State."[122] The slippage between SS soldiers standing in for Jewish victimhood, and the IDF as the refusal of victimhood manifest as victimizers, demonstrates how Jewish Israeli citizens' traumatic histories underpin rhetorical justifications for ongoing colonization and land annexation.[123]

In another commemorative speech, Prime Minister Naftali Bennett, who is on the far right, draws a link between victims of the Holocaust, emplacement, and the need for a strong military. Before an audience of government officials and Holocaust survivors on Holocaust Martyrs' and Heroes' Remembrance Day, Bennett tells the story of a young Jewish girl who was killed at Auschwitz.

Following the story, he proclaims,

> We have built a strong and prosperous Jewish state in the Land of Israel. The goal—which we have no choice but to meet—is that the State of Israel must be the strongest. Always. To have the strongest army, with the best air force, with the bravest fighters, with the most sophisticated Mossad and Israel Security Agency, and above all, with the deepest conviction in the righteousness of our path. . . . But alongside our friends and allies near and far, we must remember a basic truth: We will only be able to exist in our country if we deepen our roots in our land. . . . The Jewish people are similar to a plant that requires a certain type of land. The plant can maybe live and even somehow survive in another place, but if it wants to fully grow and blossom, it must be rooted in its own land. . . . Building the State of Israel, the Jewish state in the Land of Israel, is in fact our victory over those who sought to wipe us out. Let us all embrace and safeguard our country.[124]

By succeeding his invocation of a murdered Jewish child with the call for unlimited military power, Bennett positions the IDF as the redeemer of the Holocaust, and the land itself as the sole place where "the Jewish people" can be strengthened. Though Bennett does not directly invoke Palestinians, his mention of military, intelligence, and security agencies silently references the perceived "threat" of Palestinian infiltration into the collective body. His speech suggests how Zionist mythology recodes anticolonial resistance as irrational threat.

Bennett's speech also reveals how discourses of fragility and vulnerability become affixed to the nation, concealing the material conditions that have increased vulnerability beyond and within the Jewish collective body. Ironically, despite how their image has been instrumentalized by the state, Jewish Holocaust survivors have not escaped the harms of state neglect under neoliberal retrenchment. A 2016 *Telegraph* article titled "Tens of Thousands of Israeli Holocaust Survivors Are Living in Abject Poverty" details the "hunger, cold and homelessness" experienced by as many as forty-five thousand elderly Jewish Israelis unable to meet their material needs.[125] Yet the neglect they face is rarely discussed alongside the material deprivation of non-Jewish populations. As trade liberalization and privatization have caused a steady rise in the cost of living since the 1980s, lack of affordable housing, the gentrification of working-class city neighborhoods, the high cost of medicine, and the marketization of eldercare services have been dwarfed by the budget allotted for annual military expenditures.[126] At the same time, government and media narratives in the United States and Israel alike portray these inequalities as "the cost of Israel's security conditions."[127] The actual vulnerability of many elderly citizens are thus recorded as national sacrifice, an inevitable cost of "protecting" the latently vulnerable collective body from injury.

Jewish Israeli elderly comprising Israel's "founding generation" are also portrayed in legal decisions as the unquestionable subjects of vulnerability and care. Ethical norms around care create ontological distinctions between those who are expected to *provide* care and those who should readily *receive* care, distinctions made evident in the lack of attention to elderly Palestinians in ongoing Israeli military invasions in the occupied Palestinian Territories. While holding transformative potential, like any "biopolitical category," care renders some bodies suitable for labor and others fit for laboring in service of another's collective future without entitling these bodies to futurity themselves.[128] As Justice Cheshin notes in his 2006 Israeli Supreme Court opinion on the "binding" of migrant caregivers to their employers, "the vulnerability of the employers, according to [the Israeli government], justifies placing certain obstacles in the path of person [*sic*] working for them to stop them resigning from their work with them." Thus, the government attributes the challenge in abandoning the binding arrangement to the likelihood that "certain persons who need nursing services[,] who are also as aforesaid a weak sector of the population," would otherwise not be able to hire a foreign caregiver due to the extensive demands of tending to the elderly and the cost of hiring a round-the-clock worker.[129] The economic difficulties of elderly citizens are thus unquestionably more constitutive of vulnerability than the freedom of employment for caregivers. Similarly, in both a 2009 and a 2013 ruling excluding migrant caregivers from overtime pay, High Court justices refer to the elderly as a "weak" population or part of a "weakened group."[130]

Even where the majority opinion justices acknowledge the vulnerable status of caregivers as "weak workers in the economy," they emphasize the difficulty elderly Israelis would have obtaining needed care if they were required to pay workers for overtime hours.[131] In the 2013 ruling, Justice Elyakim Rubinstein even notes, "My heart goes out to the foreign caregivers buckling under the burden [of carework] . . . but my heart also goes out to the patient who often has no real voice, even if he is Israeli."[132] Judging the very real physical, economic, and cognitive vulnerability of elderly citizens as paramount to the same for migrants, Justice Rubinstein reinforces the ontological status of citizens as the rightful subjects of care, regardless of the physical and economic burden on largely rightless workers. The precarity that, according to Justice Rubinstein, is a necessary condition for keeping the elderly alive contrasts with the greater access to medical, elderly, child, and disability care afforded to Jewish Israelis. As I argue in the subsequent chapter, under neoliberal labor formations, migrant caregivers must often lessen the vulnerability of elderly and disabled citizens precisely at the cost of their own bodies and their ability to care for themselves.

The strengthening of the collective body depends upon not only pro-natalism and the enduring narratives of Holocaust survivors, but also the preservation, prolongation, and multiplication of elderly life more broadly. Tellingly, Zionist agencies such as Nefesh B'Nefesh, an organization funded by the Jewish National Fund that facilitates the settlement of Jews in Palestine, advertises the benefits of retiring and growing old in Israel through, in part, the possibility of long-term care done by a "foreign worker" (notably, a page of their website on moving elderly parents to Israel is dedicated to "Hiring a Foreign Care Worker").[133] Selling Israel as an optimal retirement community, Nefesh B'Nefesh, Hadassah, and other organizations advertise the opportunity for seniors "to be closer to family," to benefit from "the incredible Israeli health care system," and to enjoy what Nefesh B'Nefesh representative Marc Rosenberg describes as "the warm spirit of the country and, of course, the awesome weather."[134] Though not among the "thousands of skilled and idealistic new citizens" participating in the workforce that Nefesh B'Nefesh and the Jewish National Fund typically recruit, retired *olim* (immigrants) nevertheless increase the Jewish presence on the land and compose a steady portion of Jewish settlers each year.

Locating eldercare as a site of colonial-capital accumulation within Israel's reproductive regime is not to deny the vulnerability of the elderly. Elderly charges often express fears of being abandoned by caregivers and are unable to sleep or eat when their caregivers go on vacation. Transitioning from independent to dependent living can be an extremely painful experience for the elderly and equally stressful for family members. A similarly difficult burden for families is finding trusted caregivers to tend to their relatives. Migrant caregivers and citizen-employers in some ways are interdependent in their vulnerability. Yet these vulnerabilities are differentially created by, visible to, and prioritized by the state, and the material implications of these divergent valuations have profound impacts on migrant caregivers' ability to support themselves and their extended networks. Rather than erasing elderly citizens' dependency needs, a focus on the differential distribution of vulnerability highlights how injury to all populations is tied to the ongoing uprooting of native homes and communities. Within Israel's reproductive regime, Israel positions Palestinians as "available for injury" through state violence and labor extraction.[135]

In subsequent chapters, I turn to the home as a site of injury, resistance, unsettling, and care in its multiple forms. By ensuring the sustenance of bodies, homes, and families, migrant caregivers safeguard the lives of those who symbolically are most vulnerable while generating their own "precarity of future" in the form of debt and the risk of injury.[136] At the same time, in the face of state surveillance and household discipline of workers, migrant caregivers strategically improve their bargaining power and navigate the structural conditions binding them to employers. These strategies reveal care to be a category of valuation in the broader landscape of settler colonial governance as well as a labor, a process, a relation to people and land, a work ethic, and a shared source of resistance and transformation.

2

Intimacy, Alienation, and Affective Automation

All jobs are hard but in different ways. You are the boss, the security guard, the dog, the daughter, the mother. . . . If something happens, if they fall, it's very hard for us because we have to lift, to change, to carry [them] all the time. That's why we're very careful also—we don't want it to happen.

Ramona, caregiver, outside Tel Aviv

In her description of the day-to-day rhythms of live-in eldercare, Ramona, a caregiver from the Philippines working outside of Tel Aviv, reveals how caregivers are at once house managers, guardians of the elderly, intimately linked to employers' bodies, and treated with suspicion. The demanding, round-the-clock work of keeping employers alive involves maintaining a schedule for one's charge, protecting employers from injury, monitoring their emotional well-being, and ingratiating oneself into the home. Yet caregivers are also surveilled, accused of theft and abuse, and treated as aliens in the household and nation. As Ramona implies, injury to one's employer could lead to job loss and greater debt. For caregivers whose visas have expired, or for those who stretch time by extending their stay, guarding the elderly from injury is a matter of subverting deportation.[1] Ramona injured her shoulder by repetitively lifting her employer, quite literally bearing the weight of her charge's bodily needs at the cost of her own. Her employer was able to demand this extracontractual labor precisely because of Ramona's intimate positioning within the small confines of the home, and her lack of rights as a non-Jewish migrant. Due to the repetitive execution of physical and emotional tasks beyond her own limits, a process I call "affective automation," Ramona faced injury as a quotidian repercussion of the job.[2]

Within the home and nation, migrant caregivers are constituted as both trusted workers doing a uniquely intimate form of labor and non-Jewish "others" alienated from territorial and temporal permanence. While their positioning as intimate members of the home blurs the line between work and rest and enables labor extraction, their treatment as non-Jewish workers alienated from long-term emplacement facilitates othering, surveillance, and accusations of criminality. In their analysis of three legal cases, Guy Mundlak and Hila Shamir argue that Israeli law includes migrant caregivers within the intimate spaces of the home while exacting "alienage" by enabling undercompensation, denying them basic human rights, and extracting maximal labor.[3] Beyond the law, experiences of intimacy and alienage emerge in worker narratives, government speeches and statements, and parliamentary proceedings, where caregivers are portrayed as both trusted and compassionate stewards of Israel's most vulnerable citizens and, at the same time, as "foreigners" threatening the Jewish constitution of the state.

Beyond a neat employer-employee dyad, or a "frontier" where settler and native sovereignty meet, caregivers navigate a topography of risk that is relational and shifting.[4] Rather than constituting an imagined public-private divide, this topography composes the Jewish home-as-nation.[5] Here, I conceptualize home and its reproduction as a form of domestication in its thoroughly colonial usage—a perceived transformation of indigenous or "foreign" space into the familiar, intimate, and "safe." Though citizens may not always articulate home in these overt terms, attempts to demarcate the boundaries of the familiar and foreign are messily entangled with civilizational missions of home-making central to European imperialism.[6] Particularly in a society of forced conscription, the Jewish Israeli home and family are sites of refuge from the perceived existential threat of native infiltration where women have long washed uniforms and cooked meals for children and husbands returning from the army, doing psychic and material labor to care for the conscripted soldier.[7] As nonnative intimate laborers in the home-as-nation, migrant caregivers inhabit the unsettled position between contingent inclusion in this sphere, on the one hand, and temporal alienation from "settler time"—a Zionist temporality that "'disappear[s]' Palestinians in the present by crafting an exclusively Jewish past and future"—on the other.[8] This unsettled positioning tethers elderly rehabilitation, survival, and well-being to migrants' physical and mental health and economic precarity.

In this chapter, I draw on workers' narratives, government statements and procedures, and court rulings to examine migrant caregivers' seemingly paradoxical positioning as both intimate helpers of the family and nation and untrustworthy strangers. Within the household, this unsettled positioning requires that caregivers engage in "affective automation," the repetitive completion of tasks beyond their own physical, emotional, and mental capacities. Affective automation is both a job requirement producing physical injury and burnout and, simultaneously, a coping mechanism involving the affective distancing of oneself from the emotional labor being performed. Taking a cue from Sara Ahmed, Brian Massumi, and feminist interpretations of affective labor, I draw on the term "affect" to highlight the presocial aspects of care and domestic labor that require workers to produce or project particular emotions within the home.[9] As distinct from conceptualizations of automation centering the role of artificial intelligence in the field of care, I use the term to highlight how caregivers are expected to repetitively produce affective states of intimate connection that cater to employers' every need—a demand that can be psychically draining and alienating.[10] The resulting burnout and injury become "expected impairment[s]" within Israel's reproductive regime, producing "debility," or the "slow wearing down of populations" through labor exploitation, withholding of resources, or military violence.[11]

This and the next chapter function as somewhat of a pair, centering household interactions between migrant caregivers and settler-employers from the vantage point of each and examining the state discourses that saturate these household interactions. In the next chapter, I turn to employers' narratives, asking how the language of kinship and economic exceptionalism naturalize a settler sense of home while obscuring dispossession of Palestinian land.[12] Across both chapters, I draw on the term "unsettled" as it is used in indigenous and migration studies. While the former stresses the "desedimenting" of seemingly innocent and quotidian interactions and relations between settler, native, and nonnative populations, the latter emphasizes the liminal, in-between, and contradictory spaces migrants hold within "host" societies that exclude and include in ways specific to particular state regimes.[13] In both registers, the project of "unsettling" reveals cracks in the settler colonial economy, whether through an ongoing "archipelago of trans-indigenous resistance" or through the creative ways migrants find to collectively survive amid state surveillance and violence.[14]

To begin this chapter, I examine how politicians' statements, government debates, and court rulings constitute migrant caregivers as national helpers doing uniquely intimate work. I suggest how Israeli imaginaries of aging liken the care of elderly Jewish Israelis to the survival of the nation and migrant caregivers to its benevolent but foreign keepers, a process of comparative racialization emerging through Israel's reproductive regime. Next, I turn to workers' narratives of intimacy and alienation in the home, showing how their positioning requires that they engage in affective automation. In conclusion, I situate the demand for affective automation within a broader field of (dis)investment that differently subjects Palestinians, asylum seekers, migrant laborers, and settler-employers to bodily risk and injury.[15] Together, both chapters illuminate how the fraught, intensive relationships between migrant caregivers and settler-employers parallel and entwine with nationalist constructions of the foreign, familiar, familial, and "modern" in ways that reproduce and sometimes unsettle Jewish entitlements to land and home.

Intimacy, Alienation, and the State

Migrant caregivers' unsettled positioning as both intimate and alien emerges across the continuum of home-as-nation. Foundational to the demographic establishment of "facts on the ground," homes are sites where nationalistic ideologies are generated and reinforced, demarcating the familiar and the foreign, the benign and threatening.[16] Here, I conceptualize intimacy as a relation, a discourse, a form of physical proxy and surrogacy, a construct contingent upon the racialized and colonial fortification of ownership and private property, and a presumed quality of labor that signifies racial similarity, domestic safety, familial closeness, and legal exception.[17] Signifiers (such as intimate, safe, danger, terrorist) "stick" to particular bodies, attributing to them qualities that constitute the very boundaries of individuals and collectivities.[18] Narratives of intimacy circulate through government discourse, popular parlance, and legal and parliamentary proceedings, painting caregivers as national helpers and protectors of the elderly—and of Holocaust survivors in particular. As Mundlak and Shamir argue, legal rulings also constitute migrant care work in Israel as *uniquely* intimate through language suggesting the work is "high-trust."[19] Further, they exceptionalize migrant care work on account of its location in the home and by categorizing both employers and workers as "weak groups."[20] Yet, as I later suggest, employers' accusations of criminality and the state's ongoing deportation efforts belie claims to intimacy, revealing the broader precarity of caregivers' positioning in Palestine.

The popular acceptance of migrant caregivers as national helpers is best captured by Yoav, a Jewish Israeli migrant advocacy worker. Yoav explains that, in contrast to Palestinians and Eritrean and Sudanese refugees, "people can accept [the presence of] the Filipinas. The saying is, 'they help us, we should help them; they took care of our parents or disabled people, we should help them.'" Such laudatory language toward migrant care and domestic workers is not unique to Israel; most famously, the Philippines government has referred to overseas foreign workers (OFWs) as "national heroines," while the South Korean government has referred to Filipina sex workers' presence as a form of diplomacy.[21] What is striking in the Israeli context is the existential tenor underlying such praise, due in part to the demographic composition of the elderly population, which includes a sizable portion of Holocaust survivors and national "founders." Yet, even social, legal, and political discourses focusing on caregivers and the elderly that do not explicitly name Holocaust survivors emphasize the latter's fragility, vulnerability, and defenselessness and the caregivers' role as lifelines to helpless citizens. These depictions suggest the role of the elderly as what Haim Hazan calls a "symbolic type" in Israel.[22] Further, in the Israeli context, where eldercare and care for the disabled are the only forms of social reproduction migrants are permitted to do, state-level discussions of the fragile, defenseless subject given life by the compassionate migrant caregiver are imbued with an existential tenor echoing descriptions of a vulnerable Israel fighting for its existence.

In political and social discourse, migrant caregivers become a symbol of friendship between sending states and Israel and a form of support for the Jewish nation. A widely covered diplomatic visit between Israeli prime minister Benjamin Netanyahu and Philippine president Rodrigo Duterte in September 2018 reveals multiple aspects of caregivers' portrayal as trusted helpers. During the visit, Netanyahu proclaimed, "I am one of those families [hiring a Filipina caregiver], Mr. President. We received incredible care. My late father died at the age of 102. In his later years, he received incredible care by a caregiver from the Philippines, a woman with exceptional compassion and intelligence, I am deeply moved by this show of humanity." After depicting migrant caregivers, and Filipinas in particular, as kind, compassionate, and irreplaceable members of the family, Netanyahu adds that the caregiver working for his own family "took care of my father's every need. And when he passed away, she took care of my brother until he also passed away."[23] In contrast to Netanyahu's characterization of Palestinians as a "demographic problem," or his closely related statement referencing a "poisonous Palestinian society that creates battalions of suicide bombers," this statement suggests how migrant caregivers are comparatively racialized and gendered as empathic, giving, and hard-working members of the Jewish Israeli home.[24]

The prevalence of the Holocaust to caregivers' temporary inclusion is evident in other moments of Netanyahu's visit with Duterte. Earlier in his speech, Netanyahu describes the presence of Filipina caregivers as a "remarkable phenomenon" through which "thousands and thousands of families have taken heart from the support given by Filipino care workers to the elderly."[25] At the beginning of his speech, he also draws a parallel between the Philippine government's support for Jewish refugees fleeing the Holocaust and the labors of care that Filipinx workers provide to the elderly, saying, "We remember the exceptional role of the Philippines that received Jewish refugees during the Holocaust. We remember that the Philippines was the only Asian country that voted for the establishment of the State of Israel in the UN resolution in 1947."[26] In his statement, Filipinx caregivers are a contemporary personification of the refuge provided by the Philippines to Jews escaping the Holocaust. During the same meeting in Jerusalem, Duterte suggests how care for the elderly metonymically transfers into care for the state, justifying "anti-terror" initiatives against threats to the health of the nation in all its forms. He states, "We share the same passion for peace, we share the same passion for human beings . . . but also we share the same passion of not allowing a country to be destroyed by those who [have] the corrupt ideologies that promote nothing but to kill and destroy. . . . In this sense Israel can expect any help that the Philippines can extend."[27] Duterte's statement likens the care of elderly Jewish Israelis to that of the Jewish collective body as a whole, such that those giving care to the vulnerable also protect the nation from external attack.

Across such statements, the precarity and activism of workers themselves is erased, as Duterte frames both Israel and the Philippines as vulnerable to the existential threat of Muslim populations living within the state's borders. Caregivers are thus positioned as not only national helpers, but also nonthreatening racial others aligning with settler society in their fear of native terror. As Sarah Willen argues, migrants and Jewish Israelis become "blood brothers" only through the common criminalization of Palestinians.[28] However contingently, migrant caregivers are aligned with the presumed "rationality and goodness of settler sovereignty," as a virtuous end that preserves life, against the seemingly immoral threats of senseless destruction.[29] By positioning caregivers this way, the state also presents Palestinian resistance to settler colonialism as unjust and irrational, rather than a response to daily suppression.

Court rulings and parliamentary proceedings also construct caregivers as contingently incorporable into the home due to the role they play as intimate proxies to Holocaust survivors, and to the elderly more broadly. A 2022 Knesset proceeding on the extension of visas for migrant caregivers is revealing in this way.[30] As Meir-Aricah, legal counsel for the Holocaust Survivors' Rights Authority states at the proceeding, migrant caregivers are part of a "holistic approach to [caring for] Holocaust survivors," a responsibility that is in and of itself "a moral duty" to Israel's most vulnerable population. Indeed, Meir-Aricha and other advocates of Holocaust survivors' rights have called for visa extensions for migrant caregivers so that they may "create stability for [Holocaust survivors]" during the last days of their lives. Arguing against their deportation, Meir-Aricha frames the retention of caregivers within the home as a duty "not to shake [Holocaust survivors'] world precisely when they are getting older, precisely when their health condition is unfortunately deteriorating."[31]

Tellingly, Meir-Aricha then describes Holocaust survivors as "almost completely dependent on [migrant caregivers]," making the issue of caregiver visas "more critical to [the survivor] than any other benefit, more than any other project and service. And that is why we consider it appropriate to participate in financing the retention of a foreign worker for Holocaust, camp and ghetto survivors with dementia."[32] Likewise, in the same proceeding, Colette Avital, chairperson of the Center Organization of Holocaust Survivors in Israel, paints migrant caregivers as intimately linked to the elderly through their role as surrogates that make up for their incapacities. Avital explains, "When it comes to people, the elderly, who have passed the age of ninety, and are disabled . . . it is impossible to replace [migrant caregivers], even if another worker is authorized for them, and even if it is possible to bring in another worker."[33] Like Meir-Aricha, Avital then advocates for the extension of caregiver visas for those tending to Holocaust survivors "so that the last Holocaust survivors do not have to immediately remain either without a worker, or perhaps in the best case with a new worker, to whom it is impossible to adapt."[34] Committee Chairperson on Foreign Workers Ibtisam Mara'ana similarly notes the intimate role caregivers play in survivors' households, saying that "some people have no life without a female or foreign worker. They are their security, alongside their nuclear families. . . . There are populations that can accommodate a turnover of female and male workers, they can wait, [Holocaust survivors are] a population that we definitely consider a special population . . . [they should be] given the ability to grow old with dignity, and live their lives, [let caregivers] be by their side, hold the trauma, embrace them."[35]

Both Mara'ana and Avital suggest that migrant caregivers have become essential to Holocaust survivors' ability to live and die with dignity, a role that involves trauma intervention, emotional and cognitive support, and physical assistance.

Importantly, the intimate connection between migrant caregivers and Holocaust survivors is not happenstance, but rather part of a broader economy of reparations between Germany and Israel. Through the Conference on Jewish Material Claims against Germany (Claims Conference), the German government provides additional long-term nursing benefits to Holocaust survivors above those granted by the Israeli government to all qualifying elderly citizens. The provisioning of nursing benefits that can be used to subsidize additional care hours done by migrants allows survivors to avoid, in the words of the Claims Conference, "being uprooted from familiar surroundings and living in an institutional setting," an event that "may be particularly traumatic for an elderly survivor of Nazi persecution."[36] It is precisely the lower cost of employing migrant rather than Jewish Israeli caregivers that allows Holocaust survivors to avoid this trauma.

Beyond their intimate connection with Holocaust survivors, Israeli medical and disaster relief programs in migrant-sending countries become sites of close connection that reinforce the role of caregivers as intimate friends of the settler state. These widely publicized missions managed by the Israel Defense Forces, whether in the Philippines or Nepal, suggest how close ties between caregivers and employers interlace with broader economies of militarism and settler exceptionalism. Brian, a caregiver from the Philippines, relates that Israel had a notable presence in relief efforts after Hurricane Yolanda in 2013:

> They [Israelis] went there immediately. There were two teams and there was a mobile hospital. Did you hear about the first newborn baby? It's the Israeli team who [was there] and the mother named the baby boy "Israel." They helped and they stayed there for one month. And when they came [back] they brought with them some children from the Philippines. . . . And that's why during that time, you'd see T-shirts, especially in *takhana merkazit* [Tel Aviv Central Bus Station], that said "thank you very much, Israel," as a sign of giving back. And there are also groups [of Filipinos] in Jerusalem making T-shirts that say thank you to the government for sacrificing themselves to be there.

Brian suggests how Israeli humanitarian missions forge ties between the Zionist state and Filipinx caregivers, who then "owe" the nation their gratitude.[37] At a household level, acts of humanitarianism can also function as a form of gift-giving or nonfinancial remuneration that exceeds individual payments from bosses to workers. Celeste, a Filipina caregiver working to send money to her seven children, relayed that her employer "sent many packages home that cost [as much as] eighty-five dollars. We were hurt by Typhoon Yolanda and lost our house. Our neighbors in Israel gave me bags of clothes and 100 shekels for sending this home." Likewise, Abigail, who hosts fundraisers and events within the Filipinx community, notes that after Yolanda, "there are employers in Israel who want to give clothes and money, they're asking for Paypal accounts." This individualized aid—a concept to which I turn in the next chapter—underlies, fortifies, and expands intimate household relations between caregivers and employers on a global scale, while naturalizing economic disparities between migrant-sending and migrant-receiving countries.

Finally, beyond the invocation of Holocaust survivors, depictions of migrant caregivers as intimate members of the household and nation also emanate from the Israeli High Court of Justice (HCJ), National Labor Court (NLC), and regional labor courts. Language within particular decisions illustrates how intimacy "sticks" to workers by virtue of their association with home spaces.[38] As Mundlak and Shamir argue, Israeli court rulings exceptionalize live-in migrant care work as a labor distinctive from all other forms, a view that enables its casualization. Notably, the prohibitive laws constituting care work as exceptionally intimate only came on the books after 1993, when live-in care work was the exclusive realm of non-Jewish, largely non-European women migrants.

In court cases addressing migrant caregivers' exclusion from overtime pay, intimacy functions as a qualifier painting caregivers as benevolent foreigners dedicatedly helping the nation's elderly and integral to the nation and family home.[39] The classification of their work as especially intimate produces a form of "care work exceptionalism" that becomes the basis of their exclusion from overtime pay.[40] As Mundlak and Shamir show, looking at a 2009 *High Court of Justice v. National Labor Court* case, migrant workers were excluded from overtime pay due to their status as "high-trust employees."[41] Since their analysis, in an appeal to the HCJ in 2013, HCJ justices have addressed the intimate connections migrant caregivers share with the elderly, and, as Justice Edna Arbel states, the "difficult, holy, dedicated and demanding work" migrant caregivers do, "which many Israeli workers are not willing to do." Arbel also invokes the biblical passage "And you shall not wrong, nor shall you oppress a stranger, for you were strangers in the land of Egypt," locating migrant caregivers as both non-Jewish others *and* deserving national guests.[42] Further, an extended reading of the 2009 ruling reveals the exceptional treatment migrant caregivers conditionally receive when attached to elderly Jewish Israelis. Depicting migrant caregivers as indispensable national helpers, Justice and High Court Deputy President Eliezer Rivlin notes, "The contribution of foreign caregivers to Israeli society in general, and to their patients, mostly elderly, in particular, is invaluable. For many patients, caregivers are the fragile thread that connects them to life, itself. These angels on earth, in addition to the difficulty they themselves experience due to separation from their country and family, are educated, through good temper and devotion, to alleviate the plight of the patients clinging to them like straw in order to survive. They ensure a good quality of life for the rest of patients' lives."[43] Strikingly, while referring to caregivers as "angels on earth" who make personal sacrifices to keep the elderly alive, Justice Rivlin nevertheless dismisses the petition brought forward by Filipina caregiver Yolanda Gluten, noting the high level of "personal trust and the prohibitive cost of overtime pay that would fall to employers."[44] In the same ruling, Justice Hanan Meltzer refers to caregivers as "a kind of family member, or at least a household member, and given the devotion and caregiving services he provides to the patient . . . a special degree of personal trust is created." He then adds that "this is why the legislature allowed such caregivers, who are foreign workers, to obtain a residency permit extension beyond the 'normal' period of five years stipulated by law."[45] A further reading of both the 2009 and 2013 rulings suggests how "personal trust" and the location of care work within the home become proxies for intimacy, exceptionalizing carework as distinctively intimate.[46] This characterization omits that migrant caregivers are required to live with employers, and they do not do so out of devotion. While trust is undoubtedly a central element of caregiving, it stems not from good will and devotion but rather from the economies and colonial relations within which money, care, commodification, and vulnerability are messily intertwined.[47]

This treatment is also evident in a 2011 petition to the HCJ for an amendment to the Foreign Workers Law. The law otherwise excludes caregivers from the protections of the Commission for the Rights of Foreign Workers, on account of the vulnerability of elderly and disabled employers. Within the ruling, Justice Elyakim Rubenstein distinguishes between migrant care work and all other labor sectors by arguing that migrant caregivers in fact hold more, rather than less, power over their employers.

> The situation in the nursing sector is different from other sectors, where the foreign worker is clearly the weak side. The picture in nursing is therefore not one-way. Many foreign workers in this field are the redeeming angel for their charges, and more than once, when we see obituary notices for a patient—god forbid—the family includes the "devoted caregiver" among the mourners. However, not every patient has a strong, supportive family—more than a few are lonely, and not every caregiver is the same. More than once, unfortunately, we also have come across cases of a foreign worker who mistreated the nursing patient, took advantage of or abandoned him.[48]

Here, Justice Rubenstein goes beyond prioritizing the care needs of elderly citizens, arguing that employers are in fact more disadvantaged than migrants living in their home. Not only does his framing elide the fact of labor extraction and the settler privilege afforded employers, it also casts caregivers as strangers in the home who can become either "angels" or threats to the very well-being of family members.

Thus, when invoked by the courts, tropes of intimacy paint caregivers as trustworthy and compassionate helpers, even as they are "strangers [among Jews] in the land of Egypt" who are suspected of mistreatment. Alongside the Law of Return, these discourses position caregivers as unsettled laborers by obviating the possibility of settlement while praising them for tending to the collective and individual Jewish body. This characterization naturalizes the effortful "labor of care," imposing an ethical obligation on workers to undertake extracontractual labor in the name of keeping the elderly alive. This form of extraction takes place through the lack of compensation for overnight work, the expectation that caregivers remain by their employer's side twenty-four hours a day, and their prohibition from taking off rest hours and vacation days. A lack of adequate legal protections for migrant caregivers increases their dependence on the good will of employers for visa renewal, work permits, time off, and sick leave. The law thus figures citizen entitlements to care as tantamount to migrants' freedom of employment.[49]

These forms of expropriation suggest the fragility of migrants' positioning as proxies for the Jewish Israeli family. Tellingly, the year before Netanyahu described Filipinx migrant caregivers as possessing "exceptional compassion and intelligence," he fired Tara Kumari, a caregiver from Nepal who worked for his father-in-law. The story broke after Kumari claimed she was injured by Netanyahu's wife, Sara. In response to the accusation, Netanyahu launched a counterclaim, stating his father-in-law was injured when Kumari left him unattended. He then characterized her as a national security threat.[50] This rhetorical shift reveals the precarious nature of migrant caregivers' status as intimate proxies for the Jewish Israeli family when resisting exploitation or making claims against the state that depart from their roles as compassionate helpers.

The transitory nature of their status as national helpers is equally evident during deportation campaigns, such as the 2002–2003 mass deportation effort, known as the *gerush*. While prior to the campaign, media representations of migrants were typically favorable, as Willen shows, once the campaign started, migrants were demonized, imprisoned, profiled, and deported, and they were treated as threats to the "Jewish character" of the state. During another period of increased surveillance in 2009, former Knesset member Eli Yishai even announced that the "hundreds of thousands of foreign workers coming in here [had] disease like hepatitis, tuberculosis, AIDS, [and] drugs," presenting migrants as a threat to the health of the collective Jewish body. He also accused migrant and refugee populations alike of "turning their children into a human shield" by including their Israeli-born children's presence in arguments for why they should not be deported.[51] Yishai's statement strikingly echoes the common Israeli *hasbara* trope accusing Palestinians in Gaza of using their children as human shields, a comparison used to justify ongoing military violence and positioning Israel as a perpetual and ontological victim of threats to destroy the Jewish character of the state. This rhetorical shift not only suggests the precarious positioning of non-Jewish workers whose presence takes on multiple significations, but also how the very colonial categories of migrant, indigene, and settler shift across political moments and movements.

While the constitution of eldercare as uniquely intimate constricts workers' ability to demand overtime wages, their treatment as intimate members of the family and nation requires an emotional performance of closeness and familiarity. The specter of unemployment and deportation imbues accusations of criminality with greater risk, particularly during periods of increased instability with Palestinians. As I suggest in the pages to come, within the household, caregivers' treatment as intimate and alien necessitates their engagement in affective automation as both a demand of the job, and as a way of emotionally and mentally managing this terrain of risk.

Intimacy and Alienation in the Household

As a requirement of the job, caregivers live in close physical proximity to their charges throughout the day for years at a time. The difficulty of maintaining spatial boundaries within the small confines of the home is exacerbated by caregivers' legal construction as workers in a "high-trust" profession whose very presence within settler society is contingent on their demonstration of care and compassion toward the elderly and disabled. Social and legal constructions of intimacy therefore intensify an already fraught spatial layout that blurs the line between work and rest. Yet the obscuring of these spatial and temporal boundaries also facilitates forms of surveillance and abuse. To highlight the intertwined nature of intimacy and alienation in the home, I examine the ways spatial intimacy enables the extraction of labor, requiring workers to engage in affective automation.

I then turn to the simultaneous sense of closeness and othering caregivers describe, sometimes within the same employment relationship. To contend with the constant demand for labor and emotional burnout, many caregivers also engage in affective automation as a coping strategy.

Spatial Intimacy, Affective Automation, and Abuse

Caregivers' treatment as trusted surrogates and round-the-clock workers unentitled to rest follows, in many ways, from the spatial layout of the home. Continual spatial proximity demands the navigation of bodily, emotional, and aural boundaries that do not cohere to legal divisions between work and rest. Proximate bodily interactions and shared smells, spaces, and sounds at once generate closeness, tensions, fondness, exploitation, resentment, and othering. Though by law, caregivers are entitled to a room of their own, some workers choose to sleep next to acutely sick employers at some point during their many jobs in Palestine/Israel so they can be available twenty-four hours a day. Workers with whom I spoke largely lived in single-story flats within larger, multistory apartment buildings, though a few had lived in two-story houses or apartments inside *b'tei avot* (elderly homes). In a standard apartment there are two or three bedrooms jutting off from a common area, one for caregivers, one for charges, and sometimes one for an adult child or guest. In the apartments I visited, living rooms were generally attached to an open or semi-open kitchen, a floor plan that creates an easy sight line from different sides of the apartment. The retirement community apartments I visited were significantly smaller, with caregivers sleeping on a couch in the common room without a room of their own. To different extremes, shared apartments, houses, and *b'tei avot* create intensely intimate encounters between charges and caregivers and unequal access to privacy. Years of physical proximity between caregivers and their employers allow the former to intuit their employers' moods, expressions, and feelings better than anyone. As Jasmine explains, "I understand [my employer] on my instinct . . . if you've been together a long time you share the same feeling, you know? . . . *Safta* [grandma], she cannot talk. She don't hear. I can understand her—she's [an] Alzheimer [patient] . . . I'm more than four years in the apartment twenty-four hours so I know when she wakes up, when she eats, what she needs, so I know. I know her face . . . when she wants to do toilet, when she wants to cry." Jasmine's experience suggests how sharing a confined space with an employer for years on end synergistically attaches

Jasmine to her employer, such that she can anticipate her every need. This dependency is, in many ways, necessary to the full-time protection, survival, and well-being of elderly life. Yet, it is also structurally predicated on Jasmine's alienation—functionally, Jasmine does three times the labor of a citizen-caregiver working one eight-hour shift a day, yet she is only paid for twelve hours of this time.

In conjunction with the legal exceptionalizing of care work as uniquely "high-trust," the spatial confines of the home hinge the revitalization and rehabilitation of the elderly on the fatigue, exhaustion, and burnout of caregivers. Ramona, like many live-in caregivers, acts as a surrogate to her employers, compensating for their physical and mental incapacities. For Ramona, the spatial intimacy of the home requires that she be "always on." Ramona describes her prior job as continually demanding of her time, regardless of mandated rest hours or whether she was in the privacy of her own room. She notes, "Even at night I don't close my door because when they go to the toilet I want to hear, because sometimes you might not know if they fell. If you are in a deep sleep you can't help. It will be too late." If her employers fall while she sleeps, Ramona's physical demands would increase, as she would need to compensate for any temporary immobility.

In her previous employment arrangement, Ramona lifted her employer by herself multiple times a day over a three-year period. After months of this repeated motion, Ramona severely injured her arm. She explains, "When I left my job before this, I worked for three years very, very hard. I did all the things—I drove, I brought [my employer] to the doctor, therapy, I did massage, I cooked, I cleaned. . . . So I thought I deserved separation pay, because three times a week I have to go to my therapist, and I could not move my arm up anymore. The agency said, 'If you leave the job and the employer doesn't release you, you're not entitled to separation pay.'" After seeking legal counsel that was ultimately unsuccessful, Ramona eventually began private physical therapy paid for by her employers. Ironically, to become eligible for therapy, Ramona had to engage in the very same form of affective automation that caused her to seek therapy in the first place. The alternative—refusing to do extracontractual labor—would transfer the risk of injury from Ramona to her employer, increasing Ramona's legal and financial precarity. The denial of separation pay and the valuing of her employer's bodily needs over her own pain underscore how alienation undergirds the assumption that she is always available. Indeed, one of the most common forms of affective automation workers describe is the continual use of physical capacities with little to no break. A regular complaint migrant caregivers voiced was chronic pain in the form of back, arm, and neck injuries due to continually lifting their charges without adequate rest. The commonality of these stories is not surprising—according to a 2009 study, 44 percent of Filipinx caregivers working in Palestine/Israel have endured job-related injuries.[52] The surrogate labor caregivers undertake allows renewed usage of employers' formerly incapacitated limbs and the regeneration of functions they have lost. From lifting and carrying employers to administering massage and physical therapy, caregivers' finite energies and bodily capabilities enable the health improvements and reinvigoration of elderly employers.

Like Ramona, Aja, a caregiver from Nepal, experiences shoulder and hand pain due to a similar form of repetitive strain. Aja describes her cleaning duties as extensive, and she details her employer's expectation that she be nearby ready to help her "whenever she wants to wake up, sit, walk, at night or in the day." She explains,

> [My employer] can walk herself with *halichon* [walker] but when she wakes up, she needs to have my hand, and when she sits herself, I need to help. In the morning, I need to take her out and I need to do catheter four times a day. I need to change and dress her and [when] she goes to the bathroom, I need to help her to bed and every day at eight she needs to shower. So many times she goes to the salon to watch TV and I need to help. I use my hand for so much time, the same work eight, ten times a day. That's why I went to physical therapy three times. I have back pain also.

Aja adds that since working in Israel, "physically, I had so many problems. I had back pain, and pain in my shoulder, so many things. But slowly after 3, 4, 5 years, *mitraglim* [we get used to it]—I get used to it." Aja's comment that she "get[s] used to it" also reveals how affective automation becomes a mechanism for coping with extreme physical and mental repetition, acclimatizing oneself to the intense repetition of physical tasks without adequate break. Indeed, caregivers are expected to repetitively perform labors and affective states that can require distancing oneself from these tasks and performances. The working assumption that both Aja and Ramona appear whenever their employers require it subjects them both to physical strain as a condition of the job. Ramona's and Aja's experiences of physical injury also suggest how affective automation can function as a form of indirect bodily discipline, forcing workers to endure exhaustion and burnout to avoid financial loss.[53]

The spatial proximity between caregivers and their employers, and the expectation that as caring professionals they be "always on," require many to automate their labor throughout the night, responding to employers' noises and calls even when they are off the clock. Often, this expectation stems from workers' inability to create adequate physical and aural distance between themselves and their employers, a lack of boundaries that can work to employers' advantage. Some workers describe fatigue, headache, and mental exhaustion as a result of sleep deprivation. Nathan, a caregiver from the Philippines, explains how continual spatial closeness to his first employer led to a lack of boundaries at night, an issue made worse by his employer's dementia. His sleep deprivation was exacerbated by his employer's outbursts during fits of anger and name-calling. Nathan explains,

> [My boss] slept in the next room. He would wake in the night asking me if he could garden and we would garden in the middle of the night and the lights would come streaming and neighbors would yell and complain. Another time my employer yelled "drive! drive!" and I'd drive and drive because I was new and afraid to say no. . . . Sometimes [I] had headaches from the lack of sleep. I complained to the agency and they said, "Don't get up when he yells," but how can I ignore? [My employer] sometimes will smash a glass and I ignore. I push the bed against the door and unscrew the lightbulb so he won't turn on the light from outside.

As Nathan suggests, saying no to employers when one is off the clock is nearly impossible when living in physical proximity to one's charge. Though his alienating treatment of Nathan stems to a large extent from dementia, Nathan's employer nevertheless benefits from continual access to Nathan at all times of night and day and the structural difficulty caregivers have refusing labor given the legal and economic risks of a dissatisfied charge. Nathan notes that establishing boundaries was especially hard when he was new to caregiving, a time he remembers as filled with exhaustion and depression. He relays, "At first I was scared not to do everything he asks." Now that he has more experience, he says, he "just ignore[s] him when he berates me and

I say to myself it's because of his sickness. . . . I just let it go in one ear, out the other." Here, Nathan automates an affective state of being unbothered, distancing himself from his employer's abusive comments.

Other caregivers discussed extreme sleep deprivation as an expected challenge that comes with the territory of sharing such intimate quarters with one's employer. Rahul communicates a sense of torment while working for a past employer, who required him to be constantly alert and ready to help throughout the night:

> My employer was 107 years old. . . . After one month he started getting up two, three times in the night so I asked [my employer and his wife] for the money and they gave me that money. But after two months he started to get up seven or eight times in the night, every hour. He woke up to pee—he was doing pee, just a little quantity—and he takes ten to fifteen minutes [*laughs*]. It was very terrible. But when I ask them for the money, which I asked, they gave me already, so I continued, but after four-and-a-half months I was feeling bad, I was feeling pain in my head. I asked them to hire someone else for the night and they don't want to because in the night they have to pay someone more than me . . . in half hour I sleep again and he called me again.

Sleeping in close proximity to his employer, Rahul cannot avoid being woken throughout the night. While his employer trusts him enough to be a surrogate for his weakening body, he and his adult children view Rahul as alienable enough to deny the request for nighttime relief and a respite from his suffering. Rahul forced himself to robotically carry out his extracontractual tasks throughout the night despite extreme exhaustion, while also automating nighttime duties for over four months to complete tasks while enduring his daytime duties amid headaches and fatigue. Suggesting how spatial intimacy can lead to disciplinary forms of alienation, Rahul also discusses how his employer would attempt to control noises Rahul made throughout the home. Rahul conveys that "he don't want to hear the noise of the dishes if I'm cleaning! Sometimes we make a noise when washing dishes and he don't want to hear! I couldn't stand there. It was a very difficult job."

Like Rahul, Pamela describes engaging in extensive physical activity to meet the demands of her employer and his wife following nights of inadequate rest, all the while enduring a sense of being constantly surveilled:

They're coupled and then I took care of the old man. At night the old man was not sleeping so I have to awake for the whole night and then at daytime I have to work everything in the house with the wife because the wife wants me to work and work. . . . Cook[ing], cleaning, she's very particular about the cleaning. Everything, even the ceiling—I have to climb up the ladder to clean the ceiling so I have no energy because I have no sleep at night. . . . The wife said, "you cannot just clean only this part, you have to clean the whole house!"

Though by contract, Pamela is only required to care for one person and do occasional, light cleaning, in practice, the presence of her employer's wife in the same restricted space of the home makes refusing extracontractual labor nearly impossible. Pamela's description of her employer's wife looking over her shoulder suggests how the spatial closeness of the home—and the bodily intimacy it enables—hinders workers' ability to refuse labor, particularly while an employer watches on as workers carry out tasks. In addition to enduring nights of sleeplessness without adequate rest, Pamela can also not escape the creeping expansion of her roles during the day, due, to a large extent, to her employers' close and constant presence.

In some cases, workers may choose to minimize the impact of sleep deprivation by sleeping next to employers. Celeste, a Filipinx caregiver working outside of Tel Aviv, explains, "I sleep with the old woman because it's easier this way than to wake in a separate room. My employer turns and twists so I know when she needs something. I prefer sleeping with her because it is easier. But also I need to clean her better because she is the one sleeping with me." For Celeste, sleeping alongside her charge, even with the lack of physical, aural, and olfactory boundaries it entails, is preferable to getting up multiple times in the night to check on her. Celeste's experience exposes the extent to which job retention hinges on round-the-clock vigilance, sometimes most safely undertaken by all but attaching oneself to one's charge. By extension, Celeste's experience suggests how round-the-clock labor becomes an unwritten expectation of the job.

Even for those not required to automate their labor throughout the night, the spatial intimacy of the home generates a sense of being "always on." Sonia listens for the sound of her nonverbal employer shifting his weight in his wheelchair, while Serene tunes into the sound of her employer trying to open cabinets. At other times, the spatial intimacy of the home turns sounds into a premise for discipline. Rina recalls the first months of caregiving when her employer would angrily shout "It's noisy!" if she heard Rina talking to friends behind the closed door of her bedroom or watching television during rest hours. Ironically, at other times, Rina notes, her employer is the noisy one: "[She] tests me by waking up and banging the closets to see if I'll wake up and come, even if it's before I'm supposed to be awake at seven." Yet at other times, she says, "my employer demands to me to be by herself." Physical intimacy within the home requires that caregivers vigilantly watch, listen to, and sense their employers' whereabouts around the clock, automating tasks throughout the day, and oftentimes, at night. Through a colonial "logic of differentiation," employers wittingly or unwittingly alienate caregivers by expecting them to work through burnout, injury, extreme exhaustion, and emotional unrest.[54]

Emotional Closeness, Surveillance, and Abuse

Another common way intimacy and alienation surface within the home is through the simultaneous praise and othering caregivers receive, sometimes back-to-back in vastly different employment arrangements, and, at other times, within the same relationship. Miranda describes her dynamic with her first employer as warm and amiable, and yet physically demanding due to the intensity of the work. She explains that "when we go to our relatives [they say], 'this is our last daughter, this is my sister,' and so this is why I don't leave the work. The only one thing is they need to change me because I can't do the lifting. It's lot of lifting every time! It's so hard." Despite referring to Miranda as "a daughter," when Miranda confronted her employer about the physical strain, he responded, "I'm not a baby to use a lifter!" Miranda thus faced the option of continuing to work for her employer by automating her labor and ignoring her pain, or switching employers, which she eventually did. Like Miranda, many caregivers describe being treated "like family," and yet they experience profound othering or demands for automated labor from the same family as a condition of retaining their employment.

Following this employment arrangement, Miranda switched to another household, where she experienced othering of a different kind: "The only problem with my employer before was the food. . . . I always asked for the food and sometimes [my employer's husband] wants me to buy what I need, want. [My employer] will hide the food in her room and toothpaste and shampoo and when she leaves to go to work she closes her room. . . . Sometimes I will buy [food] and hide in my room, like biscuits and noodles."

Miranda's distinctive experiences with both employers show how alienation can take different forms, from the inability to recognize a caregiver's work-related pain and burnout to the denial of basic needs. Emma, a Filipina caregiver working outside of Tel Aviv, conveyed a similar dynamic of othering and warmth within the same relationship: "My old employer didn't let me drink tea. If I drank more than once a day, she would say, 'you can take one a day.' In my new employer's house, she's not mentally well so she'll yell and get mad and I'll just be quiet. Then sometimes the employer will be super nice and say 'honey, sweetie,' and touch me, but I know she doesn't mean it, she's only scared, she's worried I will leave." As both Miranda and Emma suggest, at moments, caregivers become aligned with the family through the rhetoric of devotion, trustworthiness, and familiarity; at other times, employers unsettle claims to familialism by treating caregivers as impermanent, non-Jewish foreigners unentitled to adequate food, space, and rest.

Like Emma, Fred, a farmer from the Philippines working as a caregiver in Jerusalem, experiences both expressions of closeness and appreciation from his employer and, within the same home, extreme surveillance. He notes, "[My employers] treat me like a son. Even as the previous employer, they treat me as a member of the family." At the same time, Fred recounts the first time he became aware of a camera inside of his employer's home:

> My problem was the son-in-law. He installed a camera. They didn't tell me about the camera. . . . The day we got into the house I saw a camera in the salon. A few days later I saw the camera in the door. But when I tell them the reason I want to leave is because of the camera, the son-in-law, the father, and the mother decided to take it down. If it's for a security reason in the room of my employer, maybe. Or in the room of the wife, maybe, yeah. But in the sitting room? How could you say that it's for security reasons?

Fred's account reveals his employer's suspicions and simultaneous hesitation to communicate this mistrust. Interviewees noted that surveillance most often took the form of hidden cameras, allegations of theft and abuse, and the manipulative use of deportation threats. By installing cameras, monitoring food intake, and supervising when caregivers are allowed to leave the house, employers suggest the contingency and limits of caregivers' positioning as national helpers.

Paradoxically, Fred's employers treat him like a son, yet fear him enough to monitor his movements around the house. More revealing of some employers' fears, and the way migrant caregivers can "come to embody distance," is Fred's story of an employer who thought he was trying to poison his food.[55] Fred describes doing the intimate tasks of bathing his employer and administering shots, yet still facing accusations of intense suspicion: "All the time he is afraid of me, that maybe I will do something to him. OK, he is blind I understand; he cannot see. But he wants me to taste his food first. . . . He didn't say it like that, but you have to know. When times come that he wants me to taste the food first, of course what you think is that he thinks you're gonna poison him. There was a time he changed his food for my food." Fred's experience suggests that despite being "like a son" in some employers' homes, his sense of feeling comfortably at home is fleeting and contingent. He notes, "He thinks I'm gonna steal something. He took out his necklace and he put it somewhere so I will think it was accidental or he forgot." The accounts Fred provides of continually alleviating employers' fears as a regular part of the job highlight how caregivers at times unsettle employers' sense of home as the realm of safety and comfort, as it instead becomes laden with their suspicion and anxiety. Fred says he makes a habit of meticulously documenting his activity within the house and sharing these records with his employment agency. As a male caregiver, the distance Fred embodies is a particularly gendered one. Fred shared more extreme experiences of mistrust than did women-identifying caregivers with whom I spoke, perhaps because of the widespread social perception among employers that women in particular are "naturally" caring. Though Fred is enough "like a son" to be entrusted with his employer's life, his likeness to the Jewish Israeli family and nation is sufficiently dissimilar that his presence must be tracked, monitored, and managed.

Much like Fred, Alice receives the praise and affections of her employers alongside their deep mistrust. Living in the basement apartment of her charge's multigenerational family home, Alice describes herself as very close with her employers, present and past. She feels especially close to her charge's adult daughter Hila, describing their relationship as warm and communicative. Alice says she is treated "like family," and notes their recognition of her indispensability to their functioning. At the same time, Alice has had to navigate accusations of theft from both Hila and Sarah. She relays one situation where Hila and a social worker involved with Sarah's care suspected Alice of elder abuse:

Sometimes I think my employer says to Hila that I hurt her. . . . I don't know if she believes her or not. Hila asked me if it's OK to put a video in her mother's room. She said it's not for checking on me. . . . Hila said, "Alice, I'm going to tell you something. I know you're honest . . . the EMS came here and they said to put a video because they saw my mother's bruises." I said, "Look, put a video, I don't care. In the video you will see what time I go to your mother's room and what I am doing. Do it, I'm not afraid! This is ridiculous!" . . . Only I am going to tell you that, you know, sometimes with the video, it only shows that you don't trust your caregiver. It only shows.

Alice's description hints at Hila's misgivings about hiring Alice as well as her anxiety over being perceived as mistrusting. The story Alice tells suggests that Hila feels unease about Alice as a foreign presence in the home and also around her own self-perception as a welcoming employer. Like Fred, Alice also discusses a time when her employer accused her of stealing:

My employer told Hila that I stole her jewelry and took her money. . . . I said, "Look, I don't come here just to steal. If it's a million dollars, maybe I will steal it." I'm crazy about the jewelry but I will not steal from somebody! . . . I told her, "You know, my last employer is American, they just leave their money, and [he works at] Mercedes-Benz. I have all these letters! Recommendation letters, letters from my former employers. I work alone. I raise my family alone. I raise my children alone. I give them education alone. So why in the world I have to ruin my life?"

Here, Hila assumes Alice is so desperate for material wealth that she will covet and try to take objects of value. Fred's and Alice's experiences illustrate how citizen-employers' homes become a spatial minefield where the burden is placed upon workers to prove that they are nonthreatening and worthy of trust. Bella likewise explains that "some employers lie also. . . . If the police come, they will investigate and believe them. They don't speak the truth. We didn't come here to be thieves. If I stole something, I don't need to work here [in Israel]. There's places to steal in our own countries." This securitizing of migrant caregivers in the home reflects and reproduces the ways migrants are policed in the neighborhoods of south Tel Aviv and throughout Israel during their days off. The home can thus function as a site of monitoring and management that protects the very boundaries of the intimate from the perceived dangers of the "foreign," with caregivers ambiguously inhabiting both. At times, employers even act as state agents of surveillance. Rina, a caregiver, factory worker, and martial artist from the Philippines, describes an instance following a fight with her employer when her employer's wife had a friend come to their home pretending to be immigration police. She recalls, "One time [my employer's] wife came in with police—or some guy who said he was the police—and said, 'He's in immigration and he'll take you back to the Philippines!' I told her, 'Really? So let's go to the airport.' I told her, 'He has no right, I'm not illegal!' and she said, 'Shut up.' It's not good to tell caregivers that." Fred relays a similar instance where employers acted as a proxy for the police. In one instance, his employer called the police because Fred, undocumented at the time, refused to work for him for fourteen hours a day:

> I cannot work with him fourteen hours a day! . . . So I packed my things. . . . So he said, "Don't leave me now, I will call the police!" So I gave the telephone to him. I said, "You can call now." . . . When I got home . . . [my flatmate] said that the police was looking for me, oh! I didn't put in my mind but he really called the police. He says that I stole his documents. . . . So the next morning I went to the agency to find another job, and the agency told me the police went to the agency, they asked about me, so I talk to them and said it's not true. I'm here to find a job. To think that I took the bag of documents, what should I do with a bag of documents? [The agency] advised me to open the telephone all the time, and when the police call me I will go. The worst is he didn't pay my salary.

Suggesting how technologies of surveillance permeate the home, these enactments of deportation buttress official state policies of jailing, expelling, and policing migrants. The requirement that Fred answer any phone calls in case it is the police tethers his daily movement to the state, whether in his employer's home, his apartment, or on his days off. As Encarnación Gutiérrez Rodríguez shows, the coloniality of migrant domestic work is upheld by contemporary migration policies that permeate household relations with hierarchical social values.[56] Assignations of home spaces as intimate, rather than exogenous and hostile, are thus equally "settler colonial technologies of space-making and race-making."[57] In the Jewish Israeli family and nation, migrant caregivers have also "come to embody distance," un-settling, by their very presence, the settler home as the site of exclusively Jewish continuity and freedom from the mistrust of the "foreign."[58] The claims to familial intimacy that both Fred and Alice have experienced thus "align individuals with communities."[59] In this sense, "the familiar is 'ex-tended' by differentiating itself from the strange, by making what seems strange 'just about' familiar," but not comfortably so.[60] Unsettling the ex-clusively Jewish constitution of the home, migrant caregivers are at once racially coded as foreign, "familiar," similar, and "safe," suggesting how notions of an "intimate" sphere belie the "racialization of intimacy," or what David Eng describes as the "collective ways by which race becomes occluded within the private domain of private family and kinship today."[61] Such coding also reinforces the colonial nature of homemaking itself, which is premised upon the expropriation of Palestinian land, and settler represen-tations of indigenous resistance to this expropriation as an irrational, "for-eign" threat. The mistrust and surveillance workers describe are reinforced by laws, regulations, and policies limiting caregivers' capacity to refuse ex-tracontractual labor and receive separation pay if they are fired. They must also weigh bodily injury and mental burnout against the economic and legal consequences of quitting.

For undocumented workers in particular, the fear of surveillance regu-larly seeps into home spaces, shaping workers' sense of alienation within employers' families.[62] Against arguments about a public-private dichotomy, the home itself is a site for the reproduction of "public discourse[s] that fa-cilitate and reinforce domestic workers' 'objectification' and 'replaceabil-ity.'"[63] Having lived undocumented for long periods when past employers have died, Alice has had to navigate when she leaves the house and how she spends her days off. Before she received a special visa regularizing her status, Alice would avoid taking weekend trips to Tel Aviv like many of her friends, as immigration police notoriously stop migrants in the city and ask for their documentation. During these periods, Alice has negotiated various domains of surveillance and alienation, both within and outside her employer's house.

Against this topography of risk, Alice, like Rina, rejects employers' at-tempts to discipline and track her movements. She notes,

> To be scared of not having a visa? I'm not. As long as I work with a
> family and they love my work and they appreciate my work, I'm not
> afraid. If someone will come and take me and send me home, I'm

not scared. Every time I said, I'm not afraid of that. Why should I be scared? I don't harm people! . . . I don't know what is really [the problem] with not having a continuous visa . . . maybe they're afraid if we stay twenty years here we will ask Immigration to be a citizen? I don't know.

Alice's experience suggests how efforts to demarcate the boundaries between foreign and intimate, foreigner and "native," further generate notions of a public and private sphere. Through a process of self-indigenizing, alienation works to push those deemed not "native" outside the boundaries of the nation. Through processes of alienation, settler-citizens, as quotidian state agents, demarcate the very external-internal division around household and territorial home, positioning migrant caregivers as territorial guests and indigenous Palestinians as infiltrators.

The small confines of the home and the lack of recourse for holding employers accountable at times also enables sexual, physical, and verbal abuse. Instances of abuse are exacerbated by the limited legal recourse migrant women in particular have to hold abusers accountable. When they attempt to do so, the burden of proof for reporting and proving one's case rests largely on the caregiver. Indeed, when recruitment agencies receive complaints of sexual abuse, they have at times responded by telling caregivers "to have 'patience.'"[64] Such responses demonstrate the often blurry line between caregiving, the "maid trade," and other intimate forms of labor within the "desire economy," one that caters to the economic purchasing power of Western consumers, migrant-receiving governments, and, in the Israeli case, settler-citizens.[65] An anonymous study conducted by Kav LaOved on sexual abuse among migrant caregivers found that 35 percent of respondents had experienced some form of sexual abuse or harassment on the job. Respondents noted that employers could get away with sexual harassment and abuse due to the physically intimate and isolated nature of care work. Engaging in physically proximate activities such as bathing, showering, and dressing one's employer in the isolated confines of the home can be some of the causes of employer abuse.[66]

Rina was very open about her experiences dealing with sexual harassment. She relates that merely one week after arriving from the Philippines, she was propositioned by her male employer, who entered her bedroom at night with his pants down demanding that she have sex with him. For the remainder of her employment, she continually feared that he would make another advance. According to Kav LaOved, migrant caregivers share stories about employers who have masturbated in front of their caregivers, propositioned them regularly when they assist them in the shower, demanded they have sex with them, and made nonconsensual physical advances.[67]

In addition to sexual harassment and abuse, many migrant caregivers report instances of physical and verbal abuse.[68] One study of Filipina home care workers indicates that 25 percent had been victims of sexual harassment, while 64 percent were subjected to abuse more broadly, and nearly half had endured injuries.[69] Sonia, a caregiver from Nepal, relays that she "worked in the past with an old lady who would scratch so much when I gave insulin shots. I have marks." Similarly, Mayra describes facing abuse from a past employer who suffered from Alzheimer's. She explains,

> She's very crazy, I'm sorry to say. She hit me and many other things. It was very difficult. They didn't give me food or shower. She's always shouting. [They] said she had Alzheimer's. That's why I was quiet. I tried to understand the situation. Not only for me. She did it to the children also. I have contact with her till now. She tells me "Come back, come back" and is crying. What can I do? She's not OK with *anybody*, not only with me. If I go today she's OK, but not tomorrow. After one or two hours, she's again not OK. But it was very painful because I'm alone there.

Maria relayed similar challenges taking care of an elderly woman with Alzheimer's who regularly threatened and attacked her:

> If I got close, she would cry and scream. If I'd come into the house, she splashed water on me. She's *balagan* [a mess]. She goes around without any clothes. She's so strong, the nails so long, and she will scratch me like this. She wants to kill me. I have a lot of scratches. She's biting. But I cannot leave because she gives me a good salary and I am live-out. . . . If I give her food, she will kill me. She throws hot water in the morning and then goes out and cries, "Look at me, look what she did!" But she's the one who threw the hot water.

Because she is undocumented, Maria works as a live-out caregiver. While this arrangement mitigates some forms of task expansion, it simultaneously weakens her ability to seek legal recourse. Maria describes an instance when her employer ran into the street screaming and crying until the police approached Maria, concerned that she was abusing her employer. On two different occasions, her employer told the police that Maria had in fact abused her, placing the burden on Maria to prove her innocence. Maria's work experience not only reveals the mental, emotional, and physical difficulty of tending to Alzheimer's patients, who are themselves vulnerable. It also suggests how quickly caretakers' intimate placement in the family can give way to the alienation of police encounters at the word of settler-employers.

Finally, intimacy and alienation are also reproduced and contested through what Tamar, a Jewish Israeli migrant advocacy worker, terms a "culture of permission." This culture requires caregivers to seek their employers' approval before going on dates, spending time with friends, attending migrant community events, or taking vacation days. Such paternalism—at times motivated by employers' claims that women caregivers in particular are "like a daughter"—is ironic when considered alongside employers' dependency upon caregivers for their survival. The de facto requirement that caregivers receive employers' approval, sometimes in personal matters such as dating and socializing, are extensions of the biopolitical management of marriage, reproduction, and migrant communal life in Israel. This burden manifests in stories told within caregiver communities about caregivers who have been fired for being pregnant, or who are expected to work around the clock even while pregnant.[70] Such demands show how the topography of risk workers navigate is differentially shaped by gendered and racialized restrictions on childbirth among non-Jewish communities. Whether abuse, paternalism, or accusations of theft, alienating interactions between settler-employers and migrant caregivers reveal how the home becomes unsettled through the presence of migrants, even when, or perhaps *because*, employers feel great fondness for caregivers.

Coping through Affective Automation

While affective automation is often a requirement of the job, it is also a mode of coping, sometimes robotically, with the emotional challenges of employer abuse, the daily repetition of tasks, longing for family and kinship networks, and death. Some interviewees described coping with exhaustion and burnout by undertaking tasks almost robotically. These automated aspects of care work require managing feelings of frustration, boredom, and bodily fatigue, a "self-management of subjectivity" characteristic of many forms of post-Fordist labor.[71] David relays dealing with the physical tedium of medical procedures through an intentional detachment: "If the person is really kind, you develop a relationship, you get attached. But I think I'm also unique in that sense because I worked, I was trained [as a nurse] to care but not to get attached, not to get emotionally attached. . . . I know how to care in a way that he feels that he is really looked after. But for me . . . I don't pour everything, it's still my job and I know how to act still professionally, even if the setting's not that professional." As David suggests, live-in care work can involve the ongoing execution of physical tasks and the accompanying emotional tedium of automating these tasks. He also suggests how live-in eldercare can be simultaneously intimate and impersonal, requiring that workers convey affectations of fondness while distancing themselves from their charges. For David, coping involves engaging a trained response of patience. He explains that as a nurse, "I was *trained* to be patient so that's where I would get it." Invocation of composure and patience thus becomes an automated response to the social and legal expectations that caregivers ceaselessly labor.

Affective automation can also include reciting the same dialogues every day, helping charges remember where they are and introducing oneself repeatedly, maintaining composure in the face of verbal abuse and depression, finding ways to cope with continual death and dying, and creating distancing mechanisms to protect against mental burnout. Pamela notes, "Every morning when [my employer] woke up I can memorize already the lines she used to say. In the morning, 'oh my God it's very painful, terrible pain, I cannot take this anymore.' Every morning, all the time . . . so every time she has to say that I have to give her a massage in her knee and talk to her just to ease the pain. . . . After you massage her, she's very thankful and smiling." Nik, a caregiver and paramedic from Nepal, likewise describes doing the same tasks each day. He recites the details as if reading a list: "In the morning at seven: tea, coffee, breakfast. At nine, ten, go to the bath, twelve or one, lunch, after lunch, two hours' nap. Four o'clock: living room, coffee, tea, biscuit. Seven o'clock: another dinner. Eight, nine, sleep. Every day's the same routine. Ninety percent of caregivers it is the same thing. Maybe in the morning we take walks or go to the clinic or hospital to get a checkup."

Other caregivers describe performing an automated facade of composure in the face of verbal abuse. In this way, affective automation can be a deliberate distancing of oneself from the requisite dispositional demands of caregiving as a mode of self-preservation. It is also a response to forms of bodily discipline imposed directly by employers or indirectly through the state-sanctioned strictures of the job. As Nicole Constable argues, drawing on Foucault, the focus of "modern, covert discipline" is not the object the worker produces but rather "the body and bodily practices."[72] Discussing the difficulties of caring round-the-clock, Pamela suggests a form of affective automation that involves "set[ting] your mind" in order to face employers with dementia or Alzheimer's who level abuses at caregivers. She explains,

> Some days you're not in a good mood as a caregiver. You have your own problems, so you get irritated, and all the time [my employer] asks and asks and asks so many things, and she doesn't know sometimes what she's saying and she's saying bad words to you, like, "You're a bitch! I don't want you to be here! Why are you here? Leave me alone! Go! Goodbye! I don't want any stranger in my house!" You have to be with her twenty-four hours and you have to bear everything, the good and the bad, so it's difficult.

To deal with her employer's erratic behavior, Pamela describes a strategic form of self-discipline that involves automating her affective comportment:

> You have to set your mind. Everything [the employer] says you have to ignore because she's ill, you're there to care not to argue. So you have to set your mind not to be depressed, not to be frustrated. . . . When she is in her climax of bad mood I have to go out and then take a deep breath and then go back again. Sometimes I don't like to go back anymore but you need to because that's your job so you have to face it . . . gather good vibes outside the house before you go back in the house and face her again. . . . Now I realize that caregiving is a very difficult job, very difficult.

Jasmine similarly relates, "I put always in my mind that I need this . . . I'm doing this for my family and to succeed also. And I always think positively. I don't think negatively, I think positively. That's my one rule. I say in my mind, 'I can do it . . . I am lucky also. I got a job like this.' . . . I say, 'Think positive' and pray." Deciding to "think positive" can be not only a coping mechanism, but also a way of constantly investing and reinvesting one's energies into one's charge each day with little or no break.

Another form of affective automation emerges in response to the pain of witnessing an employer die. As Maria suggests, joking can be one mechanism for coping with continual loss. She explains that a common joke among her friends is to ask each other, "How many employers have you killed?" Treating the subject of death with humor, she says, is perhaps the only way of processing the profound pain of separation that occurs when charges continually die. The boundary work within the intimate spaces of the home can be painful for caregivers who deeply love their employers. The process of nursing charges through the end of their life and being with them during the final moments of their life can be markedly difficult. Abigail describes her relationship with her current and former employer as loving and close, and she remembers vividly the trauma arising in the days after she watched her employer die of cancer:

> Especially the last night when you hear the last breath. For two nights it was like that—you can hear her breath, and suddenly it stopped. I was suffering from it for a few months because I was hearing it every night, the breathing. And then one night, it just stopped. I'm drinking wine to fall asleep . . . I cried more than her children. I dunno, it's part of the job. It's like, you get attached with the one you give care [to], more than your parents I think sometimes, because you know how they suffer and we see everything, even the hardship.

For caregivers who did not deal as consistently with death, close encounters with employers' pain and dependency were nevertheless difficult. Kamal expressed that the pressure to enact composure in the face of death, dependency, and aggression without break can also be long-lasting, shaping their lives after they leave Palestine/Israel. Kamal explains that "by giving of yourself, sometimes we also give ourselves punishment. There is a problem—the financial crisis [in Nepal] and we are here to support our family, our parents, but after all, actually you have to look after yourself and your health. Many people working in Israel moving back to the countries find themselves slowly getting different kinds of mental issues after working a long time." The pressure to display patience and resilience as "part of the job" can also lead to feelings of apathy and detachment. Rahul explains, "When I started the job, I thought that at the end of my job I will not be human anymore. Now also I feel I am less human than before. . . . Now I will not help if I saw some old lady. Before when I came if I saw some people if they are carrying something I help them myself." Rahul's feeling of detachment and indifference underscores the extent to which caregiving requires displaying the patience and good-heartedness that employers expect, regardless of one's own shifting emotional state.

Intense isolation and loneliness can also be exacerbated by the physical separation from families and loved ones, feelings caregivers must often separate from their work. Nina, a caregiver, former airline employee, and self-described community organizer and social worker from Nepal, sees her son only every few years. She has now been away from him for so long that he refuses to speak with her except on rare occasions, a development she says causes her pain on a daily basis. She shares, "It's so hard. We are not living, we are surviving. We don't have our own life. I have a baby; I have a husband. I'm only working here for the money. What will happen tomorrow, we don't know. When I go to restaurants, when I eat pizza, I think about my son, my daughter, if they were here, how tasty. When a child is on the road and crying, I want to pick it up and hold it because I miss them. This is what I mean by surviving." The distinction Nina draws between living and surviving reveals the weighty choice many caregivers must make between visiting their loved ones and losing their right to reenter Palestine/Israel, and as a consequence, their means of providing for families. Nina also suggests how she has adjusted her expectations of living and working in Israel to account for the distance she feels from her family, which she associates with living, and the financial incentives for being in Israel, where she is surviving. Her description also underscores the risk of depression and burnout many migrant caregivers weigh as they decide for how long they can be away from loved ones while providing for family members.[73]

Similarly to Nina, June struggles with the sadness of being separated from her three-month-old son. Faced with the risk of losing her visa and livelihood, June was forced by the government to send her newborn child back to the Philippines when he was two months old. She explains,

> I want to [visit him], I would love to. But now I need to wait for the visa on my passport, cuz now I have a special visa and I'm afraid to go out. I don't want to take the risk. If they do not allow me to get in, what can I do? You know, to separate your son after two months for the first time, *zeh meod, meod kasheh* [it's very, very hard], but

what can I do? Some people ask me, "How can you cope *kacha* [like this]? He's your son and he's your first child!" I say, "I need to sacrifice. How can my son live? How can I support him?" So for the meantime, it's like *kacha* [this].

The risk June faces is shaped by Israeli policies preventing migrant workers from having families, on the one hand, and her own feelings of guilt and sadness being far from her son. As one form of affective automation, June adopts the language of sacrifice to mitigate these continual feelings. The language of sacrifice June invokes suggests how June must distance herself from feelings of sadness as a mode of coping, all while caring for her employer. As a means of preventing injury, abuse, and burnout, affective automation becomes both a requirement of the job and a set of emotional responses mitigating the topography of risk caregivers face. Precisely *because* of their fungible positioning between intimate laborer and benignant foreigner, labor extraction, burnout, injury, and detached coping become a condition of the job.

Illness and Alienation

In explaining the lack of adequate health access for migrant caregivers, Rahul tells the story of friends from the Philippines he came to know when he donated his employer's old medicines to them. Because they became unexpectedly ill and were unable to work for more than the three month "grace period" granted by the state to ill caregivers, they lost their health insurance coverage, cleaning houses while ill to offset the cost of their medical treatments. Rahul explains:

> When my employer died, his daughter told me to throw [out] all the medicine. He has a lot of medicine, like a small pharmacy [*laughs*]. . . . What I did, I went to the hospital. There was some Filipina caregivers. They were doing dialysis. I asked them if they needed medicine. They are paying for the medicine and it was a big help for them. So I took all the medicine and gave it to them and they were very happy. . . . The bad rules here are that if something happens to you, the insurance company will not renew your insurance and they will not extend your visa anymore, [and then] you have to

go back. They didn't come with these diseases because they did medical [exams] first. Now they cannot extend the insurance. The [insurance] company will not extend because they know it's a net loss. That's why they have to pay from their pocket. They are suffering a lot—they want to die.

As Rahul suggests, beyond the work-related injuries and burnout that he himself has experienced—forms of stress that constitute what Puar calls a "normal consequence of laboring"—migrant caregivers facing unexpected illness must labor through the duration of their sickness to pay for their own treatment.[74] The difference between Rahul's experiences of burnout and that of his friends calls into question the very constitution of "normal" and "abnormal" times in relation to workers and their health and well-being.[75] Indeed, even during "healthy" times, caregivers lack the same comprehensive public health insurance as citizens, and despite the many forms of stress and burnout migrant caregivers face, mental health services are not covered through the private insurance packages employers are required to provide. The injuries and burnout caregivers endure as a "normal consequence" of in-home, round-the-clock eldercare suggests, in Puar's terms, "the violence of what constitutes 'a normal consequence.'"[76] The emergence of unexpected and prolonged illnesses that characterize "unhealthy" times—such as those Rahul's friends face—ironically require caregivers to labor as a way of covering their own care. Illustrating how disability becomes enveloped into liberal narratives of "progress" and "inclusion," Puar, drawing on Livingston, argues that the concept of "debility" better captures is "the slow wearing down of populations." Debilitation hinges on the "biopolitical scripting of populations available for injury, whether through laboring or warring or both."[77] Thus, whereas disability ascribes a temporal "before and after" to otherwise healthy bodies, debility highlights the "racialization of bodies that are expected to endure pain, suffering, and injury" as "endemic" rather than "epidemic" conditions.[78] While Rahul's employer can recuperate with the help of a caregiver, caregivers themselves are not entitled to the same recovery and rehabilitation. Rahul relays:

Three times in a week they are doing dialysis, and after, they are doing cleaning. In my experience, my employer was also doing dialysis and after that he was very tired. It's not easy—all the blood is going through the muscles. It makes them stressed and tired and in that situation, they are doing cleaning jobs. . . . I am healthy, I am good, and strong enough, but I can't do that job. They are sick and they are doing this job and I cannot imagine. . . . They also cannot take care of themselves and also for the employer.

For caregivers fighting with insurance companies to cover the costs of doctors' appointments and physical therapy for their injuries, rehabilitative resources are especially difficult to access.[79] Rahul's anecdote suggests how debility hinges on the biopolitical distribution of risk within Israel's reproductive regime. While, as Puar argues, Palestinian debility is a necessary condition for sustaining settler colonialism, debility among migrant caregivers becomes an expected negative externality of reproductive labors under settler colonial capitalism. Debility among caregivers profoundly contradicts caregivers' positioning as praised and appreciated national helpers.

For undocumented migrants, receiving diagnostic tests for new illnesses can also be prohibitively costly. A Physicians for Human Rights study shows that undocumented migrant caregivers dealing with cancer diagnoses have little bargaining power to ensure their employers provide health care, making it difficult to receive an early diagnosis.[80] These barriers to accessing health care place the onus of payments on caregivers, potentially delaying diagnosis until a later stage of metastasis. Widespread violations by employers refusing to grant sick days exacerbate the timely receipt of diagnoses.[81] Rina, for instance, lost her sister to breast cancer and worries that she is a genetic carrier of a mutation that can cause breast cancer, but between her work schedule, finding medical practices that accepted her insurance, and the closure of particular facilities on Shabbat, she was unable to find time to get a mammogram while working in Palestine/Israel. Not until she migrated to Canada in 2018 did she start to get annual mammograms.

In the courtroom, too, the right to adequate health care for migrant caregivers has hinged upon not only their care of elderly citizens but also the extent to which they can demonstrate "strong ties to Israel."[82] In a 2014 petition to the HCJ for extended health coverage for migrant caregivers, Justice Arbel underscores how the legal construction of migrant caregivers' right to adequate health care is contingent upon their perceived social embeddedness within Israel:

> Their social ties and community life are centered in Israel; their permanent place of work is in Israel and they pay taxes as required; their

assets are managed in Israel, even if money is sent to family members in the country of origin; and sometimes also their immediate family are in Israel. The prolonged stay of these workers in Israel creates a strong bond between them and the state, and at the same time cuts off their bond from the country of origin from which they came. This connection to the State of Israel cannot be ignored, even if formally those workers are not considered residents in light of the provision of Section 2A of the National Insurance Law. . . . Admittedly, their connection to Israel may be severed immediately after the death of their charge, in which case it is not expected that their residence permit in Israel will be renewed. However . . . we are talking about people who have been staying in Israel for many years, paying their taxes and tying their fate to it. . . . The nursing workers who stay in Israel for a long period of time are, in my opinion, very close to being residents of the country.[83]

Here, Justice Arbel suggests how exceptions to racial/colonial exclusion cohere around caregivers' demonstration of deep embeddedness within Israeli society. These "strong ties" are evidenced through tax payments, child-rearing, strong emotional and social connections to the state, and loyalty. Yet, in the same opinion, Justice Arbel also highlights the inherent alienability of caregivers, invoking the policy requiring them to rapidly abandon any "strong ties" and leave the country in the event of an employer's death. They are "very close to being residents," and yet, unlike residents, their informal residency is contingent upon their keeping the elderly alive. This fundamental contradiction underwrites Justice Arbel's claim earlier in the ruling that preventing caregivers from receiving adequate health-care coverage "has a dimension of exploitation that is incompatible with the values of a Jewish and democratic state."[84]

The dual treatment of migrant caregivers as intimate surrogates for the incapacities of elderly citizens and threats to settler futurity thus produces migrant injury as an unavoidable outcome of care for the elderly. Even when injuries do not directly result from these labors of care, workers' lack of access to care for non-work-related diagnoses or mental health needs follows from their assignation as migrants working in the eldercare sector.

These structural limitations can also exacerbate barriers to choice migrants face in the areas of family and reproductive planning. A common discussion among caregivers who wish to become pregnant is when and how to conceive given the great lengths of time spouses or partners may not be able to see each other while working abroad. Ivy, a caregiver living in Tel Aviv, says she has tried for years to become pregnant. She explains, "I got married two months before I came here . . . and have been home for vacation twice, but both times I couldn't get pregnant. I want a baby but this distance makes it hard. I don't know if I still can." Beyond the pain and difficulty for those who desire—but are unable—to conceive, those who are pregnant may fear a loss of health insurance or deportation altogether. Ivy tells me about a friend who "went home to the Philippines for forty-eight days and got pregnant. Now she's seven weeks pregnant and hasn't told her employer. She will tell in the next week or two. But it's hard because she doesn't feel well and can't tell and has to keep doing work." Given the state prohibitions on migrant pregnancy, one's sexual and reproductive choices can also become a liability detracting from caregivers' state-assigned function as compassionate and productive workers.

While some employers are willing to thwart policies harming migrant health, such as providing more comprehensive health insurance than is legally required, migrant caregivers must rely upon the benevolence of employers when they face unexpected illness. Though employers may feel love, affection, and admiration toward caregivers, the structural terms of exchange alienate caregivers by making their injury, enervation, and mental health challenges an acceptable price to pay for protection of the elderly. The hinging of health to employers' good will suggests how settler subjectivity "coheres through rehabilitation from disability," not only through "the systemic debilitation of Palestinians," as Puar suggests, but also the reproductive labors of noncitizen, nonnative feminized and racialized migrants.[85] Through a "three-pronged biopolitical logic" differentially and incommensurably situating settlers, Palestinians, non-Jewish migrants, and refugee populations, caregivers are allowed transitory proximity to the Jewish Israeli collective, even as they, like Palestinians, remain outside of the collective's temporal and territorial claims to an exclusively Jewish future.[86]

Locating care work within a broader Israeli "economy of injury" is not to suggest that the employer-caregiver relationship is only experienced by caregivers as exploitative and harm-inducing nor that the only currency through which the labor of care is valued is monetary.[87] Beyond direct financial remuneration, some caregivers receive gifts, legal assistance, and leniency around their work schedules. Leela, for instance, says that when her employer's late wife wanted to "show love," she would send chocolates to Leela's two daughters in Nepal. Sam describes how his former employer's son, a "very rich man" with "an airplane *prati* [private airplane]," would offer to take him on extravagant trips. Kyra says that sometimes employers donate clothes and money to caregivers' families and hometowns, and Lina relays how employers have also given to her mutual aid fund for Nepali women. Likewise, she notes, "my employers know what I like and buy me dresses because I have been there more than ten years." Orly, a Jewish Israeli employer, sends packages to Layla's two children in Nepal, and Sharon has helped buy school supplies for Isabella's two children in Palestine/Israel. While forms of gift-giving can provide additional material benefits to workers, they are nevertheless laden with coloniality, reinforcing the discretionary power of Jewish Israelis to determine who embodies a threat to territorial sovereignty and who deserves appreciation and support for their labors. As Nina articulates, "Some people are very nice—everywhere some employers are nice and some bad, but caregivers' rights is not enough."

Alongside migrants in other labor sectors, caregivers face vulnerability to injury and precarity as part of the same field of disinvestment and injury that, through occupation and military violence, injures, maims, and kills Palestinians.[88] The triangulation of indigenous, settler, and migrant populations through the expropriation of labor and land thus also differentially normalizes precarity and attendant ethical and moral claims about which populations' lives matter. This comparative positioning illustrates how a logic of racial, indigenous, and gender differentiation undergirds Israeli settler colonial capitalism and the differential risks non-Jewish migrant laborers face within Israel's reproductive regime.[89] What is more, the very meaning of the intimate, familiar, alien, and foreign materialize within a broader biopolitical field that normalizes settler emplacement and health. In the next chapter, I turn to employers' perceptions of their relationships with caregivers as a lens into this normalization.

3

Reproducing the Settler Home

By legally employing migrant workers as caregivers, the patient can stay in their familiar surroundings, keep their routine, enjoy a personal, warm attitude and constant attention, and remain in their home environment that is so important to them at this time. . . . Employing migrant workers is more economical and provides a better outcome for the patient than moving to a nursing home, sheltered housing or any alternative other than the familiar beloved home. . . . We are conscious of the sensitive nature of letting a stranger into your home. In our experience, positive co-operation with the caregiver benefits the patient receiving warm, professional, adequate care.

Men-Tal Nursing Services, "Caregivers"

One of many placement agencies matching migrant caregivers to elderly Israelis, Men-Tal Nursing Services suggests how the provisioning of eldercare is shaped by the specific meaning of home in Palestine/Israel. As the advertisement suggests, eldercare requires that workers make employers feel at ease within the "familiar beloved home," as it is a space of emotional, political, and religious significance. Under Israel's turn to aging-in-place, migrant caregivers are a salve within the Jewish Israeli family, easing tensions when adult children struggle to divide their caring and professional duties.[1] Whereas prior to the 1970s more Jewish Israeli women stayed home to tend to children and aging parents, greater numbers began earning an income outside of the home after this turning point.[2] Especially for Israel's "sandwich generation"—adult children ranging from forty to sixty-five years of age whose parents are part of the exploding elderly population—migrant caregivers enable life to proceed with fewer interruptions and family members' careers to continue unabated.[3]

Employer narratives, legal decisions, placement agency websites, and popular discourse portray aging-in-place as key to the cohesion of the Jewish Israeli home in an economically liberalized Israel. Within this framing, migrant caregivers become the only affordable option that allows Jewish Israeli women to work outside the home and adult children to move abroad and live lives free of full-time care. Upholding the structures of full-time aging-in-place, migrant caregivers' labors allow women in particular to fulfill reproductive roles vested with ritual and cultural significance. Israel's fast-growing aging population and the option of outsourcing has thus enabled a gendered reworking of the family that structurally shifts the Jewish constitution of the home, even as this shift is thought to be a financially feasible way of maintaining and reproducing its cohesion.

Building on my analysis of intimacy and alienation, I argue in this chapter that employers' dual accounts of caregivers as "one of the family" and as agents of development reinforce Israeli settler modernity and exceptionalism. Exploring one element of the ongoing regularization of settler emplacement under Israeli neoliberalism, I turn to employers' narratives of caregivers working in the home, asking how they converge with and refute government depictions of Israel as an exceptionally developed and entrepreneurial stronghold in the Middle East. This chapter offers somewhat of a quotidian "theory of the dispossessor," investigating how employers' tropes of kinship and modernity mystify migrant caregivers' exclusion from settler time and place.[4] In contrast to my examination of intimacy and alienation, I am interested in tracking what Rifkin calls "settler common sense," the "ways the legal and political structures that enable non-native access to Indigenous territories come to be lived as given, as simply the unmarked, generic conditions of possibility for occupancy, association, history, and personhood."[5] Through such elisions, Jewish Israeli homes become unremarkable sites of care outsourcing under neoliberal restructuring and ongoing bastions of safety against "the foreign." Unsettling this approach to care outsourcing—an approach that predominates within Israel Studies scholarship—this chapter centers citizen-employers' quotidian narratives, as well as state representations of Israeli economic development, as a lens into the ongoing regularization of settler emplacement. Against historiographies in the mainstream American academy and media that spotlight Israel's 1967 occupation while glossing over the foundational history of land expropriation, this chapter looks inside homes to denaturalize the presence of Jewish Israelis within Israel's imposed 1948 borders.[6] If settler colonialism is an "ongoing process making settlers desire the certainty and comfort of emplacement," then unsettling care is a method of showing how comfort in the home is produced through non-Jewish and nonindigenous labor.[7]

Throughout, I take for granted that settler-citizen complicity in ongoing indigenous erasure is often a form of "induced amnesia" taking place through unexamined passing references to indigenous land as the Jewish national home rather than unfolding through overt political statements.[8] Settler anxiety appears in everyday discussions about employers' own positions of power in relation to the "mobile" migrants tending to their family members. Notably, 78 percent of Jewish Israeli elderly settled in Israel in their lifetime and 23 percent have settled since the 1990s.[9] Still, the state and citizens alike take for granted the "stable ontological core" of the Jewish Israeli citizen and migrant workers' perpetual impermanence.[10]

The first trope employers draw on, the flip side of workers' stories of proximity, hinges on their declarations of familial closeness to caregivers and a concomitant expectation that migrants culturally assimilate in particular ways. The second trope portrays caregivers as mobile agents of development, a depiction exposing how migrants are, in fact, politically othered as foreign and transient, unentitled to territorial permanence. Together these narratives constitute two different "moves to innocence."[11]

The first discourse, what I call the kinship trope, invokes familial proximity, one premised upon the notion of a common Jewish past and future, obscuring the legal and temporal impossibility of caregivers ever joining the national (racial/colonial) family.[12] This trope also contrasts sharply with narratives of Jewish Israeli women as "national reproducers" and non-Jewish women as reproductively threatening.[13] These discourses of racial unity not only reinforce the role of Jewish Israeli citizens as the arbitrators of emplacement, they also erase the roughly 20 percent of Israelis who are Palestinian, whitewash Mizrahi Jewish identity, construct Mizrahi Jews as racially distinctive from Palestinian citizens of Israel, and represent Palestinians as a racially and religiously unified monolith.

The second discourse depicts Jewish Israeli employers as "natural" managers and migrant caregivers as "transnational development agents" alleviating poverty in the Global South.[14] Casting Israel as a modernized, gender progressive, advanced capitalist state for all its economic citizens, this trope paints over the ways Israel's turn to outsourcing and shifts in development following the Oslo Peace Accords become strategies for carrying out settler colonial policies.[15] As Linda Tabar and Omar Jabary Salamanca show, a settler colonial analysis must be central to any consideration of the post-Oslo turn to neoliberal development policies in Palestine.[16] The image of migrants tending to the elderly signifies an economic advancement and multicultural cosmopolitanism inextricable from rhetoric situating Israel as an exceptional "start-up nation," a bastion of gender equality in the Middle East, and a progressive leader helping impoverished nations through its humanitarian aid.[17] The development trope thus exceptionalizes Israel as a site of "settler modernity" in the Middle East, temporally relegating both indigenous and migrant populations to an "underdeveloped" part of the world.[18] Both discourses reinforce caregivers' liminal status as workers whose presence is contingent upon their role as a solution to the neoliberal eldercare crisis that does not threaten a permanent Jewish majority.

I begin by analyzing the Israeli government's self-portrayal as both an exclusionary ethno-racial national family ordained with biblical purpose and an exceptional "start-up nation."[19] I then suggest how the biological, cultural, and military reproduction of settler citizenship is contingent upon "redemption" of the racial family through temporal and territorial control. Next, I examine how the kinship and development tropes function within the migrant caregiver and citizen-employer relationship and their gendered and racialized resonances within Zionist discourse. In conclusion, I suggest how employers' political orientations as liberal Zionists shape their articulation of who is entitled to citizenship as one technology of emplacement.

"Settler Nativism" and the Neoliberal Family

While kinship metaphors and development discourse are ubiquitous in migrant-receiving countries, when used together in the Israeli context, they mystify Zionist claims to the land-as-home by invoking the language of economic modernity. Within the Jewish Israeli home, "one of the family" tropes are encoded with territorial and temporal exclusivity as the lynchpin of a Jewish national future. Depictions of the first Zionist settlers as having a "unique ability to survive and preserve their racial purity through difficult conditions" predicates the racial survival of the national family on this exclusivity.[20] This racial family, in turn, is brought together by what Nur Masalha calls "the invention of a new Hebraic consciousness and the historicization of the Bible as a collective national enterprise."[21] Through the lens of messianism, "history virtually stopped in the 'Land of Israel'" immediately after Jewish exile, and a collective future can only be made through territorial reclamation.[22] This messianic temporality, one transformed into a national mission within secular Zionist temporality, normalizes dispossession of indigenous land while "[deligitimizing] Palestinian spatiality and presence."[23] Absent from this history of exile and plan for future redemption, Palestinians are treated as "illegitimate tenants and squatters" outside of Zionist time, while temporary migrants are conceived of as irrelevant or instrumental.[24]

From language describing kibbutz life to biblical tropes about shared ancestry,[25] since the early days of Zionist settlement, the survival of the Jewish national family has hinged upon processes of self-indigenizing.[26] Israel's "founding generation" has been crucial to this process as a population that sometimes fought in Israel's "war of independence" while shedding diasporic names and identities for new, Hebraicized identities and garnering "moral authority for having 'been there'" at this "foundational event."[27] For Eve Tuck and K. Wayne Yang, such self-justificatory "settler nativism" obscures complicity in dispossession, often through claims to an indigenous ancestor, a move that, in the Israeli context, is evident in biblical invocations of shared forefathers and mothers, and the resultant "birthright" this ancestry accords.[28] Contemporary descriptions of Israel as a "permanent war society" and constructions of the military as a "family-in-arms" likewise hinge national unity upon the surmounting of Palestinian challenges to Jewish Israeli sovereignty.[29] Zionist narratives of familial lineage date back to the biblical Land of Israel, *Eretz Yisrael*, framing land redemption as a shared "common destiny."[30] As Nadia Abu El-Haj argues, the fortification of "the link between biology, national self, and soil" at the start of the twentieth century and, in shifting ways, through the declaration of statehood function as evidence of the "ethno-national myth of common descent" while leveraging biology toward the project of building an imagined Jewish national family.[31]

Discourses of land redemption encouraging the numerical and military strengthening of the national family become an ex post facto justification for settlement. Invocation of indigeneity is thus inseparable from claims to familial belonging as a fulcrum of redemption, survival, and a (racial) strengthening of the land.[32] This linkage between family and land also transposes Jewish futurity onto settler futurity, and anti-Semitic violence against diaspora Jews onto national vulnerability, serving as a justification for ongoing "spacio-cide."[33] Palestinian claims to land thus become an existential threat to the Jewish Israeli family itself. Settling the land generates, in the words of Theodore Herzl, "an unhoped-for accession of strength for the land."[34]

In the national project of realizing a "common [racial] destiny," Jewish women and wives have long been the symbolic bearers of the Zionist national family and its ongoing regeneration.[35] Jewish women's role as reproducers of the nation is historied within modern political Zionism. Since the early days of European Jewish settlement in Palestine, self-identifying liberal factions of the Zionist movement have celebrated the role of Jewish women pioneers, invoked as cultivating land and building the nation alongside settler men. Figures such as Henrietta Szol, Bessie Gotsfeld, Rachel Yanait Ben Zvi, and Golda Meir have been lauded for being "equal partners in the founding of the state of Israel, the Labor movement and the future of the Jewish people."[36] Organizations such as Hadassah and Pioneer Women (now Na'amat) uphold the role of Ashkenazi women in the Zionist colonial project as evidence of the state's founding commitment to "gender modernity."[37] Contemporarily, in addition to passing down historical memories associated with Jewish diasporic experiences and the founding and settling of the state, women keep diasporic and Israeli cuisines alive within the home as a "way of exerting power, sharing tradition, and understanding the nation through the way food is served."[38] They also care for enlisted family during military breaks and, importantly, host Shabbat, a cornerstone ritual for celebrating the centrality of the Jewish Israeli family to Jewish continuity and the nation.[39] For families whose children are of conscription age, Shabbat is also a chance to come home and engage in civilian life with one's family, as a respite from the perceived realm of war and national defense.[40] The presence of live-in caregivers has enabled women in Israel's sandwich generation to maintain these aspects of their cultural and religious role as reproducers, continuing with greater ease the secular and religious traditions that are part of the fulcrum of the nation.

In addition to gendered transformations in familial reproduction, bio-medical initiatives aimed at strengthening the health of the population position Israel as an exceptional site of technological modernity. Israel's burgeoning USD $6.4 billion "longevity industry" frames the nation as a leader in "geroscience," the biotechnological rehabilitation of the elderly.[41] A strategic merging of start-up companies, academic experts, transnational business partners, and the Israeli government, this industry works to re-habilitate the collective body and reproduce the national family by making aging "a condition amenable to biomedical intervention."[42] Involving over five hundred companies, the industry is aimed at "not [just] slowing the decline" of the elderly but also "going backwards in time."[43] By investing in this expanding "geroscience landscape," the government and private sector work to make Israel into a "longevity-progressive country" that is "outpacing the rest of the geographical region" as the state with the fifth-highest longevity rate in the world.[44] Reproduction of the national family and strengthening of the collective body are thus not only matters of the (re)generation of Jewish life, old and young, but also the promulgation of Israeli economic and technological exceptionalism. Echoing this positioning of eldercare as a site of modernity, the Conference on Jewish Material Claims against Germany (Claims Conference) notes that long-term care funds for Holocaust survivors have not only "revolutionized geriatric care in Israel" but also provided "modernized care for elderly Nazi victims."[45] Through in-vocations of high-tech exceptionalism, Israel's "founding generation" takes on a dual symbolism as both evidence of Israeli innovation, and at the same time, a reminder of the country's latent vulnerability. Against this framing, migrant caregivers have been symbolically conscripted into state projects of affordably bringing rehabilitation and "strength to the land" in an era of neoliberal capitalism.

"Gender Modernity," Development, and Migrant Cosmopolitanism

In addition to facilitating the cohesion of many Jewish Israeli homes, migrant caregivers are treated by employers as evidence of Israeli economic and gender modernity. Such representations appear through broader claims to technological innovation outside the field of biomedicine, humanitarian progressivity, gender equality, and economic reductionism. As Christine B. N. Chin argues in her analysis of migrant domestic workers in Malaysia, the presence of migrant domestic workers in middle-class homes signifies who can partake in "neoliberalism's version of the good life."[46] Similarly, in Tel Aviv, the "migrant-worker capital of Israel," migrant women have become a status symbol associated with well-to-do Askhenazi citizens living in the affluent suburbs of north Tel Aviv.[47] Yet unlike Malaysia, the presence of migrant caregivers also facilitates "settler modernity"—the self-portrayal of settler colonial states as comparatively more progressive than the indigenous societies they displace.[48] As status symbols, migrant caregivers signify the relative economic health of Jewish Israeli families whose adult members can maintain their careers regardless of their gender.[49] Articulated by the state and employers as a turn away from the old ways of Zionist collectivism, claims of gender progressivity, start-up culture, and development exceptionalize Israel as an international destination with a booming economy thoroughly integrated into global markets.[50]

Through Israel's turn to economic liberalization and emphasis on Jewish Israeli mothers—and Ashkenazi women in particular—as career women, Israel has become a mainstay of gender progressiveness in nationalist discourse, even as various protocols reinforce the centrality of biological and cultural reproduction to settler survival.[51] In addition to sizable wage and occupational disparities, many Jewish Israeli women occupy "mommy-track" jobs and are still expected to bear children, be primary care providers, and uphold their role as military mothers.[52] Through a logic of "neoliberal feminism," Jewish Israeli career-holding women may even turn a "'progressive' critical eye" on Israel itself while failing to challenge the underlying imperialism of settler colonial governance.[53] Rabab Abdulhadi notes that such depictions of Israel as a "liberator of women" depend upon "making

Palestinian women disappear," a form of "feminist-washing" that normalizes the displacement and marginalization of Palestinian women inside and outside of 1948 Israel.[54] Likewise, these tropes reinforce what Nada Elia has identified as a tendency among liberal feminists to obscure how "the greater oppressor of Palestinian women is not Islamic fundamentalism, but Zionism."[55]

On the one hand, migrant workers are enfolded into many receiving states' "modernity project[s]."[56] In Palestine/Israel, these narratives are part of a longer colonial trajectory categorizing non-European subjects as "premodern" to justify dispossession. Beyond claims to gender progressiveness, the Zionist establishment has fashioned itself a "modernizing agent" since early settlement at the start of the twentieth century, when Zionist leadership depicted Palestinians as in need of technological, agricultural, scientific, economic, and cultural improvement through the expertise of European settlers.[57] As Ahmad Sa'di and Rashid Khalidi argue, Theodore Herzl, Chaim Weizmann, Zev Jabotinksy, and other key Zionist leaders viewed Palestinians as in need of the economic and political tutelage that Zionism, as a European colonial project, could offer.[58] From late nineteenth-century settlement to its selective memorialization in later decades, a colonial "rhetoric of hierarchical coexistence" among Jewish settler-employers has emphasized the employment of Palestinians as a form of "interethnic harmony" and a way to commemorate *moshavot* as "having 'always' been peaceful."[59] Zionist colonization was also thought by Weizmann to increase the "spread of knowledge and learning" and to lead to superior forms of science and education.[60] Drawing on familiar orientalist binaries such as East and West, Arab and European, "uncivilized" and "civilized," and "undeveloped" and "developed," Herzl likewise thought that colonization would improve technological know-how and property value in Palestine.[61]

Under late capitalism, such rhetorical emphases on development take the form of the common claim that Israel is a "start-up nation," exhibiting what Getzoff calls a "unique cultural entrepreneurialism" that "reimagines tropes of Israeli ingenuity that have long been used to legitimize ongoing settler colonial expropriation."[62] Against the orientalist imaginary of an "underdeveloped" and monolithic Palestinian society, "start-up discourse" "refigures the image of the pioneering settlers laboring on land as a forerunner to a high-tech entrepreneur, adaptive to the global market's needs."[63] This start-up discourse extends to Palestinian citizens of Israel, who are targeted by Israeli firms as in need of integration into the high-tech economy for the sake of economic development.[64] As Dan Senor and Saul Singer revealingly write in their widely quoted bestseller *Start-Up Nation*,

> As they do in Israeli society (and have throughout Israel's history), the pioneering and innovative impulses merge into one. At the heart of this combined impulse is an instinctive understanding that the challenge facing every developed country in the twenty-first century is to become an idea factory, which includes both generating ideas at home and taking advantage of ideas generated elsewhere. Israel is one of the world's foremost idea factories, and provides clues for the meta-ideas of the future . . . while Israel has much to learn from the world, the world has much to learn from Israel.[65]

Within this description, displacement of Palestinians through Jewish homemaking is recast as the plucky ability of pioneers to survive by way of their creativity and innovation. Contemporary settler society—and the colonial-capital accumulation upon which it depends—thus becomes the genealogical inheritor of an innocent pioneering spirit.[66] Recourse to such mythos obscures the strategic "intertwinement of inclusion and exclusion" that underwrites the Israeli economy.[67]

Other aspects of Israeli development discourse circulate through public relations campaigns, including Israel Defense Forces (IDF) media on humanitarian interventions and government declarations of investment in global gender equality. Like the IDF, Israel's Agency for International Development (MASHAV), the Israeli government's main development agency whose mission is "to share with developing countries the know-how and technologies which provided the basis for Israel's own development in order to empower them in their own development efforts," has extensive humanitarian aid programs in countries from which migrant caregivers originate, including India, Nepal, the Philippines, Colombia, and Romania.[68] Attributing their many areas of capacity-building programming to Israel's "development challenges" that "transformed subsistence agriculture into an advanced, modern and efficient economy," MASHAV focuses on "sharing relevant expertise accumulated during Israel's own development experience to empower governments, communities and individuals to improve their own lives."[69] It is thus that, according to their mission, "supporting those who face great development challenges goes to the heart of what it means to be a Jewish State."[70] MASHAV furthers the narrative of Israeli technological and economic acumen, linking the common refrain that settlers "[made] the desert bloom" to its ongoing successes in venture capitalism. MASHAV, like the IDF, also attempts to normalize Israeli occupation by framing the state's ability to empower seemingly less developed nations as an inherently Jewish value.[71]

Israeli claims to "gender modernity" also abound through rhetoric painting Palestinian women, and Arab women more broadly, as in need of the cultural expertise of settler society. As Israeli ambassador Lironne Bar-Sadeh declared to the UN Committee on the Status of Women, "In a region where women are all too often excluded from public life, Israeli women stand out as leaders in politics, law, mediation and conflict resolution."[72] Casting "Arab women" as victims of a monolithic, patriarchal society, the Israel Ministry of Foreign Affairs likewise notes that, "as in other countries with traditional communities, Israel faces challenges in regard to polygamy" with respect to its Palestinian women citizens of Israel.[73] Each of these aspects of Israeli development discourse shape the affective presence of migrant caregivers in the home and reinforce depictions of Israel as a unique site of modernity. While the kinship trope buttresses Zionist temporal exclusion from a Jewish redemptive future, the development trope shapes employers' ideas about where workers come from, while categorizing native and non-Jewish populations as illiberal and undeveloped. Both reinforce "temporal boundaries" between indigenous, migrant, and refugee populations, on the one hand, and settler society, on the other.[74] Through these temporal imaginaries, employers become "settler-consumers" buying care service from the international care market.[75]

Taken against the colonial casting of Palestinian society as premodern, patriarchal, homophobic, and economically regressive, this rhetoric treats Palestinians as unfit for incorporation into the neoliberal cosmopolitan fold. Through this move, Israel becomes a bastion of progressivity in the Middle East while Jewish Israelis both "disavow and transcend indigeneity."[76] In reality, racial and economic hierarchies among Ashkenazi, Mizrahi, Palestinian, migrant, and refugee communities belie this portrayal. Alongside articulations of migrants as one of the family, neoliberal discourses of "gender modernity" and economic opportunity become "settler common sense," eliding the connection between the reproduction of the Jewish Israeli family and home and the regularizing of settler nation-building.

"Benevolent" Settler-Citizens and Kinship
as Mystification

Within Jewish Israeli households, employers' claims that caregivers are one of the family constitute a form of "settler common sense" mystifying the territorial control upon which the national family is predicated. Though intended to demonstrate a close connection with caregivers, for women caregivers in particular, refusal to perform according to an employer's desire for familial intimacy carries significant risk. Tellingly, among the descriptions employers used to characterize the migrant women whom they felt to be one of the family were "devoted," "very cooperative," "loves a laugh," "patient," "a sweet girl," "warm," "has intimate talks with my mother," and "knows how to serve us." They described those they felt less close to as "not so warm," "distant," "minding her own things," "talking a lot of rubbish," "doesn't speak Hebrew," "took her time to understand this relationship," "not enough respect," and "really busy with her family and her own stuff." Using familial rhetoric to display affective orientations that align with employers' gendered and racialized expectations thus becomes as much a job requirement as bathing and feeding. Notably, recourse to tropes of familial closeness are not only globally ubiquitous in domestic worker-employer relations, they also have their own history in the context of racialized and gendered reproductive labor in Palestine. As Nahla Abdo shows, academic depictions of relations between early Ashkenazi women settlers and indigenous Palestinian women that emphasize sisterhood through the boss-worker relation reinvigorate notions of the "benevolent colonialism" of Ashkenazi women.[77] Such recourse to the employment relationship as an evasion of colonial relations in the past and present obscures the very ways dispossession, labor, and the gendered racialization of laborers uphold the settler present.

The Kinship Trope and "Voluntary" Labor

Leah, an elderly Jewish Israeli employer from Bulgaria, describes Jennifer, the caregiver tending to her for the last eight years, as one of the family. She fondly remarks that Jennifer, who worked as a nurse in the Philippines, "knows my daughter" and "knows my grandchildren" and even has knowledge of Bulgarian movies. Leah has three adult children, one of whom lives in the United States, one of whom lives in her home but works during the day, and one of whom works full-time elsewhere in Palestine/Israel. Given her family situation and the amount of care Leah needs, if she did not employ Jennifer or another migrant caregiver, she would have to live in a senior living facility, an option she says her children refused to consider. Leah describes Jennifer as "the kind of person I like to have at home." She notes,

> It happened to me that I fell down two months ago on the floor. I couldn't get up. . . . I phoned [Jennifer]. I told her, "I fell down, please come home." In ten minutes she took a taxi and she came and then she took me back here, picked me up, put me on the chair and didn't go out. She stayed all the day because she was afraid it would happen again. Not everyone would do it. Because it was her *hofesh* [vacation] she could have come, got me up, and gone away. She didn't. I appreciate it.

While Leah depicts Jennifer's willingness to work during her vacation as voluntary, under the Law of Return facilitating Jewish settlement, Jennifer's ability to remain in Palestine/Israel is contingent upon Leah's bodily health and satisfaction with Jennifer's care. For Jennifer, making Leah feel happy and safe in the "beloved" home is thus dependent upon maintaining her status as one of the family.

On the one hand, Leah's narrative reflects a desire some caregivers possess to be treated in a familial manner. Yet, depicting Jennifer's extracontractual labor as voluntary obscures the legal and economic consequences she faces if she fails to act like one of the family. Because Jennifer's work visa has expired, these risks include deportation and the inability to remit money and pay off high-interest loans accrued during migration. Not only does the kinship trope obscure Jennifer's lack of recourse to shared common ancestors in Palestine, but as evidenced by the surveillance, policing, and deportation of politically active migrant leaders, declarations of political dissonance *from* the national family evoke settler anxieties around the legitimacy of the Zionist project itself.[78]

Despite and because of the expectations of closeness invoked through the kinship trope, Jennifer helps keep Leah's household afloat. Leah describes how Jennifer dresses her every morning, makes her coffee and three meals, brings her outside for walks, and accompanies her to family events. Jennifer also helps Leah maintain her home as a specifically Jewish Israeli one. Leah proudly comments that Jennifer "knows how to cook Bulgarian food. I taught her." Like many other employers, Leah expects Jennifer to replace her in the realm of cooking. Since moving in with Leah, Jennifer has learned to make Bulgarian pastries, eggplant dishes, schnitzel, and Israeli salad. As Claudia Pietro Piastro notes, among both secular and religious Jewish Israeli women, the Jewish Israeli kitchen is a crucial space of national reproduction.[79] Notably, Leah comments that Jennifer "also makes Filipino food. Egg rolls, noodles, rice. I eat some of it, Filipino food. She knows how to make many sauces."[80] Through Jennifer's presence, Leah has been able to continue eating the forms of Jewish cuisine with which she's most familiar while also being introduced to non-Jewish foods in her home.

Leah also explains that Jennifer helps her maintain the centrality of Shabbat to her life, accompanying her to family dinners on Friday evenings and occasionally Saturday lunches, as well as to synagogue. Preservation of Shabbat rituals and traditions, whether secular or religious, are central to the reproduction of the nation as a time when Jewish Israeli families travel to each other's homes to spend the evening or weekend together. It is also a time when many settler-citizens reaffirm a commitment to Jewish communal values, whether through meals or by attending synagogue.[81] Leah relays, "I go with [Jennifer] to reform synagogue twice a week [on Friday night and Saturday morning]. I hear twice a week *Tanakh* [Hebrew Bible]. There are many women who come with caretakers and they [caregivers] stay in the foyer. And they laugh, they are very glad to be there." Leah's observation that Jennifer stays in the foyer also suggests how migrant caregivers are othered through Jewish rituals, even as they are central to elderly participation in them.

Like the majority of Jewish Israeli elderly, Leah was not always considered an a priori fixture of the land, but was, like Jennifer, "mobile." She explains that like "all the Bulgarian Jews," she "came to Israel after the [1948] war" in the early 1950s to escape anti-Semitism and because her father was "all his life a Zionist." Upon arrival, Leah's family settled in the city of Jaffa, which had fallen under Zionist control, resulting in the expulsion and fleeing of Palestinians and the eventual transformation of the surrounding area into the "First Hebrew City" of Tel Aviv, also promoted by early settlers as the "New York of *Eretz Yisrael*" [the Land of Israel].[82] Leah's family took on a Hebraicized surname in place of the family's diasporic last name, a form of self-indigenizing that began in the first waves of settlement at the start of the twentieth century. This common story of self-indigenizing suggests how dispossession itself, as Robert Nichols argues, is a recursive process through which land is imbued with new legal and political significance it may not have before held.[83] The land on which Leah and her family made a home became property through the process of theft itself. This home then took on meaning as a sphere of safety from attack and a refuge from world-wide anti-Semitism.

While in Jaffa, Leah lived in a one-bedroom apartment with no bath-room and recalls Palestinian neighbors living nearby. Eventually, her family opened a factory in Jaffa, allowing them to generate more income. Suggesting historical and ongoing forms of settler fears around the proximity of indigenous Palestinians, she remarks that her family "preferred not to take Arabs" as workers in the factory. Leah later describes France and other areas of Europe as being "spoiled" by "Muslims and Arabs," revealing how global Islamophobia converges with indigenous erasure in the Israeli context. She then notes that, unlike Filipinx migrants, "Arabs don't want to work in Israel" because "they think it's a sort of shame to work here." Here, Leah frames the lack of migrant Muslims and non-Jewish Arabs as a matter of dishonor or embarrassment rather than a result of visa allocation policies making unlikely the entrance of demographically "threatening" populations. Covered over are the ties of transnational solidarity between Palestinians and other Arabs in the region, formed against a history of European colonialism in the Middle East. Also significant is Leah's use of the term "Arab," a descriptor commonly used to refer to Palestinians that erases the Jewish Israeli Arab population, thereby racializing Jewish Israelis as more "European" than Palestinians.

In Leah's account of her relationship with Jennifer, the taken-for-granted household environment within which labor unfolds is predicated upon Leah's "birthright" status. By contrast, migrant care work is a preferrable economic arrangement for ensuring her safety through in-home care. Like many elderly Jewish Israelis, Leah's own story is one of escaping the horrors of anti-Semitic violence and fascism, and then she herself becoming enfolded into European imperial projects in the Middle East as a Zionist settler. While her story documents her family's conversion from diaspora Jew to "indigenous" *sabra*, Palestinians only appear in her narrative as threats to her physical home and homeland. In contrast, Jennifer's perceived lack of attachment to the land and status as a mobile worker seems self-evident—during the afternoon we spent together, Leah showed me several pictures of the home Jennifer is building in Manila, explaining to me that the home is the product of Jennifer's hard work in Palestine/Israel;

through this narrative, Israel is a temporary site of opportunity allowing Jennifer to improve the conditions in her "real" home. In this context, characterizations of Jennifer as one of the family constitute a "move to innocence" by obscuring the conditions of possibility for Leah's lifelong emplacement while painting over Jennifer's legal exclusion from the national family and her closely related economic precarity.

Like Leah, Dina, an Orthodox Jewish Israeli woman living outside Tel Aviv, also refers to her mother's caregiver as one of the family. Among interviewees, Dina was the most insistent on demonstrating that her relationship with her mother's caregiver was familial. Dina's mother, too, was not born in Israel, coming from North Africa by way of Europe. Despite her family's relatively recent arrival, Dina describes her relation to Palestine/Israel as an inevitable extension of her Jewish observance, while depicting the woman caring for her mother as a benevolent non-Jew in proximity to—but definitionally outside of—the Jewish collective body. Throughout our conversation, Dina expresses profound appreciation for Sheyla, a woman from Sri Lanka whom she hired to live with and care for her mother at the end of her life. Dina was able to hire Sheyla with money allocated to her mother through the Holocaust fund for elderly Jewish Israelis established by the Claims Conference. She lovingly describes how Sheyla tended to her mother at the end of her life and their conversations about religion, each other's families, and the ways Sheyla learned to communicate with Dina's mother using a combination of French, English, and Hebrew. Unlike some employers, Dina articulates an awareness of the structural conditions shaping Shelya's life, as she is ultimately "here to earn money." Dina also acknowledges some of the multiple identities Sheyla holds beyond caregiver, noting that it was "difficult to know that she was away from her mother and [she, Dina] couldn't do anything." She explains that "[Sheyla] was working in a mental health hospital and for communities in small villages in Sri Lanka, working with people with HIV. She's really amazing. She came to send money for her family and to save money for a pension. . . . People helping are amazing and they deserve our respect and recognition. . . . It's very difficult to see people dying and dying and ill and ill and not go home because it's expensive, so I don't know where you get strength from." Unlike Leah, who expresses awe at Jennifer's infrequent trips home, Dina names the economic strictures delimiting Sheyla's ability to visit her family. She also calls for the valuating of care work as a skilled job.

Despite these words of appreciation, like many citizen-employers, Dina describes Sheyla as "part of the family" and "like a daughter to my father." Yet, like Leah, she also takes care to represent these feelings of kinship as mutual, despite the impossibility of Sheyla ever benefiting from the settler privilege of permanence: "For [Sheyla,] it was important to feel part of the family. . . . [The relationship] can't be only professional. She felt the same to my mother as her own. She would talk about how it was hard to be away from her mother and that she could not travel, and I know the situation of her mother is not good . . . it was also a responsibility on our side to fill this role of family because they need that." A central function of the kinship trope in Dina's narrative is to portray Sheyla's extracontractual work as voluntary. Alluding to the phenomenon of task expansion, Dina explains that Sheyla "was just [hired] for my mother, but naturally and spontaneously she was preparing food for my father and was taking care of the house, but this is something that she did by herself . . . I never asked her to." Her reference to uncompensated work as "natural," "spontaneous," and voluntary reveals an unwillingness to acknowledge the economic and legal strictures that require migrant caregivers, and women in particular, to mitigate their job precariousness through feminized performances of patience, generosity, and tenderness. Though Dina relays deep appreciation for Sheyla's labors, and the presence of migrant caregivers in Palestine/Israel as a whole (she notes, "in Israel there is something special happening with caregivers"), she nevertheless mystifies Sheyla's labor by attributing it to her kind personality. By extension, this mystification depoliticizes Sheyla's labor by hiding the many structural forces that require caregivers to perform emotional and physical labor to mitigate job precarity. Here, the kinship trope can also serve a disciplinary function, imposing a moral onus on workers to act like one of the family, particularly as elderly family members' health declines.

Similar to Dina, Orly, a woman in her fifties living in Tel Aviv, is intentional about projecting a sense of kinship onto Layla, a caregiver from Nepal tending to her mother. Orly has a successful career as a writer and social commentator, and she has two adult children of her own who have finished their army service. Though Orly's mother lived with her and her children during the early stages of her mother's illness, as her mother's condition worsened, Orly decided to hire a migrant caregiver so she could maintain her career. By employing Layla, Orly resolves the conflicting gender roles proscribed by the imperative to join the workforce and the necessity of culturally and materially reproducing the Jewish Israeli home, whether through care, cooking, or ritual. Suggesting her role as both career woman and bearer of family cohesion and tradition, during the afternoon that I spent with Orly in her Tel Aviv apartment, she was preparing and cooking for the Friday night Shabbat dinner she hosts for her family, who would be arriving in the evening. (She was also generously feeding me as we talked.) Orly states that as a working woman, she "didn't have the luxury" to do anything but hire the first migrant caregiver she met. Like Dina, she expresses gratitude for the care her mother receives and an awareness of the separation between Layla and her own family. Orly identifies as politically liberal and is quick to critique the ruling conservative Likud party and the poor treatment of migrant caregivers. She relays great appreciation and admiration for Layla, both for the care she gave to her mother and for her work beyond her role as caregiver. She relays, "[Layla] was very involved with political organizations that support workers who are sexually harassed by their employers. She had an article she was involved in issuing also, [in] a paper for Nepali workers and had an article in one of the newspapers. . . . She was very loved by [her friends] and they appreciated her." Like Dina, Orly also expresses an awareness of the structurally imposed sacrifices Layla must make to work in Palestine/Israel. She makes clear that "[Layla] is not seeing her children grow up. She won't see her mother. She would talk to them a lot, a lot. She was very involved in their life. . . . I never saw [her children] on Skype, but [I saw] pictures. Maybe I should've asked her to talk to them, now that I think about it." Hinting at feelings of guilt, Orly speaks about Layla's presence in her family as both a blessing and the cause of family separation.

Like Dina, Orly views Layla's presence as a function of economic necessity, though perhaps unsurprisingly, neither of them articulate migrants' presence as one shaped by Jewish Israelis' relationship to indigenous Palestinians. Also like Dina, Orly frames Layla's extracontractual labor as voluntary. Recounting her presence at various family functions, Orly comments that "she would come to my brother's on Friday nights and was of course treated like a guest, but she insisted on washing the dishes and we wanted to stop her. And then we said, 'No, she's like family; if she wants to do the dishes, it's OK.' But we didn't want her to think she *had* to do it. She was really like family. I think she didn't feel like a worker. She didn't feel obliged; she did it really as a friend." Orly's narrative belies a similar desire to portray extracontractual labor as an extension of her familial closeness rather than a manifestation of a tenuous employment situation. These conditions are made more insecure by Israel's de jure exclusionary citizenship regime and the impossibility of Layla ever being "converted," through ancestral claims, into an immovable subject.

The portrayal of care work as "voluntary" may also serve to mitigate guilt as Orly and Dina outsource traditionally feminized tasks to other women. On the one hand, Orly expresses undoubted fondness for Layla, describing her conversations with Layla about her children and appreciation for the freedom Layla's presence provides. At the same time, reducing her ingratiation into Orly's family to a matter of instinctive closeness erases the emotional labor caregivers must undertake to mitigate job insecurity while avoiding acknowledgment of bosses' own position as gatekeepers of the national family.

Shmuel, a settler-employer self-identifying as politically liberal, hired Sara, a migrant caregiver from the Philippines, to tend to his elderly mother, Chava. Like most elderly Jewish Israelis, Chava was not born in Israel, arriving, in her case, in the 1950s from Morocco. Facing economic hardship and anti-Semitism, Chava and her husband and three children, including Shmuel, left Morocco to settle in Palestine shortly after the Nakba. According to Shmuel, his parents were also motivated by Zionist ideology. He recalls his family uttering the religious phrase "*b'shana haba'ah b'yerushalayim,*" meaning "next year in Jerusalem," as a mandate to settle Palestine in the present.[84] This common phrase, one repeated at the end of Passover seders and near the end of Yom Kippur, takes on a redemptive, future-oriented quality in the context of modern political Zionism, underscoring collective return as the lynchpin of Jewish futurity and survival. Chava first lived in a *ma'abarah*, or transit camp for new Mizrahi settlers, outside the town of Netanya, where she gave birth to her fourth child. Notorious for poor living conditions, *ma'abarot* were predominantly inhabited by Mizrahim and remain a symbol of Ashkenazi Zionist leaders' colonial attitudes toward Arab Jews. After leaving the *ma'abarah*, Chava and the seven members of her family lived in a one-bedroom apartment before eventually moving to a wealthier neighborhood. As Shmuel remarks, "That's the way it was then . . . if you came from the right country it was a better situation indeed." Chava's story echoes that of many Mizrahim arriving in the 1950s, who were treated by the Zionist Ashkenazi elite as incorporable into Jewish society as "working-class settlers" who added to the total "quantity" of Jews inhabiting the land while not contributing to the "quality" of settler society overall.[85]

Despite the many hardships Chava and her family faced as working-class Mizrahim, they, too, eventually took part in self-indiginizing rituals in their lifetime, albeit in ways distinct from those among European settlers.[86] Poignantly evident of this conversion is the relationship of Chava and her family with migrant caregivers arriving four decades later under neoliberal restructuring. While Chava and her family, as Mizrahim arriving in the 1950s, were settlers whose underpaid labor subsidized Israel's "racial Fordist economy" prior to the adoption of neoliberal policies,[87] they were nevertheless capable of becoming settlers, albeit in uneven ways. In contrast, migrant caregivers are unsettled workers whose praised and expropriated labor subsidizes welfare retrenchment without a similar guarantee of settlement. The "conversion" of Shmuel's family from "immigrant" to "native" is thus also a conversion in class status, evident in the increased purchasing power of lower-middle and middle-class families when migrants are providing care. In recounting the relationship between Sara and his mother, Shmuel illustrates one aspect of this purchasing power, suggesting the steep consequences for *not* fulfilling an employer's gendered expectations of familial assimilation:

> Three years ago, we wanted to fire Sara and some of my brothers and sisters didn't trust her. They were afraid that she's violent. Sarah didn't really understand her role and we didn't think we had to explain our expectations because she's very intelligent. . . . Sara was really busy with her family, with her own stuff, and she didn't really understand that her job is not just giving and preparing food. I told her, "You don't caress [my mother], you don't sit next to her and hold her, you don't give her the emotional support she needs. If you're not capable we will have to replace you." After this [discussion], she changed. Now Sara knows the family very well, and since she started functioning on the emotional level and not only the physical, everybody likes and adores and appreciates her. She's become an angel.

To "become an angel" like Sheyla and Layla, Sara had to exhibit signs of "know[ing] the family very well" and stop being "really busy with her [own] family." In fact, "becom[ing] an angel" was elemental in reassuring Shmuel and his siblings that Sara was not "violent." Whether performative and strategic or not, this "becoming" is enmeshed with the structural conditions of care in Palestine/Israel.

Paradoxically, demands for these performances of familial and cultural assimilation do the work of othering Jewish and non-Jewish household members while (re)producing settler-employers' gendered positioning as managers within the home and, by comparison, that of caregivers as foreign. In addition to obscuring the effortful nature of care work, the kinship trope also devalues migrant caregivers' gendered subjectivities in relation to their own families and the "double duty" they undertake while simultaneously tending to children or parents abroad. When I ask Orly why Jewish Israelis are not live-in caregivers, she replies, "If you live in Israel, you have to have very special circumstances to live in a person's house; you have your *own* family. It's different." Her comment suggests that it is somehow more natural for migrant women to live thousands of miles away from their families as intimate strangers in someone else's home; the caregiver is a priori a migrant, and the Jewish Israeli woman the logical "care manager" whose proximity to her family is the logical extension of her unquestioned permanency on the land. In a telling illustration of how this belief permeates recruitment agencies, in 2009, Shmuel Armon of the National Association of International Manpower Companies noted, "I'm sure there are not many Israelis who would be willing to work as a caregiver for 24 hours a day. Most [Israeli] workers are only willing to work for eight hours, and they would never want to live away from their families."[88] This normalization becomes part of the "moral economic justifications of overseas employment" that simultaneously sustain the rhetoric of "gender modernity" and the cohesiveness of the national family.[89] The growing elderly population and the presence of migrant caregivers has created a gendered reworking of the family that structurally shifts the ethno-religious and racial constitution of the home, even as this shift is allegedly a financially feasible and demographically non-threatening way of maintaining its cohesion.

In contrast to the accounts of care work told by Orly and Dina, Idan, a self-described anti-Zionist, illustrates how some citizens attempt to unsettle settler logics, articulating a need to interrupt the reproduction of the Jewish Israeli home, even as their resistance may never transcend the colonial relation. In marked contrast to other interviewees, Idan articulates great skepticism toward the kinship trope and metaphors of Jewish Israeli society as one large, extended family. Reflecting on the performative aspects of caregiving within his father-in-law's home, he says, "Saying 'she's like family' is the same thing as the guy who goes to the prostitute and thinks she's in love with him." He then describes the relationship as inherently asymmetrical, stating that "the relationship is full of fears and racism. There are daily clashes over how to use the kitchen and if the smell is good or bad, to the opposite—whether you can eat the food the employer makes. Every little intimate problem of your daily life. It is a very personal, intimate relationship." As Idan suggests, settler-employers possess a power to determine who does and does not blend into the household and nation. Their very ability to determine who is "familiar" enough to approximate the Jewish Israeli family—whose futurity is realized and continuity ensured through territorial conquest—unveils an unquestioned "settler common sense" about their role as heirs to the land.[90] In the context of modern political Zionism, the kinship trope, as a "move to innocence," elides how the bodily health of individual citizens and the maintenance of the intergenerational Jewish Israeli family hinges upon the expropriated labor of migrants.

Kinship and the Masking of Difference

Despite her acknowledgment of economic and religious differences between her and Sheyla, like other settler-employers, Dina represents their relationship as one of intercultural exchange among equals. As Caroline Hodes argues, one way of "preserv[ing] a settler colonial status quo" is through recourse to "sameness," an evasion similarly found in discourses of racial colorblindness.[91] Eliding the effects of global restructuring and the Law of Return on their own positions of privilege, employers wittingly or unwittingly paper over the conditions of violence that position them as indigenous in relation to "foreign" workers. Dina noted that "from the first day, we asked [Sheyla] to come eat with us around the table and said that she didn't have to stay in the kitchen." Dina also spoke at length about the many spiritual similarities between herself and Sheyla, whose religious practices she says mirror many of her own: "She was Buddhist, but it was very interesting because we were talking about God's providence leading and ruling the world. . . . She even respected Shabbat . . . she learned how to separate milk from meat. It was very interesting because as religious and believing persons, we thought a lot about God and felt we had the same relation to God. It was natural. She really was an angel." In addition to describing their natural connection, Dina portrays Sheyla's familiarity with the laws of *kashrut*—or keeping kosher—as an example of cultural understanding. Importantly, various religious rituals and traditions—from the laws of *kashrut* to observing Shabbat—are central to nation-building in Israel, imbuing the state with primordial importance that links a Jewish past to a secure settler future. Since the first days of Zionist settlement, "Zionists gave religious symbols a new nationalist meaning," a phenomenon that continues to this day, from court rulings codifying the importance of Shabbat, to the enforcement of *kashrut* and Shabbat observance in the IDF.[92] Unlike migrant caregivers working for secular families, those within religious homes face more pressure to culturally assimilate in order to facilitate ritualistic activity and learn religious laws as the intergenerational need for care changes. Sheyla must learn how to separate milk and meat, put particular foods in specific cabinets and sinks, and decide how long to wait in between meals before serving different kinds of foods.

Working for religious families can also entail facilitating employers' observation of rules around working, cooking, and resting on Shabbat. While some of this information on religious observance is available through predeparture orientation programs, most comes from on-the-job learning after hours. Like many other Orthodox women, Shabbat dinner is Dina's responsibility. Beginning on Thursdays, she plans the menu and cooks. Dina describes her mother's need for full-time care as a reorienting process that has required integrating Sheyla into these routines while occasionally accommodating Sheyla's needs. At the same time, one of the ways Dina differentiated between herself, as a settler-employer, and Sheyla, was through her discussions of Shabbat. As Piastro notes, Friday night Shabbat dinners are not only a way to "showcase the national roots of a family" and perform diasporic continuity as the "New Hebrew" in contemporary Israel. They are equally a way to "socialise newcomers into Israeli society and the family," a process of "Israelisation" that women undertake as "one of their nationalist duties, and a key aspect of private life in which the nation is performed."[93] In this way, "Shabbat has kept Israel," and Friday night meals in particular have served as a way of reinforcing the Jewish Israeli family's core importance to the national project.[94]

At one point in our conversation while discussing Shabbat, Dina refers to Sheyla as a *shabbos goy*, the Talmudic term for a non-Jew completing tasks Jews cannot do on Shabbat. Paradoxically, Dina characterizes Sheyla as a member of the family by invoking the term for a non-Jew who, by virtue of being not Jewish, may be asked to undertake particular forms of reproductive labor. Yet, at other moments, Dina reinforces the division of labor between her and Sheyla, explaining that because of religious law determining food cooked by non-Jews to be unkosher, Sheyla would prepare and chop foods, while Dina would light the fire on the stove herself before the start of Shabbat to ensure the food was technically cooked by a Jew. Such tensions, ambiguities, and inconsistencies between an observant employer and a non-Jewish employee are infused with settler dominance in the Israeli context, ascribing new meaning to religious rituals than they would otherwise hold in a diasporic context. These interactions also serve as a form of othering, reinforcing Dina's role as a cultural and religious reproducer of the Israeli "nationalist family," which treats Jewish Israeli women, and Orthodox women in particular, as progenitors of the nation's religious borders and future survival.[95] As Attiya Ahmad notes, "Differences are not only produced through what a domestic worker does—that is, through her laboring, which is socially reproductive of her employers' household members—but in domestic workers' very doing of it—that is, the fact that it is she, the domestic worker, who is undertaking this work, and not her employer."[96] In the Israeli context, the distinctions Dina draws between tasks a Jew and a non-Jewish employee can and cannot do also suggest how Dina others Sheyla as a laboring outsider to the Jewish nation, even as she is necessary to the cultural and religious reproduction of Dina's home.

Notably, after describing the work Sheyla does in her home, in an unwitting "move to innocence," Dina adds, "She enjoyed it." Dina's account reinforces her own gendered self-construction as "an organic part of the family of the Jewish people."[97] At the same time, Dina hints at how Sheyla's very presence unsettles her own self-understanding as a Jew and a settler-employer, noting, "You ask yourself questions when they ask, 'What is Holocaust Remembrance Day?' and you have to explain to a person, 'What is a Jew?'" Taking for granted her unquestioned role as household manager and national "host," Dina engages in a form of "settler nativism" that normalizes both the relatively recent settlement of her own family and the mobility and impermanence of migrant workers.

Dina also admits to being "really struck" that Sheyla "would say 'Shabbat Shalom' when we were lighting candles." Yet as non-Jewish precarious laborers inside Jewish Israeli homes, it is imperative that migrant caregivers absorb aspects of Jewish culture and law to ingratiate themselves into employers' families. Several caregivers told me that during premigration trainings, they were tested on their knowledge of Israeli recipes, elements of Israeli culture, Hebrew catchphrases, Jewish holidays, and the laws for keeping kosher. Rather than bespeaking a harmonious intercultural exchange, their deep knowledge reflects the extent to which this relationship functions upon migrants' fluency in the ethnic, religious, and cultural practices of settler society. Later, Dina also unwittingly expresses awareness of the dissimilarities, noting that she "didn't care so much about the differences." Rather, she "felt like [she] was talking to a Jewish person."

The unequal demands on caregivers to learn their boss's cultural practices is not to suggest that employers' views are not also shaped by caregivers, nor that caregivers' needs never influence daily household routines. Nor does this inequality mean employers never attempt to accommodate some of the needs of caregivers. Within the strictures of her strictly kosher home, Dina explains that Sheyla "didn't eat meat so we have to adjust," and she notes that on Shabbat, "either we were doing things with fish or with no meat for her or she was cooking alone . . . we eat traditional couscous and dishes and sometimes we'd make something special for her." Dina also explains feeling a sense of shared religiosity with Sheyla over dietary observance: "Sometimes I'd ask her if the fact that she doesn't eat meat was related to Buddhism or not. . . . She said, 'You know, this is god's will and this is for the best' and god protects her . . . and this is the same sentence I would say; it's what somebody who believes would say. It's something that really strikes me." While at times, Dina reinforces Sheyla's temporary status by distinguishing between Jewish and non-Jewish and citizen and migrant labor, here, she suggests how the employer-caregiver relationship can unsettle the exclusively Jewish character of the home, even as it may not fundamentally alter religious practices or racial/colonial divisions of labor. Dina conveys respect for Sheyla's religious customs, creating some space for them within her weekly Shabbat ritual. Dina also describes how during the first Shabbat meal she shared with Sheyla, "for the first *kiddush* [blessing over the wine] we said, 'Feel free not to say it,' but she said 'Yes, I will say it.' At the end when we passed her the wine I asked her, 'Do you want to drink wine?' and she said 'No.' [It was] no problem." Dina's recounting illustrates how caregivers' needs require that settler-employers adjust their practices in limited ways, even as Sheyla's presence helps Dina maintain religio-national customs as the family's intergenerational care needs compound.

The story of Yocheved, a Modern Orthodox Jewish American settler in Jerusalem, reveals the impossibility of managing both tasks if a caregiver and her charge are both Jewish. Like Dina's family, before settling in Jerusalem, Yocheved was constructed, through Israeli citizenship law, as a lifelong "citizen-in-waiting" by virtue of being born Jewish.[98] Having recently "made *aliyah*," the term for Jews claiming their "right" to citizenship through the

Law of Return, Yocheved now lives in Nachlaot, a neighborhood of West Jerusalem inhabited by many religious Anglo-American Jews, and works as a live-out caregiver. Yocheved has been quickly enfolded into the Zionist project of making a home in Palestine. While non-Jewish migrant caregivers are expected to work around the clock for employers, Jewish Israeli caregivers like Yocheved live separately from their employers and work carefully regulated shifts each day. Throughout our conversation, Yocheved conveys her deep love for her profession and charges, the compassion required to care for the elderly with the dignity they deserve, and the sense of fulfillment she finds in giving them her attention. She also mentions the surprise some employers express when learning she is not a migrant from South or Southeast Asia. In explaining her decision not to accept one particular job, she notes,

> I could tell they were looking for somebody to do whatever they wanted, whatever hours they wanted. They were looking for people over Shabbat and I'm *shomer Shabbat* [Shabbat observant] and I've struggled a lot with this in caregiving. . . . I've always been very connected with the law in Judaism so to finally be in Israel and not do the things that are natural to do is really hard because then it's like if you were to go to somebody's house and caregive, it's like what type of expectations are they gonna ask [of] you if they expect you to break Shabbat?

So central have South and Southeast Asian migrants become to Israeli imaginaries of aging that, according to Yocheved, her own identity as a Jewish American is undesirable to employers. This imaginary is predicated as much upon the racialization of non-Jewish migrants as it is their exploitability as around-the-clock workers. Yet the expressed naturalness of Yocheved's emplacement is also the condition entitling her to refuse work that migrants do. By virtue of their territorial presence, Yocheved's and Dina's religious observance is converted from religious practices with sacred connections to the land to a political project of expropriation and displacement. Becoming emplaced in Palestine vests Dina and Yocheved with power and privilege as employers and as workers.

Unlike Dina and Orly, who stop far shy of locating migrant care work within broader structures of settler colonial capitalism, Idan views migrant labor as symbolic of wider patterns of racism. He notes that Israel "creates a permanent fear of the foreigner, thinking this foreigner only wishes to come and break the Jewish majority." In contrast to other employers, Idan has been painted as a traitor by the state for his activism, facing arrests for protesting against Palestinian human rights abuses and refusing military service. While other employers obscure their positions of power, Idan, as a "care manager," ascribes it to the Israeli government's broader treatment of non-Jews and its project of demographic management, which he sees as another effect of racial and religious supremacy enabling land annexation. He thus views the treatment of migrant caregivers as an effect of Jewish Israeli colonial claims to inalienability from the land.

Migrants as Development Agents

Another trope naturalizing settler-employer household relations portrays Jewish Israelis as inherently suited to the role of managers and migrants to the role of live-in care workers. As a "move to innocence," this trope echoes transnational discourses depicting migrants as "transnational development agents" alleviating poverty in their home countries through employment abroad.[99] This discourse casts migrant caregivers outside of settler time by characterizing them as subjects from regions of the world that are economically and politically "behind" Israel. Repeating depictions of migrant laborers within a "migration-development" framework—a set of strategies assumed to raise the economic prosperity of low-income countries—these narratives paint migrants as human capital who, by sending remittances, can "move" their home countries along a linear trajectory from poverty to "modernity."[100] As migrants come to stand in for the outsourcing of labor "traditionally" done by citizens, disproportionately women, their presence also promotes notions of "gender modernity" that present migrants' presence in the home as a "win-win" solution to global poverty.[101] In contrast to the kinship trope, development language acknowledges inequalities but presents them as an inevitable outcome of Israel's transformation from a Zionist collectivist state to an individualistic, liberalized economy.[102] Employers thus explain migrant caregivers' presence in their homes as a result of Israelis' "preference" for being managers, viewing the stigmatization of care work as an originary cause rather than an effect of neoliberal labor formations under settler colonial capitalism.

Sharon, a secular Jewish Israeli woman working full-time in the outskirts of Tel Aviv, employed Isabella, a domestic worker from Colombia, while her children were young. Because work visas in the nursing sector are not granted to migrants from Colombia, Isabella was forced to work without documentation. Sharon reflects a liberal Zionist sensibility and willingness to fight for Isabella's right to remain in Israel, even describing a period of time when Isabella and her children lived with Sharon's family while hiding from immigration police. She notes that she "can't understand the *medinah* [state], because who is staying here, let them stay here by law, and close Ben Gurion Airport or the border from new [people] to come in." Here Sharon unwittingly reaffirms Jewish Israelis as the arbitrators of who merits emplacement. She also suggests how migrants' presence can be justified by their utility to labor markets: "It's a very sad situation, because they know a little bit [of] Hebrew, they can help the old people, they are working in the *kibbutz*, they can help us, [caregiving] is a job nobody wants to do. . . . Everybody wants to be *minhalim* [managers]. Because the country is young, we are only sixty years old, and now the generation becomes older so we need someone to take care of the old people and we the Israelis don't want to do that. Because when the country was young, then everybody did everything, and now we need help." Alluding to Israel's shift from a "racial Fordist" to a market-based economy driven by capital investment, Sharon identifies migrant caregivers as a logical solution to citizens' changing socioeconomic expectations of acceptable jobs.[103] Through this denigration of live-in care work, migrant caregivers become alienated from the citizenry; while the former symbolize a permanent supply of noncitizen labor enabling the Israeli transition away from a statist economy, the latter represent the citizen-turned-managers of a liberalized Israeli economy. In Sharon's description, Israel is a place for migrant workers to be incorporated into the Israeli economy, even as it is a territory where they are excluded from narratives of permanency and emplacement.

Like Sharon, Dalia, an elderly employer from Germany, describes live-in care work as a stigmatized profession. Dalia employs Ellen, a caregiver from the Philippines, in a small two-bedroom apartment on the outskirts of Tel Aviv. Dalia relays how Ellen accompanies her everywhere, from trips to the bathroom to the shopping mall, daily walks around the block, and bridge games with friends. Dalia excitedly notes that they have even started to play Scrabble, and that while "her dietary habits are completely different . . . [Ellen] watched [Dalia] preparing recipes and [now] she can do it in a jiffy." Dalia expresses deep appreciation for the care she receives and also acknowledges that Israelis would prefer unemployment to caregiving, as "it's dirty work for Israelis to do." In contrast, Dalia describes her former part-time caregivers, all Israeli women, as impatient, inattentive, and less willing to remain by her side. She relays one incident that was emblematic of her displeasure with Israeli caregivers:

> Before [Ellen] I had Israeli *mitaplot* [female caregivers] from the national insurance three times a week for three-and-a-half hours. The last ones were completely unreliable. For instance, I went somewhere on the bus and on the way back I told her where to get off to change buses. She was not sitting next to me because I was sitting on a special seat. I told her what station; the announcement said the name of the station. I got off and she didn't. I had to get home by myself. I managed, I managed but it was risky and she phoned my daughter to tell her what happened and everybody was worried. So we complained and she was offended that we complained [*laughs*].

Dalia's story suggests how employers' sense of safety, ease, and companionship is contingent upon the constant presence of migrants, whose right to remain in the country rests upon their round-the-clock proximity to employers. Unlike the purchase of citizen-delivered eldercare, that of migrant-delivered eldercare stretches over more hours, a guarantee that the elderly will be vigilantly guarded from such "risky" situations at all times. Dalia's mention of the offense her former caregiver takes also uncovers the differing degrees of power citizen caregivers and migrant caregivers possess to refuse unfavorable labor conditions. Orly likewise suggests the undesirability of carework among citizens: "[Migrant caregivers] don't take the work of Israelis 'cause no one wants to do this work. People appreciate it; they think good things about them . . . people say, 'oh, they need the money, they come to work here, they have a license, let them do it.' This is how they're treated, not as people taking places of Israelis." Sharon's and Dalia's comments illustrate how migrant caregivers, and women in particular, fill a care gap created by the entrance of more Jewish Israeli women into the labor market at a time when Israel's elderly population is exploding. Alongside this shift is an accompanying dismissal of this labor as incompatible with the "modern" Jewish Israeli woman's lifestyle. Migrants thus facilitate the reproduction of daily life for the elderly in a way Israeli citizens are thought to be incapable of and unwilling to do. As recruitment agency Natan states on their website, "Foreign caregivers can significantly improve the quality of life of the elderly or nursing patient they care for. They provide nursing services inside the home, accompany the patient outside the home, assist in performing routine activities, and maintain [the patient's] safety around the clock. Hiring a foreign caregiver is a good and effective solution to give the elderly parent or nursing patient the help he needs while keeping him in his familiar living environment. This removes the burden from the patient's family, such that their only responsibility is to monitor and follow what is happening at home."[104] Underscoring both the significance of aging at home—something 95 percent of Israeli elderly prefer to do—and the alleviation of the "burden" of full-time eldercare, Natan hints at the sorts of cost-benefit decisions that Sharon, Orly, and others make.[105] Significantly, both Sharon and Orly work outside the home and state in almost identical terms that Israelis "[don't want] to do this work." Their assertions also echo the notion, articulated by Justice Edna Arbel in a 2014 HCJ ruling, that hiring a migrant caregiver "allows the patient to stay in his home, often with his family . . . and saves him the necessity of moving to a nursing facility which will force him to leave his familiar environment, and share care with many like him," thereby enabling a "better quality of life" and letting "the patient's family members continue their normal lives, work, and leisure, while knowing that their loved one is under close and proper supervision and care."[106] The choices Sharon and Orly make to outsource care highlight how policy and rhetoric emphasizing the workplace as a site of gender equality normalize the "femininity," "raciality," and modernity of disproportionately middle-class, affluent, and Ashkenazi women who no longer see themselves fit for eldercare. In reality, the transition of Jewish Israeli women, and Ashkenazi women in particular, from care*givers* to "care managers" emerges through the broader "market-based strategy of colonization" under neoliberal restructuring that has increasingly predicated the "benefits, salaries, and profits" of Ashkenazim on Palestinian and other non-Jewish workers while creating higher unemployment in—and segmentation of—the West Bank.[107] At the same time, post-Oslo restructuring was as much about the extraction of labor and resources as the "de-radicalization" of Palestinian popular resistance.[108] Accomplished in part through the introduction of a larger playing field of foreign donors in occupied Palestinian Territories governance and development projects, this goal is an inextricable part of the turn to migrant labor, one that connects the normalization of migrants in Jewish Israeli homes to ongoing attempts to suppress Palestinian resistance.[109]

Other settler-employers allude indirectly to the impact of these economic and political shifts on the division of caring labor, portraying Israelis as "unnatural" caregivers and describing them as too impatient, "thinking they are too smart," or as "completely unreliable." Throughout our conversation, Orly discusses her own feelings of guilt in ensuring her mother had care when she did not want to sacrifice her career to provide it herself. Yet she also draws an interesting parallel between the aging of Israel's population and the "maturing" of the state itself, referencing not only the "aging" of Israel as a state but also a shift in the Zionist ethos from a welfare-based, communitarian collectivity (for Jews) to an individualistic society where younger generations no longer "do everything."[110]

> When I was a child I was one of the rare families in our neighborhood who had grandparents. People who came from Eastern Europe, they didn't have grandparents. When my grandmother was here, we took her to a home, but this was the way. An Israeli caretaker came in the morning, and my mother came in the afternoon and took care of her. We all took care of her. The old age in Israel started to be in higher percent, and now Israelis live longer. So [there are] more old people, so this was a solution that was to be found. Because in the modern family you don't live in—how you call it? *Hamulah* [extended kinship network], like the Bedouins . . . Israelis cost more and there's fewer persons. The only economic solution for a family is a caretaker who lives there and has a salary, and you don't have to rent for him. This is the only way you can do it.

In her account, Orly contrasts Palestinian Bedouin with Jewish Israelis, the latter of whom have become too "modern" to take on full-time care work. Drawing temporal borders around settler society, this distinction echoes the beliefs of Zionist leaders that Jewish settlers would bring "modernization, progress, industry and industriousness" to Palestinians, who were thought to be antithetical to this "progress."[111] The characterization of Palestinian society as "primitive" thus functions as a virtue or asset in asserting the uniqueness of the Israeli national project.[112] Further, the framing of pre-1985 Israel as akin to a socialist economy overlooks not only the exclusion of Palestinians as beneficiaries of this economy, it also elides the role of Labor Zionism in underwriting and helping consolidate an Israeli capitalist class despite its proclaimed commitment to socialism.[113] As a "move to innocence," this binary of "modern" and "past" ignores gender disparities between Jewish Israeli Ashkenazi men and women and ethnic and class disparities among Jewish Israeli women, and most pointedly, between Jewish Israeli women, Palestinian women, and migrant women.[114] Through the invocation of gender modernity as a *form* of settler modernity, migrant women become "heroines" earning money for their countries, and employers are the benevolent bosses enacting a form of "mini-aid."[115] Here the development trope reproduces the Jewish Israeli home as a site where the global cosmopolitan citizen can increase their purchasing power of care through outsourcing.

Like Sharon and Orly, Nadav, a Jewish Israeli citizen who hired a caregiver for his father, explains that before Israel became a "modern" society, hiring a non-Jewish, live-in migrant would have seemed "unnatural." Nadav's parents came to Israel from Iraq, and his mother now lives in Jerusalem. He states, "Nobody even *thought* to take somebody strange to take care of one of the family. Now there's modern life—it's more materialistic and family members don't have time to take care of an elderly relative. You bring someone else to care for them." In contrast to the contemporary perception that lower-middle-, middle-, and upper-class elderly Jewish Israeli citizens will be cared for by migrants, Nadav recalls an era before privatization when Jewish Israeli citizens were not "natural" managers. Nadav's insight hints at how settler-employers have been *made* into managers and "citizen-consumer[s]" as the Israeli government has embraced liberalization.[116]

As Sharon, Orly, and Nadav reveal, descriptions of Jewish Israeli households—and their outsourcing of care—as "modern" and "material-istic" (a close proxy for capitalistic) relationally temporalizes Bedouin, and indigenous Palestinians more broadly, as outside of "modern" time. Nadav's suggestion that having "someone strange" tending to the elderly is part of "modern life" reveals how migrants signify a cosmopolitanism that draws workers from around the world, while simultaneously casting indigeneity as part of settler society's prehistory. Nadav's narrative also reveals that Jewish Israelis' "preferences" for avoiding round-the-clock labor are not merely the cause of the gendered racialization of live-in care work but also its effect. Taken together, the Law of Return, enactment of the Long-Term Care Insurance Program (LTCIP), and the binding arrangement economically and affectively engineer a new class of Jewish Israeli "care managers" whose positioning turns on migrant caregivers' status and their own territorial fixity. Attributing the employment of migrants to Israelis' desire to be managers overlooks how the convergence of neoliberal governance and settler colonial dispossession shape these preferences in the first place.

Politicians' speeches also portray "foreign workers" and asylum seekers in particular—whom politicians regularly refer to as "infiltrators"—as personifications of a less "developed" geography. This characterization is especially prevalent in discussions about Eritrean and Sudanese asylum seekers, who regularly contend with state anti-Blackness and its closely entwined relationship to state exploitation of labor. Whereas Prime Minister Benjamin Netanyahu has many times celebrated migrant caregivers as compassionate helpers, he has called for the use of "a firm hand" against "illegal" migrants and asylum seekers, whom he depicts as a threat to Israel's "First World" status.[117] In a 2010 speech to the Manufacturers Association of Israel, Netanyahu avowed that "we have become almost the only First World country that can be reached by foot from the Third World. We are flooded with surge [*sic*] of refugees who threaten to wash away our achievements and damage our existence as a Jewish democratic state." He added that "anyone walking around Arad, Eilat, or even south Tel Aviv today, can see this wave, and the change it is creating, with their own eyes. They are causing socio-economic and cultural damage and threaten to take us back down to the level of the Third World."[118] Netanyahu's comments position the "Third World" as a contagion attached to all non-Jewish migrants that threaten Israel's newly achieved liberalized status. Simultaneously, Netanyahu comparatively racializes noncitizen, nonindigenous temporary populations as less threatening to Israel's "First World" status.

A related narrative emerging out of caregiver-employer labor relations is one of economic reductionism. This discourse characterizes migrants as entrepreneurs whose sole reason for migrating is poverty. It thus alienates migrant caregivers as a racialized underclass who stand in for "underdevelopment" and a Global South alterity. Dina tells of her own trip to South Asia, which she visited as part of a humanitarian rehabilitation project. Dina comments, "You really feel from their situation that they have nothing." Esther, an elderly woman who hired a man from Sri Lanka to tend to her late husband, likewise asserts that "[migrant caregivers] have it good here because Israel is more modern than the Philippines. They live very well. A great life, they receive a good salary. They require a lot; they develop themselves more." Though economic considerations are often a motivating factor, in reality, so is the desire to escape political conflict, follow family or romantic partners, build houses, start businesses, and join communities abroad. Pamela, a science teacher from the Philippines, explains, "Employers think we come here because of poverty. That's the bottom line that they always say. . . . But I came here not because of poverty. . . . I have a job already in the Philippines. I came here because I *want* to come here, and my boyfriend is here, and I have another intention. I don't have poverty. I came here not because of what I'm earning. I come here because it's Jerusalem and my boyfriend is here." Despite the range of economic and noneconomic factors for migrating that Pamela highlights, Israeli recruitment and placement agencies echo these reductionist economic narratives. This economic reductionism is also evident within recruitment agencies and supportive websites for the elderly. Likewise, Israeli nursing website Nursing and Nursing Care, an informational resource for families with elderly members in need of long-term care, notes that "it is usually cheaper to employ foreign workers and also, rare Israelis dedicate their world to live-in, nursing care and living in a place that is not their home. Foreign workers usually come from low-income third world countries. In order to support their family, they have to live away from them; for them this is the only option to provide for their children."[119] Despite such representations of caregivers as solely motivated by poverty, as I discuss in the subsequent chapter, Christian Zionist caregivers come to Israel as much to tend to the elderly as to be in a land of religious significance, a commitment that positions care for elderly Jewish citizens as a kind of religious care for a sacred place.[120] Economic reductionism also decontextualizes the feminization of migration from a broader history of failed structural adjustment programs in migrant-sending countries, which, through conditional aid and widespread debt, force countries such as the Philippines to adopt labor export economies.[121] As Idan notes, "Israelis really feel they're in a Western, developed society and these foreigners come because they want to live in this society. Perhaps this is the predominant purview. It comes out of ignorance." Employer characterizations of migrants as racialized others from an "underdeveloped" part of the world thus reinforce caregivers' "foreignness" as a form of settler self-indigenizing.

Citizenship as Technology of (Dis)emplacement

Employers' descriptions of Israeli society as a "developed" bastion of gender modernity normalize settler-employer emplacement and the demographic management of territory required for its maintenance. Notably, this normalization happens across the political spectrum. With the exception of Idan, employers with whom I spoke identified as Zionist and as politically liberal or left-of-center, suggesting how the "liberal Zionist" position treats expropriation and occupation as "an extrinsic aberration or corruption of something essentially good."[122] Employers' articulations of entitlements to citizenship suggest how a liberal Zionist perspective regularizes citizenship as a technology of settlement.[123] Michael, who identifies as secular, liberal, and "very Zionist," describes Israel's "Jewish character" in circular terms, as if by its very self-designation as a Jewish state, its permanent alienation of non-Jewish migrants, asylum seekers, and native Palestinians becomes a fact as accepted as the nation-state form itself. Michael hired a caregiver from Nepal to take care of his mother, a Holocaust survivor who escaped Poland and settled in Palestine after the Nakba. Michael grew up in a Zionist youth movement founded by the Histadrut, the Jewish labor union. Michael speaks of himself proudly as both Zionist and firmly against the right-wing identifying political parties. His parents, too, were involved in the Zionist settlement of Palestine, even traveling to Russia in the 1960s to encourage other Jews to come settle Palestine. Explaining why migrant caregivers cannot attain citizenship, Michael notes, "I guess let's say in Europe for sure but in the US if someone is illegal for many years it takes a while and sometimes afterwards [they] get citizenship. But here if you're not Jewish, it's only by chance. You can't get citizenship. Let's say two Filipinos are getting married here. No way they can get citizenship. It's different. No, no. Same with refugees—Since it's a Jewish state, it doesn't accept immigrants, non-Jews." He adds soon after that "there is a fear of non-Jews coming here." Tellingly, later in our conversation, Michael conveys exasperation that a Jewish American family member "making *aliyah*" was required to procure multiple letters from rabbis to prove his Jewishness (he notes, "This is crazy!"). While preventing migrant caregivers from permanency is so natural as to not warrant explanation or debate, the demand that Jewish Americans' authenticity be questioned before taking up their "birthright" sparks outrage. Michael's story belies the reality of the Law of Return, which the government views as a matter of "national security"—so much so that it invests in the silencing of Palestinians expressing a rejection of this law.[124]

Demonstrating a somewhat more critical distance from Israel's treatment of migrant caregivers, when I ask Orly whether she thinks migrant caregivers want to be citizens, she states, "Listen, Israel does not want them to be citizens, because they are not Jewish. So from the beginning they are second-rate people." In contrast to both Michael and Orly, when I ask Idan whether migrants should have a right to citizenship, he explains, "Remember that you are in a racist, ignorant society. People feel superior to all those 'natives' that come. There's not talk of citizenship. In many societies with these types of [caregiving] services this happens. [They're] classist, racist . . . you feel the racism." The only employer with whom I spoke who referred to Israel as a settler colonial state, Idan illustrates how settler anxieties emerge not only in relation to Palestinians but also with respect to "refugees, migrants, et cetera." Explaining how the trauma of Nazi genocide becomes projected onto the Israeli state, he reiterates that "all of them [Palestinians, refugees, and migrants] are gentiles from the purview of the *shtetl*-threatened Jew, though . . . there is an imaginary of the non-Jewish foreigner as a vibrant threat." Yet Idan also offers a critique of how Palestinians and migrant workers are *comparatively* racialized, noting, "Palestinians? It is a national liberation struggle. Refugees, migrants, et cetera are now in a struggle of survival. . . . Palestinians are terrorists and migrant workers are criminals. The government places a lot of feelings on being threatened. It's in discourse. Today the written press is more and more xenophobic." Idan suggests how the imaginary of the "terrorist" is underwritten by the existential threat native populations pose to settler legitimacy. In contrast, the "criminal" migrant worker is perpetually alien, even as caregivers may not pose the same threat to intensive and ongoing processes of settler self-justification.

Idan's comments also suggest how the invocation of citizenship, as a central tenet of liberal universalism, normalizes the projects of displacement and emplacement. Looking at the case of Israeli settler colonialism, Lana Tatour calls citizenship "an institution of domination, functioning as a mechanism of elimination, a site of subjectivation, and an instrument of race making."[125] Through this reading, the jus sanguinis nature of citizenship in Palestine/Israel is perhaps a more legally obvious form of domination, but it is not exceptional to the workings of citizenship as a vehicle of empire.[126] Citizenship makes the suturing of the Jewish Israeli nuclear family to the land benign, unremarkable, and innocent, in line with the liberal Zionist assertion that Jews, like all nations, deserve a territorial homeland.[127] Interestingly, some employers also invoked ethno-racial particularism in positioning themselves as gatekeepers of the land, underscoring how settler-employers understand Israel as both a state like all other civic states and, simultaneously, as an explicitly "Jewish state" with a justifiably exclusionary citizenship regime. Sharon, a self-identified Zionist who says she is in support of migrant rights, draws on this particularity by invoking the unique experiences of the Holocaust. Discussing the time she helped an undocumented caregiver hide from deportation police, she relays,

> There is a difference between Jewish and other people because the Jews, I think, because of the Holocaust, might think different. Because every time [my caregiver] is in trouble I think, "the Holocaust, I need to help her." . . . Maybe you can find a difference between Jewish people and the others. Sometimes I'm looking at the old people, how they behave to their *mitaplot*, and I feel at times like they passed through the Holocaust, and sometimes I am watching them and I think that they behave with the *mitaplot* differently because of what they passed through. I think that I am doing so with [my *mitapelet*] because I'm always thinking about if I was in the Holocaust and I'm not Jewish, what shall I do if someone Jewish comes to my place and asks me to hide them? I don't know why but I think that every Jew, it passes through their mind. And I can see that here, and I behave the same. Immediately I thought, "Come to my place, it doesn't matter what time." I want to hide and protect her from the bad guys. I'm here in Israel, it's my place.

Referring to Israel as "my place," Sharon depicts Jews' presence in Palestine as equivalent to those of non-Jewish populations helping Jews escape Nazi persecution and death throughout Europe. This description inverts the metaphor of caregivers tending to Israel's most vulnerable population, suggesting instead that elderly Holocaust survivors' own traumas uniquely attune them to migrants' vulnerable status as non-Jews. While Sharon's claim may indeed be accurate for some employers, it nevertheless promulgates the notion of settlement in Palestine/Israel as a panacea for the horrors of the Holocaust. Sharon is willing to act in solidarity against Israel's deportation regime, yet, in line with liberal Zionist ideology, she also treats migrant deportation as an aberration to, rather than a constitutive part of, Israel's settler regime, suggesting the centrality of "founding generation" mythology to liberal and right-wing employers alike.

Such invocations of the Holocaust can be—and have been—successfully leveraged to rally Jewish Israelis in solidarity with groups targeted by the Israeli state. Yet Sharon's observation overlooks how migrant caregivers' own economic and physical well-being hinges at all costs on their ability to care for Holocaust survivors and the elderly and disabled more broadly. It also reproduces discourses that situate Jews as the rightful guardians of the land by virtue of their experiences *as* Holocaust survivors, erasing ongoing traumas experienced by Palestinians through displacement, land expropriation, and military violence. Such representations disavow the physical conditions of possibility for Jewish Israeli homemaking as a material and symbolic practice. Unsettling such narratives requires asking how migrant eldercare arrangements are constructed at the nexus of neoliberal and settler colonial ideologies and locally incorporated into projects of developmentalist modernity that exceptionalize Israel as uniquely entitled to make ethno-racial exclusions while painting it a nation like all other nations. Rather than constituting a contradiction, this dual logic reveals the functioning of citizenship itself as a vehicle of conquest and displacement. Against the unquestioned acceptance of citizenship in employers' homes, workers disrupt the most immediate effects of settler colonial capitalism, a topic to which I turn in the final two chapters.

4

Household Resistance and National Love

They become more attached to you than you to them . . . they really are like children. They see you as their food, as their life, as their everything . . . you have to base everything on whether he's awake, he's asleep, he needs something. It's like you're twenty-four hours on standby.

David

I said [to my boss], "What? I need to change *my* attitude? You need to change *your* attitude! . . . If you are good to me, I am more good than you, but if you are like that, oy va voy, I am more devilish than you!"

Rina

In my language, they say bread and meat do not come together, but here [in Israel], it comes together.

Sam

David, a twenty-six-year-old nurse, migrated to Palestine/Israel in 2012 to "explore the place, get to know the culture, and earn some money in the process." In describing his job as a caregiver for Abraham, a ninety-seven-year-old retired doctor, David identifies a fundamental schism between his and Abraham's experiences of their relationship. Abraham relies on David for his continued existence, while David ultimately views his presence in Abraham's home as short-term employment that provides economic stability and allows him to explore the ancient cities of Palestine.

Over years of providing care, David has become essential to Abraham's survival. As David explains, being indispensable means helping Abraham around the clock and anticipating his every need. At the same time, Abraham's reliance on David mitigates the legal and economic effects of labor flexibilization. In the absence of labor protections, a strong union option, and a common boss against whom to organize, migrant care and domestic workers often combat labor flexibilization individually, catering their strategies to particular bosses. Like many caregivers, they are their "own bargaining agent[s]," creatively finding ways to shape household relations to improve their material conditions.[1] As a "tacit skill," forging a relationship of indispensability is a strategy that increases bargaining power and the chances of "stretch[ing]" time by acquiring a special visa that extends the length a caregiver can stay past four years and three months.[2] In a state with no right to permanent residency, naturalization, or substantive cultural membership, stretching time unsettles the authority settler-citizens attempt to claim through the rigid setting of temporal boundaries.[3]

Using a different tactic to counter flexibilization and racial/colonial exclusion, Rina chooses at moments to contest her employer's racism and exploitation head-on. Refuting racist comments her employer makes about how she thinks a Filipina caregiver "ought" to act, Rina promises to match her employer's rudeness by being "more devilish." Rina explains that with some employers, quitting—even at a financial cost—is a better option than being subjected to unfair demands. Even so, at other times, Rina says she tells her employers only what they want to hear. For Rina, direct contestation, quitting, and strategic deference are alternating strategies for mitigating precarity in ways that make space for her presence, needs, and limits. While in the past Rina has participated in workers' rights seminars, she describes herself as apolitical.

Both David and Rina situate their own interests as distinct from that of their employers. In contrast, Sam, a caregiver and math teacher from Nepal, articulates strong alignments with his employer and love for the Israeli state. He says that it "hurts [him] inside" when caregivers try to "show that they're good caregivers" without truly loving their employers. "If it is really hard," he asks, "and they don't enjoy their work, why don't they leave their job and go back? If they need money they also should honor their duty and also love the employers and take care of the employers with *ahava* [love]." While Sam and Rina hold opposite orientations toward their bosses, both express great admiration for the Israeli government. Sam describes Israel as the "*medina kama yafah!*" (such a beautiful state) and echoes tropes that situate Israel as the only democracy in the Middle East. In contrast, Rina conveys a love and respect for Palestine/Israel *as* a "Jewish state," wearing a *magen David* (Jewish star) necklace and, on many occasions, Israel Defense Forces (IDF) T-shirts. In contrast, David takes trips to the West Bank on his days off to visit Palestinian friends and conveys disapproval of Israel's ongoing occupation.

The varying narratives of David, Rina, and Sam suggest how workers' articulations of their material interests in relation to bosses do not map neatly onto their political orientations toward the state. They also trouble simplistic or romanticized notions of worker subjectivities as monolithic and necessarily in opposition to employers, even as workers creatively resist the most immediate effects of settler colonial capitalism on a daily basis.[4] Caregivers' strategic navigation of labor precarity and demographic management unsettle employers' expectations of care work as an unquantifiable "labor of love" that is the natural domain of nonsettler, nonindigenous workers. Simultaneously, their strategies disrupt Israel's temporal boundaries by allowing caregivers to extend their time in Palestine/Israel for months and sometimes years after their initial visas expire.

This chapter excavates the many strategies migrant caregivers adopt to resist, transform, and refuse their material conditions within employers' homes. Through tactics such as direct contestation, strategic deference, and fostering indispensability, workers engage in "everyday resistance," navigating surveillance, debt, and exploitation. Workers' refusal of extracontractual labor and resistance to their treatment as disposable denaturalizes the linkages between "migrant," "non-Jew," "non-European," and round-the-clock care. By repositioning live-in, migrant eldercare as unequivocally attached to remuneration, workers also lengthen their stay in a state that reaffirms its "right" to the land by recognizing the territorial futurity of one exclusive group. Caregivers deftly shift relations of power to make themselves less expendable and to create more space for their own needs in the otherwise unequivocally Jewish space of the home. In drawing on the concept of "everyday resistance," I follow Stellan Vinthagen and Anna Johansson's readings of James Scott and Michel de Certeau, highlighting those forms of opposition to domination that manifest in a "*way of using* a system" creatively.[5] Workers may resist and refuse demands on their labor, time, and capacity while also articulating broader political alignment with bosses that reproduce employers' positioning as rightful heirs to the land.

To ground these forms of "everyday resistance" within a broader politics of Israeli exceptionalism, in the second half of the chapter, I explore caregivers' orientations toward the state, drawing on Ahmed's concept of "national love."[6] For Ahmed, migrants are a "breach in the ideal image of the nation" that threaten its constitutive character, particularly when migrants fail to show adequate appreciation to the nation for permitting them to remain within its borders.[7] At times, expressing support for Zionism—whether through praise for "the Jewish State" or the disavowal of Palestinian sovereignty—may be a form of national love that diminishes precarity, even as it reinforces Israeli settler sovereignty. At other times, support for Israel can reflect ideological, religious, or political commitments. At still other times, workers' expressions of love for Israel may be prompted in our conversations by my own position as a white, Jewish American whom workers see as a proxy for the state. My aim is not to definitively categorize or reduce workers' approval of the state to a risk mitigation tactic or ideology, to romanticize workers' tacit skills, or make legible these forms of resistance for the sake of academic inquiry. Rather, understanding how nonindigenous, noncitizen workers understand their own relationships to their work and to the state is crucial for engaging in transnational solidarity that supports the immediate struggles of workers, themselves. Further, I intend to highlight how global tropes casting Israel as a victim of Muslim violence, or regularizing Palestine/Israel as the contemporary Jewish homeland, messily intertwine with the limited forms of contestation available to non-Jewish, nonindigenous temporary workers. Expressions of sympathy and support for the Zionist project suggest how the normalization of Israel as a "Jewish national home" emerges from multiple vantage points beyond the state and those inhabitants it most privileges. I also aim to foreground the comparative lack of political space for directly contesting state policies in Palestine/Israel, a state whose temporal restrictions are significantly more stringent than other migrant-receiving regimes. While many if not most host states prevent the naturalization of migrant workers, few limit migrants to one nonrenewable visa that is only extendable by exception.[8]

In foregrounding caregivers' forms of everyday resistance, I draw on James Scott's adaptation of Erving Goffman's concept of a "frontstage" arena—the highly surveilled site of power where workers navigate domination under the direct gaze of bosses.[9] In chapter 5, I turn to migrant caregivers' "backstage" and collective modes of risk mitigation outside the home, which often take the form of community service-provision and mutual aid rather than sociopolitical protest. As Scott suggests, the assumption that resistance needs to be overt misunderstands the workings of power itself while overlooking the presence of "hidden transcripts"—"those offstage speeches, gestures, and practices that confirm, contradict, or inflect what appears in the public transcript."[10] Scott calls Goffman's "frontstage" (or "on-stage") arena the site where "subordinates" adopt performances of deference or contestation that are "disguised or otherwise seemingly invisible" and the "backstage" or "off-stage" world as that area out of earshot or sight of the oppressor where "rejoinders to that public transcript" unfold.[11]

I draw on Scott's framework for two reasons. First, the language of domination and resistance most closely parallels that used within the ongoing global movement for Palestinian liberation. As such, it juxtaposes migrants' navigation of oppressive household dynamics alongside a larger economy of occupation and everyday struggles against land expropriation and military violence. Second, by using the language of everyday resistance and domination, I wish to highlight how workers' job skills are also resistance skills through which they contend with their positioning as "flexible" and "mobile" non-Jewish subjects. In adopting Scott's framework, I do not suggest that there is a neatly delineable boundary between a frontstage and backstage or that resistance needs to be intelligible in the first place. The messy terrain of resistance often collapses the public and hidden, overt and covert, particularly as technologies of state surveillance render further ambiguous an imagined public-private distinction. Instead, my goal is to center how migrants narrate the starkly different worlds of employers' homes, a task I take up in this chapter, and community spaces outside of them, one I undertake in the next.

I begin by highlighting migrant caregivers' tactics for contesting, coping with, and resisting the difficult relationships and working conditions they often enter into when they are first hired. I focus in particular on the strategies of creating indispensability, employing strategic deference, engaging in avoidance, directly challenging employers, and quitting. I then examine how these strategies shape and are shaped by workers' orientations toward Zionism, the state, and political involvement. I locate some workers' articulated pro-Israel stances in relation to Christian Zionism and the comparative status of Israel as a "second-tier" migrant-receiving state. I ask in particular how workers' support for Israel diverges from and echoes global tropes of Israeli exceptionalism. Throughout, I highlight how workers forge relationships that require employers to take workers' needs into account, even as they may not directly wish to take on employers' roles as beneficiaries and agents of colonial emplacement.

"Frontstage" Strategies

Within citizens' homes, migrant caregivers maneuver between employers' changing moods, levels of cognition, and physical needs, deciding how to best create an atmosphere of safety and comfort for themselves and their charges. For caregivers who have surpassed their visa length, switched employers more than twice in two years, or shoulder debt, failing to ensure employers' well-being and happiness carries great financial and legal risk. Despite the potentially negative consequences of doing so, migrant caregivers regularly refuse employers' unreasonable demands, deciding whether to overtly refuse abusive treatment or foster relationships that increase their bargaining power. As I suggest in the following pages, determining when and how to use particular strategies is itself a "tacit skill"—one often unacknowledged or mistakenly coded as "soft"—that improves migrants' unequal positioning in the home.[12] Deploying expertise that "employers need and value," workers mitigate precarity and minimize risk while securing future job recommendations and employment opportunities.[13]

Creating Indispensability

The sense of disposability caregivers articulate is an effect of the short-term nature of contracts with shifting provisions, the binding of caregivers' legal status to their work permits, and the exclusion of migrants from the Zionist national family. The "biopolitical availability" of migrant laborers transnationally intersects with particular tropes of non-Jewish alienability positioning migrant caregivers as inherently mobile, flexible, and expend-able.[14] Nina alludes to this feeling of disposability in describing her relation-ships with her first two employers. Nina's first position in Palestine/Israel was with a religious family in Jerusalem where she "had to cook, clean the house, clean the baby" for "almost twelve hours a day" for an employer who "brought [her] on a flying visa so I didn't have a contract." The flying visa scheme left Nina with little to no legal recourse to counter her employers' extracontractual demands. After moving to a second job, Nina's employers fired her before a year's time so that they did not have to pay her annual va-cation salary and recuperation fees, entitlements that accrue after twelve months of work. As Nina frankly states, "They are selling us here." In addi-tion to her treatment by employers, Nina also references the "*shiva* rules"— the policies forcing caregivers to leave employers' homes, and sometimes the state, immediately following the seven-day Jewish mourning period after an employer dies, regardless of the close relationships they may have developed with families. She notes, "If we finish our work and we work very hard and have emotional attachment, if the Israeli people don't like [it], they will throw us like a dustbin. They will say, '*T'lech, lo tzarich* [Go, I don't need you].' . . . 'We don't want you.' The rules are very hard." Referring to the same policy, Lina, a caregiver from Nepal who has been in Palestine/Israel for ten years, exclaims, "It's like we're garbage! . . . Here, too many people, when the contract is finished, they're thrown like it's garbage. It's not nice." Bella, a caregiver from Nepal who has worked in Israel for fifteen years, likewise ex-plains, "If there's a death in the family, the Israeli government says we have to leave Israel. If the *baal bayit* [head of household] dies, if the family doesn't want us, they say to leave Israel. If they don't want us, they put money at the airport [in a deposit fund] . . . even if I don't want to leave Israel. It's not good for us. For example, I want work. The family doesn't want me. They want someone else. I didn't make any mistakes . . . people's life is not just money." Here, Bella refers to the deposit fund, a unique feature of Israel's mi-gration regime, as evidence of caregivers' disposability. A state-sanctioned disincentive for staying in Israel beyond one's visa length, the deposit fund requires employers to put 16 percent of caregivers' monthly salaries into an account that caregivers cannot collect until they leave the airport upon exit from the country. As an impediment to "stretch[ing] time," the deposit fund—which expires after six months—functions as a way of reinforcing the impermanence of non-Jewish migrants and asylum seekers. Bella sug-gests how such arrangements treat caregivers as "just money," ignoring the many connections they have formed while working in Palestine/Israel, including with employers' families.

If disposability takes for granted caregivers' temporal impermanence, then creating indispensability is a way of shaping the frontstage arena to better benefit workers. It is also a mode of extending time and unsettling the temporal relation between non-Jewish workers and the state. Nancy, who has been in Israel for ten years, notes that "some employers may also take advantage of the fact that an employee is on a last employer because there's no chance for a salary increase. [Caregivers] have to stay because if they quit there will be no benefits, no pension." Nancy's point is corroborated by Ivy, who explains, "I have to play the game and be extra nice and sweet because I'm on my last employer and can't get a special visa. I smile, take pictures and do posts on Facebook like I'm having fun." While caregivers may not wish to remain permanently, many want to stay beyond four years and three months in order to generate enough income for the shifting financial needs of families and networks at home. Others wish to stay longer to spend additional years living alongside communities, romantic partners, or friends.[15]

Creating indispensability means reading bodily cues; becoming physical proxies for disabled employers; anticipating employers' needs before they voice them; memorizing their likes and dislikes; and fostering closeness with employers' families. It involves knowing what questions to ask one's charges to find out how they are feeling; knowing how to probe sensitive topics without upsetting them; and understanding how Alzheimer's disease, Parkinson's disease, intergenerational trauma, and different stages of dementia impact employers and their families. Each of these "tacit skills" become resistance skills through which caregivers can transform their labor conditions while living and working under the direct gaze of employers.

Like many other caregivers, Sam, who works in a small city outside of Tel Aviv, describes a transformation in his relationship with past employers. His job was marked in the beginning by feelings of isolation and fear, and eventually, a sense of his own irreplaceability as a caretaker, interpreter, and manager of his charges' needs. Sam conveys an atmosphere of trepidation when he moved into his first employer's home, where he endured threats of being fired and felt so nervous that he would drop and break plates:

> When I first came to Israel it was really hard. Very, very tough and being a boy also I went to my room in the corner, I sat there and I cried. . . . They get angry *maher maher* [very quickly]. . . . *Eyn*

l'hem harbeh savlanut [they didn't have a lot of patience]. . . . In my work even if unintentionally it happens to make a mistake they never give a warning and they get angry. . . . I didn't know Hebrew, what is caregiving, what kind of disease old people are suffering from. . . . One day I was dressing [my employer's] wound and he asked some questions in Hebrew. I didn't understand. I wasn't answering because I didn't know what to say. He was smiling, making fun of me. But after a while he started shouting and I was not doing anything, just making a bandage. I said, "I need to learn Hebrew at any cost. That's my first priority." I put down in my diary how *alefbet* [the alphabet] was written. . . . When people were talking to each other, I was eavesdropping, I was listening to them. Slowly I started to imitate as they speak. Within six months I was a good Hebrew speaker, and after that it was very easy for me because when I took my employer to the hospital it was not a problem.

Beyond learning Hebrew, Sam also taught himself "how to clean the house and to cook Iraqi food. I taught myself to help *ima* [mother] in cooking also and about taking care of *aba* [father] to support him mentally and to take care of the wounds. . . . I joked to *ima*, 'Now you have to give *me* more shekels every month!' . . . Then we were friends. If you start liking me, you don't care about the small things. . . . Everyone started loving me, saying, 'C'mon *motek* [honey]' and 'He knows everything!'" By learning Hebrew during his rest hours, teaching himself over time to cook Iraqi food, and ascertaining his employer's medical needs and emotional states, Sam forges a space for himself in the home where he is respected and appreciated, and where he feels comfortable broaching the topic of his salary. Sam says that to this day, in addition to becoming kinder and more receptive to Sam's presence, his former employer's wife still treats him like a family member: "They call me and they say, 'Still now you are not out of my family—that's why we remember you. Can you talk to [your employers] and manage a few hours to visit the *kever* [grave]?' And I said, 'It's my pleasure.'" Sam also says that he still feels like their son.

The skills Sam developed with his first employer also helped him "stretch time" by extending his visa with other employers. With his current employer, Sam also went through a transition period where he intentionally learned his employers' needs, whims, and moods. Like many caregivers, Sam originally worked for his current employer's wife, but received a special visa when she died so he could transfer his work permit to his current employer and stay longer. Though not part of the contract, some caregivers hope to be employed by their employer's spouse in the event that they are widowed as a way of extending their stay through a special visa. Describing his relationship trajectory with his current employer, Sam explains,

> Slowly and slowly I started understanding him. . . . I started talking to him about what he used to do when he was young and when he lost his parents, what was he remembering the most about his wife . . . but I was screening my questions, you see? If I ask about his parents or wife, if he becomes more sad or something like that, I try to get my answer through his mouth spontaneously and not from my direct question. I did not ask, "When did your wife pass away?" I said, "How long have you been single here?"

Sam notes that once he began to memorize his boss's schedule ("waking up, taking a shower, mealtime preferences") and learning small phrases in Shirazi, a Jewish dialect of Farsi, his employer became calmer around him.

Like Sam, Aja, who has worked in Israel for fourteen years, says she knew no Hebrew and had no knowledge of Israeli cuisine when she first arrived. She notes, "When I arrived in Tel Aviv I know nothing. It's very hard, communication with each other. . . . I don't know how to say *shalom* [hello], nothing!" After moving into her first employer's home, her employer's son expected Aja to regularly lift his mother, a woman who weighed over ninety kilograms (almost two hundred pounds). Aja describes being scared to say no to her first employer's son and terrified to make mistakes. She began teaching herself Hebrew and learning "what to do with *savta* [grandma]," including "how to change her diaper, how to cook, how to give her food and what she wants to eat for breakfast, lunch, dinner and how to cook *marakai* [Moroccan food]" and clean a "*dati* [religious] kitchen," skills that slowly forged a place for her in the home. Aja describes taking these skills into subsequent jobs, including her job with her current employer, an elderly Polish Holocaust survivor, and her employer's husband, a German Holocaust survivor. Aja explains that "it was very hard when I started with her, very complicated" but that "now they are a good family and they teach me a lot." When she first arrived, Aja says her boss "was afraid, so I need[ed] to be with her always," remaining on alert during her rest hours and at night. She also says her boss imposed restrictions on where in the home Aja could keep her possessions and prevented her from cooking Nepalese food. Aja relays how she slowly ingratiated herself into her employer's home, teaching herself the ins and outs of her employer's medical insurance benefits, holidays her employer observed, the names of her employer's grandchildren, and the foods her employer likes best: "When I started, [my employer] has MS [multiple sclerosis], and I need to take her to the hospital every time. Sometimes operation, sometimes checkup, sometimes *bikur rofim* [doctor's visit]. I now know so many hospitals: Tel-HaShomer, Holon, and a lot of *kupat holim* [Israeli health insurance institution]. . . . Every time we went to hospital, I need to take *savta* [grandma], I need to call and see which doctor it is and to make appointment. I know every *pinah* [corner] of hospitals and *kupat holim*!" In addition to her vast knowledge of the Israeli medical system, Aja adds, "I know where to shop for meat, bread, chocolate they like. I learn what they are eating on *Pesach* [Passover], what is the *hanukkiah* [menorah], *Purim*, *Sukkot*." Aja laughingly says that now her boss "never complains, never, never, never," as she has learned to ascertain what she needs without verbal communication:

> Sometimes she doesn't like to tell me [what she needs], but I see her face and I know what she thinks. Sometimes we sit in the salon and I clean everything we have in the salon. Sometimes I move right to left, left to right. I see her face and she wants to tell me, "[Aja], not like this!" She doesn't tell me, but I know her face. Her son told me, *Lifne ema tagid mashu, Aja kvar yodaat* [before she tells me something, I know what she wants!]. I've spent a long time with her and stayed there so many years.

Through the careful cultivation of their relationship, Aja was able to secure another special visa through her employers, extending her stay in Palestine/Israel. For Aja, creating indispensability was also key to setting her own boundaries in the home. Tellingly, Aja shares an anecdote about a fight with her employer where Aja asserted her right to physical boundaries by directly daring her employer to fire her:

> When I was in my room, she told me, "Why do you need so many things, so many dresses here, shawls, so many shoes here?" I told her, "You are eighty-four years, *savta* [grandmother], and I am young, I need so many things, I'm younger, I like to use every day something

new. I'm not like you." She told me, "OK, I don't want you." I told her, "OK, it's good for me because if you tell me you don't want *me,* I get *pitzuim* [separation pay], but if I tell *you,* I don't get anything, so better you tell me."

Aja's refusal to back down when her employer threatens to fire her speaks to her position of influence in the home. Her brushing off of her employer's comment suggests that Aja is keenly aware how important she is to her employer's survival and how unlikely her employer is to fire her. The relationship she describes contrasts markedly with her first job in Palestine/Israel, where she continually feared being fired. As Aja's and Sam's anecdotes suggest, the strategy of nurturing indispensability transforms the home into a long-term living space for non-Jewish migrants who, though they in many ways must assimilate into employers' worlds, nevertheless create a space where, within a structurally unequal relationship, they are more respected and valued. Their creation of indispensability fortifies their continued presence in the home as non-Jews, unsettling the elderly charge's home as a site exclusively inhabited by Jewish Israelis and their needs. This is the case even as, paradoxically, their indispensability also ensures its functioning and reproduction. This seeming paradox underscores the fine line caregivers toe between making intergenerational reproduction possible within the home—itself a fulcrum of the state as a "Jewish state"—and from a Zionist ideological perspective, "threatening" its demographic future.

Like Aja, James paid an exorbitant amount in illegal brokerage fees—roughly USD $12,000—to come to Palestine/Israel. To ensure that he can remit more money than the fees he was initially charged, James must retain his job for another three years. Throughout our conversation, James spoke with affection about his employer, with whom he discusses philosophy and looks at the moon at night. At the same time that he attributes these warm feelings to many memorable conversations, he also describes their relationship as a product of his labor. He explains, "I've met situations where without me, it's impossible for [my employer] to survive. I've created that situation with my employer. . . . I fight for rights. I'm good with my employer. With my heart I take care of him. That's my duty; he loves me; I love him. Until early in the morning we talk about the planets, about Jupiter." James, who does not talk about his material interests as aligned with those of his employer, forges a bond that eliminates the chances of him being replaced if he takes his vacation days. He notes that in the past when his employer refused to compensate him fairly, he left the job and wouldn't return until his employer's daughter agreed to honor his request for a raise:

> Before one year I decided to leave the job because my salary was very low. I kept the condition if you want to increase my salary, it's OK, I'll stay and continue work. But if you don't, I'm forced to leave the job—I'll find somebody to replace me, but I'll leave the job. They told me OK and didn't give me the money. I left the job. One-and-a-half months, I left the job. The daughter gave me a call, [saying], "My father is very impossible without you, he needs you, he cries!" Because the father was used to me. So they called me and told me, "Whatever salary you had, we'll give you two hundred *shekel* more than that, but you come."

In this instance, James was able to quit precisely because of the symbiotic relationship he cultivated. James developed "tacit skills" such as communicating, providing emotional support, administering medical attention, and triaging his employer's relationship with his family. These skills allowed James him to "job jump" as a strategy for increasing mobility and mitigating exploitation.[16] Often, such an option is more readily available for workers whose employers are afraid of caregivers leaving. When James's attempt to thwart labor expropriation directly fails, he adopts a less confrontational mechanism of relationship-building alongside his more direct approach of quitting.

Other caregivers related similar stories of using "tacit skills" to resist disposability. These skills involved learning to anticipate employers' needs before they spoke, the subtleties of their moods, their food cravings, and how to quell their nightmares and physical symptoms. Workers thus cultivated a form of care that only they could deliver. Ramona describes creating a symbiotic dynamic with her employers:

> If I'm upstairs, I'll hear, "I feel like eating fruit," so I have to rush and say, "What do you want?," like I'm next to them. If I hear the chair moving I know they're standing up, so I run and look. They're old so they don't want to feel like they can't manage. So I watch my employer go to the toilet, and after he sits down I come, because I

know he wouldn't like it that all the time I come and say, "I will help you." That's why they say, "She's fantastic, I was about to ask but she's here already!"

The air of magic that Ramona's employers use to describe her presence reveals how the deliberate, effortful acts required to be readily available become naturalized as an effortless, desirable quality of a "good" caregiver. Suggesting the coloniality of migrant care work, attached to such perceptions are imaginaries of workers helping employers realize their every need and always placing the employer's need for care above their own. Like James, Ramona says she quit her job at one point when her employers demanded that she do tasks beyond her contract: "I couldn't keep patience so I told the husband I want to go to another job because this is not good. . . . So I left, and later she always called me, saying, 'How are you? I want you to come back to me; I'm so sorry.' . . . She phoned me all the time until she stayed in the hospital, saying every night, 'I love you.'" Despite the expanding list of unpaid tasks Ramona's boss gave her, she eventually expressed remorse when Ramona quit, suggesting both the extent to which she took Ramona for granted, and how essential Ramona was to her functioning. The indispensability Ramona cultivates with her employers also grants her the ability to inhabit the house and make it more her own. In Ramona's current employment arrangement, she hosts eight friends for dinner each week, a ritual Ramona also invited me to join. During a dinner I attended, Ramona and her friends used her employer's kitchen to cook Filipino food, played music, and sat in a large circle in the living room telling funny stories from the week. Ramona's employer remained in another part of the house throughout the evening, suggesting her respect for the space Ramona claims within the Jewish Israeli home.

Caregivers also create relationships of indispensability to diminish the chances of being replaced by a reliever, or stand-in caregiver, who covers shifts when a caregiver goes on vacation.[17] Because caregivers are required to find relievers to care for their employers during vacation days, some fear that employers may decide to fire their full-time caregivers and hire relievers whom they connect with instead. David explains that "when old workers come back, that is an issue for caregivers. Some are afraid—the term that they use is sometimes relievers steal their jobs. It happens, a lot of times it happens. Especially if the reliever finds that the job is very good." He then describes a time he encountered this issue:

I recently went on vacation a month ago. I went back to the Philippines. . . . So I had a reliever to replace me for two weeks. . . . I've
been with him for almost a year so we know each other. We, uh, sometimes I would try to run his life, as he says, and he says he doesn't
like it that much, if I do what is good for him rather than what he
wants. . . . My reliever followed everything that he said, and it was a
breath of fresh air for him because when I came back, he told me that
he wanted the reliever instead of me. I said, "OK, if that will make
you happy." But of course the family will not, because they've seen
how I was able to make him better.

In this instance, the respect David gains from Abraham's family becomes
insurance against David's own replaceability. David's job is to manage Abraham's daily schedule and medical regimen as much as to build trusting relationships with his family. As a tacit skill, forging relationships with David's
family counters the structure of disposability that otherwise shapes the field
of migrant care work.

Nurturing relationships of indispensability is also a way of making an
employer's home less a minefield of injury and risk and more a space for
caregivers' needs and demands. Ita, an elementary school teacher from
Nepal, works an hour north of Jerusalem for a woman she estimates to be
eighty-five years old. Her employer, who has dementia, would shout at Ita
when she first arrived, reprimanding her for placing dishes in the wrong
cabinets, not understanding Hebrew or Moroccan Arabic, and speaking with
her friends on Skype. Ita has two children in Nepal and wishes to stay beyond
her visa expiry to earn more money to pay for her children's schooling, and
to be near her husband, who works outside of Tel Aviv. "Stretching" time
for Ita involves learning the daily foods, schedules, and tones of voice that
make her charge feel calm and taken care of. Ita relays, "This is my first
employer. First it was very difficult. I don't know the language. Very difficult
and I was homesick. It takes time. First when I come she's very angry with
me. She tells me, 'I don't need you, you go.' . . . But now it's good—she's
also good. She knows me and I know her, all is good. . . . If I go [on break]
Friday, Saturday she don't want to eat. And [her daughter] tells me, 'How
do you cook?! My mother don't want to eat!'" [laughs]. So attached to Ita
is her employer that she will not eat when Ita is not present. To transform
their relationship, Ita learned to speak Hebrew and several phrases in Moroccan Arabic and to cook couscous, soup, and Moroccan-spiced fish, foods

her employer has eaten her whole life. She explains, "Before [coming to Israel] I learn Hebrew one month only but it don't help. When I come here I talk with her, I talk with the children and learn. Slowly, slowly, *le-at, le-at* [slowly, slowly] I learn. . . . When somebody calls me here and I tell them I'm a caregiver they say, 'Oh! I thought you were Israeli.'"

Beyond building their relationship through language and food, Ita adopted routines that made her employer feel comfortable and at ease in her home, sacrificing her rest hours on difficult days to stay by her side rather than leaving her with a reliever. She also learned how to navigate difficult moments when her employer's mood unpredictably shifted: "Sometimes she's crazy. I say like this [*softly, quietly*], '*Mah kara, ima, ma kara*? [What happened, mother, what happened?].' And after a minute or hour she's good. And I tell her, 'If you yell *like this* [*loudly*] I cannot stay here; I'll want to go to my parents and children [in Nepal].' And then she stops." Drawing on these interpersonal skills, over months and years Ita slowly transformed the home into one where she was respected. She explains that now they're "like daughter and mother. If I go [on break], she tells me, 'When you come?! I miss you, I miss you!.' . . . I tell her, '*Ima* [mother], you love me?' And she says, '*Ani ohevet otach meod* [I love you a lot].'"

Like Sam, Leela cared for her employer's spouse before she died, and was able to receive a special visa due to her close relationship with her employer's late wife. Leela relays a similar transformation in the relationship with her employer, an elderly Holocaust survivor from Germany: "It's so hard with him at first, to understand him and he would be always *atzboni* [irritated]. . . . Sometimes I'm crying but I need work. Always I think if I give him love. . . . I will massage him, give him medicine, change him, change his position in bed. When he wakes up, I give him food, bath, pray." Like Ita, Leela also learned to cook foods her employer's wife was used to eating, teaching herself how to make Hungarian soups, schnitzel, and Israeli salad. Whereas at the start of their relationship Leela's employer would often call out to her during the night, now, she says, "He tries not to wake me. He always tells me, 'God brings you. I love you, sometimes I'm angry.' I tell him, 'I love you too much.' . . . His family loves me also and calls me 'my daughter.'" She adds, "When I'm gone, he cries and says '[Leela, Leela],' he calls me. He doesn't eat, sleep when I'm gone." Learning her employer's likes and dislikes and establishing an intimate daily routine become strategies for building a relationship that mitigates labor extraction and partially reinstates the boundary between work and rest.

As David explains, strategies for building indispensability also allow caregivers to become decision-makers over more areas of the household: "As a caregiver you are actually the one who will—how do I say it? It falls upon you to do the schedule or to do the routine in the house because an old person is dependent upon you already so it falls upon you to set up everything. It's really your—it's like you play the music. . . . It's like you have to take charge. You lay out everything and if you're good with that then everything will be smooth. And then the family just has to work around with what you do." Over time, as caregivers forge trust, dependability, love, respect, and indispensability, they shape not only their working conditions, but also the home itself into a space that, however unequally, accommodates some of their interests and needs. In this way, they interrupt the home as a site that is necessarily the exclusive and exclusionary site of Jewish Israeli citizens and their needs. As non-Jews within a space that is legally, religiously, and ideologically the organic unit of the Zionist national project, they gain limited power in the day-to-day lives of Jewish Israeli families through the cultivation of indispensable relationships with the elderly. Through the skilled and creative cultivation of these relationships, caregivers also sometimes shift their own temporal relation to Israel, unsettling the rigid temporal boundaries of the state itself. At the same time, resisting disposability involves reading and assessing a continually changing emotional landscape and, as I suggest in the pages that follow, deciding when to directly challenge employers and when to perform deference.

Direct Contestation and Strategic Deference

While the cultivation of indispensability is in many ways a less risky frontstage resistance strategy than overt contestation, at times, direct confrontation can be more effective. Ascertaining when to deploy which strategy is itself a tacit skill that involves knowing employers' expressions, the phrases and insults that anger them, the compliments that make them happy, the times of day they are most likely to be in a good mood, and the moments they may be upset or unpleasant. At other times, strategic deference is a safer frontstage strategy for protecting one's employment status, whether in the form of projecting a willingness to complete extracontractual tasks or avoiding overt discussion of legal rights.

Rina describes instances of both challenging employers directly and pretending to admire them. When recounting confrontational conversations she has had with past employers, Rina repeats in a satirical tone, "Oh right, I'm a caregiver." In between her employer's utterances of the phrase *hafilipina sheli*, or "*my* Filipina," are times when Rina overtly unsettles her employer's stereotypes about the "migrant caregiver." A self-described *nudnik*—the Yiddish word for a persistent nag—Rina characterizes her relationship with her employer as "like a rat and a cat"; when her employer screams at her, she says, "I scream right back!" Rina says she is intentional about establishing transparent boundaries around the tasks she will and will not do early on in her relationship with employers. She explains that when her employer asks her to do her husband's laundry, or to thoroughly clean the house, she responds directly with "No, it's not part of my job." She also refuses to do the housekeeping work that many employers assume a caregiver should gladly undertake: "I say, no, this is too much. And then she asks me to hand-wash her clothes. I say, 'No,' and she says, 'It's only three clothes!' I say, 'It's only three clothes, but you are going to do it more and more. And you are going to bring more for ironing the clothes of your daughter.' Cleaning her house she says is part of my job. Clean the house? It's OK. But don't do cleaning like you're just the *mitapelet* [maid] of the house."

The "rat and a cat" relationship Rina describes requires that she continually disrupt her employer's expectations that she must do extracontractual labor. Such stories suggest how employers come to embody their roles as settler-consumers who have access to a pool of workers with few rights. The extent to which Rina's employer expects her to be agreeable is evident in Rina's observation that her employer "seems surprised I can say no." She adds, "Maybe she thinks I can do whatever she wants. She says I'm the most hardheaded caregiver she's had. . . . Maybe the other ones wouldn't answer her back." Rina often insists upon regularly treating her employer the way her employer treats her. These direct challenges have consequences for Rina, who says her employer becomes "so mad" that "it seems [she] wants to kill me." Despite the risks to her job security and legal status, Rina insists that even in such moments of anger, "she cannot pacify me."

While Rina adamantly frames her interests as a worker as distinct from those of her employers, she also expresses deep love for Israel and support for right-wing politician Benjamin Netanyahu. As Attiya Ahmad suggests, household interactions between employers and employees not only produce hegemonic relations; they can also be sites of "everyday conversion," a process "marked by emergent subjectivities, affinities, and belongings that complicate conventional understandings of both the feminization of transnational migration and religious conversion."[18] While not converting religiously, Rina, like some other caregivers, embraces aspects of Israeli culture, not in place of but alongside her affinities with the Philippine state and the broader Filipinx community in Palestine/Israel. Rina participates actively in *krav maga* classes, a form of Israeli martial arts first used by the IDF; celebrates Israeli independence day, Hanukah, and Passover; and learns Hebrew, both so she can listen in on her boss's conversations and so she can partake in Jewish Israeli culture. These "everyday conversions" carry over to the realm of national politics, as evident in Rina's assertion that "they [Palestinians] started the trouble" and that "Israel has the right to defend themselves." Given Rina's love of and interest in participating in Jewish Israeli culture, her unapologetic contestation of her employer's disrespect and demands for extracontractual labor are tightly circumscribed to the realm of the worker-boss relation while not extending to the source of her boss's power as it is rooted in her role as a settler-citizen.

Ella, a migrant caregiver and devout Christian Zionist from the Philippines, likewise engages in direct confrontation with her employer. Ella overtly contests her employer's expectations that she do extracontractual labor because she is a non-Jewish migrant. She has worked in Israel for twelve-and-a-half years and has successfully "stretch[ed] time" by obtaining special visas. Ella cares for a woman with paralysis and diabetes and is often asked to also tend to her employer's chronically ill husband. She explains,

> Sometimes I fight with them. They shout at me. I say, "My visa is with your mother, I don't have to do this." Sometimes my heart pours because of the mother. . . . Sometimes I also scream and I also shout. I tell them I'm just human. Some time ago the son was in the army and he doesn't have much money and lots of clothes so I wash his clothes and Saturday I let the machine run. It's Shabbat. And [the son] screamed at me and I screamed back, I said, "I'm not your maid, I'm your mother's *mitapelet*." . . . One time I said, "We Christians can scream if it's our right, it's not only Jews." I said, "I'm also a Jew now!" . . . I am a tough policeman to [my employer].

As Ella intimates, her employer's son disrespects her for breaking a law of Shabbat observance that forbids the use of electricity. Ella's anecdote suggests how the son's disrespect stems from his feeling of comparative entitlement as a Jew in a Jewish Israeli home. Against the son's presumption that the home should be the incontrovertible space of Jewish religious and cultural observance, Ella shouts that she is "also a Jew now," "troubling" and "making uneasy" the unquestioned connection between Judaism, blood, home, and homeland.[19] While resisting the most immediate effects of labor exploitation, Ella also implies that non-Jewish migrants can permeate this seemingly uncontestable border. As I address in the subsequent pages, Ella is perhaps the most direct in her contestation of exclusionary boundaries within the home, while also remaining fervently supportive of the Zionist state.

Unlike Ella, Sana, a writer and community organizer from Nepal, uses strategic deference to mitigate risk and protect her status in the home. Sana describes her employer as "so rude" and relates the various ways he condescends to her. She notes, "If sometimes I want to go outside he doesn't speak to me. That I don't like. [Spending] all the time in the home is boring and sometimes I want to go [outside]. Sometimes I have meetings or something so I want to go for an hour and they don't like it." Despite her frustration, Sana says she "only [does] good things" for her employer. She adds, "If they don't like it, I don't do another time. . . . What he needs, I do." Her performances of respect and deference are especially important in helping continue to pay her child's college tuition.

Like Sana, Rina also states that sometimes, "I just need to please." Though in our conversations Rina refers to her employer as "the pig," she adds that when her employer asks "'Do you like me?' I say, '*Betach* [Of course].' I need to pretend *betach*." Though their frontstage relationship at times requires such pretentions, behind the scenes, Rina learns Israeli labor law and studies Hebrew in a weekend class against her employer's wishes so she can understand what her employer says about her. She also files complaints with her recruitment agency when her employer refuses to honor the terms of their contract. At moments where refusing to complete unpaid work is too risky, she documents violations of the employer-employee relationship in writing and photographs, taking pictures of large laundry piles she has folded, or before-and-after shots of bathrooms she has cleaned. At other times, she completes tasks deliberately slowly.

Avoiding direct discussions about workers' rights can be another frontstage strategy that mitigates precarity. Sana suggests that the best approach to improving a hostile work environment in her employer's home is to avoid legal language altogether. This hesitation is due to the particular legal and economic liability migrant caregivers face and the strict political consequences for migrant activism in Palestine/Israel.[20] A refusal to engage in politics can also stem from caregivers' own desires to eventually return home and their lack of expectations for integrating permanently into the Jewish collective. Bella deploys strategic avoidance as a strategy for extending her time in Palestine/Israel. Like Sam, Ella, and Rina, this form of everyday resistance is a strategy for unsettling the strict temporal boundaries that relegate migrant caregivers to four years and three months in Palestine/Israel. She notes, "The *misrad* [Ministry of Interior] doesn't listen to my problems. I asked for my bonus and my severance [pay] and they were not giving it. Three families I had this problem with. I don't discuss this anymore in the Ministry because I am not an Israeli person. I cannot have citizenship, so I am silent. If I were an Israeli citizen I would fight in court, I could go to the lawyer, but I am foreign, and I have no money for charging the lawyer. Too many friends have this problem. It's a problem." While Bella, like many caregivers, has stayed in Israel far beyond the length of her first visa, she discusses this extension as a practical matter that could lengthen the amount of time during which she can remit money rather than an ideological desire. She also attributes an avoidance of politics to her temporal relation to the state: "I like politics, but I'm not a leader. . . . I came to Israel to work, and to do my work. I'm here and I don't want to start doing all that. . . . If I am all the time discussing [problems], that doesn't help. I'm scared . . . we're scared inside. . . . I want my money, my salary, my separation pay, my bonus." Bella's decision to pursue disagreements outside of the realm of rights organizing is also one based upon skepticism of advocacy efforts and her own logistical constraints. She adds that migrant worker advocacy organization Kav LaOved is too far away from where she works in Ashkelon and too expensive to reach by bus, while "[labor] lawyers is lots of money and they only talk, they don't *do*."

Like Bella, when I ask Sana whether she discusses migrant caregivers' rights with her employers, she responds, "They don't like to talk [about it]. I only talk with my agency if I need something because I don't want to fight and I don't want some problems. I don't talk in front of them ever in case they don't like it. So many of my friends are like this—if employers mind the law, they can give us rights, but if they don't like, we can't force them. So what law they can give us, we can manage and that's it." For Sana, relying upon her employers' good will is a more effective frontstage strategy than direct contestation. She addresses worker precarity by lessening the chances of a long-term strain on the employment relationship: "If something happens, it's so frightening. What to do? We need money and want a job so we need to keep quiet. We are without family, without nothing, so of course it's a challenge. We do everything here. What we do they don't like, and sometimes they can scold us. Sometimes we think, 'I can't live, I can't go on,' but when we came here we thought we could do it. That's why we accepted these challenges."

Like Sana, Amita, a caregiver from Sri Lanka, explains that caregivers "don't have time to think about the politics, and they want only to save their country." Amita expresses that her main political concern is the "very big political problems" in Sri Lanka and the violence ensuing over a six-year period during the Sri Lankan civil war. She describes the fighting that results each time there are national elections, and the fact that her property outside Colombo was destroyed during fighting between the Sri Lankan military and the Tamil Tigers. Discussing the inevitability of her involvement in politics when she returns to Sri Lanka, Amita notes, "I will have to come into politics because my friend works in politics for the party and I want to help him." Memories and discussions of political struggle in Sri Lanka thus play an integral role in Amita's life, yet she intentionally avoids discussing Israeli politics with her employer. She prioritizes "want[ing] only to save [her] country" and runs various mutual-aid initiatives among the Sri Lankan community in Palestine/Israel, yet she deliberately circumvents discussions with her employers about her rights or Israeli politics. Like Amita, Jasmine notes, "I don't like politics. I'm not concerned. Rules about our salary and everything, the rules, that's all we're concerned with." Such strategic avoidance can lessen fears of job loss and poor employer recommendations while allowing caregivers to bend the state's temporal boundaries. By doing so, they also unsettle the role of the settler-citizen as the incontrovertible arbitrator of emplacement.

Beyond direct confrontation, strategic deference, and quitting, caregivers relay other important ways of contesting the worst effects of their precarious positioning in the frontstage arena. Several caregivers who were or have been undocumented, or who have friends who have lost legal status, shared that they possess a breadth of knowledge of immigration police—where they tend to be, how they look, and spaces they less often frequent—and revealed creative ways of choosing families to work for based upon the likelihood of being surveilled. Following Eve Tuck and K. Wayne Yang's notion of "pedagogies of refusal," I exclude these discussions from the book, though I note the importance of communal knowledge-sharing practices as an essential form of resistance that mitigates the state-designed fears of living undocumented.[21]

Absent the option to bargain through unions, engage in organized strikes on a shared factory floor, or make collective demands of a common boss, caregivers navigate the frontstage world of the home by forging qualified acceptance and respect within the home and contingent appreciation within the nation. Frontstage resistance to the worst effects of flexibilization does not necessarily translate into a contestation of the broader colonial relations within which worker precarity arises. Everyday resistance on the frontstage arena of the home can manifest in less overt forms of defiance such as developing work skills that diminish disposability or strategically avoiding contentious topics, even as—and precisely because—they may not challenge the fundamental emplacement of settler-employers.[22]

National Love

While caregivers engage in many forms of everyday resistance, these modes of contestation do not necessarily extend to direct resistance to the state. Against a monolithic or romanticized representation of worker resistance, the expressions of love for "the Jewish state" that several caregivers share complicate Scott's notion of a hidden transcript that necessarily rejects the interests of the dominant collectivity. Building on the previous pages, I turn from caregivers' frontstage strategies to workers' diverse orientations toward the state. Workers' stories push against Scott's notion that engagement in everyday or hidden forms of resistance, as an alternative to direct rebellion, are necessarily a way of muting particular ideological disagreements that workers would voice were they otherwise allowed. At times, expressing national love for Israel as a declaredly Jewish state may be a strategy for garnering closeness with employers under the constraints of Israel's reproductive regime. As a state tied to and defined by which bodies "inhabit the nation" in relation to the "ideal image" of the Jewish Israeli settler, migrants ontologically fall short in their inability to live up to the Jewish character of the state.[23] Expressing ideological support for the Zionist project diminishes "disturbances" in the racial/colonial fabric of the nation that migrants are perceived to cause.[24] Given the discursive significance of elderly Israelis to Israel's "ideal image" as a beleaguered victim, Israel needs migrant caregivers to preserve and uphold Holocaust testimony as a fulcrum of Israeli nationalism. Yet migrant precarity requires them to "need" the nation as well, in order to navigate the worst effects of flexibilization, alienation, legal exclusion, and criminalization.

At the same time, national love and support for Zionism can also stem from ideological or religious commitments. I therefore locate migrants' various orientations toward the state within a complex and shifting nexus of worker precarity, racial/colonial exclusion, political commitment, religious conviction, workers' attachment to their own employers and experiences in Palestine/Israel, and my own presence as an interviewer. Some workers suggested a firm commitment to Christian Zionism, directly or indirectly reinforcing Israeli tropes of Palestinians and Muslims as "threats" to settler society. At other moments, support for Israel and characterizations of settler society as victim to perpetual attack arise from workers' intimate positioning inside Jewish Israeli homes during instances of rocket fire while living in employers' homes during the second intifada or due to the "multilayered forms of affinities and belongings" they develop through their relationships in Israel.[25] In her discussion of power and dissimulation in Syria, Lisa Wedeen notes that "power does manifest itself in the ability to impose the regime's fictions upon the world. No one is deceived by the charade, but everyone . . . is forced to participate in it."[26] In the same way, while some caregivers may ideologically support the Israeli regime, others may strategically make public claims of admiration and loyalty—in front of employers, in spaces that settler-citizens inhabit, and in front of me. Each of these dynamics shapes the ways caregivers navigate and resist their unsettled positioning as both celebrated and surveilled temporary workers.[27]

War, Christian Zionism, and Islamophobia

Some caregivers' support for Israel extended from their experiences of rocket attacks or proximity to violence during the second intifada. For Jasmine, working in Haifa during the second intifada strongly shaped her portrayal of Jewish Israelis as living under the constant threat of Palestinian-perpetrated war. Describing how she sought shelter during long nights of rocket attacks, Jasmine conveys the inescapable feeling of war:

> All the time there is a war, there is a problem. First time in my life
> I experience war was here in Israel, never in the Philippines. When

I finished my second job, I went to Haifa, in Haifa there is a war! So I looked for a job there, there is a *beit avot* [elderly home]. In one month, the missiles and the warnings started. I shook. I'm nervous, really! I think I will be dead or I think the missiles will come to us in our place, so I decide to go to another place, to find another job. . . . Because also the woman I took care of is—not good. She don't want me to go outside and she don't want also to go outside. So we will be in the one room, in twenty-four hours, we stay like this!

Jasmine's description illustrates the centrality of war and violence to some caregivers' experiences of Palestine/Israel, and at the same time, the extent to which they may experience violence from the perspective of Jewish Israelis given the location of their work. Like Jasmine, when I ask Mayra about her time working in Ashkelon, a town by the Gaza border, she simply states, "Too much war. That's the problem." June, a migrant caregiver from the Philippines working on a kibbutz near the border with Gaza, also describes her experiences living under rocket fire:

Before November last year, you are here? You can see up there the *katush* [rocket]! . . . When you're scared like that, you don't know if it falls what we're gonna do. . . . *Kol yom yesh* [there were rockets every day]. . . . You can feel the shake from *adamah* [ground], you can feel it all. Last year a few *aravim* [Arabs] entered into the kibbutz, and we hear they killed soldiers. You can see all of Gaza. You see the trees, the light. We are in a danger zone. You get used to it there. All day, all night.

June describes shuttling her elderly charge into the basement multiple times a night during rocket attacks, calming her employer even as she herself attempted to remain calm. At the same time, her description of "*aravim*" as a menacing outside threat demonstrates the extent to which migrant caregivers can become, by virtue of their delimited role in Palestine/Israel, aligned with Jewish Israeli narratives about the sources of political conflict. June's experiences of rocket fire while inside Jewish Israeli homes echoes settler anxieties about imminent native Palestinian violence as irrational and devoid of historical context. Also significant is June's relationship with her Jewish Israeli boyfriend who was stationed in Gaza during Israel's 2005 military disengagement from illegal settlements.

The narratives of June and Jasmine suggest how workers' experiences in Palestine/Israel are shaped by their close relationships with Jewish Israelis who participate in broader structures of settler complacency and military violence. These interactions often form a backdrop against which discourses of settler fragility circulate from the bottom up and beyond the Jewish body politic. Rather than necessarily always rejecting Israel for the impact of its racial/colonial exclusions on non-Jewish migrants, some workers express direct and indirect forms of solidarity with and empathy for Jewish Israeli society, due in large part to the nature of the job—forming affective bonds with Jewish Israeli families. At other times, however, solidarity with Israel is shaped by religious and political commitments that may precede the process of migration.

Indeed, some articulations of national love can stem from a firm rootedness in Christian Zionism. As scholars of migration to Israel suggest, for religious Filipinx caregivers in particular, Christian Zionism can be a way for non-Jewish migrants to stake claim in the nation.[28] Though emerging from multiple origins, Christian Zionism as a religious and political philosophy reinforces Israeli exceptionalism, whether by positioning Israel as "exceptional by divine fiat," by claiming it as a bastion of human rights in the Middle East, or by defending the connection between a biblical Israel and the contemporary state.[29] Christian Zionist narratives of Israeli exceptionalism also position evangelicals as defenders of Jewish claims to sovereignty against indigenous Palestinian claims to the same. In its contemporary political context, global Christian Zionism is also a driver of both anti-Arab racism and anti-Semitism.[30]

Paula, who is very involved in Tel Aviv's Filipinx Catholic community, says that having Christians care for Jewish Israelis is one way of "showing them the love of Jesus." This framing of the caring relationship suggests how non-Jewish Christian migrants are comparatively racialized in relation to Jewish Israeli citizens and Palestinians, the latter of whom are racialized within particular iterations of Christian Zionism as Muslim regardless of their religion. She explains, "[Caregiving] lets you show you're part of the body of Jesus. . . . It is spiritual work. It allows you to enter the home of the Jew where you otherwise wouldn't be allowed. Sometimes you're allowed to have altars in rooms in houses, sometimes not. When not, caregivers keep Jesus's words at heart. . . . You don't need to preach to them or convert them, it's enough to spread the good news by being more patient, taking care of them, showing rather than telling them that Jesus loves them." By "showing rather than telling them" about Christianity, caregivers can introduce the idea of Jesus into Jewish Israeli homes, a space that is, ironically, a guarded site of Jewish continuity. Simultaneously, Paula indicates how the meaning of care labors done by Christian caregivers takes on a national importance tied to the survival of Israel and its unique role. Here, Paula simultaneously unsettles and reinforces Israel's exceptional status, on the one hand introducing Christianity into the Jewish Israeli home, and on the other hand, aligning with the Jewish Zionist aim of "returning" worldwide Jewry to the land and normalizing the presence of Jewish settlers. Echoing Paula's sentiment, in an interview for a Catholic news service, Father Jayaseelan Pitchaimuthu, the chaplain for Indian migrants in Israel, refers to himself as a "carer of all carers," guiding migrants in their evangelizing process like a "good shepherd." He notes, "Through their generous, affectionate, kind service to the sick, bed-ridden, physically and mentally challenged, they are witness to the Christian faith. Many Jews come to know of Jesus, the Gospel and the Christian faith through these kinds of migrant workers. There are many Jews who ask them to pray for them when they are in difficulties and sick. Many Indian migrants offer Masses for the well-being of their Jewish employers and ask for our prayers at the time of their death. It is real evangelization."[31] Importantly, such depictions do not emerge entirely anew in Palestine/Israel; they circulate across transnational religious networks and home countries. As Claudia Liebelt suggests, religion is a driving motivation for many migrants from the Philippines who see their work in Palestine/Israel as "caring for the Holy Land."[32] Pamela notes, for instance, that she chose to come to Palestine/Israel because it is a place where she can "walk where Christ walked." Likewise, Brian relays his love of traveling around Palestine/Israel and visiting sites from the Bible: "My favorite place really here in Israel is in Galilee where I believe in that place Jesus performed his miracles. And also it's the place where we believe he multiplied the fish and the bread to feed people." Jasmine, too, chose to come to Israel because, she says, "It's in the Bible! Everything that you read I already experience. Because before every time you read Bible it's only imagination. But now, you can *see*. . . . Other places, I don't want to go [*laughs*]. If this is Hong Kong or Cyprus or another country, I don't want to go. [Even] because of human rights? No. I just want to see Jerusalem." The importance of Christian Zionism as a motivating force for migration underscores how Israeli settler exceptionalism is tied to broader circuits of Christian Evangelism and Zionism, of which the modern political state of Israel is a large, but not an exclusive, part.

The comparative racialization of Palestinians, Christian migrants, and Jewish settler-citizens emerged most clearly through the stories shared by Ella. Though raised Catholic, Ella became an apostolic Christian when she was a teenager and centers her life in Palestine/Israel around her church. Like many devout Christians, Ella gives 10 percent of her salary as a caregiver to the church in the form of a tithe. She explains that "the Jews for us are a special people," and it is through her belief in God and ideological commitment to the "special" status of Jews that she finds strength when her day-to-day life as a caregiver feels difficult. Ella relays a story of being stopped by undercover immigration police while walking one day in transit and sharing a sense of solidarity with them about the imminent threat of Palestinians. She notes that "[the police] said, 'Good morning, I'm immigration police!' and I said, 'Ah, good morning!'" After asking where she worked, she told the police she was employed in Ramleh, a city in Israel's central district. Testing her, the police then asked her, "'Ah so you're working in Ramallah?' I said, 'No, it's not in Ramallah, it's in Ramleh!' And he said, 'Not in Ramallah?' I said, 'No, I don't want Ramallah because there is Abu Sayyaf!'" As Ella's story implies, the immigration police test Ella by asking her to confirm that she works in Ramleh rather than Ramallah, a Palestinian city in the occupied Palestinian Territories. Strikingly, Ella likens Palestinians in Ramallah to Abu Sayyaf, an Islamic separatist group in the Philippines that has called for independence. In contemporary representations of the Muslim minority struggle for sovereignty, Abu Sayyaf has been associated with the Moro people, the Philippines' Muslim minority, and the Moro National Liberation Front. In comparing the Palestinian struggle for liberation with that of Abu Sayyaf, Ella portrays Jewish Israel as a safe haven from "irrational" Muslim violence. This depiction also paints all Palestinians as Muslim, despite the 25 percent of Palestinians in Ramallah that are Christian, while racializing Ella as firmly on the side of Christian and Jewish Zionism.

Beyond Christian Zionism, some caregivers expressed national love of a more secular nature. Perhaps most ardent in his support for Israel was Sam. Sam cares for an elderly Mizrahi Jewish Israeli man with advanced Alzheimer's disease. Toward the start of our conversation, Sam remarks, "In my language, they say bread and meat do not come together, but here [in Israel], it comes together." Interestingly, Sam's description echoes the trope—originally Toraic and transformed into Zionist political terms—that paints Israel as the "land of milk and honey," one of abundance and opportunity. In describing how he chose to work in Palestine/Israel, Sam notes, "I studied in Google what is the condition here, is this an Arab country? I looked in the encyclopedia and it is not a Gulf country and it is not an Arab country. . . . It is democratic and developed, but from time to time there is *milchama* (war), fights with the neighbors, but Israel is a very powerful country and no need to worry." Sam's portrayal of Israel as "developed" and "not an Arab country" closely replicates Western media depictions of Israel as an emblem of modernity and economic opportunity in an otherwise hostile, Arab-majority region: the "only democracy in the Middle East."[33] It also mirrors Zionist discourses comparatively racializing Jewish Israelis as European and Palestinians as Muslim Arab, erasing the presence of Mizrahi Jews and Christian Palestinians. Such distinctions not only construct Israel's racially and ethnically diverse Jewish citizenry as unified; they also portray the collective Jewish Israeli body as necessarily European.[34]

In addition to stating that "the media is more sophisticated" in Israel, and economic prosperity more accessible than in "Arab states," Sam also expresses enthusiasm for Zionist nationalism:

> Nepalese caregivers love Israel and Israeli people and Israeli culture. I am almost five years in Israel and now I am enjoying Israeli food and Israeli culture. *Chag ha'atzmaut* [Independence Day] and *zeekukin* [firecrackers]. They celebrate it and every house puts the *degel* [flag] on the top of their houses and also this feeling unites the Jewish people. They feel that Israel is our house and we are the single family and our enemies are surrounding us and we are between the Arab countries and that's why we need to be strong. . . . We don't need to fear any terrorists.

Sam's depiction of *Yom Ha'atzmaut*, Israeli Independence Day, strikingly replicates the Zionist narrative of the "birth" of Israel. In describing Israelis as a "single family" facing an outside enemy, Sam echoes the "family-in-arms" trope that simultaneously biologizes a racial distinction between Jews and Palestinians and ties cohesion of the family to the retention of land.[35] More broadly, we could understand Sam's love of the state as a form of "everyday conversion," one "inextricable from [his] everyday activities and relations" inside Jewish Israeli homes and equally shaped by relationships and views he espoused before and through processes of migration.[36] As Ahmad suggests, the belongings generated through everyday conversions do not necessarily revolve around "equal participation in political and social life" but rather stem from the quotidian affective labors with which caregivers engage in the home.[37] Despite his own lack of legal, political, or social membership in the nation, Sam expresses a profound political and cultural love for the state, one shaped by Islamophobic views he held before migrating and his close relationships with Jewish Israeli employers. Reinforcing Jewish Israelis' status as inheritors of the land, Sam situates himself as temporally outside of, yet closely aligned with, the Zionist project.

Sana articulated similar admiration for Israeli patriotism, attributing Israel's "developed" economic status to its nationalistic ardor. She explains, "Here people are so for [their] country they live [in], they don't care about anything as much, they love country . . . that's why it's so developed . . . because here for their country they contribute, they do anything. I like people here, they are devoted." Like Sam, Sana also depicts Palestine/Israel as more "developed" and respectful of human rights than Nepal. At the time we spoke, she was writing an essay "about Nepali people who work here and how we can learn from [Palestine/Israel] for our country." She notes that "in Israel, there [are] human rights for women. . . . Where there's a bank or a supermarket, where it's a good place, Israeli women are working. In our country it's not like that. They don't give us rights."

While some workers conveyed appreciation and praise for the Israeli government, others voiced skepticism over the Israeli government's treatment of Palestinians. In contrast to Sam, Saul notes that "[Israel] should make a peace agreement with Gaza so both can live in peace." More than any other interviewee, David talked considerably about Palestinian narratives beyond those offered by employers and the Zionist mainstream media. David regularly visits the West Bank to spend time with Palestinian friends, an experience he says is "like being in a different country." David has also refused caregiving work in West Bank Jewish settlements, noting, "When I left my old job I was choosing to work here or at another place, Efrat. . . . It's supposed to be beautiful but I did not choose that job because it's in a settlement." Importantly, David's political commitments and his visits to the West Bank are not something he shares with his employer. When I ask whether he discusses Israeli-Palestinian politics with his employer, he answers, "Not that much, because his daughter and all of his grandchildren by his daughter live in settlements, which I don't really like."

While sympathetic to Jewish Israeli perspectives on Israeli-Palestinian politics, David also expresses great disapproval of Israel's occupation of the West Bank, though not of its broader colonial project. During our interview David asks me, "Have you been [to the West Bank]?" When I answer "Yeah, I've spent a lot of time there," David asks, "It's sad there, right?" I answer honestly, "It makes me angry. To see the military everywhere there." David replies,

> Me too. I don't like it. What I don't like is the occupation. I don't see the purpose of it, I don't see the purpose of . . . because, if you're here on the other side—I call it the other side because it's like being in a different country—they're very poor there, they're miserable, and here [in Israel] you see that, yeah, they're kind of rich. . . . Especially in tourist season you see people scrambling to the bus to tour you in Manger Square [in Bethlehem], and then you realize that that is the only chance of income that they get. And it's so strict.

While articulating deep investment in an end to the occupation of the West Bank, David expresses sympathy with Jewish Israeli fears toward Palestinians. David also conveys the dissonance he feels between time spent with Palestinian friends and with his Jewish Israeli employers: "But also you can't blame what they're doing here [in Israel] because I used to live in a city where there was no wall bordering the West Bank and [the town where I worked] between Arab villages. And there were also a lot of bombings there during the second intifada. I was asking them how it was. And they said that the [location] near where we live, there's bombings there. . . . So it's really difficult because they both have their reasons so it comes down to a matter of if they could just get along." He later adds that "especially if you're there [in the West Bank], you have to be really careful there. We are being told [by Jewish Israelis] that if we are there we don't speak Hebrew at all, any Hebrew word. So I learned only one word, *shukran*, which is thank you in Arabic, because you don't talk Hebrew there."

David reveals the extent to which caregivers' embeddedness in the Jewish Israeli home can shape political orientations, and relatedly, how separate most caregivers' lives are from the everyday experiences of Palestinian families. While very uncommon, exceptions to this structure exist. On very limited occasions, caregivers are placed within Palestinian homes inside Israel. Among social workers, caregivers, and NGO workers, it seems to be an understood fact that workers occasionally assigned to Palestinian families more often come from Nepal, due in part to preexisting relationships between Nepali recruitment agencies and Palestinian communities. Aja was one interviewee who worked in the past for Palestinian families. She relays great appreciation and fondness for these employers:

> I was in *Nazaret Ilit* [upper Nazareth] with an Arab family, Christians, but they spoke Arabic. I learned Arabic there and worked for eight months, and after that the employer died. Then I went near *Tiveria*, to an Arab village and worked with a grandmother who couldn't stand herself, had paralysis. . . . I didn't need to cook, just for myself . . . for bath twice a week, some of her family members came to help me. . . . I didn't need to work there so much and they lived with their family. I spoke Arabic there. There were so many Nepali and Filipino girls there in the village. . . . Arab people, they are good people.

Since working for these two families, Aja's interactions with Palestinians have been limited. She explains, "When I see *aravi* [Arab] people they are coming to take the *zevel* [trash] and to clean the *geenah* [garden]." Here, Aja suggests how racial/colonial divisions of labor limit caregivers' interactions with Palestinians. During a follow-up interview one evening, Nina asked me what I thought of the situation in Gaza and the West Bank. When I told her honestly that I believed the occupation to be brutally violent, Nina offered that "the only thing we hear about Palestinians in Nepal is bad stuff." Living in close proximity to Jewish Israelis, many caregivers read and hear about the occupation through bosses and Israeli newspapers. Undoubtedly, as David and Aja suggest, exceptions to this segregation exist in the form of friendships, work relations, and romantic relationships. They can also take place in religious spaces where services for Christian migrants, asylum seekers, and Palestinians are held, often separately, and according to languages spoken.

While some articulations of national love surface through religious or ideological commitment, others arise contingently and comparatively in relation to other "destination" countries. Though Sana at times echoes tropes of Palestine/Israel as a site of "gender modernity," later in our conversation, she also states that Israel is "like a prison."[38] Qualifying this assertion, she explains the comparative treatment of migrant caregivers in Canada, who are granted permanent residency after working for two years as caregivers.[39] While in Canada "you can go wherever you like" and "you have freedom," Sana explains that in Palestine/Israel you are confined to the home and prevented from taking root. The complex economic, social, political, and legal strictures shaping caregivers' choices of destination countries change and transform as they navigate shifting forms of economic and social risk.[40] Migrant caregivers' expressions of praise for the Israeli state must therefore be comparatively contextualized in relation to the broader ambiguities of migration as a process that is both laden with economic, professional, and personal opportunity, and characterized by challenges, precarity, inequality, and the pain of separation from loved ones.

Within a broader "hierarchy of destination countries" that takes shape around earning potential, citizenship and residency rights, human rights, recruitment fees, and preexisting social networks, workers often consider Palestine/Israel to be a "second-tier" destination.[41] Some situate Palestine/Israel as the best second-tier option for migrants and the most desirable destination country in the Middle East, based on either their own previous experiences working in the UAE, Cyprus, Saudi Arabia, and Kuwait, or that of their spouses, family, and friends. As Anju Mary Paul suggests, many migrants follow a "stepwise" or "multistage migration trajectory," working jobs in the Middle East as a way of ultimately pooling the social and financial resources to reach Canada, Italy, or the United States.[42] Interviewees communicated love for Israel within broader conversations about the difficult working conditions they or their friends or family faced in the Gulf States and appreciation for the comparative earning potential in Palestine/Israel.

Some workers spoke about Saudi Arabia, Kuwait, UAE, Cyprus, Malaysia, Singapore, and Hong Kong as the least favorable places to work.[43] Yet they also discussed this hierarchy as a comparative trade-off. While agency migration fees are generally much lower for Gulf countries, the monthly salary is also significantly less lucrative. Workers I spoke to who had previously been in Saudi Arabia, Kuwait, or the UAE had earned between USD $200 and $500 a month, compared to an average of USD $1,000 in Palestine/Israel. As Nathan explains, "In Canada you can make $600 a month net, which is less than Israel, but people still want to go there because you can bring family and get better jobs after two years."

Reflecting on this set of trade-offs, Nik, a caregiver and community leader from Nepal, explains that "some friends go to Canada, America, Portugal, Europe. Most Nepalese want Europe first, then Israel, Japan, or Korea, then if there's nothing in Nepal, the third rank is Qatar, UAE, Malaysia, Saudi, the Gulf." He adds that typically there is "harder physical work" in the Gulf, as compared to Israel. Some also describe Palestine/Israel as better at enforcing rights than the UAE, Kuwait, and Saudi Arabia. Saul says that in Palestine/Israel, "human rights are also good. Not one hundred percent, but 90 percent. I think more than other countries of the Middle East like Saudi Arabia, Kuwait. But not like Europe." Nancy explains, "They say that the best payment and treatment Filipinos get is in Israel, better than in Canada. They say it's the best way to look for money because Israel is an open, democratic country. They'd still like to go to Canada because of time or visa. But even compared with Canada, Israel is good because they're not taxed in Israel like in Canada." These estimations of Israel are far from uniform. Emma, a caregiver working for an elderly woman outside of Tel Aviv, bluntly notes, "I hate Israel. I was in Cyprus before and liked it much better even though it was less money. What's money? Money's nothing."

Discourses of national love among migrants thus emerge unevenly as an effect of multiple ideological, political, and personal commitments and from various socioeconomic locations. The convergence of pro-Israel narratives can reinforce the state's self-fashioning as a site of cosmopolitan progress in the Middle East and portrayals of Israel as uniquely modern, even as workers regularly unsettle the worst effects of disposability, temporariness, and exclusion.

Temporal Boundaries

In a 2005 speech about the presence of non-Jewish migrants in Israel, then Interior Minister Eli Yishai referred to migrants as "a Trojan horse in the heart of the Jewish glow" and "a pipe bomb against the character of the Jewish nation."[44] While the former metaphor paints migrant workers as sly smugglers with machinations of altering the Jewish makeup of the state, the latter invokes temporality as the ultimate resource to be guarded, one that is a decisive threat to Israeli territorial legitimacy. Yishai's language emphasizes the existential tenor of Zionist anxieties around entitlements to more time for non-Jewish, non-native populations in Palestine, an anxiety shaping how caregivers navigate their own positioning in the home and nation. His language suggests how "time and mobility are weaponized" under Israeli settler colonialism, whether through the application of legal categories such as citizen, infiltrator, temporary worker, and asylum seeker, or the "imposed waiting" Palestinians face at checkpoints, the waiting of families with relatives in prison, or the extension or anticipation of military violence.[45]

Significantly, even as caregivers unsettle the rigidity of Israel's temporal boundaries, many express acceptance of their impermanent positioning. That is, comparative love or appreciation stems from workers' own expectations of what the state owes to them as non-Jews and the limited horizons for any kind of substantive belonging. As Sana states, "We don't have a future here . . . in Canada they give us two passports and a license. We do business, and they let us leave. Here there's nothing to do . . . we can't do nothing." June echoes this sentiment: "[It's] unlike America and Canada, [where] you can get married and automatically get citizenship. But *po* [here], *kama Filipiniot* [some Filipinas], nine, ten years in Israel. They send them back home! Let's say in Canada if you get pregnant and deliver a baby there, your baby is supposed to be Canadian citizen, but *po* [here]? No. *Zeh kasheh* [it's hard]." Commenting on the same policy regulating migrant families, Ita likewise explains, "Maybe they think if we become husband and wife we'll stay here. But we don't want to stay here! We have children, family. If we can't bring our children, we can't come here." She then compares this reality to Canada, where migrants can bring their families after two years.

Some caregivers said that they would want citizenship for practical rather than ideological terms, were it an option. Citizenship would allow freedom from immigration police and the ability to leave the country to visit family and reenter without hassle, even if Israel weren't a place they would want to stay forever. Kamal explains that "in another country, three, four years if you are willing to pay for taxes, the government gives you certain legal title or citizenship, but here there's nothing. . . . I don't know if there was a possibility [for citizenship] tomorrow if I would apply or not. . . . It's already a small country and they don't want many populations, so there is a reason." Kamal conveys both ambivalence toward citizenship and a distant sympathy with the state for having the citizenship laws they do. He later clarifies that his daughter was born in Palestine/Israel, and was forced to go back to Nepal when she was three because she was not eligible for citizenship.

Others articulate their desires to remain impermanent as an effect of job immobility. Nik says he looks forward to going back to Nepal where he was trained as a paramedic, even though his employers have offered to help him secure a special visa. Even if his employer doesn't die, he says, he needs to go back. "I am representative of 80 percent [of caregivers]," he says. "If I go back, I can't come back again because of Israeli law. I'm excited to go home."

Skepticism of Israel as a permanent home also stems from a certain degree of cultural alienation. Lina, for instance, explains that even though migrant caregivers are entitled to take their own holidays off, many employers are unaware of this rule: "Here there's many kinds of family that don't understand this [rule]. And sometimes if it's a Jewish holiday, they say, 'It's *my* holiday, you get a holiday.' But we'll not need this holiday! It's *my* festival, a Nepali festival! We're all saying, like, 'It's my festival, it's my culture!' What can I do with a Jewish holiday?" Here, Lina suggests how exclusionary Jewish claims to a future in Palestine inform workers' own expectations of what they can reasonably demand or receive from the state, and how to increase their own power while they are there.

The emphasis on non-Jewish impermanence in Palestine/Israel requires that caregivers deploy different strategies at contextually distinct moments to guard against replaceability, deportation, and injury.[46] Thus, frontstage forms of everyday resistance may not necessarily lead to transformational political outcomes, even as these resistance strategies improve caregivers' immediate working conditions.[47] Workers' diverse orientations toward the Israeli settler project challenge romanticized "partial or reductionist theories of power" that imagine violence and domination to produce a unitary consciousness among subjects marginalized by the state.[48] In many national contexts, worker isolation and the perceived informality of household labor prevent care and domestic workers from adopting organizing strategies typical of other labor sectors. In the Israeli context, this isolation is compounded by a strict investment in preventing non-Jewish migrants from pushing temporal boundaries and reproducing collective non-Jewish communities, whether biologically or culturally. Nancy's critique of caregivers' limited space for family-building in Palestine/Israel and their treatment as "national heroines" by the Philippine government in many ways captures the positioning of migrant caregivers at the intersection of neoliberal outsourcing and Zionism. She notes, "You can bring a sibling to Israel, but not a husband or wife, because if it's your husband or wife you can multiply." Her use of the word "multiply" also aptly echoes that of the biblical call to "be fruitful and multiply," one often invoked within Zionist discourse and pronatalist calls to secure a Jewish future in *Eretz Yisrael*. Offering an equally pointed critique of the Philippine government and their casting of migrant women as "national heroines," Nancy says, "It's shameful when the [Philippines] government says they're heroes. That's not why they go abroad. They're victims of corruption of the Filipino government. They send back eleven billion in remittances. They're originally accountants, doctors, dentists, engineers." Rejecting Israeli discourses of Jewish reproductive nationalism and the language of migrant heroism and sacrifice, Nancy suggests how structures of neoliberal labor export overlap with Israeli concerns over reproductive purity and territorial control. Both of these strictures shape the resources available to migrants to navigate the transnational flows of capital and accumulation of resources within which caregivers' labor is situated. Rather than indicating a romanticized "dignity or heroism of resistors," workers' strategies are indicative of how settler colonialism and neoliberal capitalism intersect within the everyday lives of workers.[49]

Given the severe quashing of migrant political activism, a topic I turn to in the final chapter, individual relationships and households become the most viable terrain for contesting employer exploitation and domination. Through everyday methods of resistance, workers shift the balance of power within employers' homes, demanding better working conditions and respect. Across the array of strategies and political perspectives caregivers adopt, they regularly cope with the isolation and atomization of the job by forging networks of care, solidarity, and support over the internet, a topic to which I turn in the subsequent chapter.

5

Collective Care and the Politics of Visibility

I care for your *savta* [grandmother]—care for me!

Protest sign, Caregivers' Rights Rally, Tel Aviv, 2014

In January 2014 in south Tel Aviv, migrant caregivers held a rally to demand equal rights, overtime pay, and observance of their rest hours and vacation days. Gathering at Levinsky Park, a popular public meeting space by the Central Bus Station where many migrants and asylum seekers spend their days off, tens of workers held signs declaring, "I care for your *savta*—care for me!" "I deserve two hours' rest!" and "*ovdot, lo avadot* [workers, not slaves]."[1] Within the public space of south Tel Aviv, protesters collectively reversed the usual equation of who produces and who benefits from the physical and psychic labors of care.

To date, the January 2014 rally has been one of the only public protests calling for better working conditions for migrant caregivers, a reality shaped by the comparative organizing terrain for temporary migrants in Palestine/Israel.[2] In contrast, several protests have taken place since 2003 against the deportation of children born to migrants in Israel.[3] Notably, after watching a documentary on the children of migrants in 2005, right-wing politician and former prime minister Ariel Sharon noted, "I was deeply touched by a television program about the children of undocumented migrants who grew up here. . . . I reached the conclusion that we must make an effort so that they can remain in Israel."[4] Sharon's comment suggests the extent to which migrant caregivers are valued by the state when they are attached to biological families—first and foremost, those of Jewish Israelis—and on an exceptional basis when they embody the role of biological mothers themselves. This prioritization of the traditional family formation prompts the question of how migrant caregivers engage in everyday forms of resistance that ensure the survival, thriving, and care of migrant communities beyond their own biological families and that of their employers, surviving collectively against the many forms of "antilife" produced through Israel's reproductive regime.[5]

Looking at caregivers' "backstage" resistance strategies away from the gaze of employers, this chapter asks how migrant caregivers meet their material needs and those of their extended communities. I examine how workers collectively mitigate economic insecurity, debt, legal precarity, and surveillance, building networks of collective care and solidarity. For James Scott, the "backstage" or "offstage" arena is the space "outside the intimidating gaze of power" where individuals can collectively come together and engage more freely and openly in subversive discussions.[6] The forms of community care that migrant caregivers adopt arise in response to the comparative landscape of migrant activism in Palestine/Israel, which is characterized by a relatively weak history of migrant sociopolitical organizing against the state, a stringent deportation regime, and a distinctively short visa period. Attention to the backstage arena highlights avenues of "possible dissent" through which caregivers unsettle barriers to collective survival that, by design, reproduce Israel as "the Jewish state."[7]

Throughout this chapter, I situate forms of mutual aid such as welfare provision, collective debt alleviation, legal defense, community protection, and emotional support as modes of "everyday resistance" that ensure the sustenance of non-Jewish collectivities for years at a time, despite the many forms of state disinvestment aimed at squelching, pushing to the margins, and expelling migrant communities. Following Asef Bayat, I suggest that resistant acts are not only those aimed at overthrowing capitalism or state power.[8] Rather, resistance involves ongoing attempts to negotiate oppressive power structures and thwart the worst threats to individual and collective existence. Ubiquitous Zionist ideologies and policies casting migrant collective life as temporally and territorially threatening often require caregivers to avoid placing demands on the state. By abstaining from such demands, workers are better able to mitigate individual precarity, spreading economic and legal risk across collective networks. The extent to which politically active migrant community leaders have in the past been criminalized or deported, and the reach of the deportation police into community spaces such as churches and homes, suggests the cost of engaging in sociopolitical organizing that directly takes on the state.

In the face of their liminal positioning between intimate laborers and criminal "others" outside of settler time, caregivers continually disrupt the demographic and temporal restrictions stymieing their collective existence through what Marlon Bailey and Valerie Francisco-Menchavez call the "labor of care"—the work of collectively providing for kinship networks and maintaining community beyond the heteronuclear family.[9] They also care for—and receive care from—informal transnational networks that include but also exceed biological kin. Away from the "frontstage" of the workplace, migrant workers' "communities of care" are a material and emotional safety net in the absence of a space for "political claims-making."[10]

To explore these aspects of community care, I begin by providing a brief layout of the comparative terrain of migrant activism in Palestine/Israel. I then discuss how migrant communities engage in mutual aid such as welfare provision, debt relief, and legal defense. Next, I examine how migrant networks, as horizontal sources of care and solidarity, provide community safety and emotional support in the face of state policing and surveillance. Over internet communication technology (ICT), migrant caregivers also give care to and receive care from chosen and biological family, romantic partners, and friends, sustaining multiple roles beyond that of caregiver. Finally, I contextualize these forms of backstage resistance by comparatively drawing out the state violence, worker exploitation, and anti-Black racism enacted against Eritrean and Sudanese asylum seekers. In conclusion, I highlight how contrasting temporal relationships to territory render the presence of asylum seekers "political" in the eyes of the state and the presence of migrant caregivers as largely apolitical.

Migrant Caregiver Organizing in Comparative Transnational Context

Migrant caregivers' backstage resistance strategies emerge comparatively in relation to other migrant-receiving states in the Middle East region and globally. Israel's migration regime possesses particular characteristics with respect to residency limits, migrant workers' "quasi-contractual" acceptance of temporariness, and the extent to which migrant networks are connected to broader regional and transnational organizations.[11] While restrictions on citizenship and permanent residency are common in migrant-receiving states globally, few states impose such a short and nonrenewable temporal cap on residency. These restrictions shape some caregivers' expectations of what they can reasonably demand of Israel as an ethnic settler state.[12] Each of these features makes welfare provision, legal defense, debt relief, and solidarity-building more prominent forms of organizing than sociopolitical claims-making against the state.

As in many Gulf Cooperation Council (GCC) countries, in Palestine/Israel, stringent forms of surveillance and control over migrant community activities stymie political activity.[13] While other states in the region also criminalize migrant political activity—some more extensively than in Palestine/Israel—instances of migrant caregiver sociopolitical protest are not more prominent in Palestine/Israel.[14] In Lebanon, for instance, there has been a more sizable and longer history of migrant domestic worker organizing, culminating in the recent consolidation of a union.[15] When compared to the instances of protest in countries outside the Middle East region that also impose restrictions on residency, family formation, and sexual autonomy, those in Palestine/Israel are also notably smaller. For instance, public protests among migrant domestic worker civil society organizations have been more numerous in Hong Kong and Singapore as well as in Denmark and Taiwan—states that, like Israel, tie workers' visas to their employment status.[16]

Beyond its distinctive management of temporal borders, Palestine/Israel is also regionally somewhat unique in the relatively late entrance of migrant domestic workers into the labor market, a feature impacting the extent to which there is historical precedent for sociopolitical organizing. For instance, in GCC countries, migrants generally entered the labor market after the 1973 oil boom, and in Lebanon, Jordan, and Mediterranean and Southern European states, they did so in the 1980s.[17] By comparison, though some Filipinx caregivers migrated to Palestine/Israel following the first intifada in 1987, most did not enter the market in larger numbers until the mid-1990s. Established networks of migrant caregiver organizing within the United States, Canada, and Italy, for instance, have allowed workers to connect more substantively to broader unionizing efforts, advocate for protective legislation, and establish numerous migrant-led workers' centers.[18] In contrast, while Israel presents fewer barriers to migrant union organizing than states such as Saudi Arabia, Malaysia, and Thailand, efforts to unionize migrant laborers in Palestine/Israel have been largely unsuccessful, failing to create any "form of industrial citizenship" for migrant caregivers.[19] Despite momentum, education, and outreach initiatives that took place between 2007 and 2011, union drives have been hampered in Palestine/Israel by caregivers' work schedules, workers' own self-understanding as highly temporary, and the perceived threat that unionizing was thought to present to "insider" elderly Jewish Israelis.[20] Notably, while several migrant worker leaders were involved in this drive, it was largely a citizen-initiated effort, a reality impeding long-term continuity.[21] Across Israel, efforts to unionize migrant caregivers have been isolated and lacking worker-led momentum to the same extent as in other states. In contrast, in Lebanon, migrant domestic worker unionizing efforts have been supported by the International Labor Organization and the European Union, and in the UK, France, Brazil, Uruguay, Hong Kong, and the Dominican Republic, national unions and regional networks play a pivotal role in union drives.[22]

Where migrant domestic workers have been able to overcome barriers to organizing in countries with restrictions comparable to Palestine/Israel, extensive regional and transnational networks have played a key role. In Hong Kong, for instance, transnational and regional organizations have provided capacity and support to migrant worker mobilizations.[23] Despite similar requirements that caregivers live with employers in Hong Kong, and the deterring effect of a militarized police presence, the region's migrant domestic worker movement has been strengthened by regional and transnational organizations such as the Asian Migrants Coordinating Body (AMCB), the International Migrants Alliance (IMA), and the Hong Kong Federation of Asian Domestic Worker Unions.[24]

Though there are a handful of well-known Israeli NGOs advocating for migrant rights, including those partially functioning as workers' centers, migrant-led groups are generally organized around hometown development projects, welfare provision, religious affiliation, recreational programming, sports, and regional and national identities, rather than workers' rights.[25] While deeply tied to formal and informal transnational networks, these groups tend to be sociocultural rather than rights-based. Though migrant rights umbrella groups have operated in the Middle East region—for instance, Philippines-based organization Migrante International has a Middle East chapter—these regional associations are less active in Palestine/Israel.[26] Thus, as in GCC states, activism around migrant domestic worker issues can often come from organizations advocating for migrant rights from locations outside of the state itself. For instance, Migrante International's Manila-based chapter has advocated for migrant caregivers' rights in Palestine/Israel, calling for protections for Filipinx caregivers during escalations in violence, condemning the deportation of migrant children, rejecting illegal recruitment fees, and drawing connections between structural adjustment, Filipinx caregivers in Israel, and Palestinian liberation.[27]

Despite a lack of overt sociopolitical organizing, the hundreds of migrant-led organizations that exist in Palestine/Israel function as networks to informally share information around rights, placement agencies, and Israeli law. Though not formally challenging state ideologies or policies, they ensure the material sustenance of communities despite state efforts to depoliticize care work.[28] Away from the gaze of employers, migrant caregivers contravene the disinvestment in non-Jewish life and the atomization and individualizing of workers, generating mutual aid networks that, as Dean Spade argues, allow people "to create systems of care and generosity that address harm and foster well-being."[29]

By far the largest number of formal community organizations exist within the Filipinx migrant community under the umbrella organizations Federation of Filipino Communities in Israel (FFCI) and National Alliance of Filipino Communities (NAFILCO). Though formally, forty-nine organizations are recognized by the embassy of the Philippines under FFCI, according to Brian, a community leader actively involved in religious and regional organizations, informal community groups number in the hundreds. Within the Nepalese community, there are thirty-two total embassy-recognized groups organized around religion, hometown region, social causes, and region of employment in Palestine/Israel. Within Indian and

Sri Lankan migrant communities, organizations are oftentimes connected to Catholic churches.

Tellingly, Abigail describes the vast Filipinx social networks she participates in as a form of "voluntary care." She states that "in every organization we become close to each other, so it's a family away from home." This "voluntary care" is at once a source of refuge, pleasure, and comfort and a "labor of care" required to maintain community amid family separation, indebtedness, and state racism.[30] These networks illustrate how social reproduction is not only the labor of reproducing households, economies, and ideologies, but also that of building what Francisco-Menchavez calls "communities of care" and solidarity—the "reorganizing [of] care horizontally, *from* migrants *to* other migrants."[31] Rather than an a priori natural affiliation, collective solidarity and care are themselves outcomes of reproductive labor—even as this work may bring forms of self-actualization and nonalienation—that sustain communities in the backstage arena away from employers' homes. Collective solidarity can also give strength and support to workers engaging in individual acts of resistance against employers.

Against Scott's notion of everyday resistance as disguised acts of subversion or rebellion that are distinct from collective and open resistance to an oppressor, the pooling of financial, legal, and emotional resources constitutes a form of quotidian resistance that is neither wholly unintelligible to employers and the state nor a form of rights-based protest. Care and domestic workers cannot easily organize against the same boss, conduct synchronous slowdowns in a factory or engage in high-risk protests, nor are these forms of resistance expressed as desirable. In between what Scott describes as subversive "foot-dragging" and open rebellion, caregivers collectively shoulder the emotional, financial, legal, and physical hazards that atomized workers face in the home without worsening the risk of deportation.[32]

Welfare Provision

The ongoing targeting of migrant community spaces such as churches, apartments, restaurants, and nightclubs illuminates the extent to which the Israeli state views migrants as a collective threat once they step beyond their legally and socially proscribed roles as workers and national helpers.[33] Across Filipinx, Indian, Nepalese, and Sri Lankan communities, organizations hold fundraisers for group members in need of food, cloth-ing, or medical care; pool money to collectively alleviate debt or compensate for lost wages; raise money for disaster relief, education, and infrastruc-ture projects in their hometowns; host sporting, holiday, and social events; organize beauty pageants; and connect new caregivers with networks of support. Migrants often leverage the communication networks already built into formal organizations during times of crisis to generate more informal, project-based participation for fundraising, whether in the wake of natural disasters, political conflict, or health crises, or for hometown development projects.

The biopolitical disinvestment in migrant caregivers' health, both through the high rate of on-the-job injuries and the lack of access to ade-quate medical care, often leaves workers in need of health services that are not covered by insurance. The risk of becoming uninsured is especially high for unemployed and undocumented caregivers who become and remain ill and cannot rely upon their employers for insurance. Because any attempts to access health care would require registration with the Ministry of Inte-rior, undocumented workers must often rely on the good will of employers for health services. For those who hold valid work permits, being fired can lead to negative employer recommendations, difficulty finding subsequent jobs, and an inability to send remittances to family or pay the high-interest loans required to migrate. Collective welfare provisioning is thus particu-larly important for terminally ill migrant caregivers lacking comprehensive health care. By helping individual migrants meet their basic needs indepen-dently of their employers, mutual aid organizations mitigate the impacts of debt bondage by reducing the costs of walking away from an abusive or exploitative employer. Ensuring the survival of individual migrants, com-munity welfare networks not only strengthen migrant social support sys-tems but also increase the total amount of remittances that communities can send to their families and home regions.

Saul, a caregiver from Sri Lanka working outside of Tel Aviv, has organized a mutual aid fund for Sri Lankan migrants living in Israel. On weekends, Saul lives in a small flat with his wife, whom he is married to in secret. In his capacity as an organizer with the mutual aid fund, Saul ar-ranges and facilitates large sporting events, cultural celebrations, beauty pageants, and fundraisers. He also collects a small fee from the monthly sal-aries and charges participation fees at all events with the aim of financially assisting caregivers whose insurance does not cover the excessive costs of hospitalization. The fund also provides food and shelter to undocumented migrants who cannot find work and supports community development projects in Sri Lanka. His wife, Amita, who also works as a caregiver and helps with the fund, notes, "The important thing is if someone's sick, everyone's working. Who helps them? Four, five, girls got cancer. It was a very bad situation. We helped them. How much we can help, we do. We raised five hundred dollars." Saul adds that "the association was our plan when we came here and saw no one was helping. The embassy cannot help us. We had to do something if we were going out [of Sri Lanka] to Israel. We are doing this from our heart, but every time we cannot do this. It's hard in Israel." Both Saul and Amita portray the fund as, on the one hand, an obligation to their community, and on the other, a necessity arising out of the absence of other forms of social support. Without the association, there would be no network to fill the gap generated by state disinvestment and the absence of help from the embassy. Saul and Amita thus describe the pooling of resources as a community responsibility to keep each other alive, as well as a practical means of sending more money home to support family networks.

At the same time, Saul's description of the welfare fund suggests an ambivalence about the role of informal networks in providing crucial services; though he feels a moral responsibility "to do something" for fellow Sri Lankans, his admission that "every time we cannot do this" suggests the toll of the reproductive labors of providing for one's community in the absence of state services. While Amita and Saul "are doing this from [their] heart," the fund is itself a "labor of care" requiring additional psychic and social energy after the workday to fill the gaps created by the state, even as the association also provides a place for celebration, relaxation, and support. Saul's articulation of his own limits highlights the constraints of the welfare fund more broadly. Rather than transforming state structures of "depletion," the fund is a panacea for the many bodily, economic, and legal risks migrant caregivers encounter, without which they could face greater precarity.

Others use organizations' preexisting communication structures to mobilize assistance for caregivers from their home region who are sick or experiencing financial crisis. Kamal explains that there are many contingent or short-term community funds available to Nepalese migrants through Facebook. These funds support caregivers who get sick and have high medical expenses or who need help with food security or medical care. He notes, "We have different societies that are raising funds for if you need some help, or if somebody gets sick and they stay a long time in the hospital, or for food if they're a long time in the apartment. So they're helping by raising funds for members. A couple of hundred shekels they're raising. . . . Sometimes we just call each other and ask on Facebook, 'somebody's having this and this and we need help.'" As Kamal relays, these fundraising efforts also take place through informal channels rather than formal organizations and large events. Though Kamal has never drawn on mutual aid funds for himself, he describes the very presence of these networks as a safety net: "If something happened to me tomorrow, they're ready to help me also. Same with everyone."

In addition to medical assistance, migrant communities also generate financial resources to compensate for stolen wages. In this way, they fill a gap created by the state that otherwise enables wage theft. Leveraging the social networks built through formal organizations, migrant caregivers pool funds equal to the amount an employer owes. Abigail explains that she has helped collect funds to alleviate the burden of debt accrued through exorbitant recruitment agency fees, asking for donations from caregivers who have already paid off their loans and pooling money for those who have recently begun working in Palestine/Israel. She adds that another common form of collective debt relief is the mutual shouldering of interest payments on loans, which then allows migrants to remit wages more quickly. Because debt is closely bound up with workers' bargaining power and the risk of exploitation and abuse, the collective ability to pay off debt more quickly increases worker power in situations of abuse, exploitation, or wage theft. Like Saul and Kamal, Abigail explains that helping those with inadequate resources in Israel is "like an obligation. If one of us is needy, we need to give."

Mutual aid can also be a way of addressing the specific concerns of community members most vulnerable to economic and political crises more broadly. Yonas, an asylum seeker active in the Eritrean community, was one of the interviewees I spoke to during the pandemic who commented on his experiences of COVID. He explains that "when Corona started in March 2020 . . . the entire Eritrean community managed to raise a lot of money *from* the community *to* the community, so we collected a lot of money from people, especially around Tel Aviv, and from people who have businesses, and this was distributed most of the time to single mothers, old people, and the disabled, until the end of 2020. A lot of women get benefits from this, especially single mothers." Yonas relates that because of their undocumented status, asylum seekers who are single mothers—most of whom work as cleaners and live-out caregivers—only labor four-to-six hours a day. Due to these limited hours, and hyperexploitation by bosses who are aware that asylum seekers have the least bargaining power of all workers, single mothers have been especially hard hit by the COVID-19 pandemic. This mutual aid "from the community to the community" has been essential in helping single mothers and others cover their basic needs since March 2020. Across communities, various forms of mutual aid enable the survival of migrant and refugee groups in the absence of state provision and in the presence of state violence. Raising money for food, medical services, and debt relief also takes place through formal pageants, church celebrations, and sporting events. For instance, at one community event I was invited to attend, workers organized a beauty pageant hosted by an organization for Filipinx migrants from the Igorot region. The event celebrated Igorot music, dress, food, and culture, while also raising money for a member of the Filipinx community in Israel who was hospitalized and in need of supportive funds. The event was attended by caregivers working throughout Israel who had traveled to Tel Aviv to attend the event as well as community leaders from organizations throughout the FFCI.

Another component of mutual aid is the hometown projects caregivers undertake. Hometown projects fulfill, in one sense, the developmentalist duties and expectations that sending country governments may place upon migrant workers. Yet they also provide key resources by directly supporting families and social networks. Such projects can also be a respite from the tedious job of live-in care work, a platform for social connection, and a way of combating political alienation. Through Facebook event pages and homepages, for instance, caregivers regularly raise money for livelihood projects that benefit their hometown associations. Brian, who is involved with a Filipinx Catholic organization, says his group raised NIS $70,000 in 2014 to buy computers and projectors for a school in Cordillera. Brian comments that sometimes individuals from the organization will also bring money donations directly to the Philippines, as was the case after Hurricane Yolanda in 2013. Abigail is involved in a regional organization for Filipinx migrant caregivers in Palestine/Israel. Though the mission of the organization is to host cultural events and fundraisers that support the construction of houses and schools in the Philippines, the group also provides a network for Filipinx migrant caregivers in Israel to share on-the-job experiences, pool resources, and provide emotional and social support. Abigail explains that mobilizing caregivers to raise money for educational and infrastructural projects in her home region is not only a way of keeping her mind stimulated during the hours she is working, but also is a way of using her leadership and writing skills to visibly improve day-to-day life for children at home. Through a Facebook page dedicated to her fundraising campaigns and cultural events, Abigail has raised enough money to build a school and buy supplies for children in her home region and to send packages to families who lost their homes after Hurricane Yolanda.

Similarly, in the aftermath of the May 2015 earthquake in Nepal, Nina helped raise more than USD $90,000 for rebuilding projects that were distributed across seven districts in Nepal. Similarly, using Facebook, Nina publicized and raised money for a separate infrastructure project in Kathmandu. Likewise, Kamal raised 500,000 Nepalese rupees for shoes for children in a mountainside village severely impacted by the 2015 earthquake. Beyond the biological nuclear families for whom migrant caregivers often work, networks of "voluntary care" unsettle the reproduction of settler colonial exclusion, exploitation, and expropriation. Migrant reproductive labor is thus as much the work of caring for elderly citizens as it is the reproduction of nonheteronuclear, non-Jewish "chosen" families.[34]

In addition to mitigating migrant precarity through the collective shouldering of risk, networks of mutual aid ensure the reproduction of migrant collectivities without exacerbating the threat of surveillance or deportation. In this way, "backstage" survival and resistance strategies are inextricable from "frontstage" strategies, in that the individual bargaining power a worker holds is deeply tied to the collective alleviation of risk and the emotional support and solidarity that "communities of care" provide.[35] Further, mutual aid, as a form of everyday resistance, is neither wholly a form of tacit, individual rebellion, nor a visible and collective rejection of state ideologies. Rather than romanticizing mutual aid as a caring practice that necessarily transforms spaces of community reproduction into ones aimed at undermining the state, I locate it as a form of resistance that unsettles the specific strictures of neoliberal precarity and settler colonial governmentality migrant caregivers face.

Legal Defense

Beyond the provisioning of basic needs through mutual aid networks, migrant "communities of care" also distribute the resources needed for legal defense and advocacy. Through the communal pooling of legal resources across informal migrant networks, caregivers contest employer paternalism, attempt to hold bosses and recruitment agencies accountable to contracts, and assert their right to live and work in Palestine/Israel free of abuse. Such forms of legal paternalism require migrant caregivers to hire expensive Israeli lawyers or to rely upon the limited legal services of advocacy organizations such as Kav LaOved if they hope to contest the legal claims of a citizen. Under the conditions of legal dependency enabled by the binding arrangement, migrant caregivers are treated as obstacles to the legal protection of citizens rather than legal subjects worthy of protection themselves. As de facto objects rather than subjects of the law, they must therefore develop ad hoc measures for defending themselves against deportation, undercompensation, exclusion from the Work and Rest Hours Law, and exploitation.

Though migrant caregivers are at a legal disadvantage even when they can afford to hire a lawyer, through extant networks, they are still able to place legal pressure upon employers who don't pay them what they are lawfully owed. In addition to raising funds for medical expenses, the welfare fund that Saul runs within the Sri Lankan community also collects money to pay lawyers' fees for caregivers who cannot afford attorneys. Collecting legal fees is especially important when caregivers are accused of mistreating their elderly employers or stealing. As Saul explains, "If the employer complains without [witness], you need a bailout. [Employers] don't need any witness or anything. The police trust that [the caregiver] did something." In contrast, whereas police officers do not demand a witness to support the claims of citizen-employers, they require that an Israeli witness support a migrant caregiver's refutation of claims made against her and sign a bail bond releasing her from prison. Saul's mutual aid fund attempts to address issues that arise out of this situation of legal dependence, providing jail support and raising funds for legal services: "When an employer has a complaint, the caregiver doesn't have a lawyer. Last Thursday one lady had a fight with an employer and then quit. After one week, police called [and said], 'Come to the police, we have a complaint against you.' She went to the Jerusalem police, and they put her in jail and told her she couldn't be let out. They told her, 'If you want to get out, bring an Israeli man for the bailout. Any Israeli, they can sign.' For nothing she was put in jail; she didn't do nothing." The requirement that a caregiver "bring an Israeli" with them suggests that, in the eyes of the state, testimony from a citizen-employer is sufficient to press charges, while a countertestimony from a migrant caregiver lacks credibility. Though in this instance, the fund could not confer the legal power accorded to Israeli citizens (Saul notes that, when he could not immediately help this association member because he was busy at work, she frustratedly stated, "You are a member of the association, why are you not doing anything?!"), it nevertheless helped her secure a lawyer and raise the NIS $5,000 for legal representation. Without this help, Saul says, the member would have had to wait in jail for fourteen days. Saul describes how the welfare fund also generates money for lawyers' fees that would otherwise be too costly for caregivers. The fund also serves as a point of communication for caregivers who are held in police custody. The sporting events, social gatherings, and beauty pageants his organization hosts thus serve the dual purpose of building community and raising money for contingent emergency situations that caregivers would otherwise have to navigate on their own.

Some caregivers also express the importance of sharing legal knowledge through organizational networks as a means of increasing their bargaining power with employers. Using the language of law as a form of leverage over employers helps caregivers not only to fight for the baseline amount of compensation to which they are entitled but also to increase their bargaining power in the long term and demand respect from employers. James's experiences reflect the familiar situation of many caregivers who learn employment and immigration law in their spare time and become lawyers on their own behalf. When he first began working for his current employer, James received less than the required minimum salary. After he quit his job for a period of one month due to undercompensation, his employer's family refused to give him the social benefits and severance pay to which he was entitled. As is commonly the case among caregivers, the recruitment agency sided with James's employer. He remarks, "I didn't keep quiet . . . I fought with the agency and I told them the law. I quoted the law. They were not accepting the fact that it was in the law. Finally they gave me what I'm supposed to get. I fight for my rights and I got it and from that time on they obey the law." James adds that leveraging the language of legality is "why they respect me." His legal knowledge has since become an asset to his broader network of friends who have migrated from his home region in India, and he helps other friends file claims against employers who violate the Law of Severance Act through local Israeli advocacy groups. For James, information dissemination takes place through a regional organization for caregivers from northeast India with over five hundred members. Commenting on the instantaneous dissemination enabled by the group's presence on Facebook, he notes, "We have a group on Facebook. . . . Now my whole group knows that you are taking my interview. Whatever new things happen in our work, we share it in the group. . . . Northeast Indians are united . . . whatever talk happens between you and me, I'll update so all my friends can know."

James's comment about the role this network could play in disseminating information about me, as an outside researcher, is revealing of how pre-existing networks allow members to caution against or welcome outsiders as required. More broadly, internet-based "information-distribution networks" facilitate this type of organizing and mobilizing despite limitations on physical and political mobility.[36]

Likewise, Lina has used her own past experiences navigating Israeli law to disseminate skills for navigating bureaucratic traps and making use of migrant advocacy groups. After learning the ropes while helping her sister recover a year's unpaid salary, a process that took months and required extensive trips to government offices and migrant rights organizations, she now accompanies other Nepalese migrants in similar situations, helping them file cases with Kav LaOved, going with them to *Misrad Hapanim* (the Ministry of the Interior), and helping them understand separation and overtime pay policies and the holidays to which they are entitled. "After this I'm starting to help people," she notes. "Every place I'm going and I'm not afraid. Because it's hard when people come not speaking Hebrew and not English." During the first two times I met with Lina, she received calls from friends whom she was planning to meet later in the day to help them with visa and unpaid salary issues, and after both of our meetings, she was headed to a migrant rights clinic with other Nepalese migrants during her day off to help them file claims against their employers. Lina also organizes a group for Nepalese women, helping them navigate their jobs in Israel and connecting with other women in Nepal to discuss issues of domestic violence and violence against women.

As Lina's and James's experiences suggest, knowledge of the law and the ability to navigate Israeli bureaucracy become a community resource, increasing caregivers' bargaining and legal power. Many caregivers go to Israeli migrant rights organization Kav LaOved during their days off from work seeking legal advice, attempting to recover unpaid wages, reporting abuse, or, when they are offered, attending "Know Your Rights" seminars. Migrant caregivers share information about how to take photographs and collect other forms of documentation that prove employers are demanding work of caregivers beyond the contract and how to file complaints with social workers at recruitment agencies. James notes, "In my community if people have problems, I go to Kav LaOved with them and I help them with what I know and I feel happy, satisfied. Last time I took one girl, she had a problem, and I solved the problem."

Nina, too, regularly accompanies community members and friends to different legal offices, sharing knowledge she picked up while volunteering at a migrant rights organization during her time off. She acknowledges the laborious nature of caring for her community, a labor that eventually stopped her from volunteering. She explains, "[This organization] is fighting for our rights. I used to go there to help. Then I was becoming a little bit unhappy because I worked nine hours [there] and then I came home [to work]." Though Nina is still deeply involved in a Nepalese cultural organization in the Tel Aviv area, balancing her regular job as a live-in caregiver with her role as a volunteer ultimately became too time consuming to maintain. For migrant communities taking on physical and economic risk, legal defense is more than an individual act reasserting the legal personhood of the caregiver. Rather, it is a measure against laws and policies refusing to recognize the value of non-Jewish migrants beyond their role as workers.

In an environment where the enforcement of labor law for migrants falls largely on civil society organizations and individual workers, Facebook has also become a crucial tool for the distribution of information about rights, changing legislation affecting migrant caregivers, and protests. Kav LaOved, for instance, has in the past coordinated "Know Your Rights" workshops and rallies and regularly assists caregivers in navigating legal issues with employers and recruitment agencies. The Kav LaOved Facebook page is a critical source of information for caregivers. It publishes updated protocol on employment and visa regulations and hosts a live comments section where caregivers can ask questions about health-care benefits, work-related injuries, severance pay, and salary calculations. When a new employment regulation is passed, there are at times over a hundred questions from caregivers in a given thread, with answers posted by staff. That these answers are publicly available means that migrants can learn from each other's employment challenges and share strategies for addressing abusive employers. Though Kav LaOved is run by Israelis, caregivers are an integral part of the volunteer system, and migrant caregiver community networks serve as focal methods of the organization's information dissemination.

Each of these aspects of mutual aid—welfare provision, legal defense, and collective debt alleviation—are forms of everyday resistance that improve caregivers' immediate material conditions without further risking their ability to stay in Palestine/Israel or to "stretch" time. Yet, in contrast to Scott's formulation, where everyday resistance is generally hidden, individual, and tacit, mutual aid is not necessarily a quiet form of "foot-dragging," nor a series of atomized acts against an oppressor that only become collective in the aggregate.[37] Tungohan asserts, in the context of migrant caregiver organizing in Canada, that at times, "individual acts are all channeled into transition moments that may form the basis for largescale political activity."[38] While mutual aid is "hidden" to the extent that it is not necessarily subject to the surveillance of household employers, nor is it under the watch of the state to the same extent as protests, it is also often what Scott calls "quasi-public," unfolding through Facebook announcements, signs posted in Neve Sha'anan, and celebrations held in parks and city streets. Mutual aid unfolds in a hybrid space beyond the atomized workplace where caregivers rehabilitate citizens, and away from political protest, where they collectively make demands upon the state.

Solidarity and Safety from the State

Migrant communities of care also leverage informal networks to provide emotional support, protect each other from deportation police and state agents, and care for family and friends. Away from the frontstage of the employer's home, horizontal care networks provide solace and comradeship, whether within churches and religious spaces, in weekend flats where caregivers live, or over ICT. Restrictions forbidding migrant workers from marrying, discouraging pregnancy, preventing spousal and familial migration, and hindering non-Jewish collective life are deliberate strategies aimed at guarding an exclusionary Jewish future and an exclusive "right" to permanency.

Spiritual Networks of Support

Migrant religious and spiritual networks, both formal and informal, engender support and respite from the frontstage stresses of the employer's home. Religious communities among Catholic, Buddhist, Hindu, and Evangelical Christian caregivers also provide a place of belonging for migrant children whose births are treated as illegal by the state and whose social right to membership is denied for years at a time.[39] As Ella explains, "[At the church] we pour out our stress—it helps. Not only that we fellowship together; we laugh together in the church . . . bonding and talking with each other about problems, knowing you can trust them, you can pour out your soul, so that helps. So sometimes when we go for a trip or something we used to laugh and then afterwards the stress is gone . . . there's lots of singing. Sometimes it's not the actual mass but we sing together, we laugh together, so it helps a lot."

Migrant church spaces also directly challenge the Israeli government's prohibition on migrant marriages and childbirth. Finding creative ways to start families, get married, and raise children thwarts the state ban on biological reproduction and sexual intimacy. Migrants plan weddings that take place inside migrant church basements, car showrooms, public parks, or small rental spaces throughout south Tel Aviv. They host baptisms, communions, and bar and bat mitzvahs for children of migrants and citizens. Often, various migrant-led religious communities play a large role in creating spaces for these life cycle events. Pamela, a teacher from the Philippines living in Jerusalem, migrated with her boyfriend of ten years, whom she married while working in Palestine/Israel. Pamela describes her deep involvement with Couples for Christ, a worldwide Catholic movement started in 1981 in Manila. She explains that she and her husband "spend all our days off in church. We do not go to other things, only to church." Detailing the busy schedule on Sundays, she notes,

> The members are all Filipinos and you can be a member here and a member there—we're united. . . . Me and my husband, we like to go to church so we always attend two churches. . . . We attend a mass in Agron Holy Rosary at 10 o'clock; after that we go to Terra Santa at 11:30; after that we have our prayer meeting; and we finish in the afternoon [at] four o'clock [or] three o'clock at the earliest. We like it so much. My favorite is our activity, Couples for Christ, after church. We have a gathering; we eat in fellowship. After that we have our bible sharing, and then worshipping, after that fellowship again, then we go home.

Pamela's extensive involvement with the Filipinx migrant Catholic community in Jerusalem sustains her when she feels depressed on the job or if she is suffering from her employer's verbal abuse. When deciding to get pregnant, her extended religious community served as a network of support for her and her husband.[40] Likewise, during his days off, Peter, a caregiver from the Philippines working outside of Tel Aviv, volunteers with a Catholic ministry for migrants by helping with service rituals. Brian describes the Catholic practice of Recollection, or a communal retreat to spiritually connect with God, as a space of emotional support: "Here in Israel I travel a lot, you know, especially every Christmas I go to Bethlehem. And during that when I am active in the church we have Recollection—in Jerusalem, and near Galilee. So we have our Recollection—that's the time we can express our feelings with our friends, our problems, so it's just like our second family, so if you are here abroad it's nice to have groups to consider your second family." Brian also spends time with his church community through planned weekend trips to Christian holy sites and by organizing activities with an organization for caregivers from his region of the Philippines.

Martha, a devout Catholic working in Tel Aviv, describes her church community as a space that does the spiritual work of supporting caregivers. Martha's language echoes that of Paula as well as the many caregivers in Liebelt's study of Christian Zionist migrants in Palestine/Israel who see their own caregiving roles as infused with religious meaning.[41] Martha explains that the church clergy "cry with them, laugh with them, sit with them, [and] help them with spiritual brokenness and loneliness." She also relays that migrant friends with children born in Palestine/Israel seek out the church as a space of acceptance for Hebrew-speaking Filipinx children otherwise excluded from and targeted by the state. At the church, migrant children can learn Tagalog and attend Catholic services in Hebrew, a religious need specific to migrant children. In instances where caregivers face moral dilemmas around intermarriage, the church community is there to "advise what to do" and to give caregivers "blessings so the wife can stay Catholic and children will be Catholic, even if the man does not have to convert." In this way, the church functions as both a site of support and a space of Christian continuity that helps caregivers deal with what Martha calls a feeling of "splitness," at once missing home and feeling attached to their lives in Palestine/Israel. She explains that "there are masses at night because that's when people get off work. Nearly every day, some in English, some Tagalog, some *ivrit* [Hebrew] for the kids. The loneliness is worse for those in Be'er Sheva, where they only get off one weekend a month, and sometimes only five hours. They get 100 shekel and will spend all of the money and time going to Tel Aviv to mass, then the time is up and they pay their own money to come back." As Martha suggests, regular masses function as a space for

solidarity and support, providing time for connection and camaraderie between caregivers experiencing "splitness." The church space is a way for
workers facing dilemmas around faith, work, dating, and raising children
in a self-declared Jewish state to come together.

Yet, church networks are not only a site of emotional support and kinship beyond the nuclear family; they also provide the reproductive resource
of childcare for single parents whose children the state labels as "illegal."
Through Catholic daycare and afterschool programs in both Jerusalem and
Tel Aviv, migrant parents are able to secure their income while ensuring
their children can be with other Filipinx children born in Palestine/Israel.
Creating belonging for undocumented children of migrants is also a pro-
grammatic priority of some churches. During one of several masses I was
invited to attend at a migrant community church in south Tel Aviv, the
service was geared specifically toward Hebrew-speaking children of migrants who were invited to participate in various ritualistic components of
the service. Unlike regular weekday masses geared toward adults, prayers
and songs were translated into Hebrew, with the words projected onto a
screen for families to sing along together. The room was overflowing with
even more participants than usual, providing a rare space for migrant families to be together away from the gaze of employers. Among regular mass
attendees, such a gathering is not one to be taken for granted; as Martha
notes, masses for this particular Catholic community used to take place
"in a religious area, and Jews thought they were too loud." Amid continual
surveillance—by employers, by neighbors, by the state—such spaces provide a rare sense of celebration and safety for migrant families whose very
right to worship together is often under threat.

Churches can also be a space for caregivers to make sense of the "splitness" that Martha identifies, drawing on specifically religious tropes. Invocation of religious figures and imagery can be a way of providing comfort to
caregivers facing loneliness and burnout drawing on a commonly shared set
of rituals and practices. During another mass I attended, a nun working at
the church delivered a homily about patron Saint Agatha, a Catholic figure
who was tortured because she refused to marry, instead devoting her life
to Jesus. Following a long period in jail, Agatha's suitor Quintian cut off her
breasts, a form of torture signaling Agatha's ultimate sacrifice to her faith.
During her homily, the nun drew a parallel between Agatha's sacrifices to
Jesus and those made by migrant caregivers working in "the Holy Land"—a
striking parallel, given the visceral nature of Agatha's torture. Following the

service, the church hosted a meal in honor of Saint Agatha for attendees, the overwhelming majority of whom were women. The invocation of Agatha, as well as regular references to the Virgin Mary, underscores how liturgical images and offerings are woven into the language of comfort and sacrifice as caregivers communally navigate their unsettled positioning.

Spiritual Networks and Community Safety

Migrant religious communities have in certain instances also doubled as hiding places for undocumented caregivers. The particularly intense wave of deportation raids in 2002–2003, and the creation of the "Oz Task Force," a deportation wing of the Ministry of Interior operating in 2009, resulted in the closure of several migrant churches and community centers and the arrest of community leaders involved in cultural programming and worker organizing.[42] Under Israel's "closed skies" policy, the government deported roughly six thousand migrants in 2002 alone.[43] Among the deportation practices reported during this and other times were the holding of migrants without documents in jails for months, the "entrapment" of migrants visiting imprisoned relatives, and the abduction of parents who leave their children behind.[44]

Sustaining migrant communities is thus a matter of physically thwarting state agents whose aim is to prevent migrants from collectively thriving reproductively, religiously, socially, and symbolically. Ella explains,

> I have been taking care of some of our people—I shelter them in the church, I help to sleep in the church with some of them, I usually buy some stuff for them. Sometimes, I every week send money for their families, and there were no private businesses who send money, only through the Western Union, so I had to go at seven in the morning and line myself up. I sent two to three [payments] a week. There was one who was caught in the church. We were sleeping at seven o'clock and one of our friends dreamed about her phone ringing. It was not actually a call but it was [someone in] the church texting me saying, "Be careful, there is immigration here." But I didn't see my message. So she said she wanted to go to the CR [comfort room] so she went. Afterwards while she was opening the door she came out from the CR because it was outside the church and at the door there is two policemen and sad to say one Filipino who guided them. . . . So she came

inside with the policemen of course because her passport is inside the church. . . . It was one good friend of mine was sleeping without her passport. Police took those without passports right away.

Ella explains that part of the mission of her church fellowship is to provide safety to all children of migrants regardless of their legal status, housing them overnight when police come to migrants' homes and collecting food to make sure they are fed. Ella's story makes clear the tenuousness of migrant community life in Israel, despite rhetoric praising the importance of eldercare. It also demonstrates how the specter of deportation penetrates into the most intimate community spaces, ones intended to provide support, solace, and solidarity. Suggesting the importance of care for extended networks beyond those in Palestine/Israel, Ella not only helps make the church into a sanctuary space for undocumented migrants but also ensures that the families of those hiding in the church receive remittances. She explains the steps she takes to ensure that people receive the money to which they are entitled if apprehended by deportation police: "And then that's it. And then sometimes when there were people being caught, I also come from my friend's boss's house and take the money and bring it on the train to the airport to make sure they have the salary they need. . . . There are instances where they're brought straight to the airport if you want, or if not you're going to be sent to prison . . . so we have to take their luggage going there."

While Ella coordinates solidarity efforts for community members who are hiding from police, providing for their families and helping them recover wages, she also suggests regret that churches must play this role in the first place. She notes, "Anyway, a church is not supposed to be a place where you sleep but for this special reason we really had to so we did." Ella's commitment to providing community protection from deportation shapes her commitments to the church, even as, drawing on her Christian Zionist beliefs, she proudly supports Israel as a homeland for Jews. Ella takes enormous personal risks to disrupt the work of deportation police, unsettling the power of the state over intimate and sacred community spaces, even as these forms of backstage resistance may not manifest in collective, public demands made of the state itself.

Migrants also build solidarity by ensuring the continuation and regeneration of community activities that are otherwise criminalized by the state. Beauty pageants, singing contests, picnics, and church services are all gatherings that enable a temporary coming together outside the confines of the employer's apartment and a break from the taxing physical and emotional elements required of the job. Spaces for collective storytelling and solidarity include dance parties thrown at Takhana Merkazit (Tel Aviv Central Bus Station), dinners hosted in shared weekend flats, and religious gatherings held in nearby parks. Shared weekend flats can also be a bedrock of community support, becoming nonbiological, homosocial sites that allow migrants to give and receive care.[45] During days spent within the flat, caregivers celebrate belated birthdays and religious holidays, cook together, share stories from the week, exchange best practices for dealing with difficult employers, and arrange weddings, birthday parties, and outings.

Communal flats can also be sites of what Manalansan calls the "queering" of care, where caregivers cultivate support and solidarity that does not revolve around "biological motherhood and its naturalized linkage to 'caring.'"[46] Flats can be safe spaces to celebrate life events that are themselves a form of resistance to Israel's deportation regime, such as birthday parties for undocumented children and anniversary celebrations for couples who are married in secret. During the many Friday evenings I was invited into one particular weekend flat in Tel Aviv, flatmates made dinner together, hosted birthday and karaoke parties, spent time with romantic partners, and told stories from the work week. Sharing stories from the week is not only a way of receiving crucial emotional support, but also of building solidarity *as workers*. As Premilla Nadasen argues, storytelling among household workers can counter the atomization of workers experienced disproportionately by those in the home care industry, creating a sense of kinship and community.[47] In Ella's weekend flat, she and her fifteen flatmates affectionately referred to the oldest member of their apartment as "mother," a term so bestowed because of her "maternal" role within the home. "Mother," a caregiver from the Philippines in her fifties, made large meals for the younger caregivers on Friday evenings, managed the apartment while others went out after dinner, and humorously and sagely guided various flatmates through dating dilemmas, problems at work, and what clothes to wear to parties. Within these spaces, there is both the reproduction of familial roles and also a departure from the biological basis of familial roles altogether, what Bailey calls a "labor of care" that "take[s] on the work of family and community."[48]

Beyond physical sites of horizontal care, migrants also forge networks of solidarity and emotional support and *receive* care through ICT. The widespread fear of deportation raids at times makes ICT the most viable medium for information dissemination and political contestation. Online "communities of care" are sites for sharing best practices, worker solidarity, and support, and for workers to virtually receive care themselves. Though not a panacea for the pain of separation from loved ones, nor to be mistaken for collective resistance to global structures of domination, it is a transnational medium allowing migrant caregivers to collectively cope with mental and emotional stress, and to give and receive care beyond the wage relation.[49] As Fred asks rhetorically, "So what are we gonna do at home? Just look at the four sides of the wall! . . . We're not just *mitaplot* [caregivers] taking care of the old woman, we are also human." In describing his day-to-day routine, Fred alludes to his desire for greater social, emotional, and intellectual engagement and stimulation, yet his ability to seek such interaction is dependent upon his employer's physical and emotional needs. Acknowledging the need to escape boredom and vent about the difficulty of the job, Fred explains that cyberspace provides a needed place for him to complain to other caregivers about his employer and seek support, especially when he is not able or allowed to leave the house: "When you get angry with them sometimes, you cannot fight with them . . . when I'm expressing my anger to my employer, [it is] just wasting time, wasting money . . . you cannot fight with them, even if they are angry . . . lately I'm playing with, enjoying my computer to talk about my employers. What I want [to know] is . . . news [of my] family. It's very big help for me."

This sense of being "always on" is a crucial means of coping with his job when he cannot directly contest his employers' actions.[50] He reiterates, "When I get angry with [my employers], sometimes . . . you cannot fight with them. I take the patience from my family." He suggests that constant communication with his sons gives him strength to undergo the sacrifice of living abroad, reminding him of the larger reasons motivating his decision to work in Palestine/Israel.

Online communities and networks of care enable caregivers to connect with family and friends across vast geographical distances, giving and receiving support that sustains them through the many challenges of the workday. As Loretta Baldassar and Laura Merla illustrate, the forms care takes across these distances are multidirectional and asymmetrical, changing throughout the course of a lifetime and, importantly, shaping migrants' relationships not only with nuclear and biological family, but also with extended kinship networks.[51] Leela receives emotional fulfillment and strength by speaking with her nine-year-old and fifteen-year-old daughters on Skype daily, monitoring what they eat, ensuring they do their homework, and telling them bedtime stories. Constant connection with her family also helps her deal with the depression of being confined to a small home on a remote kibbutz, in contrast to the many caregivers who live near fellow co-nationals in cities like Tel Aviv. Through ICT, Leela simultaneously tends to her employer and continues to mother her children from afar. She explains that as soon as she finishes her morning routine with her employer, "I call my mother and daughters on the phone." Although she cannot be physically close to her children, Skype, Viber, and Facebook allow her to establish a source of ongoing support for her family. These platforms allow her to instill in her children the lessons she would otherwise teach were she in Nepal, while earning money for their education and the construction of a new house: "My younger daughter asks to tell her a story." When she starts, her daughter says, "'*Nachon, ima*! [that's right, Mom!].' I'm always worried about them and need to tell them what's good and bad. I tell them [about] good morals, read, don't go outside. . . . I tell them to eat apple, drink water. . . . I'm here and I have difficult work. I tell them I don't want them to have that—[I want them to] be [a] doctor, be [an] engineer." For Leela, continual communication with her daughters over Skype also allows her to monitor her kids while she earns money abroad so they can have greater class mobility. Beyond her family, Leela receives support from other Nepali caregivers in Israel, despite her remote work location. She notes, "[I do] Viber, Skype with friends in Israel when I have time. We do joint calls. This is life every day." Continual conversations with her family and social networks over ICT help Leela manage the emotional and physical difficulties of the job.

Workers also take part in ICT communities of care that create a shared sense of solidarity through humor. Maria notes that when her employer, who suffers from severe dementia, talks abusively to her or, as on a few occasions, attempts to slap her when Maria gives her meals, she uses humor to complain to her friends on Facebook. "We put a picture of our employer, [saying,] 'Look how this devil looks!'" she says. Community leaders working as caregivers in Palestine/Israel also use Facebook to promote upcoming events organized around and across lines of multiple affinities. The Facebook group "Overseas Filipino Lesbian and Gay International" is but one example of a contingent community based primarily on sexual orientation. With members living in many countries across the world, this closed group is a virtual space for socializing with LGBT Filipinx conationals and sharing experiences about working abroad while navigating sexuality in different national contexts. Similarly, one Facebook page dedicated to butch-identifying

Filipinx caregivers disseminates information about galas and fashion shows across Palestine/Israel. After events take place, the Facebook page also becomes a repository for event photos and videos, generating new affective responses among viewers and instantiating the page as a growing community.

Migrant married couples also receive care and emotional support over ICT in the face of Israel's ban on spousal migration. Kyra, a caregiver from India who works for a woman with Alzheimer's in Herzliya, says she uses WhatsApp throughout the day to communicate with her boyfriend, who works in the UAE. Because she is only allowed to take her vacation day once a month, communication with her boyfriend is a form of connectivity sustaining her for days at a time. Alongside communal alleviation of debt bondage, the joint leveraging of legal power, and the protection provided by formal and informal networks, online communities of care lessen the emotional impacts of worker atomization by fortifying the sharing of experiences that extend the spaces in which caregivers can find respite from work. ICT thus functions as a site for caregivers to prioritize the representation of their own experiences and needs for care rather than catering their actions to the whims and desires of their employers.

Visibility, Risk, and Anti-Blackness

The same night that the 2014 caregivers' rights protest took place in Tel Aviv, a much larger demonstration proceeded through the streets a few blocks away. Marching throughout the evening, hundreds of participants of an asylum-seeker-led action declared the start of a three-day general strike. Speakers called for states around the world to pressure the Israeli government to grant them refugee status, holding signs that read "Yes to Freedom, No to Jail" and "No More Prison," referring to the Holot detention center where asylum seekers were detained.[52] Unlike caregivers, who often position themselves as temporary, asylum seekers, by virtue of their very condition of de facto statelessness, cannot distance themselves from the perception that they desire and require permanent settlement. Despite the physical proximity of both protests, the two struggles have remained overwhelmingly separate. The differential positioning of asylum seekers and migrant caregivers within the state, and their distinctive relationship to permanent settlement and anti-Blackness, shapes how they ensure collective survival and articulate their demands.

Though deportation raids can happen at any time or place, the majority of activity occurs in Neve Sha'anan, where migrant workers are most collectively visible. In contrast to their employers' houses, where they live as individual workers throughout the week, Neve Sha'anan is where many migrant caregivers socialize during their days off, shop, catch up with friends, and send money to their families at one of many remittance offices. Home to Levinsky Park, a central spot for political organizing among Eritrean and Sudanese asylum seekers, the neighborhood offers lower rent than other quickly gentrifying areas of Tel Aviv and a chance for migrants and refugees to eat food from their home regions and inhabit a space where they face less atomization and surveillance. Within the neighborhood, caregivers live alongside migrant laborers from China and Thailand, working-class Mizrahi Jews, and, since 2005, asylum seekers from Eritrea and Sudan. Precisely because Neve Sha'anan is a vibrant center of migrant community life, it is also a site of surveillance and risk. Several migrant caregivers mentioned the lurking fear of deportation police in the Neve Sha'anan area, and the need to carefully navigate Takhana Merkazit, the Central Bus Station in the middle of Neve Sha'anan and a port of entry for migrants beginning their days off, as it is notorious for immigration police.

Against this backdrop of anti-Blackness and state anxieties over non-Jewish permanence, caregivers strategize the best forms of risk mitigation in the backstage arena. When I ask Brian whether he attended the caregiver rights protest, he notes that "mostly you will see the Filipino community here, we are concentrated on our work. During their occupancy, the Filipinos, they go to church, they are in their flats, that's all. We don't join Israeli protests." Two other caregivers said that they didn't attend due to fear that their employers, whom they must live with, would see them. These reactions hint at the threat that migrant communities face when perceived to be making collective demands of employers, as their legal link to the state, and the state itself. Keren, a Jewish Israeli advocacy worker organizing for migrants' rights, similarly articulates the lack of political space in Palestine/Israel for visible, collective migrant worker organizing. When I ask whether there are solidarity efforts across migrant worker sectors, and between migrant workers and asylum seekers, she notes, "There are many organizations in the community but we don't see an uprising or a grassroots situation—there are not many [political] organizers. We do see organizers in terms of helping with humanitarian situations and stuff like that but not really organized work. I think the issue is there are 56,000 caregivers and 53,000 employers. . . . I'm sorry to say that the only [cross-sector] solidarity that we really saw was when three migrant workers were killed in the last missile attack that we had. One of them was a caregiver." Referring to the deaths of Thai agricultural workers Weerawat Karunborirak and Sikarin Sa-ngamrum and Indian caregiver Soumya Santosh, Keren alludes to the limited political space for collective action amid the dangers of criminalization and deportation. As national helpers, migrant caregivers are "grievable" through a "biopolitical trope of innocent victims united against a demonized cast of 'Real Others.'"[53] Additionally, as Keren aptly describes, a near ubiquitous organizing problem domestic workers face is having multiple bosses and no shared workplace.

Memories of deportations and the imprisonment of well-known political organizers circulate among migrant caregivers. A Ghanaian migrant worker interviewed in a 2003 study on migrant organizing in Israel notes, for example, "We were invited to join the Histadruth, [the Israeli Trade Union] but it's too dangerous: A Filipino worker and a South American each tried to create a union for foreign workers, but each was sentenced to deportation."[54] Further indicating migrants' marginal political space for organizing within the state, Filipino community leader Elmer Cainday faced deportation not long after starting the Filipino Foreign Workers' Organization, a union that is part of a transnational Filipinx organization. Though the state has denied that the deportation of leaders is part of its official policy, as Israel Drori suggests, the government has "an undeclared goal of frightening foreign workers away from additional attempts to organize and claim their right."[55] Two months after Cainday's brother Albert replaced him as the leader, he too was arrested and deported.[56] In a news feature on the deportation of migrant leaders, Albert explains, "Nobody told me that was the reason, but the fact is that they didn't arrest me in the street just by chance. . . . The policeman who came to arrest me had an address, and they were holding a copy of the newspaper I edited, which had a picture of me. The deportation is part of the price I am paying for my activity. I know I'm not the first leader to be deported, and I'm probably not the last."[57] The consecutive deportations of the Cainday brothers concede the personal risk non-Jewish migrants absorb when they step into visible leadership roles. To be deported is not only to lose one's ability to earn a living in Palestine/Israel, but also to be removed without warning from community networks of kinship and care. An environment of fear thus underlies collective migrant gatherings.

The state's differential disciplining and management of Palestinians, migrant caregivers, and Eritrean and Sudanese asylum seekers reveals how non-Jewish populations are comparatively racialized in relation to labor demands and demographic management. Whereas Eritrean and Sudanese refugees draw upon the language of international human rights and refugee law to demand that the Israeli state grant them asylum, migrant caregivers at the 2014 protest drew on International Labor Organization Convention 189 on domestic workers' rights, focusing on the issue of labor over residency. Sara Ahmed suggests how migrants must prove they are not threats to the state by demonstrating they are worthy of inclusion through the productiveness of their labor. Through this demonstration, they will "receive the welcome they deserve."[58] The hierarchical categorization of "good" and "bad" noncitizens and nonsettlers thus suggests that it is through the "intensification of the border that the nation can be secured as an object of love, which can then be given to others."[59] In Palestine/Israel, where the nation as "object of love" cannot be fully given to others, deservedness is tied to productiveness of labor and degree of political distance from the state's temporal borders.

In contrast to the state's characterization of migrant caregivers as atomized, temporary workers, the government has criminalized Eritrean and Sudanese asylum seekers whose requests for permanent status they treat as a direct threat to the Zionist project.[60] This perceived threat has led to the imprisonment of asylum seekers, racist government statements, and a rise in hate crimes—including the firebombing of asylum seekers' apartments and a kindergarten attended by asylum seekers' children.[61] Since their arrival, the Israeli government has adopted a combined policy of extended incarceration without trial, sweeping harassment, and forced deportation.[62] Tellingly, the very reference to Eritrean and Sudanese asylum seekers as "infiltrators" stems from the 1954 Prevention of Infiltration Law designed to criminalize Palestinians attempting to reclaim their homes in the newly established State of Israel. Government statements by party leaders and Knesset debates regularly liken asylum seekers to Hezbollah and Palestinians in the Occupied West Bank and Gaza.[63] As Sharon Weinblum shows, such comparisons, evident in a 2010 speech by Prime Minister Benjamin Netanyahu, racialize asylum seekers in a similar way to Palestinians, painting both as inherently threatening: "We must also lay the infrastructure that will prevent the free movement of illegal infiltrators [crossing the borders from Egypt]. We are going to erect an obstacle in the South, as this issue is no less important for our national security than the other things I mentioned [on the topic of national security—i.e., Hezbollah and the Iranian threat]."[64] Such depictions contrast starkly with Netanyahu's reference to the presence of Filipinx caregivers as a "remarkable phenomenon in Israel" and a symbol of Israel-Philippines friendship.[65] Though racialized through distinctive relations of anti-Blackness and coloniality, Netanyahu's comments momentarily tie Eritrean and Sudanese asylum seekers to indigenous Palestinians through the perceived threat that their differently articulated claims to permanency pose to the Zionist project.

Zionist claims to exclusive Jewish sovereignty thus cast asylum seekers as outside "infiltrators" and indigenous Palestinians as threats from within. Notably, government representatives and right-wing citizens alike commonly to refer to Eritrean and Sudanese asylum seekers as "labor migrants" as a way of dismissing their claims to permanent settlement as refugees on the basis of international law.[66] As Yoav, a Jewish Israeli migrant advocacy worker notes, "In Israeli discourse . . . there is no legal reason for [asylum seekers] to stay here or even moral reason—they're 'illegal' migrant workers [to the government]. . . . There's no mercy for 'illegal' migrant workers—economic reasons are not good enough to migrate, that's the [Israeli government's] approach. . . . A lot of people say they came for economic reasons, and that's not a good enough reason to stay." Yoav's description reflects not only government attitudes toward asylum seekers in comparison to migrant caregivers, but also that of Israeli popular discourse. Beyond the vociferous protests in south Tel Aviv demanding asylum seekers be deported, a 2019 Center for International Migration and Integration (CIMI) report reveals that only 7 percent of Israelis believe asylum seekers have a permanent right to remain in Israel.[67] By contrast, migrant caregivers' presence evokes far less settler anxiety, even as they also face racism and exploitation.

These comparative forms of state racism and violence also travel across broader global circuits of anti-Blackness and Islamophobia that take a particularly gendered form in Palestine/Israel. Because migrant caregivers are predominantly women while asylum seekers are disproportionately men, the former are more often gendered within social discourse, print media, and government statements according to orientalist tropes of docility, while the latter are painted as sexual predators threatening the moral opprobrium and honor of Jewish women as biologically reproductive citizens.[68] Such rhetoric draws upon notions of Jewish female sexuality as the "vessel of reproduction" of the Jewish body politic, and a marker of racial continuity and purity, and asylum seekers as the "alien bodies" who wish to enter the body politic "from without."[69]

For migrant caregivers who have lived in Neve Sha'anan since before the arrival of asylum seekers in 2006, the criminalization of Eritrean and Sudanese inhabitants has led to a rise in policing in an area already flooded with deportation agents, an increase in racist media coverage of the neighborhood, and the transformation of Levinsky Park into a center of community-led political activism. Tellingly, a police station sits at the north end of Levinsky Park, feet away from several Sudanese, Eritrean, Ethiopian, Indian, Filipino, and Nepali restaurants and grocery stores. The differential positioning of asylum seekers and migrant caregivers in relation to the state, and the fears of association with a highly criminalized migrant population, was reflected in some migrant caregivers' depiction of their own presence in Palestine/Israel as "legal" and politically uncontroversial and that of Eritrean and Sudanese asylum seekers as "illegal." Some compared the "illegal" crossing of the Egyptian-Israeli border by asylum seekers to their own entry by visa, describing the agency fees they paid as a form of legal and financial legitimacy. Characterizations of asylum seekers as "illegal" also arose from the large percentage of Eritrean and Sudanese workers who are denied work permits and therefore work without documentation, earning income under poor labor conditions and many times being forced into situations of housing insecurity.[70]

While discussing asylum seekers, some workers attempted to express the distance and difference between migrant caregivers' location in Palestine/Israel and those of asylum seekers. When I asked Sana whether migrant caregivers and asylum seekers ever engage in joint political action, she responded: "We are not joined. Refugees have their own life and caregivers have their own life. It is Israelis' country and their rules they can follow as they like. When we come, we come only for five years, not seven, nine, ten." Sana adds that while migrant caregivers pay money to work in Palestine/Israel, asylum seekers "come for free." Notably, Sana contrasts the position of migrant caregivers with that of asylum seekers by emphasizing her own desire to return home to Nepal. This positioning parallels the state's own portrayal of migrant caregivers as "legally" doing temporary work that Israelis don't want to do, and that of asylum seekers' presence as comparatively more threatening to, in former Shas party leader Eli Yishai's words, "the Zionist dream."

The contrast in state responses to migrant caregivers and asylum seekers facing injury and violence is revealing in this respect. In a widely covered story from October 2015, Eritrean asylum seeker Haftom Zarhum was shot and beaten to death by Israeli security forces and a mob at a bus station in Be'er Sheva after being mistaken for a "terrorist." In rationalizing why they did not subsequently list him as a terror victim on their website, the Ministry of Defense indicated that it was because Haftom entered Israel "illegally."[71] In contrast, when Soumya Santosh, a caregiver from India, was killed by a Hamas fired rocket in May 2021, government officials were quick to reach out to her family and the Indian government alike, comparing her death to that of victims of the 2008 Mumbai attacks by Islamist organization Lashkar-e Taiba. Noting that "the whole country is mourning her loss," Israeli ambassador to India Ron Malka called the incident an "indiscriminate terror attack on innocent lives."[72] While Santosh's tragic death is grievable, and Santosh herself is included within the fold of national victimhood and innocence, the murder of Haftom, stemming from gratuitously violent anti-Blackness, is beyond grievability. In this context, "illegality" becomes a thinly veiled dog whistle for anti-Blackness.

Some caregivers also described a heightened sense of fear living in Neve Sha'anan, couched in anti-Black and Islamophobic rhetoric. Amita notes:

> It's not good for Israel. They come for nothing; they didn't pay anything. They are doing very bad things. Before they came I'd come home at two, three in the night, it's no problem. But two weeks ago I come to the park at ten at night. They are saying very bad things and following me . . . they don't know I know Arabic . . . I'm not afraid of them, and I asked, "What do you want?" If someone is coming I know what they will do . . . I think it's not good, the Sudan[ese] people. The woman is no problem, with the children, they are innocent. But men, the Muslims, they don't care about responsibility.

From a very different standpoint, Amita echoes particular government tropes that criminalize and hypersexualize Black migrant men, attributing a lack of safety in the neighborhood to the presence of Eritrean and Sudanese men. She also attributes to their presence an increase in muggings and theft caused by the rising cost of living in Tel Aviv, growing inequality, and municipal disinvestment:

It's a very big problem in Tel Aviv. One time they robbed my house. They know to follow us because we have money in the bags and we don't have a place to keep it. A lot of girls they steal from, they come on the bikes and they steal, even the passport. . . . If they want to stay, Israel can put them in camp and stay inside, not in the park. If we want to rest and go to the park, we cannot go to the park. They are very dirty. . . . It's not dirty before.

Such characterizations mystify the deteriorating economic conditions of south Tel Aviv that stem from decades of municipal neglect, gentrification, and state racism.[73] As Taj Haroun, a Sudanese asylum seeker and community activist, notes in a 2018 press interview, "[Because] we are the vulnerable people with no one to protect us, we became the scapegoat. . . . You can understand from the beginning that the plan of the government was to send everyone to south Tel Aviv because south Tel Aviv is considered the backend. There they have no responsibility, they don't have to take care of anyone."[74] A long history of government neglect of the area—one disproportionately inhabited by Mizrahi Jews—becomes pinned to asylum seekers through tropes of anti-Blackness perpetuated by the government and echoed among portions of the citizenry alike.

Though not expressed in sexualized terms, Brian's description similarly suggests a racialized anxiety about "the Africans," whom he also perceives as making the neighborhood more dangerous:

We don't have a relationship . . . there are some Israelis who are fighting for their rights. But for us, for the Filipinos living in [Neve Sha'anan] for six years, we didn't encounter problems when they were not in the area. But now the Filipinos, they're afraid. Caregivers walk in the evening, and you'll see how Filipina girls hold their bags. It's a dangerous place because in the evening, the Africans, not all of them, but many are snatching bags. I have experienced this also myself. They tried to take my bag . . . that's how I started to be scared of them also.

The accounts that Brian, Amita, and Sana offer also illustrate an anxiety about being associated with the nonpermanent population most stigmatized and marginalized by the Israeli government. Their accounts of Neve Sha'anan suggest how state power operates in a working-class migrant neighborhood, where national strategies of racial categorization and disinvestment disincentivize multiracial working-class solidarity. Anti-Black racism also circulates among employers, potentially impacting how migrant caregivers talk about their own presence inside the state. James points to the anti-Black racism of past employers, suggesting that they "always see Blacks as a negative sign—they don't care what they are facing." Such attitudes reinforce the notion of "good" and "bad" migrants, casting the former as hard-working, temporary, feminine, and "legal," and the latter as unwilling to work, permanent, "illegal," and masculine. While the former are associated with political neutrality, the latter are associated with political conflict at home and in Palestine/Israel.

Caregivers' strategies of service provision, legal defense, and community care are in important ways a "diagnostic of power" revealing the landscape of risk produced through settler colonial capitalism.[75] As part of its core logic, the very production of categories such as "asylee" and "migrant" create a tier of deservedness within the imperially imposed borders of the nation.[76] State policies differentiating between Black asylum seeking populations and South and Southeast Asian migrant populations are inextricable from the "racial coding of immigration policies" and border regulations, in the context of not only Israeli settler colonialism but also middle and high-income states benefiting from the labor of migrants under structural adjustment.[77] This coding shapes the topography of risk that caregivers negotiate outside employers' homes and the many ways workers unsettle their instrumentalization by the state. Absent cross-sector alliances, union power, or legal mechanisms for mitigating the risks of temporary labor, such collective action, even if desirable, comes with substantial risk and danger, both long- and short-term. Against conceptions of individual "everyday resistances" as diametrically opposed to collective action, migrant caregivers demonstrate how collective networks of care capacitate the navigation of risk and contestation of abuse within the employer-employee relationship.[78] These everyday forms of emotional support are not a replacement for collective political demands on the state made by those with the least to lose, yet they allow workers to increase their bargaining power, improving their material conditions and establishing collective forms of life against and beyond the state.

Epilogue

Since the start of the global pandemic, caregivers, front-line workers, and feminist commentators have emphasized that while the era of COVID-19 is an exceptional period of heightened disparity and loss, it is not itself the genesis of a care crisis. By "care crisis" I refer not only to the lack of adequate childcare, eldercare, and health-care resources for those who need it, nor to the lack of remuneration for those providing these services. While "care crisis" encompasses these terms, it also denotes the ways that state violence, colonialism, ongoing capital accumulation, and the racialized and gendered segmentation of labor markets structurally shape the need for and access to care. In Palestine/Israel, the extenuating health inequities that the pandemic has wrought across settler, native, and migrant populations demystify the differential allocation and depletion of resources that are central to Israel's reproductive regime under "regular" times. Since the onset of COVID-19, Israeli forms of colonial-capital accumulation have persisted in the form of land confiscation, house demolitions, and the withholding of medical and economic resources.[1] Israeli authorities have continued to annex land and demolish homes in the West Bank; block access to medical care, food distribution, and clinics; conduct home arrests; administer surveillance technology throughout the occupied Palestinian Territories (OPT); and imprison Palestinian detainees in facilities without COVID safety precautions in place.[2] These developments have worsened the economic insecurity of already precarious families and communities in the West Bank and Gaza while providing further pretense for surveillance and military incursion by Israeli authorities.[3]

The pandemic has similarly surfaced the differential exposure to exhaustion and burnout that migrant caregivers face during "non-crisis" times. Though I periodize my project as one that is prepandemic, questions around who the state sees as worthy of care have been brought into sharp relief since March 2020. One interviewee I spoke to during the spring of 2021, Kamal, suggested how his day-to-day routines have changed little under COVID. For Kamal, the pandemic is not the root cause of the intensity of time he spends in isolation at his place of employment, even as it has exacerbated these conditions. Kamal explains,

> I was also working weekends and . . . if someone is willing to pay us *shishi/shabbat* [Friday/Saturday], that's extra money for us. And my conditions was I was working already on *shishi/shabbat*—full time I was working. Once a month, twice a month I take only one day off. I have community friends, I ask them, "How are you?" We don't feel—I don't feel it that much. If you look from the outside, the world is on lockdown, the street is empty, the coffee shop is empty, coming from the outside. But we don't feel that much pressure of this COVID because we are already—if people are already involved with the family, have intimacy with the family, the patients, I don't think they feel that so much.

Kamal locates COVID as a moment of intensification in his regular working conditions rather than a wholly new set of demands on his labor. He qualifies his experiences under COVID, noting that for caregivers whose employers do not pay overtime, the pandemic has enabled the additional extraction of unpaid labor. Kamal also stresses how difficult the mental load can be for caregivers who are not allowed to leave their employers' home: "Every week taking off [work] for them—it's difficult because the people were in fear. Not only caregivers; the world was in fear because we didn't know what was going to happen at that time. Somehow the psychological effect—everybody is effected by that and we are also." Kamal's experiences ask us to consider how the crises of care that COVID unveils have their genesis in a settler colonial labor market that relies in different ways upon both land theft and the production of value by non-Jewish temporary migrants. Kamal describes his first job in Palestine/Israel in 2012 as a process of slowly getting used to the isolation and loneliness of working round-the-clock inside his employer's home. He explains, "If tomorrow somebody put me in a jail, I have to act as a prisoner; if we have to do something and there's no other option, we deal with it. So there were no other options at that time." His description contextualizes his COVID experiences, suggesting that he has found creative ways of navigating what have already been difficult and isolating conditions over a period of nine years.

I name these continuities not to take away from the enormous loss of life wrought by the pandemic, nor the exacerbation of mental stress, financial loss, and increased exposure to injury for workers. As migrant rights advocacy worker Keren explains, the isolation specific to in-home caregiving was made more extreme due to COVID restrictions:

> So the two things were you couldn't take a day off, you couldn't go back home for vacation, and everyone was very afraid for their parents and siblings. And the situation was where caregivers were not given any rest within the family, were working extra hours they were not getting paid for, and also because during lockdown the regulations constricted them to stay in their employer's apartment, one hundred meters close. It's not like they sat all day and did nothing, but many of them were not being paid for these hours because they were expected to stay anyway. So this was one of the biggest problems that we saw during COVID.

In addition to the exacerbation of labor extraction and isolation, some caregivers have also faced increased financial precarity due to the unpredictable closing of borders. Keren explains that "the second thing that we saw [under COVID] was caregivers that were stuck abroad after they went for maternity leave or sick leave or just visiting home. Until today there are many of them that can not come back to Israel. So we saw people that paid thousands of dollars for brokerage fees to come to Israel but they couldn't finish the four years and three months because they couldn't come back." Keren notes that caregivers' lack of insurance coverage for mental health issues has been especially difficult under COVID, creating obstacles to case work.

The ruptures Keren identifies are also present in public debates about the elderly and the meaning of care within Israeli society. In a February 2021 opinion piece in Israeli news outlet Walla, Doron Raz, Chairman of the Association of Nursing Services Providers, suggests how COVID has made plain, rather than created, crises of care that have always existed. Raz states that "every 55 hours, the body of a helpless elderly man is discovered in Israel. Without corona the situation would have been worse . . . were it not for the coronavirus, apparently the plight of the elderly would have continued to be ignored by decision makers."[4] Later in the piece, Raz underscores how the pandemic presents Israel with "an opportunity to improve the treatment that the founding generation deserves." The COVID-related care dilemmas Raz raises are a lens into the workings of Israel's reproductive regime as it unfolds through the triangulation of migrant labor, settler emplacement, and indigenous dispossession and resistance. Invoking the "the founding generation," Raz frames the duty to care for (Jewish Israeli) elderly as an extension of their value as witnesses to—and agents of—the birth of the state. Explicitly excluded from this framing are elderly Palestinian witnesses to and resistors of the Nakba, whose own right to end-of-life dignity is obviated when care is predicated upon one's status as a "founder." Though beyond the ambit of Raz's essay, his emphasis on the "founding generation" also confesses the uneven ways that resources required for social reproduction are distributed across settler, indigenous, and migrant populations. These resources include childcare, eldercare, care for the disabled, community care, freedom from state violence, economic security, adequate housing, freedom of movement, and the right to a collective identity.

Interestingly, even as Raz echoes tropes of Jewish Israeli exceptionalism, he also suggests how the state does not, in fact, adequately care for its elderly citizens, citing the shamefully inadequate care that they themselves have received during the pandemic.[5] Indeed, as evidenced in the 30 percent of Holocaust survivors who live under the poverty line—a number that has expanded under neoliberal restructuring—population-level priorities of investment and disinvestment instrumentalize even those bodies whose need of legitimate care and protection serve to justify the state's existence.[6] Following what Gabriel Piterberg identifies as a liberal Zionist pattern of critique, Raz names the lack of adequate care for the elderly as an aberration rather than a byproduct of austerity measures that are inseparable from the siphoning off of health-care resources—and the resources necessary for social reproduction—from Gaza, the West Bank, and Palestinians within Israel 1948.[7]

Such examples belie how nationalist narratives shape perceptions of who is the deserving subject of care. The impact of the ongoing occupation on elderly Palestinians—both in OPT and in communities around the world—reveals the effects of ethnic cleansing, militarization, and displacement on access to adequate care at the end of one's life.[8] So, too, has the pandemic exacerbated these conditions among displaced populations already resisting state violence and among workers disproportionately subjected to injury due to the nature of their work. Under COVID, the high representation of Filipinx migrants in home care, eldercare, and nursing has exacerbated their chances of injury and illness, "expos[ing] the elder care industry's exploitation of racialized migrant workers and the government's neglect in protecting them."[9]

In the same vein, the pandemic also lays bare how activists from the Philippines to Palestine have long fought the ravages of colonialism and labor exploitation as part of the same struggle. As Migrante International's most recent May Day statement explains, "The Filipino labor and migrant movements both have a rich anti-imperialist and nationalist history," one that fights against state austerity measures, colonialism, the ongoing US military presence in the Philippines, authoritarianism, structural adjustment, and the exploitation of workers abroad as part of the same fight.[10] Likewise, the recent May 2021 strike that spread across the OPT was the latest in a genealogy of Palestinian workers organizing against the inextricability of labor exploitation and colonial occupation.[11] Taking up an explicitly gendered lens, in a February 2020 statement, Palestinian feminist movement Tal'at members Hala Marshood and Riya Alsanah affirmed, "In addition to posing a direct threat to life and social reproduction, to further entrench its control, Israel has strategically worked to crush and fragment Palestinians socially, politically and economically. . . . An actuality which cannot be sidelined from this matrix of oppression, is the systematic crippling of Palestinian economic development and the engineering [of] Palestinians, including women, into a cheap and exploitable workforce."[12] Marshood and Alsanah's statement suggests how the accumulation of resources required for social reproduction takes place, in part, through the gendered racialization of the workforce. Under COVID, the "direct threat to life and social reproduction" is doubly pronounced, as Israeli forces have seized the moment of crisis to exact more extensive forms of surveillance.[13]

Indeed, the COVID pandemic underscores in other ways how migrant eldercare is intertwined with Israeli militarism and colonial expansion. During the pandemic, the Israeli government tasked a special Israel Defense Forces (IDF) unit, entitled the Guards of Gold, with caring for the elderly.[14] Tellingly, pro-Israel public relations group StandWithUs, an organization whose mission is to "ensure that Israel's side of the story is told in communities, campuses, libraries, the media and church," has covered the work of the Guards of Gold in its media campaigns.[15] To this effect, a March 2020 StandWithUs Facebook post features a picture of two hands clasping each other, one aged and wrinkled, and the other, youthful. Under the photograph in large font reads the caption, "The Israel Defense Force has stepped up to take care of the elderly in the country during the coronavirus crisis." The Facebook caption next to the picture reads, "*Kol Hakavod* [well done] and thank you to the Israel Defense Forces." Immediately underneath the heading is the StandWithUs logo in blue and white, Israel's national colors.[16]

Underwriting this figurative and literal image of military care for the elderly is a form of moral exceptionalism that appears in other media outlets covering the plight of elderly Jewish Israelis during the pandemic. An April 2020 opinion piece by Jerusalem-based pundit Renee Garfinkel also invokes the Guards of Gold as exemplary of the exceptional love and respect Israel shows its vulnerable elderly. Comparing treatment of the elderly in Europe and the United States to that in Israel, Garfinkel notes that "the Secret Service protects the US president. Teenage army draftees in the IDF, Guards of Gold, protect Israel's elders. Society chooses to provide special protection to certain citizens not just because of their vulnerability, but also because of their importance." Garfinkel then draws on this purported difference to contextualize European critiques of Israeli human rights, noting, "Europe has a nasty habit of wagging its high-minded finger at Israel. During the pandemic, Europe ought to look to Israel for moral guidance." The piece also suggests that "under stress, Europe is reverting to its long history of deeming some groups worthy of life; others, not so much. Eugenics flourished at the turn of the 20th century. . . . Happily, Israel is not Europe."[17] Garfinkel unironically distinguishes Israel from Europe by suggesting that the latter preserves hierarchies of race, nationality, and colonial status, while Israel rejects such eugenic commitments. Garfinkel's selective retelling of Israeli histories of race-making suggests how state responses to the pandemic have updated familiar tropes of Israeli exceptionalism to the present moment of crisis, from those around the "humane" treatment of the vulnerable to the techno-scientific excellence of vaccine development.

As in the years prior to the pandemic, since March 2020, Israeli state officials have painted migrant caregivers as a lifeline to Israel's most vulnerable citizens. In September 2020, Israeli Minister of Foreign Affairs Gabi Ashkenazi announced the government decision to increase the number of visas for home care residents from Nepal and Georgia, suggesting that this influx would "ensure national resilience" and serve as a "protective shield for nursing home residents." Evocative of "Operation Protective Edge" and "Operation Defensive Shield," both deadly military campaigns that the IDF carried out in the OPT, Ashkenazi's description likens caregivers to a military asset protecting the state. In the same announcement, Minister for Social Equality Meirav Cohen states that "until we succeed in recruiting local manpower for these tasks, and in view of the urgent requirements [under COVID-19], this decision is unavoidable and represents an oxygen tank that will enable the proper functioning of the institutions that care for our elderly."[18] Cohen's metaphorical invocation of caregivers likens migrants to the lungs of the Israeli institutions whose capacity to assist the "founding generation"—and the elderly more broadly—has been severely hampered by the pandemic.

In reality, the heroizing of migrant caregivers that Ashkenazi and Cohen take up reinforces the imperative workers face to individually absorb the responsibility of tending to the aged, thereby avoiding the "unethical" practice of refusing extracontractual work. But the structural inability to easily refuse work is part of a biopolitical regime managing access to the preservation of "life itself." Here "life," as Heike Schotten argues, is not a "prepolitical" biological category but rather a moral one, where the very meaning of Palestinian "life" emerges through the dialectical construction of settler society as "good," "rational," and morally worthy.[19] Through Israel's reproductive regime, Palestinian life becomes an "immoral" threat to Jewish Israeli collective "life itself," in the form of settler futurity. The unquestioned vulnerability of Jewish Israeli elderly and their right to individual and collective health over that of other populations must be read through this broader moralizing regime.

In response to the heroizing of frontline workers, since the onset of the pandemic, media outlets globally have featured stories of overworked and underpaid hospital workers, op-eds about nursing home staff unable to adequately care for the elderly, and editorials about underfunded hospitals. Feminist critics globally have called for the adequate remuneration of caregivers and revaluation of their work and, at times, for the socialization of care, both proposals that are crucial to the betterment of workers' immediate conditions. While they are key points in broadening public discussions around reproductive labors, in the Israeli context, both proposals leave untouched the modes of deliberate devitalization and uneven resource allocation that fundamentally constitute the Israeli state as a settler project. Further, as the "conquest of labor" period suggests, socialist commitments to shared labor responsibilities that are expressed through the language of Zionism reinforce a European Jewish vanguardism while fundamentally dispossessing indigenous populations of land and resources. Other public debates have centered on the gendered allocation of care work, another important lynchpin in the valuation of care. Yet such debates leave unaddressed how gendered and sexualized constructions of settler-citizens and their national roles have played a central role in building and maintaining the state. This is as true for the "pioneering" Ashkenazi woman central to Zionist mythology as the virile Ashkenazi "New Jew" "strengthening" the land through manual labor.

Fundamentally, addressing the exacerbation in working conditions that migrant caregivers face requires squaring with the twin forms of colonial-capital accumulation undergirding Israel's care crisis—global colonial histories of labor outsourcing, on the one hand, and Israel's ongoing campaign to amass Palestinian land and resources while taking Palestinian life, on the other. Yet, as I suggest in chapters 4 and 5, the assertion of such a critique is not necessarily desirable to temporary non-Jewish migrants, nor is it individually strategic to those workers who most readily face deportation and debt. Speaking to the risks of migrant advocacy efforts, during a follow-up interview with Abigail, she explained why she no longer publicly speaks out against the high fees recruitment agencies charge. Just before we met, a friend had encouraged her to speak to a reporter for an exposé on recruitment agencies in Israel, telling her, "You'll be a hero!" Abigail explains that, though she would have once agreed to talk to reporters about this phenomenon, she now realized that doing so carried too many risks. Authorities would perhaps "forgive her," she explained, for exposing the exploitative practices of agencies at first, but "once [coverage] fades, that's the time they'll do something."

Though focusing on the role of agencies, Abigail's point holds for critiques of other Israeli state policies and colonial practices. Many of the workers whose narratives make up this book are no longer in Palestine/Israel. Rina eventually migrated to Canada, working at first as a live-out caregiver in a senior living facility and then at an Amazon warehouse. Sam and Ita moved to Portugal, where—unlike in Israel—they are permitted to be married to each other. Nina has plans to return home to Kathmandu to reunite with her nineteen-year-old son, an aspiring DJ who was three when she first left him. Leela moved back to Nepal to work in the tourism industry, and Kyra returned to West Bengal to build a home for her aging parents. Migrant caregivers' temporal connection to the Israeli state shapes not only the risk of speaking out against it; for those who have left, it shapes the very ordering of political priorities. For Abigail, pressure against Israel must therefore come from those outside of the state with the least to lose and, importantly, must take into account the differential degrees of historical power held by migrant-sending and migrant-receiving states. As Abigail explains, "That's how they did it with [migrant] children's rights. They brought pressure from outside Israel. . . . And you know, it really works when the international community pressures the country so the politicians will get a sermon and be pressured by the president or higher-ranking officials. Because it's already our country that is at stake."

NOTES

Introduction

1   I use the terms "Palestine," "Israel," and "Palestine/Israel" in different
contexts throughout the book. When referring to ongoing settler colonial
logics propagated by the Israeli government, I draw on the term "Israel."
A central aim of this project is to show how everyday modes of settler
colonial governance unfold in ways that naturalize and take for granted
Israel's declared borders while treating the occupied Palestinian Territories of the West Bank, Gaza, and East Jerusalem as the sole location of
colonial displacement. When I use the term "Palestine" I am referring to
the historic land of Palestine prior to Zionist colonization, dispossession,
and settlement and to ongoing efforts to recognize the territory within Israel's declared borders as part of this land. Finally, combining these two
meanings, at times I use the term "Palestine/Israel" when denaturalizing
and naming ongoing settler practices while also denoting the territory
within which migrant caregivers are subjected to the strictures of Israeli
labor and citizenship laws. The most blatant, recent example of these settler colonial practices has occurred since this book went into production,
as Israel undertakes a project of genocide in Gaza with the backing of the
United States government. In the aftermath of the October 7, 2023, attack
by Hamas, which followed a seventy-five-year occupation, and the killing of
1,200 Israelis, Israel has indiscriminately bombed the Gaza Strip, including
hospitals, schools, and civilian neighborhoods. As of May 22, 2024, Israeli
bombs and its ground invasion had killed more than 35,000 Palestinians,
disproportionately children, according to the Gaza Health Ministry. Since

this book was already written when these events unfolded, I am unable to more thoroughly address them throughout each chapter. That said, these events further highlight the naked brutality of Israel's settler colonial regime and the impunity with which it acts.

2   Masalha, "Settler-Colonialism, Memoricide and Indigenous Toponymic Memory."

3   Glass, *From New Zion*, 219. Following Rabab Abdulhadi, I use the term "indigenous Palestinian" to reference "the totality of the Palestinian people, whether they became refugees after being expelled from their land by Zionist militias when Israel was founded in 1948 or they live under Israel's colonial rule in the areas defined as such in 1948 and 1967." Abdulhadi, "Israeli Settler Colonialism in Context," 542.

4   Brodsky et al., *65+ Population*. In Israeli Central Bureau of Statistics and National Insurance Institute literature, the term "elderly" denotes those age sixty-five and older.

5   Harper and Zubida, "Living on Borrowed Time," 108.

6   After four years and three months, migrant caregivers can work in short-term arrangements as substitute caregivers (known as "relievers") for workers who go on vacation, for up to thirty days at a time, until sixty-three months after their arrival. Otherwise, they can apply for a special visa to care for the "extremely severely" disabled, which they can renew until sixty-three months, or until the employer they work for at or after this juncture passes away. See PIBA, *Foreign Workers' Rights Handbook*, 16.

7   Following reforms to the Law of Return in 1970, grandchildren of Jews and their immediate family members may also apply for the "right of return." See Adalah, "Law of Return."

8   Ben-Israel, *Revisiting CEDAW's Recommendations*.

9   Arlosoroff, "Filipina Workers"; Margalit, "Israel's Invisible Filipino Workforce"; Hotline for Migrant Workers, "Children of Migrant Workers."

10   Kav LaOved, "New State Deposit Fund."

11   PIBA, *Foreign Workers' Rights Handbook*.

12   ACRI, "Slavery Law."

13   These areas include the Peripheral Region, Central Region, and Tel Aviv Region. See PIBA, *Foreign Workers' Rights Handbook*.

14   Rifkin, "Settler Common Sense."

15   Bailey, *Butch Queens Up in Pumps*, 19; Francisco-Menchavez, *Labor of Care*.

16   Mohanty, "Women Workers," 5. For a discussion of the treatment of Ethiopian Jews in Palestine/Israel in comparison to Vietnamese refugees, see Gandhi, *Archipelago of Resettlement*.

17   Willen, *Fighting for Dignity*, 8.

18   Here I take a cue from Lisa Lowe's conceptualization of intimacy as "scenes of close connection in relation to a global geography that one more often conceives in terms of vast spatial distances" (*Intimacies*, 18) and David Eng's notion of the "racialization of intimacy" as "the collective ways by which race becomes occluded within the private domain of private family and kinship today" (*Feeling of Kinship*, 10).

19   I take a cue from Kevin Bruyneel's concept of a "third space of sovereignty," a site on the boundaries of colonial governmentality and Native sovereignty that is neither external nor internal to the colonial state's jurisdiction and reach. See Bruyneel, *Third Space of Sovereignty*.

20   According to a 2022 interministerial Knesset staff report, of the 46,000 citizens eligible to hire migrant caregivers, only 6,000 receive entitlement through the disability benefit, and another 750 according to the disabled child benefit. Knesset, "Staff Report."

21   I am grateful to Rhacel Salazar Parreñas for suggesting this term, which broadens my original formulation of the "coloniality of reproductive labor."

22   See Giacaman et al., "Politics of Childbirth"; Hasso, *Buried in the Red Dirt*; Kanaaneh, *Birthing the Nation*; Yuval-Davis, "National Reproduction." Abdulhadi further discusses the "gendered and sexualized narrative of the defeat, subjugation, and submission of Palestinians" ("Israeli Settler Colonialism in Context," 559).

23   Hasso, *Buried in the Red Dirt*.

24   See Jiryis on land expropriation in the years following the Nakba and for a broader discussion of these processes of "Judaization." Mahmani, leader of the Jewish National Fund from 1935 to 1965, authored the "Project for the Judaization of the Galilee." Jiryis, "Land Question in Palestine," 12. See also Nakhleh, "Two Galilees."

25   On this topic see Griffiths and Repo, "Biopolitics and Checkpoint 300"; Giacaman et al., "Politics of Childbirth"; Abusneineh, "(Re)producing the Israeli (European) Body"; Joronen and Griffiths, "Affective Politics of Precarity"; Kanaaneh, *Birthing the Nation*; Kravel-Tovi, "National Mission"; Parsons and Salter, "Israeli Biopolitics"; Shalhoub-Kevorkian, "Stolen Childhood"; Willen, "Citizens, 'Real' Others."

26   Grassiani, "Families in Arms."

27 Lentin, *Traces of Racial Exception*; Said, *Covering Islam*.

28 I use the terms "unsettled" and "unsettling" interchangeably.

29 Eshkol, "Eshkol: A Reply to Nasser," 53.

30 Tuck and Yang, "Decolonization Is Not a Metaphor," 4; Arvin, Tuck, and Morrill, "Decolonizing Feminism"; Wynter, "Unsettling the Coloniality of Being"; Abdo and Yuval-Davis, "Palestine, Israel."

31 Murphy, "Unsettling Care," 722, drawing on Unsettling Minnesota, *Unsettling Ourselves*.

32 Kauanui, "A Structure, Not an Event," drawing on Wolfe, "Settler Colonialism." See also Gnaidek, "Times of Settler Colonialism."

33 Hilal, "Rethinking Palestine," 2; Khalidi, *Hundred Years' War*; Tamari, "Normalcy and Violence"; Abu El-Haj, *Facts on the Ground*; Elia, *Greater than the Sum*; Salamanca et al., "Past Is Present."

34 Tamari, "Normalcy and Violence"; Ayyash, *Hermeneutics of Violence*, 203.

35 Chatterjee, "Immigration, Anti-racism," 647.

36 Byrd draws on the term "arrivant," building on the work of Kamau Brathwaite, as a "process" rather than "an identificatory category to claim alongside settler, Native, slave, savage, or settler ally." Byrd, "Weather with You," 210.

37 Tuck and Yang, "Decolonization Is Not a Metaphor," 18.

38 Trask, "Settlers of Color."

39 Englert, "Settlers, Workers."

40 Gandhi develops this term in relation to Vietnamese refugees in Palestine/Israel and Guam. *Archipelago of Resettlement*, 4.

41 Chatterjee, "Immigration, Anti-racism." On the positioning of (im)migrant/settler/Native subjectivities, see Day, *Alien Capital*; Byrd, "Weather with You"; Lawrence and Dua, "Decolonizing Antiracism"; Saranillo, "Why Asian Settler Colonialism Matters"; Pulido, "Geographies of Race"; Madokoro, "Peril and Possibility"; Thrush, *Indigenous London*; Glenn, "Settler Colonialism as Structure"; Karuka, *Empire's Tracks*; Sharma and Wright, "Decolonizing Resistance."

42 Rifkin, *Beyond Settler Time*.

43 Willen, "Citizens, 'Real' Others."

44 For this reason, Israel has granted refugee status to less than 1 percent of Eritrean and Sudanese asylum seekers. Raijman, "Warm Welcome for Some."

45   Kaplan, "Manifest Domesticity"; Yuval-Davis, "National Reproduction."

46   Day, "Settler Colonialism."

47   Tadiar, "Uneven Times."

48   Busbridge, "Messianic Time," 5.

49   Parreñas, *Unfree*.

50   Lori, *Offshore Citizens*.

51   On temporality, migration, and waiting, see Bryan, "Wait and While You Wait, Work"; Auyero, *Patients of the State*; Ibañez Tirado, "We Sit and Wait"; Lori, *Offshore Citizens*; Mountz, "Where Asylum-Seekers Wait."

52   Ahmad, *Everyday Conversions*.

53   See also Jackson, "Belonging against the National Odds"; Harper and Zubida, "Living on Borrowed Time."

54   On the legal construction of migrant care work in Palestine/Israel (a concept I expand in chapter 2), see Mundlak and Shamir, "Between Intimacy and Alienage."

55   Exceptions are extremely rare and include permanent residency through marriage to a Jewish Israeli citizen and an Orthodox conversion, followed by an application for citizenship. In 2006, the government said that children of non-Jewish migrant workers who were born in Israel, or who have been in Israel for six years, could receive status. This led to nine hundred children being regularized and granted eligibility for citizenship application upon turning twenty-one or serving in the Israel Defense Forces. In 2009, deportations of migrant children began, and in 2013, a decision similar to that of 2006 was made. See Hotline for Migrant Workers, "Children of Migrant Workers."

56   Willen, *Fighting for Dignity*, 118; Jackson, "Belonging against the National Odds."

57   Ahmad, *Everyday Conversions*.

58   On Christian Zionism among migrant workers, see also Liebelt, *Caring for the "Holy Land"*; Kemp and Raijman, "Christian Zionists"; Jackson, "This Is Not the Holy Land."

59   Ahmed, *Cultural Politics*, 134.

60   Tuck and Yang, "Decolonization Is Not a Metaphor."

61   Abu El-Haj, *Facts on the Ground*. See also Abdo, *Women in Israel*; Yuval-Davis, "National Reproduction."

62   Anderson, *Imagined Communities*.

63   Parreñas, "Indenture of Migrant Domestic Workers."

64   Constable, "Tales of Two Cities"; Banerjee et al., *Assessing the Changes*.

65   Chin, *In Service and Servitude*; Lee, *Service Economies*; Truong and Quesada-Bondad, "Intersectionality"; Constable, "Tales of Two Cities."

66   Constable, "Sexuality and Discipline."

67   Chen, *Marginalized*; Parreñas, *Unfree*.

68   Parreñas and Silvey, "Precarity of Migrant Domestic Work."

69   Parreñas and Silvey, "Precarity of Migrant Domestic Work."

70   Workforce Development Agency, "Work Qualifications." Parreñas, "Unfree."

71   Ben-Israel, *Revisiting CEDAW's Recommendations*; Arlosoroff, "Filipina Workers"; Berkovitch, "Motherhood as National Mission"; Kanaaneh, *Birthing the Nation*.

72   Senor and Singer, *Start-Up Nation*.

73   Hughes, "Unbounded Territoriality," 217.

74   Ahmad, *Everyday Conversions*.

75   OECD, "Spending on Long-Term Care." This data is based upon thirty-five reporting countries.

76   Kemp, *Reforming Policies on Foreign Workers*; Halperin, "Aging, Family, and Preferences," citing Bar-Zuri, *Holders of Permits*. This data comes from 2010 and, given the growth in the elderly population, is a low estimate for the contemporary percentage. See also Arlosoroff, "World's Highest Rate," drawing on Tamir and Avraham, "Minimizing the Use of Foreign Workers."

77   By comparison, only 20.3 percent of employers in a study of migrant domestic workers in Lebanon hired workers explicitly to do eldercare, and 19.5 percent hired workers to tend to the disabled. ILO, *Study of Employers*. In Jordan, many migrant women also work in the garment industry. ILO, *Migrant Domestic and Garment Workers*.

78   As measured by the UN, the "Western Asia" region includes Armenia, Azerbaijan, Bahrain, Cyprus, Georgia, Iraq, Israel, Jordan, Kuwait, Lebanon, Oman, Qatar, Saudi Arabia, Palestine, Syria, Turkey, UAE, and Yemen. See United Nations DESA, *World Population Ageing 2019*.

79   Brodsky et al., *65+ Population in Israel*, drawing on Central Bureau of Statistics, National Insurance Institute, Ministry of Health, and Ministry of Labor and Social Affairs data.

80   This estimate is based on a growth rate of elderly age seventy-five and older between 2002 and 2007 and the rate of increase of government-issued permits for migrant caregivers. Eckstein, *Subcommittee on Foreign Workers*.

81 Busbridge draws the distinction between civic and ethnic settler states. "Settler Colonial 'Turn,'" 107–8. See also Robinson, who argues that Israel is a liberal settler state (*Citizen Strangers*).

82 For a discussion on Israeli efforts to be seen as a "normal" liberal state and to be seen simultaneously as exceptional, see Lloyd, "State of Exception." In the Israeli Declaration of the Establishment of the State of Israel, the right to establish "a national home for the Jewish people" is derived from the "natural and historic right" of Jews to "Eretz-Israel," or the biblical land of Israel. Though equal social and political rights for non-Jews are invoked, these rights are to be distributed in service of the "Ingathering of Exiles" and the "establishment of a Jewish state." Though Israel has no constitution, its Basic Laws, which serve functionally as its constitution, reaffirm that Israel is "a Jewish democratic state." Masri, "Colonial Imprints."

83 Adalah, "Discriminatory Laws Database"; Ben-Youssef and Tamari, "Enshrining Discrimination."

84 Knesset, "Basic Law—Israel"; Pappé, *Ethnic Cleansing*.

85 Day, "Settler Colonialism"; Hughes, "Unbounded Territoriality"; Abu-Laban and Bakan, *Israel, Palestine, and the Politics of Race*. Importantly, following Bhandar, I do not suggest by this comparison that settler states such as the United States, Australia, and Canada no longer expropriate indigenous land. Bhandar, *Colonial Lives of Property*. I also do not suggest that Israel is "singular or exceptional among settler colonies" but, rather, that borders and annexation in Palestine/Israel form a central part of ongoing public debates within settler society itself. Hughes, "Unbounded Territoriality," 228.

86 Clarno, *Neoliberal Apartheid*; Lloyd and Wolfe, "Settler Colonial Logics"; Veracini, "Settler Collective," citing Lawson, *Unhomely States*, 157.

87 Clarno, *Neoliberal Apartheid*; Farsakh, *Palestinian Labour Migration*. See also Hilal, "Rethinking Palestine."

88 Clarno, *Neoliberal Apartheid*; Farsakh, *Palestinian Labour Migration*. This post-Oslo period has also seen the "NGOisation" of the Palestinian women's movement, as an emphasis on "good governance" under pressure from international donors has replaced certain segments of the grassroots left. Jad, "NGOs," 622, drawing on Alvarez, "Women's Movements"; Kuttab, "Palestinian Women's Movement."

89 See Jamal, *Arab Minority Nationalism*; Shalhoub-Khevorkian, *Security Theology*; Pappé, "Shtetl Colonialism." Due to Israel's strategy of blatant and ongoing expansion—and the high percentage of indigenous as compared to settler citizens (approximately 21 percent of Israeli citizens are Palestinian, according to Haddad Haj-Yahya et al., "Statistical Report on

Arab Society in Israel")—Jewish Israelis' relationship to Palestinians is in many ways discursively distinct from the settler-Native relation in the United States. See Sayegh, "Zionist Colonialism in Palestine"; Hughes, "Unbounded Territoriality"; Veracini, "Settler Collective"; Piterberg, *Returns of Zionism*.

90   Bartram, "Foreign Workers, Refugees."

91   Gandhi, *Archipelago of Resettlement*.

92   Kravel-Tovi, "'National Mission,'" 74. This survivalist logic has justified the Knesset's annual renewal of a state of emergency since 1967. On this topic, see also Lentin, *Traces of Racial Exception*; Lloyd, "State of Exception"; Pappé, "Shtetl Colonialism"; Yiftachel, *Ethnocracy*. State laws, policies, and protocols that follow from this defensive stance have been given as justification for house demolitions, prevention of Palestinian family reunification, extrajudicial killings of Palestinians, administrative detention of Palestinians without trial, expropriation of Palestinian Bedouin land in the Naqab, censoring of Palestinians' right to free speech, and ongoing military attacks. Hilal, "Rethinking Palestine"; Sa'di, "Modernization as an Explanatory Discourse"; Gordon and Ram, "Ethnic Cleansing"; Zureik, *Israel's Colonial Project*; Rouhana, *Palestinian Citizens*; Shalhoub-Kevorkian, *Militarization and Violence*.

93   On the role of international law in ongoing colonization, see Erakat, *Justice for Some*.

94   Lebovitch and Friedman, *Black Money*.

95   Kemp, "Labor Migration and Racialisation."

96   See Oran, "Pensions and Social Reproduction."

97   Bhattacharya, "How Not to Skip Class"; Oran, "Pensions and Social Reproduction."

98   Litwin et al., "Religiosity and Well-Being," 209.

99   Knesset, "24th Knesset, Protocol 26."

100   Zertal, *Israel's Holocaust*, 18, 21.

101   I am grateful to Jasbir Puar for helping me think through this angle of Israeli settler colonialism.

102   Sperling, "Be Fruitful and Multiply," 363.

103   Raz-Krakotzkin, "Exile within Sovereignty"; Abusneineh, "(Re)producing the Israeli (European) Body," 108. See also Puar, *Right to Maim*, 102; Piterberg, *Returns of Zionism*, 94; Boyarin, *Unheroic Conduct*.

104   Aging Analytics Agency, *Longevity Industry*.

105   Anderson, *Doing the Dirty Work?*

106   Hardt, "Affective Labor"; Anderson, *Doing the Dirty Work?*; Gutiérrez Rodríguez, *Migration, Domestic Work and Affect.*

107   Kav LaOved, *Shadow Report*. See also Ayalon, "Evaluating the Working Conditions."

108   Hobart and Kneese, "Radical Care," 2.

109   On this topic, see also Ruddick, *Maternal Thinking*; Held, *Ethics of Care*; Nadasen, "Rethinking Care Work"; Ticktin, "Care beyond Innocence"; Yuval-Davis, "Nationalism, Belonging, Globalization."

110   See Hartman, *Scenes of Subjection*; Threadcraft, *Intimate Justice*; Morgan, *Laboring Women*; Davis, "Women and Capitalism."

111   Palmer, *Domesticity and Dirt*; Rollins, *Between Women.*

112   Crenshaw, "Mapping the Margins."

113   Brah, interview by Bhandar and Ziadah, 41; Bhandar and Ziadah, introduction to *Revolutionary Feminisms*; Davis, *Freedom Is a Constant Struggle*, 19.

114   Hobart and Kneese, "Radical Care," 3.

115   Gandhi discusses these "archipelagos" in the context of Vietnamese refugees in Palestine/Israel and Guam. Gandhi, *Archipelago of Resettlement.*

116   hooks, *All about Love*; hooks, *Sisters of the Yam*; Lorde, *Burst of Light*; Caldera, "Challenging Capitalist Exploitation"; Nash, "Practicing Love," 3; Woodly, "Black Feminist Visions."

117   Lorde, *Burst of Light*, 130. Piepzna-Samarasinha, *Care Webs*; Threadcraft, *Intimate Justice*; Narayan, "Colonialism"; TallBear, "Caretaking."

118   Liebelt, *Caring for the "Holy Land"*; Parreñas, "Migrant Domestic Workers as 'One of the Family.'"

119   Manalansan, "Queering the Chain of Care Paradigm."

120   Francisco-Menchaves, *Labor of Care*; Parreñas, "Long Distance Intimacy"; Tungohan, "Reconceptualizing Motherhood."

121   Tronto, "The 'Nanny' Question," 48. See also Tronto, *Caring Democracy*; Gould, *Interactive Democracy.*

122   Shalhoub-Kevorkian, "Education under Siege"; Shalhoub-Kevorkian, "Human Suffering in Colonial Contexts"; Elia, *Greater Than the Sum*; Kravel-Tovi, "'National Mission.'"

123   Day, *Alien Capital*, 16.

124   Coulthard, *Red Skin, White Masks*, 14. See also Federici, *Caliban and the Witch*; Mies, *Patriarchy and Accumulation.*

125 Abu El-Haj, *Facts on the Ground*, 17–18; Kotef, *Colonizing Self*.

126 Abdo, *Women in Israel*; Meari, "Roles of Palestinian Peasant Women"; Abu Awwad, "Gender and Settler Colonialism." The term "Mizrahi" generally refers to Jews of Middle East and North African origin. The term has a distinctively political connotation, denoting a "hybrid identity" that contests the racialization of the categories "Jew" and "Arab" as mutually exclusive. Shohat, "The Invention of the Mizrahim," 5; Lavie, *Wrapped in the Flag*.

127 See Bakan, "The 'Jewish Question'"; Rouhana and Sabbagh-Khoury, "Settler-Colonial Citizenship"; Abdo and Yuval-Davis, "Palestine, Israel and the Zionist Settler Project." For a discussion of Zionism and the making of a national home, see Shalhoub-Kevorkian, "Infiltrated Intimacies."

128 Day, *Alien Capital*, 24, 31; Karuka, *Empire's Tracks*; Hilal, "Imperialism and Settler Colonialism," 53.

129 Rosenhek, "Political Dynamics," citing a 1995 issue of formerly circulating Israeli newspaper *Davar*.

130 Bartram, "Foreign Workers in Israel"; Farsakh, *Palestinian Labour Migration*.

131 Beinin, "Palestine and Israel." See also Farsakh, *Palestinian Labour Migration*, 136.

132 Clarno, *Neoliberal Apartheid*, 40; Farsakh, *Palestinian Labour Migration*.

133 Farsakh identifies "bantustanisation" as the post-Oslo period wherein the West Bank and Gaza Strip became "*de facto* population reservoirs reminiscent of South Africa's bantustans insofar as they are unsustainable economically and unable to separate viably from Israel to form an independent contiguous state." Farsakh, *Palestinian Labour Migration*, 2. On neoliberal retrenchment and inequality, see Maron and Shalev, introduction to *Neoliberalism as a State Project*.

134 Clarno, *Neoliberal Apartheid*, 39.

135 Hasso, *Buried in the Red Dirt*; Morgensen, "Settler Homonationalism."

136 Farsakh, *Palestinian Labour Migration*.

137 Hall and Massey, "Interpreting the Crisis," 55. Hall describes a conjuncture as "long or short" and "not defined by time or by simple things like a change of regime—though these have their own effects." Bartram describes the entrance of migrant laborers into Israeli labor markets somewhat similarly, as a "product of congruence." Bartram, "Foreign Workers in Israel," 322.

138 Day, *Alien Capital*, 33.

139 Morgensen, "Settler Homonationalism," 119; Goldberg, *Threat of Race*, 114.

140   Arlosoroff, "World's Highest Rate"; Shapiro, "Development of a 'Privileged Underclass'"; Eckstein, "Hiring Foreign Workers."

141   Chernichovsky et al., *Long-Term Care*.

142   Morgensen, *Spaces between Us*, 36.

143   Benjamin, *Gendering Israel's Outsourcing*.

144   Kemp and Fuentes, "Between Border Policies," quoting Kemp and Raijman, *Foreign and Workers*.

145   Iecovich, "Long-Term Care Insurance Law," 84.

146   Benjamin, *Gendering Israel's Outsourcing*; Hacker, *Legalized Famlies*.

147   Parreñas and Silvey, "Precarity of Migrant Domestic Work," 432. On these phenomena more broadly, see Trimikliniotis and Fulias-Souroulla, "Informalisation and Flexibilisation."

148   Brodsky et al., *65+ Population in Israel*. This 13 percent also includes the smaller population of non-Arab Christians and religiously unaffiliated elderly.

149   Brodsky et al., *65+ Population in Israel*.

150   Ayalon, "Perceived Discrimination," citing National Insurance Institute. See also Khalaila and Litwin, "Modernization and Future Care Preferences"; Khalaila and Litwin, "Modernisation and Filial Piety"; Halperin, "Aging, Family, and Preferences."

151   See Baron-Epel, Garty, and Green, "Inequalities in Use of Health Services"; Kanaaneh, *Birthing the Nation*, 48, quoting Swirski, Kanaaneh, and Avgar, "Health Care in Israel"; Keshet, Popper-Giveon, and Liberman, "Intersectionality"; Rouhana, *Palestinian Citizens*.

152   Khatib and Muhammad, "Health Status of Palestinians." See also Sa'ar, *Economic Citizenship*.

153   In drawing on the term "apartheid," I take a cue from Elia, who argues that apartheid is the legal system upholding settler colonial theft. Elia, *Greater than the Sum*.

154   Parreñas, "Migrant Filipina Domestic Workers," 561; Ong, *Neoliberalism as Exception*, 7. See also Ehrenreich and Hochschild, introduction to *Global Woman*; Ehrenreich, "Maid to Order."

155   ILO, *Decent Work for Migrant Domestic Workers*; Standing, "Global Feminization."

156   Choy, *Empire of Care*.

157   Fifty percent of revenue under Marcos, for example, went to interest payments on foreign debt. Parreñas, *Children of Global Migration*, 15, referencing

Mendoza, *Debt Management Approach*. The Philippines is thus the third-largest remittance-receiving country in Asia.

158 Rodriguez, "Migrant Heroes," 347. See also Guevarra, *Marketing Dreams*; Oishi, *Women in Motion*.

159 Raijman and Kushnirovich, *Labor Migrant Recruitment Practices*, 7.

160 Raijman and Kushnirovich, *Labor Migrant Recruitment Practices*.

161 Lebovitch and Friedman, *Black Money*. Numbers reflect the period within which I conducted interviews before the introduction of bilateral agreements. On the importance of bilateral agreements, see Kushnirovich and Raijman, *Impact of Bilateral Agreements*.

162 See also Liebelt, *Caring for the "Holy Land."* Paul, "Stepwise International Migration."

163 Williams, "Transnational Political Economy of Care"; Williams, "Care: Intersections of Scale."

164 Melnyk, *Regulating International Labor Recruitment*. A bilateral agreement between Israel and the Philippines in the home care sector exists as of 2018. As of 2020, general bilateral agreements exist between Israel and Nepal and Israel and Sri Lanka.

165 Boris, *Making the Woman Worker*; Fish, *Domestic Worker Organizing*.

166 Boris and Fish, "Domestic Workers Go Global"; IDWF, "About Us."

167 Roseware discusses the symbolic nature of these shifts more broadly in "The ILO's Domestic Worker Convention."

168 Mahon, "Through a Fractured Gaze," 572.

169 Roseware, "The ILO's Domestic Worker Convention"; Mahon, "Through a Fractured Gaze."

170 Melnyk, *Regulating International Labor Recruitment*.

171 Lowe, *Intimacies*, 21.

172 Wedeen, "Reflections on Ethnographic Work," 264.

173 See Mills, *Racial Contract*; Hayward, *How Americans Make Race*.

174 hooks, *All about Love*; Ackerly, *Just Responsibility*; Ackerly et al., "Unearthing Grounded Normative Theory," 5.

175 Foucault, *History of Sexuality*; Foucault, "Birth of Biopolitics"; Schotten, *Queer Terror*, xiii.

176 Kotef, *Movement*, 5; Lentin, *Traces of Racial Exception*; Abu-Laban and Bakan, "Social Sorting."

177   Bakan introduces the term "citizen-in-waiting" to refer to the status granted world Jewry with respect to becoming citizens in Israel. Bakan, "The 'Jewish Question,'" 261.

178   Hodes, "Gender, Race, and Justification," 74; Veracini, "Introducing 'Settler Colonial Studies.'"

179   Palestine Remembered, "District of Haifa"; Decolonizer, "Tel Aviv and Its Palestinian Localities."

180   Byrd, *Transit of Empire*; Elia, *Greater than the Sum*; Salaita, "Inter/Nationalism."

181   Coulthard, *Red Skin, White Masks*.

182   Ahmed, *Cultural Politics*, 113.

183   Puar, *Right to Maim*, xvii.

184   Rifkin, "Settler Common Sense."

185   Gonalons-Pons, "Modern Domesticity," 40; Morgensen, "Settler Homonationalism."

Chapter 1. The Coloniality of Israel's Reproductive Regime

1   Litwin et al., "Religiosity and Well-Being," 2.

2   See Mazuz, "Beauty Contests"; Shapiro, "Development of a 'Privileged Underclass'"; Weissbrod, "'Translated People.'"

3   Rosenhek, "Political Dynamics," 243.

4   Norton, "Israeli Cleaning Company."

5   Applied Research Institute, *Beit Surik*; Applied Research Institute, *Biddu*; Applied Research Institute, *Qatanna*.

6   Kershner, "Palestinian Gunman"; Lieber, "Man Who Cleaned Our House."

7   Rubin, "Palestinian Kills 3."

8   Lieber, "Man Who Cleaned Our House."

9   Weiss, *Chosen Body*, 128.

10   Abusneineh, "(Re)producing the Israeli (European) Body," 100. See also Abu El-Haj, *Genealogical Science*.

11   Weiss, *Chosen Body*, 1; Abusneineh, "(Re)producing the Israeli (European) Body," 109. See also Piterberg, *Returns of Zionism*, 94; Boyarin, "Homophobia"; Puar, *Right to Maim*; Presner, *Muscular Judaism*. For Weiss, the collective body is premised upon the "chosen body"—that of the youthful,

hypermasculine pioneer, worker, and soldier. My focus here is on the invocation of vulnerability to the collective body as a justification for its reproductive regime.

12   Hirsch, "Zionist Eugenics," 592, citing Falk, *Zionism* and Hart, *Social Science*.

13   Raz-Krakotzkin, "Exile within Sovereignty"; Abusneineh, "(Re)producing the Israeli (European) Body," 108. See also Puar, *Right to Maim*, 101–4; Boyarin, *Unheroic Conduct*; Presner, *Muscular Judaism*.

14   Weiss, *Chosen Body*, 20; Hirsch, "Zionist Eugenics."

15   Abu El-Haj, *Genealogical Science*, 82, 85.

16   Zertal, *Israel's Holocaust*, 18.

17   I am grateful to Jasbir Puar for helping me conceptualize this point as it fits into my broader argument about the coloniality of Israel's reproductive regime.

18   *I24 News*, "Israel Counts 180,000 Holocaust Survivors" (emphasis mine).

19   Weiss, *Chosen Body*, 66, 19.

20   Rai, Hoskyns, and Thomas, "Depletion."

21   Hasso, *Buried in the Red Dirt*; Chilmeran and Pratt, "Geopolitics of Social Reproduction," 586. Internal displacement of Palestinians in 1948 has yielded greater instances of chronic stress, trauma, and socioeconomic inequality (Daoud et al., "Internal Displacement"). Stress, trauma, and poor health outcomes also result from land confiscation, house demolitions, and military violence that leave Palestinians permanently wounded. See Khatib and Muhammad, "Health Status of Palestinians"; Puar, *Right to Maim*; Shalhoub-Kevorkian, *Incarcerated Childhood*.

22   Hasso, *Buried in the Red Dirt*, 244.

23   Coulthard, *Red Skin, White Masks*, 12, 14. On accumulation and settler colonialism in Palestine, see also Englert, "Settlers, Workers."

24   Quijano, "Coloniality of Power," 533; Lugones, "Heterosexuality"; Gutiérrez Rodríguez, "Domestic Work—Affective Labor"; Gutiérrez Rodríguez, "Coloniality of Migration" (drawing on Quijano). In centering coloniality, I draw on the work of Anibal Quijano and María Lugones. I draw on Gutiérrez Rodríguez's argument that contemporary forms of migrant domestic labor are imbricated in histories of extractive colonialism and settler colonialism. In dialectical relation, the *affective* value of migrant care work justifies and enables its *economic* devaluation and the accumulation of wealth by the state. Through the "coloniality of migration," "colonial system(s) of

classification" reveal themselves in contemporary migration generating a distinction between "citizen" and "alien" that echoes an older white Christian European and colonial "Other" classification. Gutiérrez Rodríguez, "Domestic Work—Affective Labor," 49.

25 On the coloniality of migrant domestic work in Europe, see Gutiérrez Rodríguez, "Domestic Work—Affective Labour" and "Coloniality of Migration." On the coloniality of migrant domestic work done by Eritrean Afro-Surinamese women, see Marchetti, "Migrant Domestic Work."

26 Salaita, *Holy Land in Transit*, 175. See also Hasso, *Buried in the Red Dirt*.

27 The recently published work of Marcelo Svirsky also helpfully uses the framework of social reproduction and accumulation to think about settler colonialism in Palestine/Israel; see Svirsky, "Reproduction of Settler Colonialism." For an analysis of social reproduction and settler colonialism outside of the Israeli case, see Goldstein, "On the Reproduction of Race."

28 Coulthard, *Red Skin, White Masks*. Recognizing migrant eldercare as enmeshed in both capital *and* land relations also necessitates a rethinking of reproductive labor as a form of *ongoing* colonial-capital accumulation. Reworking Marx's concept of primitive accumulation—the violent separation of peasants from their means of subsistence and their subsequent proletarianization—Angela Davis ("Women and Capitalism") and Silvia Federici (*Caliban and the Witch*) show how the accumulation of wealth is ongoing, and takes place not only on the factory floor, but also through the material and psychic sustenance of workers and families.

29 Abdo, *Women in Israel*; Zu'bi, "Development of Capitalism in Palestine"; Svirsky, "Reproduction of Settler Colonialism." For a discussion of land cultivation and colonization in the Israeli context, see Bhandar, *Colonial Lives of Property*.

30 Shafir, *Land, Labor*.

31 Day, *Alien Capital*, 53.

32 Day, *Alien Capital*.

33 Here, I draw on the work of Gershon Shafir, Nahla Abdo, Smadar Lavie, Zachary Lockman, and Jamil Hilal, among others, to locate eldercare in a longer genealogy of the management of labor *and* land expropriation. As Shafir notes, there are three meanings to "conquest of labor": that of "self-conquest," or the reconnection of Jewish settlers with agriculture; that of the conquest over working conditions; and finally, the replacement of indigenous Palestinian labor with Jewish labor. Shafir, *Land, Labor*, 60.

34 Gordon and Ram, "Ethnic Cleansing," 23, citing Wolfe, "Settler Colonialism." For a discussion of the "conquest of land," see Shafir, *Land, Labor*.

35 Veracini, "Settler Collective," citing Lawson, *Unhomely States*, 157.

36 Shalhoub-Kevorkian, "Infiltrated Intimacies," 167.

37 Khalidi, *All That Remains*.

38 Abu El-Haj, *Facts on the Ground*; Shalhoub-Kevorkian, "Human Suffering in Colonial Contexts"; Shalhoub-Kevorkian, "Infiltrated Intimacies."

39 Shalhoub-Kevorkian, "Infiltrated Intimacies," 167

40 There is disagreement about the origins of this phrase. British author Israel Zangwill is credited with first citing the term, according to Edward Said. Others say it was first used by Christian writers of the Victorian era. See Said, *Orientalism*; Muir, "Land without a People."

41 Shafir, *Land, Labor*; Lockman, *Comrades and Enemies*.

42 Halperin, *Oldest Guard*.

43 Druyan, "American Zionist Efforts."

44 Shafir, *Land, Labor*; Lavie, *Wrapped in the Flag*. While Yemenite Jews were officially recruited as laborers during the "conquest of labor" period beginning in 1908, they began settling Palestine long before, in the 1880s. Halperin, *Oldest Guard*, 11.

45 Bhandar, *Colonial Lives of Property*, 124; Lavie, *Wrapped in the Flag*; Shafir, *Land, Labor*; Lockman, *Comrades and Enemies*. While Shafir emphasizes the period 1904–1914 and the pure settlement model as the foundational logic to the Zionist project in subsequent decades, Lockman suggests that various forms of state coercion and violence following this period also crucially influenced the Zionist project and state formation.

46 Hilal, "Imperialism and Settler-Colonialism," 53; Abdo, *Women in Israel*; Zu'bi, "Development of Capitalism in Palestine"; Abu El-Haj, *Genealogical Science*.

47 Shafir, *Land, Labor*, 99–100, quoting a letter written by Aharon Eisenberg in 1909.

48 Lavie, *Wrapped in the Flag*, 49; Shafir, *Land, Labor*, 109.

49 Shafir, *Land, Labor*, 99–100.

50 Shohat, "Sephardim in Israel," 5, quoting Smooha, *Israel: Pluralism and Conflict*, who quotes Meir.

51 Khalidi, *Hundred Years' War*, 10, quoting Arthur Hertzberg's translation of Herzl.

52 Seikaly, *Men of Capital*, 7.

53 Lavie, *Wrapped in the Flag*; Bar-Yishay, "Women in the Yishuv Work-force"; Pfefferman, "Separate Spheres"; Imhoff, *Lives of Jessie Sampter*; Halperin, *Oldest Guard*, drawing on ha-Po'el ha-tza'ir, 1913.

54 Lavie, *Wrapped in the Flag*.

55 Lavie, *Wrapped in the Flag*, 53.

56 Imhoff, *Lives of Jessie Sampter*, 175, citing Sampter, *Modern Palestine*.

57 Lavie, *Wrapped in the Flag*.

58 Seikaly, *Men of Capital*; Kahlenberg, "New Arab Maids."

59 Lavie, *Wrapped in the Flag*; Abdo, *Women in Israel*, 85, quoting Katz, *Women and Gender*, 118.

60 Boyarin, *Unheroic Conduct*.

61 Lavie, *Wrapped in the Flag*. For a critique of scholarly representations of Ashkenazi women as a pioneering vanguard, see Abdo, *Women in Israel*.

62 Imhoff, *Lives of Jesse Sampter*, 174, citing Sampter, *Guide to Zionism*, 160.

63 Abdo, *Women in Israel*.

64 Kuttab, "Paradox of Women's Work," 233; Abu Awwad, "Gender and Set-tler Colonialism"; El Zein, "Developing a Palestinian Resistance Economy."

65 Al-Botmeh, "Palestinian Women in the Labor Market."

66 Seikaly, *Men of Capital*; Kahlenberg, "New Arab Maids"; Meari, "Roles of Palestinian Peasant Women"; Kuttab, "Paradox of Women's Work"; Abu Awwad, "Gender and Settler Colonialism"; Samed, "Proletarianization of Palestinian Women"; Al-Botmeh, "Palestinian Women in the Labor Market."

67 Meari, "Roles of Palestinian Peasant Women." See also Hasso, *Buried in the Red Dirt*.

68 Kuttab, "Paradox of Women's Work"; Abu Awwad, "Gender and Settler Colonialism."

69 Samed, "Proletarianization of Palestinian Women"; Zu'bi, "Development of Capitalism in Palestine."

70 Samed, "Proletarianization of Palestinian Women," 13. See also Daoud, *Palestinian Women and Politics*. Elite and middle-class Palestinians also hired working-class Palestinian women as maids in pursuit of this goal. Palestinian working-class women also labored as maids in Jewish and British homes, a source of income for rural Palestinian women in par-ticular. Seikaly illustrates how during the 1940s, many elite Palestinian women viewed their role in the home as domestic managers with purview

over the family budget and training family. Seikaly, *Men of Capital*. See also Abdo and Yuval-Davis, "Palestine, Israel"; Hilal, "Imperialism and Settler-Colonialism."

71 Weiss, *Chosen Body*, 20.

72 Samed, "Proletarianization of Palestinian Women," 15, citing a December 13, 1974, *Haaretz* article.

73 Kuttab, "Community Development Under Occupation"; Abu Awwad, "Gender and Settler Colonialism."

74 See Kuttab, "Paradox of Women's Work"; Kuttab, "Palestinian Women in the Intifada"; Abdulhadi, "Palestinian Women's Autonomous Movement."

75 Samed, "Proletarianization of Palestinian Women."

76 ILO, *Assessment of the Domestic Work Sector*; Al Gherbawi, "Bleak Economy Pushes Gazan Women."

77 ILO, *Assessment of the Domestic Work Sector*.

78 Kuttab, "Paradox of Women's Work."

79 Englert, "Settlers, Workers"; Abdo and Yuval-Davis, "Palestine, Israel."

80 See, e.g., Sa'ar, *Economic Citizenship*; Motzafi-Haller, Benjamin, and Bernstein, "Emotional Politics"; Kraus and Yonay, *Facing Barriers*; Abdo and Yuval-Davis, "Palestine, Israel."

81 Stasiulis and Yuval-Davis, "Introduction: Beyond Dichotomies"; Lavie, *Wrapped in the Flag*.

82 Coulthard, *Red Skin, White Masks*; Issar, "Theorizing 'Racial/Colonial Primitive Accumulation.'"

83 Silvey and Parreñas, "Precarity Chains."

84 Benjamin, *Gendering Israel's Outsourcing*, 13. Benjamin notes that approximately 70 percent of women in the Israel labor market are employed in these services.

85 Benjamin, *Gendering Israel's Outsourcing*.

86 Silvey and Parreñas, "Precarity Chains"; Parreñas and Silvey, "Precarity of Migrant Domestic Work."

87 Clarno, *Neoliberal Apartheid*, 198.

88 Clarno, *Neoliberal Apartheid*, 83; Farsakh, *Palestinian Labour Migration*; Daoud, *Palestinian Women and Politics*.

89 Hever, "Night Watchman."

90 Clarno, *Neoliberal Apartheid*, 30.

91 Clarno, *Neoliberal Apartheid*, 90.

92 Gutiérrez Rodríguez, "Domestic Work—Affective Labor."

93 Lebovitch and Friedman, *Black Money*.

94 Drori, *Foreign Workers in Israel*, 29. See also Raijman and Kushnirovich, *Labor Migrant Recruitment Practices*.

95 POEA, "New Standard Employment Contract"; Kav LaOved, "Migrant Caregivers in Israel."

96 Udell, "Denied Basic Labor Rights."

97 POEA, "New Standard Employment Contract."

98 RavGil, "Looking for Caregivers?"

99 POEA, "Recruitment Specification Form."

100 Mandal, "Everything You Want to Know."

101 Tungohan, "'Ideal' Female Migrant," 37.

102 Parreñas and Silvey, "Precarity of Migrant Domestic Work," 435.

103 Tungohan, "'Ideal' Female Migrant," 38.

104 Constable, "Sexuality and Discipline," 553; Constable, *Maid to Order*.

105 See, e.g., Anderson, *Doing the Dirty Work?*; Parreñas, *Servants of Globalization*; Romero, *Maid in the U.S.A.*; Hondagneu-Sotelo, *Doméstica*; Lutz and Pallenga-Möllenbeck, "Care Workers, Care Drain."

106 See Kav LaOved, *Shadow Report*.

107 See Kemp, *Reforming Policies on Foreign Workers*.

108 Berg, "Honest Day's Wage," 173.

109 *Aba* is Hebrew for "father" and *ema* for "mother," terms many caregivers adopt when referring to their employers.

110 Employers' gender preferences in hiring a caregiver are also shaped by their physical condition and level of religious observance.

111 See, e.g., POEA, "Recruitment Specification Form"; POEA, "New Standard Employment Contract."

112 Karuka, *Empire's Tracks*, 97.

113 Zertal, *Israel's Holocaust*, 2.

114 Zertal, *Israel's Holocaust*, 3.

115 Knesset, "24th Knesset, Protocol 26." Over half of the total elderly population employing migrant caregivers are Holocaust survivors, a number approximating 19,500.

116 Zertal, *Israel's Holocaust*, 16.

117 Zertal, *Israel's Holocaust*, 174.

118 Steinberg, "Israel at Sixty."

119 On this topic see Lentin, *Traces of Racial Exception*; Pappé, "Sthetl Colonialism"; Said, *Covering Islam*.

120 Pappé, "Sthetl Colonialism," 47.

121 Pappé, "Sthetl Colonialism," 47.

122 Sharon, "Speech at Birkenau."

123 Lentin, *Traces of Racial Exception*.

124 Israel Ministry of Foreign Affairs, "PM Bennett's Holocaust Martyrs."

125 Sanchez, "Israeli Holocaust Survivors."

126 Beinin, "Palestine and Israel"; Maron and Shalev, introduction to *Neoliberalism as a State Project*; Clarno, *Neoliberal Apartheid*.

127 Krampf, "Israel's Neoliberal Turn," 229.

128 Aizura uses the term "biopolitical category" to refer to the closely related concept of vulnerability. Aizura, "Affective Vulnerability," 124.

129 See HCJ, Worker's Hotline v. Government, para. 16, of the supplementary statement of the respondents of May 21, 2003. See also HCJ, Yolanda Gluten v. National Labor (1678/07); HCJ, Yolanda Gluten v. National Labor (10007/09).

130 See HCJ, Yolanda Gluten v. National Labor (1678/07); HCJ, Yolanda Gluten v. National Labor (10007/09).

131 HCJ, Yolanda Gluten v. National Labor (10007/09).

132 HCJ, Yolanda Gluten v. National Labor (10007/09).

133 Nefesh B'Nefesh, "Informal Guide."

134 Ghert-Zand, "Making the Dream."

135 Puar, *Right to Maim*, 64.

136 Silvey and Parreñas, "Precarity Chains," 2.

Chapter 2. Intimacy, Alienation, and Affective Automation

Selected paragraphs from this chapter appeared in Brown, "Multiple Modes of Care."

1 Harper and Zubida, "Living on Borrowed Time," 108.

2   I am grateful to Rhacel Salazar Parreñas for suggesting the term "affective automation." This term appears in the fields of neuropsychology and cognitive science, but to my knowledge, it has not been applied to discussions about care work or affective labor.

3   Mundlak and Shamir, "Intimacy and Alienage."

4   See Bruyneel, *Third Space of Sovereignty*; Vimalassery, Pegues, and Goldstein, "Colonial Unknowing."

5   Kaplan, "Manifest Domesticity."

6   McClintock, *Imperial Leather*.

7   Herzog, "Family-Military Relations"; Herzog, "Homefront and Battlefront."

8   Rifkin, *Beyond Settler Time*; Busbridge, "Messianic Time," 2.

9   Ahmed, "Affective Economies"; Massumi, *Politics of Affect*.

10   Folbre, "Nursebots to the Rescue?"; Folbre, *Who Pays for the Kids?*

11   Puar, *Right to Maim*, xv. Puar draws on Livingston's work on "debility" and "expected impairments." Livingston, "Insights," 3, 20. On "debilitation" and "the slow wearing down of populations," see Puar, *Right to Maim*, xiv. In the Palestinian/Israeli context, Puar argues that "mutilation and amputation . . . are part of the biopolitical scripting of populations available for injury, whether through laboring or through warring or both." Puar, *Right to Maim*, 64.

12   In addition to Mundlak and Shamir, "Intimacy and Alienage," on the simultaneously close and alienating nature of domestic work in Palestine/Israel, see Rosenthal, "Terms of Endearment." Outside of Palestine/Israel, see Lan, *Global Cinderellas*.

13   Murphy, "Unsettling Care," 732. See also Tuck and Yang, "Decolonization Is Not a Metaphor," 4; Moreton-Robinson, *White Possessive*; Abdo and Yuval-Davis, "Palestine, Israel"; Alloul, "Signs of Visual Resistance"; Kotef, *Colonizing Self*; Fortier, "Unsettling Methodologies/Decolonizing Movements." As Abu El-Haj argues, it is "at the level of everyday life" that settler society remakes a place and naturalizes its connection to the land. Abu El-Haj, *Facts on the Ground*, 19. For incorporation of the concept of "unsettling" in the context of migration, see Tang, *Unsettled*; Raghuram, "Which Migration?"; Hausermann et al., "Unsettled Belonging"; Zetter, "Refugees."

14   Gandhi, *Archipelago of Resettlement*, 6.

15   Here I draw on the work of Jasbir Puar in *Right to Maim*.

16   Abu El-Haj, *Facts on the Ground*.

17 Lowe, *Intimacies*.

18 Ahmed, *Cultural Politics*, 4.

19 Mundlak and Shamir, "Intimacy and Alienage," 167. In addition to the 2009 *Yolanda Gluten* case that Mundlak and Shamir identify, see also HCJ, Kav LaOved v. Minister of Welfare et al., which involved a petition for extended health coverage for migrant caregivers. Several other cases hinge on the question of whether migrant care work is quantifiable and whether the plaintiff can prove that they were uncompensated for overtime work; see HCJ, Todroangan v. Moshe Maayan; Regional Labor Court in Haifa, Molnar Atalka v. the Estate of the Late Zelucivar Penny, Mali Kesner, et al.; National Labor Court, Elena Zachariah v. the Estate of the Late Liza Kimmelman; National Labor Court, Aryeh Zetlman v. Valentina Petrov.

20 HCJ, Sharmila Liangi et al. v. the Knesset et al., petition for a conditional order. See also the dissenting opinion of National Labor Court vice president Elisheva Barak in HCJ, Todroangan v. Moshe Maayan; National Labor Court, Aryeh Zetlman v. Valentina Petrov. See also Knesset, "Staff Report"; Knesset, "24th Knesset, Protocol 38"; Knesset, "24th Knesset, Protocol 19"; Knesset, "19th Knesset, Protocol 21."

21 See for example Lee, *Service Economies*, 127.

22 Hazan, "Victim into Sacrifice," 77.

23 Caduaya, "Filipina Caregiver Took Care."

24 Benn, "Netanyahu."

25 Prime Minister's Office, "PM Netanyahu Meets with Philippines President."

26 Prime Minister's Office, "PM Netanyahu Meets with Philippines President."

27 Ahren, "Duterte, Accused of Mass Killings."

28 Willen, *Fighting for Dignity*, 182.

29 Schotten, *Queer Terror*, xv; Ayyash, *Hermeneutics of Violence*.

30 Knesset, "24th Knesset, Protocol 26." In addition to this proceeding, see also HCJ, Sarah Ravid v. Population and Immigration Authority, which involves a request for permission to appeal a Court of Administrative Affairs judgment, wherein Justice Uzi Fogelman argues that "in certain cases, which are difficult by their nature, severing the relationship between the patient and the foreign worker treating him may in itself harm the patient and increase the amount of suffering the patient is already in (*Gama* case, paragraph 57 of the opinion of Justice A. Procaccia). Therefore, it was also determined that in appropriate cases it would be possible to allow the continuation of the therapeutic relationship, even at the cost of the foreign

worker's continued stay in Israel beyond the maximum employment period (Fogelman opinion, 19n21)."

31 Knesset, "24th Knesset, Protocol 26."

32 Knesset, "24th Knesset, Protocol 26."

33 Knesset, "24th Knesset, Protocol 26."

34 Knesset, "24th Knesset, Protocol 26."

35 Knesset, "24th Knesset, Protocol 26."

36 Claims Conference, "Our Work around the World."

37 Ahmed, *Cultural Politics*.

38 Ahmed, *Cultural Politics*, 4.

39 See Mundlak and Shamir, "Intimacy and Alienage."

40 Mundlak and Shamir, "Bringing Together," 294.

41 Mundlak and Shamir, "Bringing Together," 291.

42 HCJ, Yolanda Gluten v. National Labor Court et al. 2013 (Opinion of Justice Arbel).

43 HCJ, Yolanda Gluten v. National Labor Court et al. 2009 (Opinion of Vice President Rivlin).

44 HCJ, Yolanda Gluten v. National Labor Court et al. 2009 (Opinion of Vice President Rivlin). See also Mundlak and Shamir, "Bringing Together," 294, which originally analyzes this case in the context of "care work exceptionalism."

45 HCJ, Yolanda Gluten v. National Labor Court et al. 2013 (Opinion of Justice Meltzer).

46 Similarly to this case, Mundlak and Shamir likewise note how statutory exceptions to overtime pay were applied in both a 2001 Labor Court case, where the court determined that caregivers were "workers whose working time cannot be monitored," and in a District Court case, which determined that the "high-trust nature" of live-in care work prevented caregivers from accurately reporting working hours, and therefore, obviated their right to overtime pay. Mundlak and Shamir, "Intimacy and Alienage," 167.

47 I do not suggest that care work does not involve intimacy of different kinds, nor that care work is not labor involving bodily proximity and emotion. As Davis argues, care, sex, and reproductive work are all forms of labor involving the "commodification of activities conventionally associated with women" and therefore generate questions about the extent to which these

labors are exceptional in nature or "just work" like any other kind. When viewing work itself as a site of subject-formation, all jobs are a locus of intimate exchange. Davis, "Regulating Sex Work."

48 HCJ, Sharmila Liangi et al. v. the Knesset et al., note 10.

49 Other cases simultaneously articulate the central role caregivers play in "the special humanitarian need of nursing patients" and the commitment to ensuring migrant workers' temporariness. See, e.g., HCJ, Sarah Ravid v. Population and Immigration Authority.

50 Ravid, "Domestic Issues."

51 Willen, *Fighting for Dignity*, 8, drawing on *Ynet*, "Foreigners."

52 Ayalon, "Evaluating the Working Conditions."

53 Constable, *Maid to Order*; Constable, "Sexuality and Discipline."

54 Gutiérrez Rodríguez, "Domestic Work—Affective Labor," 48.

55 Ahmed, *Queer Phenomenology*, 121.

56 Gutiérrez Rodríguez, "Domestic Work—Affective Labor."

57 Smith, "Settler Colonialism," 1.

58 Ahmed, *Queer Phenomenology*, 121.

59 Ahmed, "Affective Economies."

60 Ahmed, *Queer Phenomenology*, 119.

61 Eng, *Feeling of Kinship*, 10.

62 Similar to Mundlak and Shamir, Rosenthal discusses the paradoxical migrant domestic worker/employer relationship within Jewish-Israeli homes using the terms "closeness" and "remoteness." Rosenthal, "Terms of Endearment."

63 Rosenthal, "Terms of Endearment," 204.

64 Kolker, "Privatizing Israel's Migrant Care."

65 See, e.g., Agathangelou, "'Sexing' Globalization," 151; Hoang, *Dealing in Desire*; Chang and Ling, "Globalization"; Cheng, *Serving the Household*.

66 Ayalon, "Evaluating the Working Conditions"; Kav LaOved, *Shadow Report*.

67 Weinglass, "Grandma's Caretaker," drawing on an interview with (then) Kav LaOved coordinator of the caregiving field Idit Lebovitch.

68 Kav LaOved, *Shadow Report*.

69 Ayalon, "Evaluating the Working Conditions."

70 Shkolnik, "Caregiver's Choice."

71   Weeks, *Problem with Work*, 31; Hardt, "Affective Labor."

72   Constable, *Maid to Order*, 14, drawing on Foucault, *Discipline and Punish*, 137–38.

73   On this topic, see also Ayalon, "Suicidal and Depressive Symptoms"; Francisco-Mencahvez, *Labor of Care*; Parreñas, *Servants of Globalization*; Parreñas, "Long Distance Intimacy."

74   Puar, *Right to Maim*, xvi.

75   Puar, *Right to Maim*, xvii.

76   Puar, *Right to Maim*, xvi.

77   Puar, *Right to Maim*, 64. Here Puar is referring to both those labors undertaken "in the service of war" that maim "national bodies," as well as maiming those "foreign" bodies deemed criminal, in addition to those labors particular populations are expected to undertake despite and because of the bodily risks they entail.

78   Puar *Right to Maim*, xiv, xvii.

79   See also Kav LaOved, "Migrant Caregivers in Israel."

80   Gutzeit, *Excluded from Care*.

81   Green and Ayalon, "Violations of Workers' Rights."

82   HCJ, Kav LaOved v. Minister of Welfare et al.

83   HCJ, Kav LaOved v. Minister of Welfare et al., note 65.

84   HCJ, Kav LaOved v. Minister of Welfare et al.

85   Puar, *Right to Maim*, 109.

86   Willen, *Fighting for Dignity*, 137.

87   Puar, *Right to Maim*, xvii.

88   Puar, *Right to Maim*.

89   Tuck and Yang, "Decolonization Is Not a Metaphor."

Chapter 3. Reproducing the Settler Home

An early version of chapter 3 appeared as Brown, "Reproducing the National Family."

1   Mazuz, "State of the Jewish Family."

2   Ajzenstadt and Gal, "Appearances Can Be Deceptive."

3   Bouhnik and Giat, "Sandwich Generation."

4   Kotef, *Colonizing Self*, 5. In focusing on the narratives of Jewish Israelis, I follow scholars who argue that the "demand side" of migrant care and domestic work exposes the formation of gendered and racial hierarchies and ideologies inhering within specific national contexts. See Rollins, *Between Women*; Staab and Maher, "Dual Discourse"; Porat and Iecovich, "Relationships between Elderly"; Ambrosini, "Employers as 'Care Managers'"; Marchetti, "'Mum Seems Happy'"; Kristensen, "Paid Migrant Domestic Labour."

5   Rifkin, "Settler Common Sense," 323. See also the recent work of Svirsky on the reproduction of settler subjectivity in the Israeli case: Svirsky, "Reproduction of Settler Colonialism in Palestine."

6   Khalidi, *Hundred Years' War*, 107. On the emergence of the settler colonial paradigm in Israeli academia, see Sabbagh-Khoury, "Tracing Settler Colonialism."

7   Morgensen, "Un-settling Settler Desires."

8   Khalidi, *Hundred Years' War*, 107. See also Rifkin, "Settler Common Sense"; Rifkin, "Settler States of Feeling."

9   Brodsky et al., *65+ Population*.

10   Simpson, "On Ethnographic Refusal," 70.

11   Tuck and Yang, "Decolonization Is Not a Metaphor," 1.

12   Abu El-Haj, *Genealogical Science*; Alam, *Israeli Exceptionalism*. For analysis of the "one of the family" trope, see Rollins, *Between Women*; Bakan and Stasiulis, "Foreign Domestic Worker Policy"; Anderson, *Doing the Dirty Work?*; Hondagneu-Sotelo, *Doméstica*; Romero, *Maid in the U.S.A.*

13   Yuval-Davis, "National Reproduction," 93; Kanaaneh, *Birthing the Nation*.

14   Faist, "Migrants as Transnational Development Agents," 21.

15   See Tabar and Salamanca, "After Oslo"; Clarno, *Neoliberal Apartheid*.

16   Tabar and Salamanca, "After Oslo," 22.

17   Getzoff, "Start-Up Nationalism," citing Senor and Singer, *Start-Up Nation*; Goldberg, *Threat of Race*.

18   Morgensen, "Settler Homonationalism," 119.

19   Senor and Singer, *Start-Up Nation*. For a critique of their book in the context of Israeli neoliberalism, see Getzoff, "Start-Up Nationalism."

20   Alam, *Israeli Exceptionalism*, 18.

21   Masalha, *Bible and Zionism*, 3.

22   Abdo and Yuval-Davis, "Palestine, Israel," 291.

23   Busbridge, "Messianic Time," 2.

24   Masalha, *Bible and Zionism*, 139; McMahon, "Temporality," 26; Chowers, "Time in Zionism." I became aware of the work of McMahon and Chowers through the work of Busbridge.

25   See Alam, *Israeli Exceptionalism*; Abu El-Haj, *Genealogical Science*; Kedem and Padva, "From Sabra to Children."

26   Tatour, "Citizenship as Domination"; Ra'ad, "Enlarging 'Palestine'"; Abu-Laban and Bakan, *Israel, Palestine*.

27   Ben-Ze'ev and Lomsky-Feder, "Intergenerational Hero," 1264.

28   Tuck and Yang, "Decolonization Is Not a Metaphor," 10. See also Tatour, "Citizenship as Domination"; Masalha, *Bible and Zionism*; Abu El-Haj, *Genealogical Science*.

29   Yuval-Davis, "National Reproduction," 100; Grassiani, "Families in Arms."

30   Stasiulis and Yuval-Davis suggests that the "myth of common destiny" is a counterpart to the "myth of common origin." Stasiulis and Yuval-Davis, "Introduction: Beyond Dichotomies" 19.

31   Abu El-Haj, *Genealogical Science*, 67, 77.

32   See also Puar, *Right to Maim*, on racialization, Jewish settlement in Palestine, and Zionism.

33   Hanafi, "Explaining Spacio-Cide."

34   In 1897, Herzl declared, "The immigration of Jews signifies an unhoped-for accession of strength for the land which is now so poor; in fact, for the whole Ottoman Empire." See Lentin, *Traces of Racial Exception*, 27, citing Herzl's 1897 First Congress address.

35   Stasiulis and Yuval-Davis, "Introduction: Beyond Dichotomies"; Sharoni, *Gender and the Israeli-Palestinian Conflict*.

36   Na'amat, "History." See also Shargel, "American Jewish Women."

37   Gonalons-Pons, "Modern Domesticity," 40. I draw on this concept throughout to discuss the particular case of employers of migrant caregivers in Palestine/Israel.

38   Piastro, *Eating in Israel*, 104.

39   Piastro, *Eating in Israel*.

40   Herzog, "Family-Military Relations."

41   Aging Analytics Agency, *Longevity Industry in Israel*.

42   Aging Analytics Agency, *National Longevity Development Plans*, 193.

43 Jaffe-Hoffman, "Israeli Scientists," quoting Shai Efrati. See also Aging Analytics Agency, *Longevity Industry in Israel*.

44 Aging Analytics Agency, *Longevity Industry in Israel*, 15, 100; Selby, "Israeli Longevity Industry 'Reaching Critical Mass,'" 2019.

45 Claims Conference, "Our Work around the World."

46 Chin, *Service and Servitude*, 10. Whereas Chin argues that in the case of postcolonial Malaysia, migrant domestic workers function as symbols of the state's export-oriented development program and growing middle class, I suggest that in Palestine/Israel, citizens see them as representing Israel's shift from an upper-middle to a high income, liberalized economy where families beyond the middle class can now afford round-the-clock live-in care.

47 Shapiro, "Development of a 'Privileged Underclass,'" 432.

48 Morgensen, "Settler Homonationalism," 119.

49 On women's labor market participation and gender inequality within the Israeli welfare state and beyond, see Ajzenstadt and Gal, "Appearances Can Be Deceptive"; Sasson-Levy, "Contradictory Consequences"; Gonalons-Pons, "Modern Domesticity."

50 See also Goldberg, *Threat of Race*.

51 Ajzenstadt, "Moral Panic"; Ajzenstadt and Gal, "Appearances Can Be Deceptive"; Sa'ar, *Economic Citizenship*; Rom and Benjamin, *Feminism, Family, and Identity*.

52 Izraeli, "Culture, Policy, and Women," cited in Rom and Benjamin, *Feminism, Family, and Identity*, 52. See also Berkovitch, "Motherhood as National Mission"; Ajzenstadt and Gal, "Appearances Can Be Deceptive"; Swirski et al., *Women in the Labour Force*; Sasson-Levy, "Contradictory Consequences."

53 Rottenberg, "Rise of Neoliberal Feminism," 432.

54 Abdulhadi, "Israeli Settler Colonialism," 570.

55 Elia, "Justice Is Indivisible," 50.

56 Chin, *Service and Servitude*.

57 Sa'di, "Modernization as Explanatory Discourse," 26; Bhandar, *Colonial Lives of Property*.

58 Sa'di, "Modernization as Explanatory Discourse," drawing on Khalidi, *Hundred Years' War*.

59 Halperin, *Oldest Guard*, 67, 70, 82.

60 Sa'di, "Modernization as Explanatory Discourse," 27, quoting Khalidi, *Hundred Years' War*, 189–90.

61   Getzoff, "Start-Up Nationalism"; Herzl, *Jewish State*.

62   Getzoff, "Start-Up Nationalism," 812.

63   Getzoff, "Start-Up Nationalism," 818.

64   Taha, "Making Cheaper Labor." Taha looks specifically at domestic out-
      sourcing within the Galilee.

65   I take a cue from Getzoff in examining Senor and Singer's *Start-Up Nation*
      as an example of "start-up discourse" and "neoliberal Zionism" in Israel
      more broadly. Getzoff, "Start-Up Nationalism," 812.

66   Coulthard, *Red Skin, White Masks*, 14.

67   Taha, "Making Cheaper Labor," 24.

68   MASHAV, "MASHAV—Israel's Agency."

69   MASHAV, "MASHAV: Aid from Israel."

70   Israel Bonds International, "A Mere 11 Years."

71   See, e.g., MASHAV MFA, "World Humanitarian Aid"; MASHAV MFA,
      "MASHAV in India"; MASHAV MFA, "TIPA Project"; IDF, "Preparations
      for IDF's Humanitarian Aid"; IDF, "IDF Aid Mission Saves"; IDF, "First
      Baby Born."

72   Israel Ministry of Foreign Affairs, "Ensuring Equal Rights."

73   Israel Ministry of Foreign Affairs, "Ensuring Equal Rights."

74   Bruyneel, *Third Space of Sovereignty*, xv.

75   I draw on Mohanty's discussion of "citizen-consumers" in my use of the
      term "settler-consumers." Mohanty, "Women Workers," 5.

76   Morgensen, *Spaces between Us*, 171.

77   Abdo, *Women in Israel*, 76.

78   For a discussion on the deportation and surveillance of migrant com-
      munities, see Willen, "'Flesh of Our Flesh'?"; Willen, "Citizens, 'Real'
      Others."

79   Piastro, *Eating in Israel*.

80   Piastro, *Eating in Israel*, 107.

81   On the national significance of Shabbat meals, see Piastro, *Eating in Israel*.

82   Berman, "Birth of Tel Aviv."

83   Nichols, *Theft Is Property*, 145.

84   This phrase is not necessarily a mandate for settlement but is also widely
      interpreted as a spiritual orientation, rather than a literal territorial
      project.

85   Englert, "Settlers, Workers"; Shafir, *Land, Labor*.

86   As Englert argues, struggle *between* settler classes is waged "over the distribution of wealth extracted from settler labor, but also over the distribution of the loot accumulated through the dispossession of the indigenous population." Englert, "Settlers, Workers."

87   Clarno, *Neoliberal Apartheid*, 13.

88   Eglash, "Government Looks to Cut."

89   Ong, *Neoliberalism as Exception*, 200; Gonalons-Pons, "Modern Domesticity," 40.

90   Rifkin, "Settler Common Sense."

91   Hodes, "Gender, Race and Justification," 79.

92   Piastro, *Eating in Israel*, 88.

93   Piastro, *Eating in Israel*, 106–9.

94   Piastro, *Eating in Israel*, 91, drawing on Dosick, *Living Judaism*, 130.

95   Jacoby, "Gender Relations," 89; Yanay and Rapoport, "Ritual Impurity."

96   Ahmad, *Everyday Conversions*, 29. Ahmad is here drawing on Vora, *Impossible Citizens*.

97   Yuval-Davis, "National Reproduction," 10, citing Knesset member Geula Cohen.

98   Bakan uses the term "citizens-in-waiting" in reference to Jewish privilege under the Israeli Law of Return. Bakan, "'Jewish Question,'" 261.

99   Faist, "Migrants as Transnational Development Agents."

100   See, e.g., Davies, "Reconceptualzing the Migration-Development Nexus"; Faist, "Migrants as Transnational Development Agents"; Raghuram, "Which Migration, What Development?"; Wise, Covarrubias, and Puentes, "Reframing the Debate on Migration," 430.

101   Gonalons-Pons, "Modern Domesticity," 40; Kristensen, "Paid Migrant Domestic Labour."

102   Shafir and Peled, *Being Israeli*.

103   Clarno, *Neoliberal Apartheid*, 13.

104   Natan Nursing, "Foreign Caregivers."

105   See Knesset, "19th Knesset, Protocol 43."

106   HCJ, Kav LaOved v. Minister of Welfare et al. (Opinion of Justice Arbel).

107   Clarno, *Neoliberal Apartheid*, 90, 30; Ambrosini, "Employers as 'Care Managers.'"

108   Haddad, "Neoliberalism and Palestinian Development," 46.

109   Haddad, "Neoliberalism and Palestinian Development," 46.

110   See Beinin, "Palestine and Israel"; Shafir and Peled, *Being Israeli*.

111   Goldberg, *Threat of Race*, 109.

112   Deloria, *Playing Indian*.

113   Hanieh, "From State-Led Growth."

114   See Abdo, *Women in Israel*; Cohen and Haberfeld, *Gender, Ethnic, and National Earnings*.

115   Rodriguez, "Migrant Heroes"; Kristensen, "Paid Migrant Domestic Labour," 222.

116   Mohanty, "Women Workers," 5.

117   Goldstein, "PM: Infiltrators."

118   Goldstein, "PM: Infiltrators."

119   Nursing and Nursing Care, "Foreign Workers."

120   On this topic, see also Liebelt, *Caring for the "Holy Land."*

121   Davies, "Reconceptualzing the Migration-Development Nexus"; Faist, "Migrants as Transnational Development Agents"; Raghuram, "Which Migration, What Development?"; Wise, Covarrubias, and Puentes, "Reframing the Debate on Migration."

122   Piterberg, *Returns of Zionism*, 56.

123   Tatour, "Citizenship as Domination," 15.

124   Sabbagh-Khoury, "Palestinian Predicaments," 178. See also Robinson, *Citizen Strangers*.

125   Tatour, "Citizenship as Domination," 10.

126   Tatour, "Citizenship as Domination." On how the freedoms that the modern state claims to distribute are coconstituted by violence enacted toward nonnormative populations, see Reddy, *Freedom with Violence*.

127   Piterberg, *Returns of Zionism*, 56.

Chapter 4. Household Resistance and National Love

Selected paragraphs from this chapter appeared in Brown, "Multiple Modes of Care."

1   Nadasen, *Household Workers Unite*, 110.

2   Hagan, Hernández-León, and Demonsant, *Skills of the "Unskilled,"* 15; Harper and Zubida, "Living on Borrowed Time," 108.

3   Jackson, "Belonging against the National Odds."

4   See also Parreñas, *Servants of Globalization*. Drawing on Foucault, Parreñas highlights how many migrant Filipina domestic workers engage in improving their immediate conditions within the systems of capitalism, racism, and sexism shaping their lives rather than directly confronting or articulating opposition to these broader systems.

5   Vinthagen and Johansson, "Everyday Resistance," 16, drawing on de Certeau, *Practice of Everyday Life*, and Scott, "Everyday Forms of Resistance." Several scholars of migration and domestic work have drawn on the concept of "everyday resistance," including Cohen and Hjalmarson, "Quiet Struggles"; Tungohan, "Politics of Everyday Resistance"; Barua, Haukanes, and Waldrop, *Maid in India*; Li, "Digital Togetherness"; and Ogaya, "Filipino Domestic Workers."

6   Ahmed, *Cultural Politics*, 137.

7   Ahmed, *Cultural Politics*, 133.

8   Parreñas, "Indenture of Migrant Domestic Workers."

9   Scott, "Everyday Forms of Resistance"; Scott, *Domination*; Goffman, *Presentation of Self*.

10   Scott, *Domination*, 4–5.

11   Scott, "Everyday Forms of Resistance," 50, 59; Scott, *Domination*, 5, 111; Vinthagen and Johansson, "Everyday Resistance," 4. Here I follow Scott's conceptualization of the "frontstage" as that site in front of the employer, and the "backstage" (or "offstage") as that site away from the employer. This inverts Scott's formulation as the "frontstage" being akin to a "public" sphere and "offstage" being a private or hidden realm.

12   Hagan, Hernández-León, and Demonsant, *Skills of the "Unskilled,"* 5.

13   Hagan, Hernández-León, and Demonsant, *Skills of the "Unskilled,"* 7.

14   Ong, *Neoliberalism as Exception*, 201.

15   See also Harper and Zubida, "Living on Borrowed Time."

16   Hagan, Hernández-León, and Demonsant, *Skills of the "Unskilled,"* 101, 139.

17   For a more recent parliamentary debate on this issue, see Knesset, "25th Knesset, Protocol 5."

18   Ahmad, *Everyday Conversions*, 6.

19   Murphy, "Unsettling Care," 721.

20   Jackson, "Belonging against the National Odds."

21   Tuck and Yang, "Unbecoming Claims."

22   See Parreñas, *Servants of Globalization*.

23   Ahmed, *Cultural Politics*, 16, 137.

24   Ahmed, *Cultural Politics*.

25   Ahmad, *Everyday Conversions*, 16.

26   Wedeen, "Acting 'As If,'" 511.

27   Wedeen, "Acting 'As If,'" 511.

28   Kemp and Raijman, "Christian Zionists." See also Liebelt, *Caring for the "Holy Land"*; Jackson, "This Is Not the Holy Land"; Guarnieri Jaradat, *Unchosen*.

29   Shapiro, "Thank You Israel," 622; Davidson, "Christian Zionism as Representation."

30   Salaita, "Beyond Orientalism"; Pieterse, "History of a Metaphor."

31   Pentin, "Terrasanta.net."

32   Liebelt, *Caring for the "Holy Land."*

33   Sadowski, "New Orientalism"; Said, *Covering Islam*.

34   Lavie, *Wrapped in the Flag*; Shohat, "Sephardim in Israel."

35   Handelman, *Nationalism and the Israeli State*, 13.

36   Ahmad, *Everyday Conversions*, 20.

37   Ahmad, *Everyday Conversions*, 69.

38   Gonalons-Pons, "Modern Domesticity," 40.

39   Changes to the Canadian Live-In Caregiver Program were implemented in 2014. There are now increased barriers to permanent residency, even as the program no longer requires that caregivers live with their employers. Banerjee et al., *Assessing the Changes*.

40   Bryceson and Vuorela, "Transnational Families."

41   Paul, "Stepwise International Migration," 1843.

42   Paul, "Stepwise International Migration," 1843. In her examination of stepwise migration, Paul focuses specifically on Filipinx domestic workers.

43   See also Liebelt, *Caring for the "Holy Land."*

44   Kalir, "To Deport or to 'Adopt'?," 374, quoting Eli Yishai.

45   Peteet, "Closure's Temporality," 44.

46 As Parreñas argues, "migrants resist larger structural forces by responding to the dislocations that these forces have generated in their lives." *Servants of Globalization*, 33.

47 Parreñas, *Unfree*.

48 Abu-Lughod, "Romance of Resistance," 53.

49 Abu-Lughod, "Romance of Resistance," 53.

Chapter 5. Collective Care and the Politics of Visibility

Selected paragraphs from this chapter appeared in Brown, "Multiple Modes of Care."

1 Udell, "Denied Basic Labor Rights." This description is also based upon my attendance at the protest.

2 Protests against an Entry into Israel Law amendment took place in 2011. Mundlak and Shamir, "Organizing Migrant Care Workers."

3 While migrants have organized several protests against the deportation of Israeli-born children of migrants in 2019, 2010, and 2003, the demands of these protests were not specifically centered around migrant caregivers' working conditions.

4 Kalir, "To Deport or to 'Adopt'?," 373–74, quoting Ariel Sharon.

5 Lorde, *Burst of Light*, 130.

6 Scott, *Domination*, 18.

7 Scott, *Domination*, 20.

8 Bayat, *Life as Politics*.

9 Bailey, *Butch Queens Up in Pumps*, 19; Francisco-Menchavez, *Labor of Care*.

10 Francisco-Menchavez, *Labor of Care*, 94; Jackson, "Belonging against the National Odds," 64.

11 Mundlak and Shamir, "Organizing Migrant Care Workers," 111.

12 Mundlak and Shamir, "Organizing Migrant Care Workers," 111.

13 Parreñas, *Unfree*; Lee, Johnson, and McCahill, "Race, Gender, and Surveillance"; International Trade Union Confederation, *Facilitating Exploitation*.

14 Qadri, "UAE's Kafala System."

15   ILO, "Domestic Workers' Union in Lebanon"; ILO, *Migrant Domestic Workers in Lebanon*.

16   See Central News Agency, "Rally Demands Better Work Conditions"; Constable, "Migrant Workers and the Many States." Though protests in Taiwan are not common, to date there have been several, focusing on migrant domestic worker issues; the most recent include those held in 2022. Martyr, "Taiwan's Domestic Workers"; CIVICUS, "Protests on Labour Rights"; Everington, "Migrant Domestic Caregivers Rally"; Morris, "Taiwain's Migrant Workers." See also Aspinwall, "Southeast Asian Workers Rally"; Parreñas, *Unfree*; Lyons, "Transcending the Border."

17   Ahmad, *Everyday Conversions*; Ireland, "Female Migrant Domestic Workers."

18   For a comparison of the field of migrant activism in Palestine/Israel in relation to that of DREAMers in the United States, see Willen, *Fighting for Dignity*. Rodriguez, "Philippine Migrant Workers' Transnationalism," also illustrates how some migrants choose countries based upon the migrant and labor rights organizing landscape. On migrant caregiver organizing in Canada, see Tungohan, "Reconceptualizing Motherhood."

19   Mundlak and Shamir, "Organizing Migrant Care Workers," 94; Human Rights Watch, "Claiming Rights."

20   Mundlak and Shamir, "Organizing Migrant Care Workers," 94.

21   Mundlak and Shamir, "Organizing Migrant Care Workers."

22   Human Rights Watch, "Claiming Rights"; Mundlak and Shamir, "Organizing Migrant Care Workers"; ILO, "Domestic Workers' Union in Lebanon."

23   See, e.g., Francisco and Rodriguez, "Countertopographies of Migrant Women."

24   UIA, "Asian Migrants Coordinating Body"; Francisco and Rodriguez, "Countertopographies of Migrant Women."

25   Mundlak and Shamir, "Organizing Migrant Care Workers," drawing on Ayalon, "Foreign Home Care." Nonprofit organizations working on behalf of migrant rights include Kav LaOved, Physicians for Human Rights, Hotline for Migrant Workers, ASAF, and United Children of Israel, among others.

26   On Migrante's Middle East chapter, see Rodriguez, "Philippine Migrant Workers' Transnationalism."

27   ABS-CBN News, "Probe High Fees"; Migrante International, "US-Israel Hands Off Gaza!"; Migrante International, "Arrest and Detention of Filipino

Migrants"; Migrante International, "Migrante International Expresses Solidarity"; Javellana-Santos, "Philippine Envoy to Israel Recalled."

28   Chilmeran and Pratt, "Geopolitics of Social Reproduction."

29   Spade, *Mutual Aid*, 2.

30   Bailey, *Butch Queens Up in Pumps*, 19; Francisco-Menchavez, *Labor of Care*.

31   Francisco-Menchavez, *Labor of Care*, 97.

32   Nadasen, *Household Workers Unite*; Scott, *Domination*, xiii.

33   Liebelt, *Caring for the "Holy Land"*; Willen, "'Flesh of Our Flesh'?"

34   Manalansan, *Global Divas*; Manalansan, "Queering the Chain of Care"; Francisco-Menchavez, *Labor of Care*.

35   Francisco-Menchavez, *Labor of Care*.

36   Vegh, "Classifying Forms of Online Activism," 73.

37   Scott, *Domination*, xiii.

38   Tungohan, "Politics of Everyday Resistance," 42.

39   Willen, *Fighting for Dignity*.

40   Churches also play an important role in filling in gaps left by the state in its denial of services to migrant communities. Through the Latin Patriarchate of Jerusalem, the Coordination for the Pastoral among Migrants oversees pastoral care among different Catholic migrant communities, liaises with embassies, connects migrants to counseling services, provides childcare and religious education for the children of working migrant mothers, and offers services for convalescent migrants. Saint James Vicariate, "About Us"; Latin Patriarchate, "Vicariate for Migrants"; Guarnieri Jaradat, *Unchosen*.

41   Liebelt, *Caring for the "Holy Land."*

42   Willen, "Citizens, 'Real' Others"; Drori, *Foreign Workers in Israel*.

43   Ellman and Laacher, *Migrant Workers in Israel*, 272.

44   Ellman and Laacher, *Migrant Workers in Israel*.

45   Francisco-Menchavez, *Labor of Care*.

46   Manalansan, "Queering the Chain of Care."

47   Nadasen, *Household Workers Unite*.

48   Bailey, *Butch Queens Up in Pumps*, 19.

49   As Francisco-Menchavez notes, as a "secondary and almost equally profitable industry" to labor export, ICT is not a solution to the terrain of risk

migrant caregivers navigate but rather a "consolation" for the widespread impacts of neoliberal globalization that helps migrants forge solidarities. *Labor of Care*, 91.

50   Madianou, "Ambient Co-presence," 188.

51   Baldassar and Merla, "Introduction: Transnational Family Caregiving," 11, 25.

52   Holot prison was formally closed in 2018.

53   Butler, *Frames of War*; Willen, *Fighting for Dignity*, 182.

54   Ellman and Laacher, *Migrant Workers in Israel*, 18.

55   Drori, *Foreign Workers in Israel*, 205.

56   Drori, *Foreign Workers in Israel*, 205.

57   Wuhrgaft, "Our Challenge," whose *Haaretz* article is cited in Drori's discussion of the Cainday brothers. Drori, *Foreign Workers in Israel*, 205.

58   Ahmed, "Affective Economies," 122.

59   Ahmed, *Cultural Politics*, 135–36.

60   For example, former interior minister Eli Yishai stated in 2012, "We need to transform military bases in which we can imprison all of them without exception." Nondangerous prisoners could be released early pending deportation to make room for "infiltrators who pose a far greater risk to public safety." He added, "The infiltrators are going to reach the promised land but they aren't going to see it at all, only through bars . . . they are going to be deported from here, either pleasantly or forcibly." Sherwood, "Israeli Minister Inflames Racial Tensions."

61   Matar, "Community Shaken"; Simpson, *Make Their Lives Miserable*. For a discussion of state violence asylum seekers face, see Guarnieri Jaradat, *Unchosen*.

62   Simpson, *Make Their Lives Miserable*. Under a 2012 amendment to the 1954 Law for the Prevention of Infiltration, the government can detain asylum seekers who cross the Sinai border into Israel indefinitely. According to the UNHCR, while Sudanese asylum seekers originally came to Palestine/Israel to escape human rights abuses in Darfur, Eritreans began migrating in 2005 to avoid forced conscription and death orders under President Isais Afwerki. As of 2017, there were roughly 27,000 Eritrean and 7,700 Sudanese asylum seekers in Palestine/Israel. Spindler, "UNHCR Appeals to Israel."

63   Weinblum, "Conflicting Imaginaries."

64   Weinblum, "Conflicting Imaginaries," 6, quoting Netanyahu.

65   Prime Minister's Office, "PM Netanyahu Meets with Philippines President."

66   Telesur, "Israel Urges Employers." On state violence inflicted upon Eritrean and Sudanese asylum seekers, see Ravid, "Making Their Lives Miserable."

67   Halon, "Half of Israelis."

68   Yuval-Davis, "National Reproduction."

69   Mills, "Body Politic, Bodies Impolitic," 602.

70   Shani et al., *No Safe Haven*; Ravid, "Making Their Lives Miserable."

71   Ben Zikri, "Parents of Eritrean Asylum Seeker."

72   *Hindu*, "Israeli President Speaks"; Asian News International, "Israeli Envoy Speaks to Kin"; Abraham, "Indian Woman Killed in Israel."

73   Bousso, "Housing Prices in Israel"; Cohen and Margalit, "'There Are Really Two Cities Here.'"

74   Berger, "Other Side of Israel's 'White City.'"

75   Abu-Lughod, "Romance of Resistance," 41.

76   Gutiérrez Rodríguez, "Coloniality of Migration."

77   Gutiérrez Rodríguez, "Coloniality of Migration," 34.

78   Vinthagen and Johansson, "Everyday Resistance"; Bayat, *Life as Politics*; Tungohan, "Politics of Everyday Resistance"; Francisco-Menchavez, *Labor of Care*.

Epilogue

1   Coulthard, *Red Skin, White Masks*. See also Al-Ali, "COVID-19."

2   Miaari, Sabbah-Karkabi, and Loewenthal, *How Is the COVID-19 Crisis Exacerbating Socioeconomic Inequality among Palestinians?*; Helbich and Jabr, "Analysis of Mental Health Response"; Giacaman et al., "Life and Health."

3   AbuMezied and Sawafta, "Analysing Care Practices."

4   Raz, "Every 55 Hours."

5   On the state of elderly Holocaust survivors in Palestine/Israel, see Ben-Zion and Scharf, "As World Marks Holocaust."

6   Ben-Zion and Scharf, "As World Marks Holocaust."

7   Piterberg, *Returns of Zionism*.

8   See, e.g., Munem, "Migration and the Aging Body"; Tina, *Violence against the Elderly*; Harsha, Ziq, and Giacaman, "Disability among Palestinian Elderly."

9   Nasol and Francisco-Menchavez, "Filipino Home Care Workers," 1380; Sales, "Activism as Essential Work."

10   Migrante International, "Labor Day 2023: Workers of the World Unite"; Sales, "Activism as Essential Work."

11   Beinin, "Palestinian Workers."

12   Marshood and Alsanah, "Tal'at."

13   Zureik and Lyon, "Coronavirus Surveillance."

14   Ahronheim, "IDF Responsible."

15   StandWithUs, LinkedIn page.

16   StandWithUs, "Dubbed 'Guards of Gold.'"

17   Garfinkel, "To Be Honored."

18   Israel Ministry of Foreign Affairs, "New Agreements Permit."

19   Schotten, *Queer Terror*, 32, xv.

BIBLIOGRAPHY

Abdo, Nahla. *Women in Israel: Race, Gender and Citizenship*. London: Zed, 2011.

Abdo, Nahla, and Nira Yuval-Davis. "Palestine, Israel and the Zionist Settler Project." In *Unsettling Settler Societies*, edited by Daiva Stasiulis and Nira Yuval-Davis, 291–322. London: SAGE, 1995.

Abdulhadi, Rabab. "The Palestinian Women's Autonomous Movement: Emergence, Dynamics, and Challenges." *Gender and Society* 12, no. 6 (1998): 649–73.

Abdulhadi, Rabab. "Israeli Settler Colonialism in Context: Celebrating (Palestinian) Death and Normalizing Gender and Sexual Violence." *Feminist Studies* 45, no. 2–3 (2019): 541–73.

Abraham, Bobins. "Indian Woman Killed in Israel Was on Videocall with Husband in Kerala When Hamas Rocket Hit." *India Times*, May 12, 2021.

ABS-CBN News. "Probe High Fees for Job Placement to Israel—Migrante." March 31, 2009.

Abu Awwad, Nida. "Gender and Settler Colonialism in Palestinian Agriculture: Structural Transformations." *Arab Studies Quarterly* 38, no. 3 (2016): 540–61.

Abu El-Haj, Nadia. *Facts on the Ground: Archaeological Practice and Territorial Self-Fashioning in Israeli Society*. Chicago: University of Chicago Press, 2001.

Abu El-Haj, Nadia. *The Genealogical Science: The Search for Jewish Origins and the Politics of Epistemology*. Chicago: University of Chicago Press, 2012.

Abu-Laban, Yasmeen, and Abigail Bakan. *Israel, Palestine and the Politics of Race*. London: Bloomsbury, 2019.

Abu-Laban, Yasmeen, and Abigail Bakan. "The 'Israelisation' of Social Sorting and the 'Palestinianization' of the Racial Contract: Reframing Israel/Palestine and the War on Terror." In *Surveillance and Control in Israel/Palestine: Population,*

Territory and Power, edited by Elia Zureik, David Lyon, and Yasmeen Abu-Laban, 276–94. London and New York: Routledge, 2010.

Abu-Lughod, Lila. "The Romance of Resistance: Tracing Transformations of Power Through Bedouin Women." *American Ethnologist* 17, no. 1 (1990): 41–55.

AbuMezied, Asmaa, and Mohammed Sawafta. "Analysing Care Practices and Policies in Times of Austerity and Conflict: The Case of the Occupied Palestinian Territories (OPT)." *Gender and Development* 30, no. 1–2 (2022): 341–59.

Abusneineh, Bayan. "(Re)producing the Israeli (European) Body: Zionism, Anti-Black Racism and the Depo-Provera Affair." *Feminist Studies* 128, no. 1 (2021): 96–113.

Ackerly, Brooke A. *Just Responsibility: A Human Rights Theory of Global Justice.* Oxford, England: Oxford University Press, 2018.

Ackerly, Brooke, Luis Cabrera, Fonna Forman, Genevieve Fuji Johnson, Chris Tenove, and Antje Wiener. "Unearthing Grounded Normative Theory: Practices and Commitments of Empirical Research in Political Theory." *Critical Review of International Social and Political Philosophy* (2021): 1–27.

Adalah. "The Law of Return." Discriminatory Laws Database Website. Accessed September 25, 2017. https://www.adalah.org/uploads/oldfiles/Public/files/Discriminatory-Laws-Database/English/36-Law-of-Return-1950.pdf.

Adalah. "The Discriminatory Laws Database." September 25, 2017. https://www.adalah.org/en/content/view/7771.

Agathangelou, Anna M. "'Sexing' Globalization in International Relations: Migrant Sex and Domestic Workers in Cyprus, Greece, and Turkey." In *Power, Postcolonialism and International Relations: Reading Race, Gender and Class*, edited by Geeta Chowdry and Sheila Nair, 142–70. New York: Routledge, 2002.

Aging Analytics Agency. *Longevity Industry in Israel: Landscape Overview 2019*. Accessed May 21, 2020. https://analytics.dkv.global/data/pdf/Longevity-in-Israel/Longevity_in_Israel_-_Full_Report.pdf.

Aging Analytics Agency. *National Longevity Development Plans: Global Overview 2019*. Accessed 25 May, 2020. https://analytics.dkv.global/data/pdf/National-Longevity-Development-Plans-First-Edition/Report.pdf.

Ahmad, Attiya. *Everyday Conversions: Islam, Domestic Work and South Asian Migrant Women in Kuwait*. Durham, NC: Duke University Press, 2017.

Ahmed, Sara. "Affective Economies." *Social Text* 22, no. 2 (2004): 117–39.

Ahmed, Sara. *The Cultural Politics of Emotion*. Durham, NC: Duke University Press, 2004.

Ahmed, Sara. *Queer Phenomenology: Orientations, Objects, Others*. Durham, NC: Duke University Press, 2006.

Ahren, Raphael. "Duterte, Accused of Mass Killings, Says Israel Shares His Passion for People." *Times of Israel*, September 3, 2018.

Ahronheim, Anna. "IDF Responsible for Taking Care of Elderly during Coronavirus Crisis." *Jerusalem Post*, March 24, 2020.

Aizura, Aren A. "Affective Vulnerability and Transgender Exceptionalism: Norma Ureiro in Transgression." In *Trans Studies: The Challenge to Hetero/Homo Normativities*, edited by Yolanda Martinez-San Miguel and Sarah Tobias, 122–40. New Brunswick, NJ: Rutgers University Press, 2016.

Ajzenstadt, Mimi. "Moral Panic and Neo-Liberalism: The Case of Single Mothers on Welfare in Israel." *British Journal of Criminology* 49, no. 1 (2009): 68–87.

Ajzenstadt, Mimi, and John Gal. "Appearances Can Be Deceptive: Gender in the Israeli Welfare State." *Social Politics* 8, no. 1 (2001): 292–324.

Akalin, Ayse. 2018. "Affective Precarity: The Migrant Domestic Worker." *South Atlantic Quarterly* 117, no. 2 (2018): 420–29.

Al-Ali, Nadje. "COVID-19 and Feminism in the Global South: Challenges, Initiatives and Dilemmas." *EJWS* 27, no. 4 (2020): 333–47.

Alam, Shaheed M. *Israeli Exceptionalism: The Destabilizing Logic of Zionism*. New York: Palgrave Macmillan, 2009.

Al-Botmeh, Samia. "Palestinian Women in the Labor Market: A Burgeoning Workforce Curbed by Israel's Colonialism." In *Interactive Encyclopedia of the Palestine Question*, edited by Camille Mansour. Beirut: Institute for Palestine Studies. Accessed April 7, 2024. https://www.palquest.org/en/highlight/16043/palestinian-women-labor-market.

Al Gherbawi, Hadeel. "Bleak Economy Pushes Gazan Women Toward Domestic Work." *Al-Monitor*, February 20, 2022.

Allen, Fern. "Informal Guide to Bringing Your Elderly Parents to Israel." *Nefesh B'Nefesh*, July 5, 2023. https://www.nbn.org.il/uncategorized/informal-guide-to-bringing-your-elderly-parents-to-israel/.

Alloul, Jaafar. "Signs of Visual Resistance in Palestine: Unsettling the Settler-Colonial Matrix." *Middle East Critique* 25, no. 1 (2016): 23–44.

Alvarez, Sonia. "Women's Movements and Gender Politics in the Brazilian Transition." In *The Women's Movement in Latin America: Feminism and the Transition to Democracy*, edited by Jane S. Jacquette, 18–71. London: Unwin Hyman, 1989.

Ambrosini, Maurizio. "Employers as 'Care Managers': Contracts, Emotions and Mutual Obligations within Italy's Invisible Welfare System." In *Employers, Agencies and Immigration: Paying for Care*, edited by Sabrina Marchetti and Anna Triandafyllidou, 17–34. Abingdon, UK: Ashgate, 2016.

Anderson, Benedict. *Imagined Communities: Reflections on the Origin and Spread of Nationalism*. New York: Verso, 1991.

Anderson, Bridget. *Doing the Dirty Work? The Global Politics of Domestic Labour*. London: Zed, 2000.

Applied Research Institute. *Beit Surik Town Profile*. Jerusalem, 2012. Accessed July 26, 2022. http://vprofile.arij.org/jerusalem/pdfs/vprofile/Beit%20Surik_En.pdf.

Applied Research Institute. *Biddu Town Profile*. Jerusalem, 2012. Accessed July 26, 2022. http://vprofile.arij.org/jerusalem/pdfs/vprofile/Biddu_EN.pdf.

Applied Research Institute. *Qatanna Town Profile*. Jerusalem, 2012. Accessed July 26, 2022. http://vprofile.arij.org/jerusalem/pdfs/vprofile/Qatanna_EN.pdf.

Arlosoroff, Meirav. "Filipina Workers Give Israel's Elderly Great Care, but They Can't Get Pregnant." *Haaretz*, August 12, 2019. https://www.haaretz.com/israel-news/business/2019-08-12/ty-article/israels-elderly-get-great-care-while-filipina-workers-pay-the-price/0000017f-f563-d460-afff-ff67b04c0000.

Arlosoroff, Meirav. "Israel May Have the World's Highest Rate of Foreign Health Aides—and It's a Luxury, Not a Need." *Haaretz*, August 14, 2019. https://www.haaretz.com/israel-news/business/2019-08-14/ty-article/israel-may-have-the-worlds-highest-rate-of-foreign-health-aides-and-its-a-luxury/0000017f-dee5-db5a-a57f-deef82b20000.

Arvin, Maile, Eve Tuck, and Angie Morrill. 2013. "Decolonizing Feminism: Challenging Connections Between Settler Colonialism and Heteropatriarchy." *Feminist Formations* 25, no. 1 (2013): 8–34.

Asian News International. "Israeli Envoy Speaks to Kin of Kerala Woman who Died in Rocket Attach in Israel, Extends Condolences." May 12, 2021. https://www.aninews.in/news/world/asia/israeli-envoy-speaks-to-kin-of-kerala-women-who-died-in-rocket-attack-in-israel-extends-condolences20210512150308/.

Aspinwall, Will. "Southeast Asian Workers Rally to Protest Sexual Abuse, Poor Labor Standards." *News Lens*, March 25, 2019. https://international.thenewslens.com/article/116085.

Association for Civil Rights in Israel. "The 'Slavery Law' and Beyond: New Bills Targeting Foreign Residents." March 24, 2011. https://law.acri.org.il/en/2011/03/24/three-proposed-bills-targeting-non-residents/.

Auyero, Javier. *Patients of the State: The Politics of Waiting in Argentina*. Durham, NC: Duke University Press, 2012.

Ayalon, Liat. "Evaluating the Working Conditions and Exposure to Abuse of Filipino Home Care Workers in Israel: Characteristics and Clinical Correlates." *International Psychogeriatrics* 21, no. 1 (2009): 40–49.

Ayalon, Liat. "Perceived Discrimination and Stigma in the Context of the Long-Term Care Insurance Law from the Perspectives of Arabs and the Jews in the North of Israel." *International Journal of Environmental Research and Public Health* 16 (2019): 3511.

Ayalon, Liat. "Suicidal and Depressive Symptoms in Filipino Home Care Workers in Israel." *Journal of Cross-Cultural Gerontology* 27, no. 1 (2012): 51–63.

Ayyash, Mark M. *Hermeneutics of Violence: A Four-Dimensional Conception*. Toronto: University of Toronto Press, 2019.

Bailey, Marlon M. *Butch Queens Up in Pumps: Gender, Performance, and Ballroom Culture in Detroit*. Ann Arbor: University of Michigan Press, 2013.

Bakan, Abigail. "The 'Jewish Question': Reconsiderations on Race, Class and Colonialism." In *Theorizing Anti-racism: Linkages in Marxism and Critical Race
Theories*, edited by Abigail B. Bakan and Enakshi Dua, 252–79. Toronto: University of Toronto Press, 2014.

Bakan, Abigail B., and Daiva Stasiulis. "Foreign Domestic Worker Policy in Canada
and the Social Boundaries of Modern Citizenship." In *Not One of the Family:
Foreign Domestic Workers in Canada*, edited by Abigail B. Bakan and Daiva
Stasiulis, 29–52. Toronto: University of Toronto Press, 1997.

Baldassar, Loretta, and Laura Merla. "Introduction: Transnational Family Caregiving through the Lens of Circulation." In *Transnational Families, Migration and
the Circulation of Care: Understanding Mobility and Absence in Family Life*,
edited by Loretta Baldassar and Laura Merla, 3–24. New York: Routledge, 2014.

Baldassar, Loretta, and Laura Merla. "Locating Transnational Care Circulation
in Migration and Family Studies." In *Transnational Families, Migration and
the Circulation of Care: Understanding Mobility and Absence in Family Life*,
edited by Loretta Baldassar and Laura Merla, 25–58. New York: Routledge,
2014.

Banerjee, Rupa, Philip Kelly, Ethel Tungohan, GABRIELA–Ontario, Migrante–
Canada, and Community Alliance for Social Justice. *Assessing the Changes to Can-
ada's Live-In Caregiver Program: Improving Security or Deepening Precariousness?*
Pathways to Prosperity Project, December 2017. http://p2pcanada.ca/files/2017/12
/Assessing-the-Changes-to-Canadas-Live-In-Caregiver-Program.pdf.

Barber, Pauline Gardiner, and Winnie Lem. "Migration, Temporality, and Capitalism: A Brief Introduction." In *Migration, Temporality and Capitalism*, edited
by Pauline Gardiner Barber and Winnie Lem, 1–19. New York: Palgrave, 2018.

Baron-Epel, Orna, Noga Garty, and Manfred S. Green. "Inequalities in Use of Health
Services among Jews and Arabs in Israel." *Health Services Research* 42, no. 3
(2007): 1008–19.

Bartram, David V. "Foreign Workers in Israel: History and Theory." *International
Migration Review* 32, no. 2 (1998): 303–25.

Bartram, David V. "Foreign Workers, Refugees and Prospects for an Israeli-
Palestinian Agreement." *Development* 43, no. 3 (2000): 72–78.

Barua, Padmaja, Haldis Haukanes, and Anne Waldrop. 2016. "Maid in India: Nego-
tiating and Contesting the Boundaries of Domestic Work." *Forum for Development Studies* 43, no. 3 (2016): 415–36.

Bar-Yishay, Hanna. "Women in the Yishuv Workforce." *Jewish Women: A Comprehensive Historical Encyclopedia*. Jewish Women's Archive. February 27, 2009.
https://jwa.org/encyclopedia/article/women-in-yishuv-workforce.

Bar-Zuri, Ronny. *Holders of Permits for Employing Migrant Homecare Workers:
An Overview*. [In Hebrew.] Jerusalem: Ministry of Employment, Commerce,
and Industry, 2010.

Bass, Michiel, and Brenda S. A. Yeoh. "Introduction: Migration Studies and Critical Temporalities." *Current Sociology* 67, no. 2 (2018): 161–68.

Bayat, Asef. 2009. *Life as Politics: How Ordinary People Change the Middle East*. Stanford, CA: Stanford University Press, 2009.

Beinin, Joel. "Palestine and Israel: Perils of a Neoliberal, Repressive, Pax Americana." *Social Justice* 25, no. 4 (1998): 20–39.

Beinin, Joel. "Palestinian Workers Have a Long History of Resistance." *Jacobin*, June 6, 2021. https://jacobin.com/2021/06/palestinian-labor-trade-unions -strike-resistance-worker-solidarity-may-18-labor-history/.

Ben-Israel, Hanny. *Revisiting CEDAW's Recommendations: Has Anything Changed for Migrant Workers in Israel in the Last Two Years?* Tel Aviv: Kav LaOved, 2013. https://www.kavlaoved.org.il/wp-content/uploads/sites/3/2014/02/KLO -Revisiting-CEDAW-Dec-2013.pdf.

Benjamin, Orly. *Gendering Israel's Outsourcing: The Erasure of Employees' Caring Skills*. London: Palgrave Macmillan, 2016.

Benn, Aluf. "Netanyahu: PA Leadership Cannot Prosper in 'Poisonous Palestinian Society.'" *Marker*, December 17, 2003. https://www.themarker.com/misc/2003– 12–17/ty-article/0000017f-dba8-d3a5-af7f-fbae0d8b0000.

Ben-Youssef, Nadia, and Sandra S. Tamari. "Enshrining Discrimination: Israel's Nation-State Law." *Journal of Palestine Studies* 48, no. 1 (2018): 73–87.

Ben-Ze'ev, Efrat, and Edna Lomsky-Feder. "The Intergenerational Hero: Carrier of Bonding Memory." *Memory Studies* 16, no. 5 (2022): 1264–79.

Ben Zikri, Almog. "Parents of Eritrean Asylum Seeker Killed in Mob Attack Sue Israel." *Haaretz*, June 16, 2016. https://www.haaretz.com/israel-news/2016– 06–16/ty-article/.premium/parents-of-eritrean-asylum-seeker-killed-in-mob -attack-sue-israel/0000017f-dfaa-df7c-a5ff-dffada850000.

Ben-Zion, Ilan, and Isaac Scharf. "As World Marks Holocaust, Some Survivors in Israel Struggle." Associated Press, January 27, 2022.

Berg, Heather. 2014. "An Honest Day's Wage for a Dishonest Day's Work: (Re) Productivism and Refusal." *Women's Studies Quarterly* 42, nos. 1–2 (2014): 161–77.

Berger, Miriam. "The Other Side of Israel's 'White City.'" *Citylab*, May 9, 2018.

Berkovitch, Nitza. "Motherhood as National Mission: The Construction of Womanhood in the Legal Discourse in Israel." *Women's Studies International Forum* 20, no. 5–6 (1997): 605–19.

Berman, Helen. "The Birth of Tel Aviv." *Haaretz*, October 31, 2005. https://www .jpost.com/travel/tel-aviv/the-birth-of-tel-aviv-3369.

Beth-Halachmy, Sharon. "Israel's Sandwich-Generation Kids Are Getting Squashed under Pressure—Opinion." *Jerusalem Post*, August 30, 2022. https://www.jpost .com/opinion/article-715859.

Bhandar, Brenna. *Colonial Lives of Property: Law, Land, and Racial Regimes of Ownership*. Durham, NC: Duke University Press, 2018.

Bhandar, Brenna, and Rafeef Ziadah. Introduction to *Revolutionary Feminisms: Conversations on Collective Action and Radical Thought*, 1–30. New York: Verso, 2020.

Bhattacharya, Tithi. "How Not to Skip Class: Social Reproduction of Labor and the Global Working Class." *Viewpoint Magazine*, October 31, 2015.

Birenbaum-Carmeli, Daphna, and Martha Dirnfeld. "In Vitro Fertilisation Policy in Israel and Women's Perspectives: The More the Better?" *Reproductive Health Matters* 16, no. 31 (2008): 182–91.

Boris, Eileen. *Making the Woman Worker: Precarious Labor and the Fight for Global Standards, 1919–2019*. New York: Oxford University Press, 2019.

Boris, Eileen, and Fish, Jennifer. "Domestic Workers Go Global: The Birth of the International Domestic Workers Federation." *New Labor Forum* 23, no. 3 (2014): 76–81.

Bouhnik, Dan, and Yahel Giat. "The Sandwich Generation in Israel—Information Needs and Benefit Awareness." *Scientific Research* 4, no. 3 (2014): 242–57.

Bousso, Nimrod. "Housing Prices in Israel Are Climbing Faster Than Wages." *Haaretz*, September 22, 2013. https://www.haaretz.com/israel-news/business /2013-09-22/ty-article/.premium/israel-housing-prices-rising-faster-than -wages/0000017f-e3c9-d9aa-afff-fbd93c0d0000.

Boyarin, Daniel. "Homophobia and the Postcoloniality of the 'Jewish Science.'" In *Queer Theory and the Jewish Question*, edited by Daniel Boyarin, Daniel Itzkovitz, and Ann Pellegrini, 149–65. New York: Columbia University Press, 2003.

Boyarin, Daniel. *Unheroic Conduct: The Rise of Heterosexuality and the Invention of the Jewish Man*. Berkeley: University of California Press, 1997.

Brah, Avtar. Interview by Brenna Bhandar and Rafeef Ziadah. In *Revolutionary Feminisms: Conversations on Collective Action and Radical Thought*, edited by Brenna Bhandar and Rafeef Ziadah, 33–54. London: Verso, 2020.

Brodsky, Jenny, Yitschak Shnoor, Shmuel Beer, and Alexa Neville. *The 65+ Population in Israel*. Jerusalem: Myers-JDC Brookdale, 2018.

Brog, Mooli. "Victims and Victors: Holocaust and Military Commemoration in Israeli Collective Memory." *Israel Studies* 8, no. 3 (2003): 65–99.

Brown, Rachel H. "Multiple Modes of Care: Internet and Migrant Caregiver Networks in Israel." *Global Networks* 16, no. 2 (2016): 237–56. https://doi.org/10 .1111/glob.12112.

Brown, Rachel H. "Reproducing the National Family: Kinship Claims, Development Discourse and Migrant Caregivers in Palestine/Israel." *Feminist Theory* 20, no. 3 (2019): 247–68.

Bruyneel, Kevin. *The Third Space of Sovereignty*. Minneapolis: University of Minnesota Press, 2007.

Bryan, Catherine. "Wait and While You Wait, Work: On the Reproduction of Precarious Labour in Liminal Spaces." In *Migration, Temporality, and Capitalism: Entangled Mobilities across Global Spaces*, edited by Pauline Gardiner Barber and Winnie Lem, 123–40. London: Palgrave Macmillan, 2018.

Bryceson, Deborah, and Ulla Vuorela. "Transnational Families in the Twenty-First Century." In *The Transnational Family: New European Frontiers and Global Networks*, edited by Deborah Bryceson and Ulla Vuorela, 3–30. London and New York: Routledge, 2002.

Busbridge, Rachel. "Israel-Palestine and the Settler Colonial 'Turn': From Interpretation to Decolonization." *Theory, Culture and Society* 35, no. 1 (2018): 91–115.

Busbridge, Rachel. "Messianic Time, Settler Colonial Technology and the Elision of Palestinian Presence in Jerusalem's Historic Basin." *Political Geography* 79 (2020): 2–9.

Busbridge, Rachel. "On Haunted Geography: Writing Nation and Contesting Claims in the Ghost Village of Lifta." *International Journal of Postcolonial Studies* 17, no. 4 (2015): 469–87.

Butler, Judith. *Frames of War: When Is Life Grievable?* New York: Verso, 2009.

Byrd, Jodi. *Transit of Empire: Indigenous Critiques of Colonialism*. Minneapolis: University of Minnesota Press, 2011.

Byrd, Jodi. "Weather with You: Settler Colonialism, Antiblackness, and the Grounded Relationalities of Resistance." *Journal of the Critical Ethnic Studies Association* 5, no. 1–2 (2019): 207–14.

Caduaya, Editha Z. "Filipina Caregiver Took Care of Netanyahu's Father, Brother in Israel." *Newsline*, September 6, 2018. https://newsline.ph/top-stories/2018/09/06/filipina-caregiver-took-care-of-netanyahus-father-brother-in-israel/.

Caldera, Altheria L. "Challenging Capitalist Exploitation: A Black Feminist/Womanist Commentary on Work and Self-Care." *Feminist Studies* 46, no. 3 (2020): 707–16.

Care Collective. *The Care Manifesto: The Politics of Interdependence*. London: Verso, 2020.

Central News Agency. "Rally Demands Better Work Conditions for Migrant Caregivers in Taiwan." *Taiwan News*, March 8, 2020. https://www.taiwannews.com.tw/en/news/3893016.

Chang, Kimberly A., and L. H. M. Ling. "Globalization and Its Intimate Other: Filipina Domestic Workers in Hong Kong." In *Gender and Global Restructuring: Sightings, Cites and Resistances*, edited by Marianne H. Marchand and Anne Sisson Runyan, 27–43. London: Routledge, 2000.

Chatterjee, Soma. "Immigration, Anti-racism, and Indigenous Self-Determination: Towards a Comprehensive Analysis of the Contemporary Settler Colonial." *Social Identities* 25, no. 5 (2019): 644–61.

Chen, Sharlene. *The Marginalized—An Overview of the Migrant Domestic Workers in Taiwan*. Humanity Research Consultancy, 2021. Accessed November 12, 2022. https://humanity-consultancy.com/wp-content/uploads/2021/07/The -Marginalised-An-Overview-of-the-Migrant-Domestic-Workers-in-Taiwan.pdf.

Cheng, Shu-Ju Ada. *Serving the Household and the Nation: Filipina Domestics and the Politics of Identity in Taiwan*. Lanham, MD: Lexington, 2006.

Chernichovsky, Dov, Avigdor Kaplan, Eitan Regev, and Jochanan Stessman. *Long-Term Care in Israel: Funding and Organization Issues*. Jerusalem: Taub Center for Social Policy Studies in Israel, 2017.

Chilmeran, Yasmin, and Pratt, Nicola. "The Geopolitics of Social Reproduction and Depletion: The Case of Iraq and Palestine." *Social Politics* 26, no. 4 (2020): 586–607.

Chin, Christine B. N. *In Service and Servitude: Foreign Female Domestic Workers and the Malaysian "Modernity" Project*. New York: Columbia, 1998.

Chowers, Eyal. "Time In Zionism: The Life and Aftermath of a Temporal Revolution." *Political Theory* 25, no. 5 (1988): 652–85.

Choy, Catherine Ceniza. *Empire of Care: Nursing and Migration in Filipino American History*. Durham, NC: Duke University Press, 2006.

CIVICUS. "Protests on Labour Rights and against Discriminatory Migrant Worker Policies in Taiwan." March 8, 2021. https://monitor.civicus.org/updates/2021 /08/03/protests-labour-rights-and-against-discriminatory-migrant-worker -policies-taiwan/.

Claims Conference. "Our Work around the World: Israel." 2013. https://www .claimscon.org/regions/israel/.

Clarno, Andy. *Neoliberal Apartheid: Palestine/Israel and South Africa After 1994*. Chicago: University of Chicago Press, 2017.

Coe, Cati. "The Temporality of Care: Gender, Migration, and the Entrainment of Life-Courses." In *Anthropological Perspectives on Care*, edited by Erdmute Alber and Heike Drotbohm, 181–205. New York: Palgrave, 2015.

Cohen, Amy, and Elise Hjalmarson. "Quiet Struggles: Migrant Farmworkers, Informal Labor, and Everyday Resistance in Canada." *International Journal of Comparative Sociology* 61, no. 2–3 (2020): 141–58.

Cohen, Nir, and Talia Margalit. "'There Are Really Two Cities Here': Fragmented Urban Citizenship in Tel Aviv." *International Journal of Urban and Regional Research* 39, no. 4 (2015): 666–86.

Cohen, Yinon, and Yitchak Haberfeld. *Gender, Ethnic, and National Earnings Gaps in Israel: The Role of Rising Inequality*. Tel Aviv: Pinhas Sapir Center for Development, Tel Aviv University, 2003.

Constable, Nicole. *Maid to Order in Hong Kong: Stories of Migrant Workers*. Ithaca, NY: Cornell University Press, 1997.

Constable, Nicole. "Sexuality and Discipline among Filipina Domestic Workers in Hong Kong." *American Ethnologist* 24, no. 3 (1997): 539–58.

Constable, Nicole. "Migrant Workers and the Many States of Protest in Hong Kong." *Critical Asian Studies* 41, no. 1 (2009): 143–64.

Constable, Nicole. "Tales of Two Cities: Legislating Pregnancy and Marriage among Foreign Domestic Workers in Singapore and Hong Kong." *Journal of Ethnic and Migration Studies* 46, no. 16 (2020): 3491–507.

Coulthard, Glen. *Red Skin, White Masks: Rejecting the Colonial Politics of Recognition*. Minneapolis: University of Minnesota Press, 2014.

Crenshaw, Kimberlé. "Mapping the Margins: Intersectionality, Identity Politics, and Violence against Women of Color." *Stanford Law Review* 43, no. 6 (1991): 1241–99.

Cwerner, Saulo B. "The Times of Migration." *Journal of Ethnic and Migration Studies* 27, no. 1 (2001): 7–36.

Dahan-Kalev, Henriette. "Mizrahi Feminism in Israel." *Jewish Women: A Comprehensive Historical Encyclopedia*. Jewish Women's Archive, February 27, 2009.

Daoud, Nihaya, Ketan Shankardass, Patricia O'Campo, Kim Anderson, and Ayman K. Agbaria. "Internal Displacement and Health among the Palestinian Minority in Israel." *Social Science Medicine* 74, no. 8 (2010): 1163–71.

Daoud, Suheir Abu Oksa. *Palestinian Women and Politics in Israel*. Gainesville: University Press of Florida, 2009.

Davidson, Lawrence. "Christian Zionism as a Representation of American Manifest Destiny." *Critique: Critical Middle Eastern Studies* 14, no. 2 (2010): 157–69.

Davies, Rebecca. "Reconceptualising the Migration-Development Nexus: Diasporas, Globalisation and the Politics of Exclusion." *Third World Quarterly*, 28, no. 1 (2007): 59–76.

Davis, Adrienne D. "Regulating Sex Work: Erotic Assimilationism, Erotic Exceptionalism, and the Challenge of Intimate Labour." *California Law Review* 5 (2014): 1195–276.

Davis, Angela Y. *Freedom Is a Constant Struggle: Ferguson, Palestine, and the Foundations of a Movement*. Chicago: Haymarket, 2015.

Davis, Angela Y. "Women and Capitalism: Dialectics of Oppression and Liberation." In *The Angela Y. Davis Reader*, edited by Joy James, 161–92. Malden, MA: Blackwell, 1971.

Day, Iyko. *Alien Capital: Asian Racialization and the Logic of Settler Colonial Capitalism*. Durham, NC: Duke University Press, 2016.

Day, Iyko. "Being or Nothingness: Indigeneity, Antiblackness, and Settler Colonial Critique." *Critical Ethnic Studies* 1, no. 2 (2015): 102–21.

Day, Iyko. "Settler Colonialism in Asian North American Representation." *Oxford Research Encyclopedia of Literature*, September 26, 2018, pp. 102–21. https://doi.org/10.1093/acrefore/9780190201098.013.795.

de Certeau, Michel. *The Practice of Everyday Life*. Berkeley: University of California Press, 1984.

Decolonizer. "Tel Aviv and Its Palestinian Localities." Accessed July 22, 2021. https://www.de-colonizer.org/tel-aviv-and-its-palestinian-locali.

Deloria, Philip J. *Playing Indian*. New Haven, CT: Yale University Press, 1998.

Dosick, Wayne D. *Living Judaism: The Complete Guide to Jewish Belief, Tradition, and Practice*. New York: Harper Collins, 2007.

Drori, Israel. *Foreign Workers in Israel: Global Perspectives*. Albany: State University of New York Press, 2009.

Druyan, Nitza. "American Zionist Efforts on Behalf of Yemenite Jews in Eretz Israel, 1912–1914." *American Jewish History* 69, no. 1(1979): 92–8.

Eckstein, Zvi. "Hiring Foreign Workers." [In Hebrew.] Institute for Israeli Democracy, 2010. Accessed October 24, 2020. https://www.idi.org.il/media/4615/העסקת-עובדימ-זרים.pdf.

Eckstein, Zvi. *Report to the Members of the Subcommittee on Foreign Workers in Israel*. September 20, 2007. [In Hebrew.] Accessed October 24, 2020.

Eglash, Ruth. "Government Looks to Cut Back on Foreign Caregivers to Help Unemployment." *Jerusalem Post*, March 12, 2009. https://www.jpost.com/israel/govt-looks-to-cut-back-on-foreign-workers-to-help-unemployment.

Ehrenreich, Barbara. "Maid to Order." In *Global Woman: Nannies, Maids, and Sex Workers in the New Economy*, edited by Barbara Ehrenreich and Arlie Hochschild, 85–103. New York: Henry Holt, 2002.

Ehrenreich, Barbara, and Arlie Hochschild. Introduction to *Global Woman: Nannies, Maids, and Sex Workers in the New Economy*, 1–14. New York: Henry Holt, 2002.

Elia, Nada. *Greater Than the Sum of Our Parts: Feminism, Inter/Nationalism, and Palestine*. London: Pluto, 2023.

Elia, Nada. "Justice Is Indivisible: Palestine as a Feminist Issue." *Decolonization: Indigeneity, Education and Society* 6, no. 1 (2017): 45–63.

Ellman, Michael, and Smaïn Laacher. *Migrant Workers in Israel: A Contemporary Form of Slavery*. Copenhagen: Euro-Mediterranean Human rights Network and International Federation for Human Rights, 2003. https://www.fidh.org/IMG/pdf/il1806a.pdf.

El Zein, Rayya. "Developing a Palestinian Resistance Economy through Agricultural Labor." *Journal of Palestine Studies* 46, no. 3 (2017): 7–26.

Eng, David. *The Feeling of Kinship: Queer Liberalism and the Racialization of Intimacy*. Durham, NC: Duke University Press, 2010.

Englert, Sai. "Settlers, Workers, and the Logic of Accumulation by Dispossession." *Antipode* 52, no. 6 (2020): 1647–66.

Erakat, Noura. *Justice for Some*. Stanford, CA: Stanford University Press, 2019.

Eshkol, Levi. "Eshkol: A Reply to Nasser." Interview by Arnaud de Borchgrave and Michael Elkins. *Newsweek*, February 17, 1969, pp. 49–50, 53, 56. Archived April 7, 2022, at Archive.org. https://archive.org/details/sim_newsweek-us_1969-02-17_73_7/page/49/mode/1up.

Everington, Keoni. "Migrant Domestic Caregivers Rally in Taipei for Equal Rights." *Taiwan News*, December 14, 2020. https://www.taiwannews.com.tw/en/news/4077258.

Fabian, Johannes. *Time and the Other: How Anthropology Makes Its Object*. New York: Columbia University Press, 1983.

Faist, Thomas. "Migrants as Transnational Development Agents: An Inquiry into the Newest Round of the Migration-Development Nexus." *Population, Space and Place*, 14 (2008): 21–42.

Falk, Raphael. *Zionism and the Biology of the Jews*. [In Hebrew.] Tel Aviv: Resling, 2006.

Farsakh, Leila. *Palestinian Labour Migration to Israel: Labour, Land and Occupation*. Abingdon, UK: Routledge, 2005.

Fatema, Shahara Islam (@S_I_Fatema). "Every Israeli city was once Sheikh Jarrah." Twitter, May 13, 2021. https://twitter.com/s_i_fatema/status/1392786841909141507.

Federici, Silvia. *Caliban and the Witch: Women, the Body and Primitive Accumulation*. Chico, CA: AK, 2004.

Fish, Jennifer. *Domestic Worker Organizing in the Global Economy*. New York: Rosa Luxemburg Stiftung, 2017.

Folbre, Nancy. "Nursebots to the Rescue? Immigration, Automation, and Care." *Globalizations* 3, no. 3 (2006): 349–60.

Folbre, Nancy. *Who Pays for the Kids?* New York: Routledge, 1993.

Fortier, Craig. "Unsettling Methodologies / Decolonizing Movements." *Journal of Indigenous Social Development* 6, no. 1 (2017): 20–36.

Foucault, Michel. "The Birth of Biopolitics." In *Ethics, Subjectivity, and Truth*, edited by Paul Rabinow and J. D. Faubion, 73–79. New York: New Press, 1997.

Foucault, Michel. *Discipline and Punish*. New York: Vintage, 1979.

Foucault, Michel. *The History of Sexuality*. Vol. 1, *An Introduction*. London: Penguin, 1981.

Francisco, Valerie, and Robyn Magalit Rodriguez. "Countertopographies of Migrant Women: Transnational Families, Space, and Labor as Solidarity." *Journal of Labor and Society* 17 (2014): 357–72.

Francisco-Menchavez, Valerie. *The Labor of Care: Filipina Migrants and Transnational Families in the Digital Age*. Urbana: University of Illinois Press, 2018.

Gandhi, Evyn Lê Espiritu. *Archipelago of Resettlement*. Berkeley: University of California Press, 2022.

Garfinkel, Renee. "To Be Honored as an Elder in Israel: Aging in the Time of Corona." *Jerusalem Post*, April 2, 2022. https://www.jpost.com/opinion/to-be-honored-as-an-elder-in-israel-aging-in-the-time-of-corona-623390.

Getzoff, Joseph F. "Start-Up Nationalism: The Rationalities of Neoliberal Zionism." *Society and Space* 38, no. 5 (2020): 811–28.

Ghert-Zand, Renee. "Making the Dream of Aliyah Come True for Retirees." *Hadassah Magazine*, July 9, 2018. https://www.hadassahmagazine.org/2018/07/09/making-dream-aliyah-come-true-retirees/.

Giacaman, Rita, Weeam Hammoudeh, Suzan Mohammad Mitwalli, Hala Khallawi, and Hanna Kienzler. "Life and Health under Israeli Military Occupation during COVID-19: Report from the West Bank, Occupied Palestinian Territory." *International Journal of Social Determinants of Health and Health Services* 53, no. 2 (2022).

Giacaman, Rita, Laura Wick, Hanan Abdul-Rahim, and Livia Wick. "The Politics of Childbirth in the Context of Conflict: Policies or De Facto Practices?" *Health Policy* 72, no. 2 (2005): 129–39.

Glass, Joseph B. *From New Zion to Old Zion: American Jewish Immigration and Settlement in Palestine, 1917–1939*. Detroit: Wayne State University Press, 2002.

Glenn, Evelyn Nakano. "Settler Colonialism as Structure." *Sociology of Race and Ethnicity* 1, no. 1 (2015): 52–72.

Gnaidek, Melissa. "The Times of Settler Colonialism." *Lateral* 6, no. 1 (2017).

Goffman, Erving. *The Presentation of Self in Everyday Life*. New York: Anchor, 1956.

Goldberg, David Theo. *The Threat of Race: Reflections on Racial Neoliberalism*. Malden, MA: Wiley-Blackwell, 2008.

Goldstein, Alyosha. "On the Reproduction of Race, Capitalism, and Settler Colonialism." In *Race and Capitalism: Global Territories, Transnational Histories: Conference Proceedings*, edited by Ananya Roy, 42–51. Los Angeles: UCLA Institute on Inequality and Democracy, 2017.

Goldstein, Tani. "PM: Infiltrators Pull Us toward Third World." *Ynet*, January 21, 2010. https://www.ynetnews.com/articles/0,7340,L-3837667,00.html.

Gonalons-Pons, Pilar. "Modern Domesticity: Why Professional Women Hire Domestic Workers in Spain." In *Employers, Agencies and Immigration: Paying for Care*, edited by Sabrina Marchetti and Anna Triandafyllidou, 35–52. Farnham, UK: Ashgate, 2015.

Gordon, Neve, and Moriel Ram. "Ethnic Cleansing and the Formation of Settler Colonial Geographies." *Political Geography* 53 (2016): 20–29.

Gould, Carol C. *Interactive Democracy: The Social Roots of Global Justice*. Cambridge: Cambridge University Press, 2014.

Grassiani, Erella. "Families in Arms: Kinship and the Military in Israeli Society." *Etnofoor*, 16, no. 1 (2003): 115–26.

Green, Ohad, and Liat Ayalon. "Violations of Workers' Rights and Exposure to Work-Related Abuse of Live-In Migrant and Live-Out Local Home Care Workers—A Preliminary Study: Implications for Health Policy and Practice." *Israel Journal of Health Policy Research* 7, no. 1 (2018): 32.

Griffiths, Mark, and Jemima Repo. "Biopolitics and Checkpoint 300 in Occupied Palestine: Bodies, Affect, Discipline." *Political Geography* 65 (2018): 17–25.

Groves, Julian McAllister, and Kimberly A. Chang. "Romancing Resistance and Resisting Romance: Ethnography and the Construction of Power in the Filipina Domestic Worker Community in Hong Kong." *Journal of Contemporary Ethnography* 28, no. 3 (1999): 235–36.

Guarnieri Jaradat, Mya. *The Unchosen: The Lives of Israel's New Others*. London: Pluto, 2017.

Guevarra, Anna. *Marketing Dreams, Manufacturing Heroes: The Transnational Labour Brokering of Filipino Workers*. Rutgers, NJ: Rutgers University Press, 2009.

Gutiérrez Rodríguez, Encarnación. "The Coloniality of Migration and the 'Refugee Crisis': On the Asylum-Migration Nexus, the Transatlantic White European Settler Colonialism-Migration and Racial Capitalism." *Refuge* 34, no. 10 (2018): 16–28.

Gutiérrez Rodríguez, Encarnación. "Domestic Work—Affective Labor: On Feminization and the Coloniality of Labor." *Women's Studies International Forum* 46 (2014): 45–53.

Gutiérrez Rodríguez, Encarnación. *Migration, Domestic Work and Affect: A Decolonial Approach on Value and the Theory of Labor*. New York: Routledge, 2010.

Gutzeit, Zoe. *Excluded from Care: Status-Less Cancer Patients in Israel*. Tel Aviv: Physicians for Human Rights, 2021.

Haaretz. "Israeli Company Pricing Cleaners by Ethnicity Sparks Online Furor." January 10, 2018. https://www.haaretz.com/israel-news/2016–02–07/ty-article/racist-cleaning-service-leaflet-raises-online-outcry/0000017f-e0e7-d7b2-a77f-e3e7ba430000.

Hacker, Daphna. *Legalized Families in the Era of Bordered Globalization*. Cambridge: Cambridge University Press, 2017.

Haddad, Toufic. "Neoliberalism and Palestinian Development: Assessment and Alternatives." In *Critical Readings of Development Under Colonialism: Towards a Political Economy for Liberation in the Occupied Palestinian Territories*, 33–66. Palestine: Rosa Luxemburg Siftung Regional Office and Center for Development Studies, 2015.

Haddad Haj-Yahya, Nasreen, Muhammed Khalaily, Arik Rudnitzky, and Ben Fargeon. "Statistical Report on Arab Society in Israel: 2021." *Israel Democracy Institute*, March 17, 2022. https://en.idi.org.il/articles/38540.

Hagan, Jacqueline, Rubén Hernández-León, and Jean-Luc Demonsant. *Skills of the "Unskilled": Work and Mobility among Mexican Migrants*. Berkeley: University of California Press, 2015.

Hall, Stuart, and Doreen Massey. "Interpreting the Crisis." *Soundings* 44 (2010): 55–69.

Halon, Eytan. "Half of Israelis Say Asylum Seekers Should Be Allowed to Temporarily Stay." *Jerusalem Post*, January 1, 2019. https://www.jpost.com/israel

-news/half-of-israelis-say-asylum-seekers-should-be-allowed-to-temporally -stay-576044.

Halper, Jeff. "Israel's Gone Way beyond Apartheid." Interview by Frank Barat. *New Internationalist*, April 26, 2012.

Halperin, Dafna. "Aging, Family, and Preferences for Care among Older Jews and Arabs." *Israel Studies Review* 28, no. 2 (2013): 102–21.

Halperin, Liora. *The Oldest Guard: Forging the Zionist Settler Past*. Stanford, CA: Stanford University Press, 2021.

Hanafi, Sari. "Explaining Spacio-Cide in the Palestinian Territory: Colonization, Separation, and the State of Exception." *Current Sociology* 61, no. 2 (2012): 190–205.

Handelman, Don. *Nationalism and the Israeli State*. Oxford: Berg, 2004.

Hanieh, Adam. "From State-Led Growth to Globalization: The Evolution of Israeli Capitalism." *Journal of Palestine Studies* 32, no. 4 (2003): 5–21.

Hardt, Michael. "Affective Labor." *Boundary* 26, no. 2 (1999): 89–100.

Harper, Robin, and Hani Zubida. "Living on Borrowed Time: Borders, Ticking Clocks and Timelessness among Temporary Labour Migrants in Israel." In *Migrating Borders and Moving Times*, edited by Donnan Hastings, Madeleine Hurd, and Carolin Leutloff-Grandits, 102–20. Manchester, UK: Manchester University Press, 2017.

Harsha, Nouh, Luay Ziq, and Rita Giacaman. "Disability among Palestinian Elderly in the Occupied Palestinian Territory (OPT): Prevalence and Associated Factors." *BMC Public Health* 19, no. 432 (2019).

Hart, Mitchell. *Social Science and the Politics of Modern Jewish Identity*. Stanford, CA: Stanford University Press, 2000.

Hartman, Saidiya V. *Scenes of Subjection*. New York: Oxford, 1997.

Harvey, David. "The 'New' Imperialism: Accumulation by Dispossession." *Actuel Marx* 35, no. 1 (2004): 71–90.

Haskel, Gil. "Statement by Ambassador Gil Haskel, Head of MASHAV—Israel's Agency for International Development Cooperation." Speech at the United Nations Third International Conference on Financing for Development, Addis Ababa, Ethiopia, July 15, 2015. https://embassies.gov.il/MFA/InternatlOrgs /Speeches/Pages/3rd-International-Conference-on-Financing-for-Development -15-Jul-2015.aspx.

Hasso, Frances Susan. *Buried in the Red Dirt: Race, Reproduction, and Death in Modern Palestine*. Cambridge: Cambridge University Press, 2021.

Hausermann, Heidi, Morgan Lundy, Jill Mitchell, Annabel Ipsen, Quentin Zorn, Karen Vasquez-Romero, and Riley DeMorrow Lynch. "Unsettled Belonging in Complex Geopolitics: Refugees, NGOs, and Rural Communities in Northern Colorado." *Sustainability* 13, no. 3 (2021): 1344.

Hayward, Clarissa. *How Americans Make Race: Stories, Institutions, Spaces*. New York: Cambridge University Press, 2013.

Hazan, Haim. "Victim into Sacrifice: The Construction of the Old as a Symbolic Type." *Journal of Cross-Cultural Gerontology* 5 (1990): 77–84.

Helbich, Maria, and Samah Jabr. "Analysis of the Mental Health Response to COVID-19 and Human Rights Concerns in the Occupied Palestinian Territories." *International Journal of Human Rights in Healthcare* 14, no. 3 (2021): 255–69.

Held, Virginia. *The Ethics of Care: Personal, Political, Global*. Oxford: Oxford University Press, 2006.

Hennebry, Jenna, Will Grass, and Janet Mclaughlin. *Women Migrant Workers' Journey through the Margins: Labour, Migration and Trafficking*. New York: UN Women, 2016.

Hertzberg, Arthur. *The Zionist Idea: A Historical Analysis and Reader*. Lincoln: University of Nebraska Press, 1970.

Herzl, Theodor. *The Jewish State*. Mineola, NY: Dover, 1988.

Herzl, Theodor. "Opening Address, First Zionist Congress, 1897. In *The Judaic Tradition*, edited by Nahum N. Glatzer, 672–78. Springfield, New Jersey: Behrman House, 1969.

Herzog, Hanna. "Family-Military Relations in Israel as a Gendering Social Mechanism." *Armed Forces and Society* 31, no. 1 (2004): 5–30.

Herzog, Hanna. "Homefront and Battlefront: The Status of Jewish and Palestinian Women in Israel." *Israel Studies* 3, no. 1 (1998): 61–84.

Hever, Shir. "Exploitation of Palestinian Labour in Contemporary Zionist Colonialism." *Settler Colonial Studies* 2, no. 1 (2012): 124–32.

Hever, Shir. "The Night Watchman Becomes a Mercenary." *Settler Colonial Studies* 9, no. 1 (2019): 78–95.

High Court of Justice (HCJ). Kav LaOved v. Minister of Welfare et al. (1105/06). [In Hebrew.] 2014. Accessed May 3, 2023. https://psakdin.co.il/Court/בתחום-הסיעוד-פס-ד בנושא-ביטוח-בריאות-לעובדים-הזרים-המועסקים.

High Court of Justice (HCJ). Kav LaOved Worker's Hotline v. Government of Israel et al. (4542/02). *Israel Law Reports* (2006): 260–316.

High Court of Justice (HCJ). Sarah Ravid v. Population and Immigration Authority (8668/17). [In Hebrew.] October 30, 2019. https://www.nevo.co.il/psika_html/elyon/17086680-M19.htm.

High Court of Justice (HCJ). Sharmila Liangi et al. v. the Knesset et al. (4007/11). [In Hebrew.] Jun6 6, 2011. https://www.odonline.co.il/עו-ד-און-ליין-עורכי-דין-פסקי-דין-פסק-דין-11-4007.html.

High Court of Justice (HCJ). Todroangan v. Moshe Maayan (001113/02). [In Hebrew.] January 25, 2004. http://www.glima.info/verdicts/A6E53725C9013FE042256E2D002DDF1E.html.

High Court of Justice (HCJ). Yolanda Gluten v. National Labor Court et al. (1678/07). [In Hebrew.] November 29, 2009. http://www.glima.info/verdicts/07016780.p13.htm.

High Court of Justice (HCJ). Yolanda Gluten v. National Labor Court et al. (10007/09). [In Hebrew.] 2013. Accessed May 3, 2023. https://www.psakdin.co.il/Court/פסק-דין-בתיק-דנגייץ-10007-09.

Hilal, Jamil. "Imperialism and Settler-Colonialism in West Asia: Israel and the Arab-Palestinian Struggle." *Utafiti* 1, no. 1 (1976): 51–70.

Hilal, Jamil. "Rethinking Palestine: Settler-Colonialism, Neo-liberalism and Individualism in the West Bank and Gaza Strip." *Contemporary Arab Affairs* 8, no. 3 (2015): 351–62.

Hindu. "Israeli President Speaks to Family of Indian Caregiver Killed in Rocket Attack from Gaza." May 19, 2021. https://www.thehindu.com/news/national/israeli-president-speaks-to-family-of-indian-caregiver-killed-in-rocket-attack-from-gaza/article34591081.ece.

Hirsch, Dafna. "Zionist Eugenics, Mixed Marriage, and the Creation of a 'New Jewish Type.'" *Journal of the Royal Anthropological Institute* 15 (2009): 592–609.

Hoang, Kimberly Kay. *Dealing in Desire: Asian Ascendancy, Western Decline, and the Hidden Currencies of Global Sex Work.* Berkeley: University of California Press, 2015.

Hobart, Hiʻilei Julia Kawehipuaakahaopulani, and Tamara Kneese. "Radical Care: Survival Strategies for Uncertain Times." *Social Text* 142, no. 38 (2020): 1–16.

Hodes, Caroline. "Gender, Race and Justification: The Value of Critical Discourse Analysis (CDA) in Contemporary Settler Colonial Contexts." *Journal of International Women's Studies* 19, no. 3 (2018): 71–91.

Hondagneu-Sotelo, Pierrette. *Doméstica: Immigrant Workers Cleaning and Caring in the Shadows of Affluence.* Berkeley: University of California Press, 2001.

hooks, bell. *All about Love.* New York: William Morrow, 2001.

hooks, bell. *Sisters of the Yam: Black Women and Self-Recovery.* New York: Routledge, 2015.

Hotline for Migrant Workers. "Children of Migrant Workers in Israel." January 15, 2014. https://hotline.org.il/en/migrants-en/%E2%80%8Fchildren-of-migrant-workers-in-israel/.

Hua, Julietta, and Kasturi Ray. "Rights, Affect and Precarity: Post-racial Formations in Carework." *Cultural Dynamics* 26, no. 1 (2014): 9–28.

Hughes, Sara Salazar. "Unbounded Territoriality: Territorial Control, Settler Colonialism, and Israel/Palestine." *Settler Colonial Studies* 10, no. 2 (2020): 216–33.

Human Rights Watch. "Claiming Rights: Domestic Workers' Movements and Global Advances for Labor Reform." *HRW*, October 27, 2013. https://www.hrw.org

/report/2013/10/27/claiming-rights/domestic-workers-movements-and-global
-advances-labor-reform.

I24 News. "Israel Counts 180,000 Holocaust Survivors at the End of 2020." April 6,
2021. https://www.i24news.tv/en/news/israel/1617722799-israel-counts-180–
000-holocaust-survivors-at-the-end-of-2020.

Ibañez Tirado, Diana. "'We Sit and Wait': Migration, Mobility and Temporality in
Guliston, Southern Tajikistan." *Current Sociology*, 67, no. 2 (2019): 315–33.

Iecovich, Esther. "The Long-Term Care Insurance Law in Israel: Present and Future."
Journal of Ageing and Social Policy 24, no. 1 (2012): 77–92.

Imhoff, Sarah. *The Lives of Jessie Sampter: Queer, Disabled, Zionist.* Durham, NC:
Duke University Press, 2022.

International Domestic Workers Federation (IDWF). "About Us." March 17, 2017.
https://idwfed.org/en/about-us-1.

International Labour Organization (ILO). *Assessment of the Domestic Work Sector
in West Bank Governorates.* Beirut, Lebanon: International Labour Office, 2017.

International Labour Organization (ILO). *Decent Work for Migrant Domestic Workers: Moving the Agenda Forward.* Geneva, Switzerland: International Labour
Office, 2016.

International Labour Organization (ILO). *Domestic Workers across the World: Global
and Regional Statistics and the Extent of Legal Protection.* Geneva, Switzerland:
International Labour Office, 2013.

International Labour Organization (ILO). "Domestic Workers' Union in Lebanon."
Last updated August 3, 2015. https://www.ilo.org/dyn/migpractice/migmain
.showPractice?p_lang=en&p_practice_id=138.

International Labour Organization (ILO). "Founding Congress: Launch of Domestic Workers Union in Lebanon." January 25, 2015. https://www.ilo.org/wcmsp5
/groups/public/—-ed_protect/—-protrav/—-migrant/documents/event/wcms
_383813.pdf.

International Labour Organization (ILO). *Intertwined: A Study of Migrant Domestic
Workers in Lebanon.* Geneva, Switzerland: International Labour Office, 2016.

International Labour Organization (ILO). *Migrant Domestic and Garment Workers
in Jordan.* Geneva, Switzerland: International Labour Office, 2017.

International Labour Organization (ILO). "Our Work." International Organization
of Migration. 2020. https://www.iom.int/our-work.

International Trade Union Confederation. *Facilitating Exploitation: A Review of
Labour Laws for Migrant Domestic Workers in Gulf Cooperation Council Countries.* Brussels, Belgium: International Trade Union Confederation, 2017.

Ireland, Patrick R. "Female Migrant Domestic Workers in Southern Europe and the
Levant: Towards an Expanded Mediterranean Model?" *Mediterranean Politics*
16, no. 3 (2011): 343–63.

Israel Bonds International. "A Mere 11 Years after the End of the Shoah and 9 Years after the Birth of Modern Israel, the Country Created a Program That Would Become a Beacon, a True 'Light unto the Nations,' for Developing Countries." February 2020. https://israelbondsintl.com/feb2020-israel-matters/.

Israel Defense Forces. "First Baby Born in the Field Hospital Established by the IDF in the Philippines." November 15, 2013. Video, 0:43. https://www.youtube.com/watch?v=yXx43HqC_dw&t=5s.

Israel Defense Forces. "IDF Aid Mission Saves Thousands around the World." January 4, 2012. Video, 0:56. https://www.youtube.com/watch?v=L7OyAb2Ozwk&t=15s.

Israel Defense Forces. "Preparations for the IDF's Humanitarian Aid Mission to Nepal." April 27, 2015. Video, 2:28. https://www.youtube.com/watch?v=k47D7Fge5Wk.

Israel Ministry of Foreign Affairs. "Ensuring Equal Rights for Women in Israel." December 31, 2013. https://embassies.gov.il/MFA/AboutIsrael/state/Law/Pages/Ensuring-equal-rights-for-women-in-Israel.aspx.

Israel Ministry of Foreign Affairs. "Statement by Ambassador Gil Haskel, Head of MASHAV- Israel's Agency for International Development Cooperation, Addis Ababa." July 15, 2015. https://embassies.gov.il/MFA/InternatlOrgs/Speeches/Pages/3rd-International-Conference-on-Financing-for-Development-15-Jul-2015.aspx.

Israel Ministry of Foreign Affairs. "New Agreements Permit Additional Care Workers from Nepal and Georgia to Enter Israel." September 30, 2020. https://www.gov.il/en/departments/news/new-agreements-permit-additional-care-workers-from-nepal-and-georgia-to-enter-israel-30-september-2020.

Israel Ministry of Foreign Affairs. "PM Bennett's Holocaust Martyrs' and Heroes' Remembrance Day Speech at Yad Vashem." April 27, 2022. https://www.gov.il/en/departments/news/pm-bennett-s-holocaust-martyrs-and-heroes-remembrance-day-speech-27-apr-2022.

Issar, Siddhant. "Theorizing 'Racial/Colonial Primitive Accumulation': Settler Colonialism, Slavery and Racial Capitalism." *Race and Class* 63, no. 1 (2021): 23–50.

Izraeli, Dafna Nundi. "Culture, Policy, and Women in Dual-Earner Families in Israel." In *Dual-Earner Families: International Perspectives*, edited by Suzan Lewis, Dafna Nundi Izraeli, and Helen M. Hootsmans, 19–45. Thousand Oaks, CA: SAGE, 1992.

Jackson, Vivienne. "Belonging against the National Odds: Globalisation, Political Security and Philippine Migrant Workers in Israel." *Global Society* 25, no. 1 (2011): 49–71.

Jackson, Vivienne. "'This Is Not the Holy Land': Gendered Filipino Migrants in Israel and the Intersectional Diversity of Religious Belonging." *Religion and Gender* 3, no. 1 (2013): 6–21.

Jacoby, Tami Amanda. "Gender Relations and National Security in Israel." In *Redefining Security in the Middle East*, edited by Tami Amanda Jacoby and Brent E. Sasley, 83–104. Manchester, UK: Manchester University Press, 2018.

Jad, Islah. "NGOs: Between Buzzwords and Social Movements." *Development in Practice* 17, no. 4/5 (2007): 622–29.

Jaffe-Hoffman, Maayan. "Israeli Scientists Claim to Reverse Aging Process." *Jerusalem Post*, November 21, 2020. https://www.jpost.com/health-science/israeli -scientists-say-they-found-a-way-to-reverse-the-human-aging-process-649798.

Jamal, Amal. *Arab Minority Nationalism in Israel*. London: Routledge, 2011.

Javellana-Santos, Julie. 2005. "Philippine Envoy to Israel Recalled after Nazi Remark." *Arab News*, June 8, 2005. https://www.arabnews.com/node/268190.

Jiryis, Sabri. "The Land Question in Israel." *MERIP Reports* 47 (1976): 5–20, 24–26.

Johansson, Anna, and Stellan Vinthagen. "Dimensions of Everyday Resistance: An Analytic Framework." *Critical Sociology* 42, no. 3 (2014): 417–35.

Joronen, Mikko, and Mark Griffiths. "The Affective Politics of Precarity: Home Demolitions in Occupied Palestine." *Environment and Planning D: Society and Space* 37, no. 3 (2019): 561–76.

Kahlenberg, Caroline. "New Arab Maids: Female Domestic Work, 'New Arab Women,' and National Memory in British Mandate Palestine." *International Journal of Middle East Studies* 52 (2020): 449–67.

Kalir, Barak. *Latino Migrants in the Jewish State: Undocumented Lives in Israel*. Bloomington: Indiana University Press, 2010.

Kalir, Barak. "To Deport or to 'Adopt'? The Israeli Dilemma in Dealing with Children of Non-Jewish Undocumented Migrants." *Ethnography* 21, no. 3 (2020): 373–93.

Kanaaneh, Rhoda Ann. *Birthing the Nation: Strategies of Palestinian Women in Israel*. Berkeley: University of California Press, 2002.

Kaplan, Amy. "Manifest Domesticity." *American Literature* 70, no. 3 (1998): 581–606.

Karuka, Manu. *Empire's Tracks: Indigenous Nations, Chinese Workers, and the Transcontinental Railroad*. Berkeley: University of California Press, 2019.

Katz, Sheila. *Women and Gender in Early Jewish and Palestinian Nationalism*. Gainesville: University Press of Florida, 2003.

Kauanui, J. Kēhaulani. "'A Structure, Not an Event': Settler Colonialism and Enduring Indigeneity." *Lateral* 5, no. 1 (2016).

Kav LaOved. "Caregivers Call for Ratification of Convention 189." December 30, 2013. https://www.kavlaoved.org.il/en/migrant-caregivers-demand-equal-rights-call -ratification-convention-189/.

Kav LaOved. "Migrant Caregivers in Israel: Problems and Recommendations." Tel Aviv: Kav LaOved and Migrant Forum in Asia, 2009.

Kav LaOved. "New State Deposit Fund for Migrant Caregivers." Kav LaOved—
Migrant Caregivers Facebook page, 2019. https://m.facebook.com/nt
/screen/?params=%7B%22note_id%22%3A1378388902552254%7D&path
=%2Fnotes%2Fnote%2F.

Kav LaOved. "Promoting Domestic Workers' Rights in Accordance with UN Convention 189." 2013. https://www.kavlaoved.org.il/en/promoting-domestic-workers
-rights-in-accordance-withun-convention-189/.

Kav LaOved. *Shadow Report on the Situation of Female Migrant Workers in Israel.*
Submitted to the Committee on the Elimination of All Forms of Discrimination
against Women, 48th Session, Geneva, Switzerland, January 17–February 4,
2010.

Kav LaOved. "Sri Lankan Migrant Workers in Israel: A Report by Kav LaOved
(Worker's Hotline)." Tel Aviv: Kav LaOved, Migrant Forum in Asia, and Migrant
Rights International, 2009.

Kedem, Eldad, and Gilad Padva. "From Sabra to Children of the Sun: Kibbutz Films
from the 1930s to the 2000s." In *One Hundred Years of Kibbutz Life*, edited by Michal Paigi and Shulamit Reinharz, 173–94. New Brunswick, NJ: Transaction, 2011.

Kemp, Adriana. "Labour Migration and Racialisation: Labour Market Mechanisms
and Labour Migration Control Policies in Israel." *Social Identities* 10, no. 2
(2004): 267–92.

Kemp, Adriana. *Reforming Policies on Foreign Workers in Israel.* Paris: OECD, 2010.

Kemp, Adriana, and Francisco Javier Moreno Fuentes. "Between Border Policies
and Welfare Control: A Comparative Analysis of Immigration Policy in Spain
and Israel." In *Spain, Israel and the EU: Human Rights and Immigration Policy*,
73–120. Be'er Sheva, Israel: Ben Gurion University of the Negev, 2010.

Kemp, Adriana, and Rebeca Raijman. "Christian Zionists in the Holy Land: Evangelical Churches, Labor Migrants, and the Jewish State." *Identities* 10, no. 3
(2003): 295–318.

Kemp, Adriana, and Rebeca Raijman. *Foreign and Workers: The Dual Political Economy of Labor Migration in Israel.* [In Hebrew.] Tel Aviv: Kibbutz Hameuchad
and Van Leer Institute Publishing, 2008.

Kershner, Isabel. "Palestinian Gunman Kills 3 Israelis at West Bank Crossing." *New
York Times*, September 26, 2017. https://www.nytimes.com/2017/09/26/world
/middleeast/gunman-kills-israelis.html.

Keshet, Yael, Ariela Popper-Giveon, and Ido Liberman. "Intersectionality and
Underrepresentation among Health Care Workforce: The Case of Arab Physicians
in Israel." *Israel Journal of Health Policy Research* 4, no. 18 (2015).

Khalaila, Rabia, and Howard Litwin. "Modernisation and Filial Piety among Traditional Family Care-Givers: A Study of Arab-Israelis in Cultural Transition."
Ageing and Society 32 (2012): 769–89.

Khalaila, Rabia, and Howard Litwin. "Modernization and Future Care Preferences: A Cross-sectional Survey of Arab Israeli Caregivers." *Journal of Advanced Nursing* 67, no. 7 (2010): 1614–24.

Khalidi, Rashid. *The Hundred Years' War on Palestine*. London: Macmillan, 2020.

Khalidi, Walid, ed. *All That Remains: The Palestinian Villages Occupied and Depopulated by Israel in 1948*. Ramallah: Institute for Palestine Studies, 1991.

Khalidi, Walid. *From Haven to Conquest: Readings in Zionism and the Palestine Problem Until 1948*. Ramallah: Institute for Palestine Studies, 1971.

Khatib, Mohammad, and Ahmad Sheikh Muhammad. "The Health Status of the Palestinians Living in Israel: A Cross-sectional Study." *Lancet* 391, no. S24 (2018).

Knesset. "Basic Law: Israel—The Nation State of the Jewish People." Accessed September 28, 2022. https://knesset.gov.il/laws/special/eng/BasicLawNationState.pdf.

Knesset. "The 19th Knesset, 2nd Session. Protocol No. 21." [In Hebrew.] November 26, 2013. https://oknesset.org/meetings/5/4/541368.html.

Knesset. "The 19th Knesset, 2nd Session. Protocol No. 43." [In Hebrew.] June 23, 2014. Knesset Special Committee Proceedings Database. https://www.knesset.gov.il/committees/eng/CommitteeHistoryByCommittee_eng.asp?com=15.

Knesset. "Staff Report, Presented in Honor of the Minister of Interior, Ms. Ayelet Shaked." [In Hebrew.] April 22, 2022. Knesset Special Committee Proceedings Database. https://www.knesset.gov.il/committees/eng/CommitteeHistoryByCommittee_eng.asp?com=15.

Knesset. "The 24th Knesset, 2nd Session, Protocol No. 19." [In Hebrew.] December 27, 2022. https://oknesset.org/meetings/2/1/2167061.html.

Knesset. "The 24th Knesset, 2nd Session. Protocol No. 26, Meeting of the Special Committee for Foreign Workers." [In Hebrew.] February 1, 2022. Knesset Special Committee Proceedings Database. https://www.knesset.gov.il/committees/eng/CommitteeHistoryByCommittee_eng.asp?com=15.

Knesset. "The 24th Knesset, 2nd Session. Protocol No. 38." [In Hebrew.] May 9, 2022. Knesset Special Committee Proceedings Database. https://www.knesset.gov.il/committees/eng/CommitteeHistoryByCommittee_eng.asp?com=15.

Knesset. "The 25th Knesset, 1st Session, Protocol No. 5." [In Hebrew.] March 19, 2023. Knesset Special Committee Proceedings Database. https://www.knesset.gov.il/committees/eng/CommitteeHistoryByCommittee_eng.asp?com=15.

Kolker, Abigail F. "Privatizing Israel's Migrant Care Puts Profits before People." *+972 Magazine*, September 13, 2015. https://www.972mag.com/privatizing-israels-migrant-care-puts-profits-before-people/.

Kotef, Hagar. *The Colonizing Self: Or, Home and Homelessness in Israel/Palestine*. Durham, NC: Duke University Press, 2020.

Kotef, Hagar. *Movement and the Ordering of Freedom: On Liberal Governance and Mobility*. Durham, NC: Duke University Press, 2016.

Krampf, Arie. "Israel's Neoliberal Turn and Its National Security Paradigm." *Polish Political Science Yearbook* 47, no. 2 (2018): 227–41.

Kraus, Vered, and Yuval P. Yonay. *Facing Barriers: Palestinian Women in a Jewish-Dominated Labor Market*. Cambridge: Cambridge University Press, 2017.

Kravel-Tovi, Michal. "'National Mission': Biopolitics, Non-Jewish Immigration and Jewish Conversion Policy in Contemporary Israel." *Ethnic and Racial Studies* 35, no. 4 (2012): 737–56.

Kristensen, Guro Korsens. "Paid Migrant Domestic Labour in Gender-Equal Norway: A Win-Win Arrangement?" In *Paid Migrant Domestic Labour in a Changing Europe*, edited by Berit Gullikstad, Guro Korsnes Kristensen, and Priscilla Ringrose, 169–93. London: Palgrave Macmillan, 2016.

Kushnirovich, Nonna, and Rebeca Raijman. *The Impact of Bilateral Agreements on Labor Migration to Israel*. New York: Ruppin Academic Center, American Jewish Joint Distribution Committee, 2017.

Kuttab, Eileen. "Community Development Under Occupation: An Alternative Strategy." *Journal of Refugee Studies* 2, no. 1 (1989): 131–38.

Kuttab, Eileen. "Palestinian Women in the Intifada: Fighting on Two Fronts." *Arab Studies Quarterly* 15, no. 2 (1993): 1–69.

Kuttab, Eileen. "The Palestinian Women's Movement: From Resistance and Liberation to Accommodation and Globalization." In *Vents d'Est, vents d'Ouest: Mouvements de femmes et féminismes anticoloniaux*. Geneva: Graduate Institute Publications, 2009.

Kuttab, Eileen. "The Paradox of Women's Work: Coping, Crisis, and Family Survival." In *Living Palestine: Family Survival, Resistance, and Mobility under Occupation*, edited by Lisa Taraki, 231–74. Syracuse, NY: Syracuse University Press, 2006.

Lan, Pei-Chia. *Global Cinderellas: Migrant Domestics and Newly Rich Employers in Taiwan*. Durham, NC: Duke University Press, 2006.

Latin Patriarchate of Jerusalem. "Vicariate for Migrants and Asylum Seekers." Accessed February 3, 2021. https://www.lpj.org/vicariates-and-parishes/vicariate-for-migrants-and-asylum-seekers.html.

Lavie, Smadar. *Wrapped in the Flag of Israel: Mizrahi Single Mothers and Bureaucratic Torture*. Lincoln: University of Nebraska Press, 2014.

Lawrence, Bonita, and Enakshi Dua. "Decolonizing Antiracism." *Social Justice* 32, no. 4 (2005): 120–43.

Lawson, Alan. *Unhomely States: Theorizing English-Canadian Postcolonialism*. Peterborough, Canada: Broadview, 2004.

Lebovitch, Idit, and Zehavit Friedman. *Black Money, Black Labor: Collection of Brokerage Fees from Migrant Caregivers in Israel*. December 2013. www.kavlaoved.org.il/en/wp-content/uploads/2014/02/Black-Money-Black-Labor.pdf.

Lee, Jin-kyung. *Service Economies: Militarism, Sex Work, and Migrant Labor in South Korea*. Minneapolis: University of Minnesota Press, 2010.

Lee, Maggy, Mark Johnson, and Michael McCahill. "Race, Gender, and Surveillance of Migrant Domestic Workers in Saudi Arabia." In *Race, Criminal Justice, and Migration Control: Enforcing the Boundaries of Belonging*, edited by Mary Bosworth, Alpa Parmar, and Yolanda Vázquez, 13–28. Oxford: Oxford University Press, 2018.

Lentin, Ronit. *Traces of Racial Exception: Racializing Israeli Settler Colonialism*. London: Bloomsbury Academic, 2018.

Li, Yao-Tai. "Digital Togetherness as Everyday Resistance: The Use of New Media in Addressing Work Exploitation in Rural Areas." *New Media and Society*, February 24, 2022.

Liebelt, Claudia. *Caring for the "Holy Land": Filipina Domestic Workers in Israel*. New York: Berghahn, 2011.

Lieber, Dov. "'The Man Who Cleaned Our House for 2.5 Years Was the Terrorist.'" *Times of Israel*, September 26, 2017. https://www.timesofisrael.com/the-man -who-cleaned-our-house-for-2-5-years-was-the-terrorist/.

Linder, Ronny. "Health Ministry: Israel Faces Horrendous Crisis Caring for Elderly." *Haaretz*, March 20, 2012. https://www.haaretz.com/israel-news/business /2012-03–20/ty-article/health-ministry-israel-faces-horrendous-crisis-caring -for-elderly/0000017f-e61f-d97e-a37f-f77f100e0000.

Litwin, Howard, Ella Schwartz, and Dana Avital. "Religiosity and Well-Being among Older Jewish Israelis: Findings from SHARE." *Journal of Religion, Spirituality, and Aging* 29, no. 2–3 (2017): 208–23.

Livingston, Julie. "Insights from an African History of Disability." *Radical History Review* 94 (2006), 111–26.

Lloyd, David. "Settler Colonialism and the State of Exception: The Example of Palestine/Israel." *Settler Colonial Studies* 2, no. 1 (2012): 59–80.

Lloyd, David, and Laura Pulido. "In the Long Shadow of the Settler: On Israeli and U.S. Colonialisms." *American Quarterly* 62, no. 4 (2010): 795–809.

Lloyd, David, and Patrick Wolfe. "Settler Colonial Logics and the Neoliberal Regime." *Settler Colonial Studies* 6, no. 2 (2016): 109–18.

Lockman, Zachary. *Comrades and Enemies*. Berkeley: University of California Press, 1996.

Lorde, Audre. *A Burst of Light*. Ithaca, NY: Firebrand, 1988.

Lori, Noora. *Offshore Citizens: Permanent "Temporary" Status in the Gulf*. Cambridge: Cambridge University Press, 2019.

Lowe, Lisa. *The Intimacies of Four Continents*. Durham, NC: Duke University Press, 2015.

Lugones, Maria. "Heterosexualism and the Colonial/Modern Gender System." *Hpyatia* 22, no. 1 (2007): 186–209.

Lutz, Helma, and Ewa Pallenga-Möllenbeck. "Care Workers, Care Drain, and Care Chains: Reflections on Care, Migration, and Citizenship." *Social Politics* 19, no. 1 (2012): 15–37. https://doi.org/10.1093/sp/jxr026.

Luxemburg, Rosa. *The Accumulation of Capital*. New York: Routledge, 2003.

Lyons, Lenore. "Transcending the Border: Transnational Imperatives in Singapore's Migrant Worker Rights Movement." In *Migrant Workers in Asia*, edited by Nicole Constable, 87–104. New York: Routledge, 2013.

Madianou, Mirca. "Ambient Co-presence: Transnational Family Practices in Polymedia Environments." *Global Networks* 16, no. 2 (2016), 183–201.

Madokoro, Laura. "Peril and Possibility: A Contemplation of the Current State of Migration History and Settler Colonial Studies in Canada." *History Compass* 17, no. 1 (2019): 1–8.

Mahon, Rianne. "Through a Fractured Gaze: The OECD, the World Bank and Transnational Care." *Current Sociology* 66, no. 4 (2018): 562–76.

Manalansan, Martin F., IV. *Global Divas: Filipino Gay Men in the Diaspora*. Durham, NC: Duke University Press, 2003.

Manalansan, Martin F., IV. "Queering the Chain of Care Paradigm." *Scholar and Feminist Online* 6, no. 3 (2008). http://sfonline.barnard.edu/immigration/manalansan_01.htm.

Mandal, Chandan Kumar. "Everything You Want to Know about Jobs in Israel." *Kathmandu Post*, January 21, 2021. https://kathmandupost.com/national/2021/01/24/everything-you-want-to-know-about-jobs-in-israel.

Marchetti, Sabrina. "Citizenship and Maternalism in Migrant Domestic Labour: Filipina Workers and Their Employers in Amsterdam and Rome." In *Paid Migrant Domestic Labour in a Changing Europe*, edited by Berit Gullikstad, Guro Korsnes Kristensen, and Priscilla Ringrose, 147–89. London: Palgrave Macmillan, 2016.

Marchetti, Sabrina. "Migrant Domestic Work through the Lens of 'Coloniality:' Narratives from Eritrean Afro-Surinamese Women." In *Towards a Global History of Domestic and Caregiving Workers*, edited by Dirk Hoerder, Elise van Nederveen Meerkerk, and Silke Neunsinger. Leiden, Netherlands: Brill, 2015.

Marchetti, Sabrina. "'Mum Seems Happy': Relatives of Dependent Elders and the Difficult Task to Employ a Migrant Care-Giver." In *Employers, Agencies and Immigration: Paying for Care*, edited by Sabrina Marchetti and Anna Triandafyllidou, 93–110. Farnham, UK: Ashgate, 2015.

Margalit, Ruth. "Israel's Invisible Filipino Workforce." *New York Times*, May 3, 2017. https://www.nytimes.com/2017/05/03/magazine/israels-invisible-filipino-work-force.html.

Maron, Asa, and Michael Shalev. Introduction to *Neoliberalism as a State Project: Changing the Political Economy of Israel*, 1–26. Oxford: Oxford University Press, 2017.

Marshood, Hala, and Riya Alsanah. "Tal'at: A Feminist Movement That Is Redefining Liberation and Reimagining Palestine." *Mondoweiss*, February 25, 2020.
https://mondoweiss.net/2020/02/talat-a-feminist-movement-that-is-redefining
-liberation-and-reimagining-palestine/.

Martyr, Kate. "Taiwan's Domestic Workers Demand Better Conditions." *Deutsche
Welle*, January 1, 2022. https://www.dw.com/en/taiwans-domestic-migrant
-workers-demand-better-conditions/video-60482922.

Masalha, Nur. *The Bible and Zionism: Invented Traditions, Archaeology and Postcolonialism in Palestine-Israel*. London: Zed, 2007.

Masalha, Nur. "Settler-Colonialism, Memoricide and Indigenous Toponymic Memory: The Appropriation of Palestinian Place Names by the Israeli State." *Journal
of Holy Land and Palestine Studies* 14, no. 1 (2015): 3–57.

MASHAV. "MASHAV: Aid from Israel." Gov.il (Israeli government website), August 3, 2022. https://www.gov.il/BlobFolder/generalpage/mashav-brief/en/PDF
_ABOUT-MASHAV-ENGLISH.pdf.

MASHAV. "MASHAV—Israel's Agency for International Development Cooperation,
Ministry of Foreign Affairs." UNECE, February 2015. https://unece.org/fileadmin
/DAM/energy/se/pp/gee21/Workshop_Israel_Feb_15/Mashav.pdf.

MASHAV MFA. "MASHAV in India Indo Israel Agricultural Project." December 3,
2018. Video, 8:18. https://www.youtube.com/watch?v=6o-Dn154wWY.

MASHAV MFA. "The TIPA Project: Empowering Small Holder Farmers in Sen-
egal." February 18, 2018. Video, 1:36. https://www.youtube.com/watch?v
=ucpJsARF_O0.

MASHAV MFA. "World Humanitarian Aid Day 2020." August 19, 2020. Video, 2:03.
https://www.youtube.com/watch?v=IYnjYVknUZE.

Masri, Mazen. "Colonial Imprints: Settler-Colonialism as a Fundamental Feature
of Israeli Constitutional Law." *International Journal of Law in Context* 13, no. 3
(2017): 388–407.

Massumi, Brian. *Politics of Affect*. Cambridge: Polity, 2015.

Matar, Haggai. "Community Shaken after Night of Arson Attacks on Refugees."
+972 Magazine, April 26, 2012. https://www.972mag.com/community-shaken
-after-coordinated-attacks-on-african-refugees/.

Mazuz, Keren. "Beauty Contests, Challenging Israeliness." *Ethnologie Française*
25, no. 2 (2015): 353–62.

Mazuz, Keren. "Folding Paper Swans, Modeling Lives." *Medical Anthropology Quarterly* 27, no. 2 (2013): 215–32.

Mazuz, Keren. "The State of the Jewish Family: Eldercare as a Practice of Corporeal
Symbiosis by Filipina Migrant Workers." In *Ethnographic Encounters in Israel:
Poetics and Ethics of Fieldwork*, edited by Fran Markowitz, 97–111. Blooming-
ton: Indiana University Press, 2013.

McClintock, Anne. *Imperial Leather: Race, Gender and Sexuality in the Colonial Contest*. New York: Routledge, 1995.

McMahon, Sean F. "Temporality, Peace Initiatives and Palestinian-Israeli Politics." *Middle East Critique* 25, no. 1 (2016): pp. 5–21.

Meari, Lena. "The Roles of Palestinian Peasant Women: The Case of al-Birweh Village, 1930–1960." In *Displaced at Home: Ethnicity and Gender among Palestinians in Israel*, edited by Rhoda Ann Kanaaneh and Isis Nusair, 119–32. Albany: State University of New York Press, 2010.

Melnyk, Leanne. *Regulating International Labor Recruitment in the Domestic Work Sector: A Review of Key Issues, Challenges and Opportunities*. Geneva, Switzerland: International Labour Organization, 2016.

Mendoza, Amado. *The Record of a Non-confrontational Debt Management Approach*. Quezon City, Philippines: UP Center for Integrative Development Studies, 1992.

Men-Tal Nursing Services. "Caregivers." 1995. Archived December 7, 2021, at Archive.org. https://web.archive.org/web/20211207182914/http://men-tal.net /eng/caregivers.htm.

Miaari, Sami H., Maha Sabbah-Karkabi, and Amit Loewenthal. *How Is the COVID-19 Crisis Exacerbating Socioeconomic Inequality among Palestinians in Israel?* IZA: Institute of Labor Economics, discussion paper no. 13716, September 2020. https://docs.iza.org/dp13716.pdf.

Mies, Maria. *Patriarchy and Accumulation on a World Scale*. London: Zed, 1986.

Migrante International. "Arrest and Detention of Filipino Migrants in Israel Refutes Duterte's 'Malasakit' and 'Serbisyo' towards Overseas Filipinos." July 24, 2019. https://migranteinternational.org/arrest-and-detention-of-filipino-migrants -in-israel-refutes-dutertes-malasakit-and-serbisyo-towards-overseas-filipinos -migrante-international/.

Migrante International. "Labor Day 2023: Workers of the World Unite and Fight for Our Rights! Onward with Our Struggle against Imperialist Exploitation and Oppression." May 1, 2023. https://migranteinternational.org/labor-day-2023 -workers-of-the-world-unitye-and-fight-for-our-rights-onward-with-our -struggle-against-imperialist-exploitation-and-oppression/.

Migrante International. "Migrante International Expresses Solidarity with the Palestinian People and Demand the Safety of Filipinos Affected by the Escalating Israeli-Palestinian Conflict." May 15, 2021. https://migranteinternational.org/migrante -international-expresses-solidarity-with-the-palestinian-people-and-demand -the-safety-of-filipinos-affected-by-the-escalating-israeli-palestinian-conflict/.

Migrante International. "US-Israel Hands Off Gaza! Free Palestine! End the Genocide!" August 6, 2014. https://migranteinternational.org/us-israel-hands-off -gaza-free-palestine-end-the-genocide/.

Mills, Charles. "Body Politic, Bodies Impolitic." *Social Research* 78, no. 2 (2011): 583–606.

Mills, Charles. *The Racial Contract*. Ithaca, NY: Cornell University Press, 1997.

Mohanty, Chandra. "Women Workers and Capitalist Scripts." In *Feminist Genealogies, Colonial Legacies, Democratic Futures*, edited by Chandra Talpade Mohanty and Jacqui M. Alexander, 3–29. New York: Routledge, 2003.

Moreton-Robinson, Aileen. *The White Possessive: Property, Power, and Indigenous Sovereignty*. Minneapolis: University of Minnesota Press, 2015.

Morgan, Jennifer. *Laboring Women: Reproduction and Gender in New World Slavery*. Philadelphia: University of Pennsylvania Press, 2004.

Morgensen, Scott. "Settler Homonationalism: Theorizing Settler Colonialism within Queer Modernities." *GLQ* 16, no. 1–2 (2010): 105–31.

Morgensen, Scott. *Spaces between Us: Queer Settler Colonialism and Indigenous Decolonization*. Minneapolis: University of Minnesota, 2011.

Morgensen, Scott. "Un-settling Settler Desires." *Unsettling America* (blog), September 8, 2011. https://unsettlingamerica.wordpress.com/2011/09/08/un-settling -settler-desires/.

Morris, James X. "Taiwan's Migrant Workers Are Finding Their Voice." *Diplomat*, June 27, 2018. https://thediplomat.com/2018/06/taiwans-migrant-workers-are -finding-their-voice/.

Motzafi-Haller, Pnina, Orly Benjamin, and Deborah Bernstein. "Emotional Politics in Cleaning Work: The Case of Israel." *Human Relations* 64, no. 3 (2011): 337–57.

Mountz, Alison. "Where Asylum-Seekers Wait: Feminist Counter-topographies of Sites between States." *Gender, Place and Culture* 18, no. 3 (2011): 381–99.

Muir, Diana. "A Land without a People for a People without a Land." *Middle East Quarterly* 15, no. 2 (Spring 2008). https://www.meforum.org/1877/a-land -without-a-people-for-a-people-without.

Mundlak, Guy, and Hila Shamir. "Between Intimacy and Alienage: The Legal Construction of Domestic and Carework in the Welfare State." In *Migration and Domestic Work: A European Perspective on a Global Theme*, edited by Helma Lutz, 161–76. Farnham, UK: Ashgate, 2008.

Mundlak, Guy, and Hila Shamir. "Bringing Together or Drifting Apart? Targeting Care Work as 'Work Like No Other.'" *Canadian Journal of Women and the Law* 23, no. 1 (2011): 289–308.

Mundlak, Guy, and Hila Shamir. "Organizing Migrant Care Workers in Israel: Industrial Citizenship and the Trade Union Option." *International Labour Review* 153, no. 1 (2014): 93–116.

Munem, Bahia M. "Migration and the Aging Body: Elderly War Refugees in Brazil between National Borders and Social Boundaries." In *Liquid Borders: Migration as Resistance*, edited by Mabel Moraña, 240–54. London: Routledge, 2021.

Murphy, Michelle. "Unsettling Care: Troubling Transnational Itineraries of Care in Feminist Health." *Social Studies of Science* 45, no. 5 (2015): 717–37.

Na'amat. "History: In the Beginning." Archived September 29, 2022, at Archive .org. https://web.archive.org/web/20220929214312/https://naamat.org/about /history/.

Nadasen, Premilla. *Household Workers Unite: The Untold Story of African-American Women Who Built a Movement.* Boston: Beacon, 2015.

Nadasen, Premilla. "Rethinking Care Work: (Dis)Affection and the Politics of Caring." *Feminist Formations* 33, no. 1 (2021): 165–88.

Nakhleh, Khalil. "The Two Galilees: Zionist Practice in the Context of Military Occupation in Palestine." Paper presented at the Fifth United Nations Seminar on the Question of Palestine, New York, March 15–19, 1982. https://www.un.org /unispal/document/auto-insert-195585/.

Narayan, Uma. "Colonialism and Its Others: Considerations on Rights and Care Discourses." *Hypatia* 10, no. 2 (1995): 133–40.

Nash, Jennifer C. "Practicing Love: Black Feminism, Love-Politics, and Post-intersectionality." *Meridians* 11, no. 2 (2011): 1–24.

Nasol, Katherine, and Valerie Francisco-Menchavez. "Filipino Home Care Workers: Invisible Frontline Workers in the COVID-19 Crisis in the United States." *American Behavioral Scientist* 65, no. 10 (2021): 1365–83.

Natan Nursing. "Foreign Caregivers." [In Hebrew.] May 7, 2015. Archived May 22, 2016, at Archive.org. https://web.archive.org/web/20160522125827/https://nathan .co.il/עובדים_זרים_לסיעוד/.

National Insurance Institute. *Implementation of the Long-Term Care Insurance Law in the Arab Sector.* [In Hebrew.] Jerusalem: National Insurance Institute. 1995.

National Labor Court. Aryeh Zetlman v. Valentina Petrov (47576-10-12). [In Hebrew.] July 7, 2016. https://www.nevo.co.il/psika_html/avoda/A-12-10-47576 -456.htm.

National Labor Court. Elena Zachariah v. The Estate of the Late Liza Kimmelman (001267/04). [In Hebrew.] July 23, 2006. https://www.nevo.co.il/psika_html /avoda/a04001267-156.htm.

Nefesh B'Nefesh. "Informal Guide to Bringing Your Elderly Parents to Israel." Last updated July 5, 2023. https://www.nbn.org.il/uncategorized/informal-guide-to -bringing-your-elderly-parents-to-israel/.

Nichols, Robert. *Theft Is Property! Dispossession and Critical Theory.* Durham, NC: Duke University Press, 2020.

Norton, Ben. "Israeli Cleaning Company Charges Based on Race and Characterizes Arabs as a Security Threat, according to Flier." *Salon*, February 8, 2016. https:// www.salon.com/2016/02/08/israeli_cleaning_company_charges_based_on_race _and_characterizes_arabs_as_a_security_threat_according_to_flier/.

Nursing and Nursing Care. "Foreign Workers." [In Hebrew.] Accessed September 21, 2022. https://www.nursing.org.il/עובדים-זרים/החלפת-עובד-זר-סיעודי/.

Ogaya, Chiho. "Filipino Domestic Workers and the Creation of New Subjectivities." *Asian and Pacific Migration Journal* 13, no. 3 (2004): 381–404.

Oishi, Nana. *Women in Motion: Globalization, State Policies, and Labor Migration in Asia*. Stanford, CA: Stanford University Press, 2005.

Ong, Aihwa. *Neoliberalism as Exception*. Durham, NC: Duke University Press, 2006.

Oran, Serap S. "Pensions and Social Reproduction." In *Social Reproduction Theory: Remapping Class, Recentering Oppression*, edited by Tithi Bhattacharya, 148–70. London: Pluto, 2017.

Organisation for Economic Co-operation and Development (OECD). *In It Together: Why Less Inequality Benefits All*. Paris: OECD, 2015.

Organisation for Economic Co-operation and Development (OECD). "Spending on Long-Term Care." November 2020. https://www.oecd.org/health/health -systems/Spending-on-long-term-care-Brief-November-2020.pdf.

Palestine Remembered. "District of Haifa." Accessed June 8, 2021. https://www .palestineremembered.com/Haifa/Haifa/index.html.

Palmer, Phyllis. *Domesticity and Dirt: Housewives and Domestic Servants in the United States, 1920–1945*. Philadelphia: Temple University Press, 1989.

Pappé, Ilan. *The Ethnic Cleansing of Palestine*. Oxford: Oneworld, 2006.

Pappé, Ilan. "Shtetl Colonialism: First and Last Impressions of Indigeneity by Colonised Colonisers." *Settler Colonial Studies*, 2, no. 1 (2012): 39–58.

Parreñas, Rhacel S. *Children of Global Migration*. Stanford, CA: Stanford University Press, 2005.

Parreñas, Rhacel S. "The Indenture of Migrant Domestic Workers." *WSQ* 45, no. 1/2 (2017): 113–27.

Parreñas, Rhacel S. "Long Distance Intimacy: Class, Gender and Intergenerational Relations between Mothers and Children in Filipino Transnational Families." *Global Networks* 5, no. 4 (2005): 317–36.

Parreñas, Rhacel S. "Migrant Domestic Workers as 'One of the Family.'" In *Migration and Care Labour*, edited by Bridget Anderson and Isabel Shutes, 49–66. London: Palgrave Macmillan, 2014.

Parreñas, Rhacel S. "Migrant Filipina Domestic Workers and the International Division of Reproductive Labor." *Gender and Society* 14, no. 4 (2000): 560–80.

Parreñas, Rhacel S. *Servants of Globalization: Migration and Domestic Work*. Stanford, CA: Stanford University Press, 2001.

Parreñas, Rhacel S. *Unfree: Migrant Domestic Work in Arab States*. Stanford, CA: Stanford University Press, 2021.

Parreñas, Rhacel S., and Rachel Silvey. "The Precarity of Migrant Domestic Work." *South Atlantic Quarterly* 117, no. 2 (2018): 430–38.

Parsons, Nigel, and Mark B. Salter. "Israeli Biopolitics: Closure, Territorialisation and Governmentality in the Occupied Palestinian Territories." *Geopolitics* 13, no. 4 (2008): 701–23.

Paul, Anju M. "Stepwise International Migration: A Multi-stage Migration Pattern for the Aspiring Migrant." *American Journal of Sociology* 116, no. 6 (2011): 1842–86.

Pentin, Edward. "Terrasanta.net: Indian Catholic Migrant Workers in Israel." Saint James Vicariate for Hebrew-Speaking Catholics in Israel. Accessed June 18, 2021. https://catholic.co.il/?cat=news&view=article&id=1504.

Peteet, Julie. "Closure's Temporality: The Cultural Politics of Time and Waiting." *South Atlantic Quarterly* 117, no. 1 (2018): 43–64.

Pfefferman, Talia. "Separate Spheres, Intertwined Spheres: Home, Work, and Family among Jewish Women Business Owners in the Yishuv." *Journal of Israeli History* 32, no. 1 (2013): 7–28.

Philippines Department of Foreign Affairs. "Filipino Caregivers Tapped as Tourism Ambassadors in Israel." February 11, 2020. https://dfa.gov.ph/dfa-news/news -from-our-foreign-service-postsupdate/26057-filipino-caregivers-tapped-as -tourism-ambassadors-in-israel.

Philippine Overseas Employment Administration (POEA). "Recruitment Specification Form," form no. 200008-V (November 2, 2019). Department of Labor and Employment. https://www.dmw.gov.ph/archives/vacancies/files/200008%20 -%20U%20-%20ISRAEL.pdf.

Philippine Overseas Employment Administration (POEA). "New Standard Employment Contract for Filipino Caregivers to Israel," memorandum circular no. 2 (February 20, 2020). Department of Labor and Employment. https://www.dmw .gov.ph/archives/memorandumcirculars/2020/MC-02-2020.pdf.

Piastro, Claudia P. *Eating in Israel: Nationhood, Gender and Food Culture*. Cham, Switzerland: Palgrave, 2021.

Piepzna-Samarasinha, Leah L. *Care Work: Dreaming Disability Justice*. Vancouver: Arsenal Pulp, 2018.

Pieterse, Jan N. "The History of a Metaphor: Christian Zionism and the Politics of Apocalypse." *Archives de Sciences Sociales des Religions* 36, no. 75 (1991): 75–103.

Piterberg, Gabriel. *The Returns of Zionism: Myths, Politics and Scholarship in Israel*. New York: Verso, 2008.

Population and Immigration Authority (PIBA). *Foreign Workers' Rights Handbook*. April 1, 2023. https://www.gov.il/BlobFolder/generalpage/foreign_workers _rights_booklets/he/foreign_workers_rights_booklets_en.pdf.

Porat, Irit, and Esther Iecovich. "Relationships between Elderly Care Recipients and Their Migrant Live-In Home Care Workers in Israel." *Home Health Care Services Quarterly* 29, no. 1 (2010): 1–21.

Presner, Todd S. *Muscular Judaism: The Jewish Body and the Politics of Regeneration*. London: Routledge, 2007.

Prime Minister's Office. "PM Netanyahu Meets with Philippines President Rodrigo Duterte." Gov.il (Israeli government website), September 3, 2018. https://www.gov.il/en/departments/news/event_philippines030918.

Puar, Jasbir. *The Right to Maim: Debility, Capacity, Disability*. Durham, NC: Duke University Press, 2017.

Pulido, L. "Geographies of Race and Ethnicity III: Settler Colonialism and Non-native People of Color." *Progress in Human Geography* 42, no. 2 (2018): 309–19.

Qadri, Mustafa. "The UAE's Kafala System: Harmless or Human Trafficking?" In *Dubai's Role in Facilitating Corruption and Global Illicit Financial Flows*, edited by Matthew Page and Jodi Vittori, 79–83. Washington, DC: Carnegie Endowment for International Peace, 2020.

Quijano, Anibal. "Coloniality of Power and Eurocentrism in Latin America." *Nepantla* 1, no. 2 (2000): 533–80.

Ra'ad, Basem L. "Enlarging 'Palestine.'" *PMLA* 129, no. 2 (2014): 274–76.

Raghuram, Parvati. "Which Migration, What Development? Unsettling the Edifice of Migration and Development." *Population, Space and Place*, 15, no. 2 (2009): 103–17.

Rai, Shirin M., Catherine Hoskyns, and Dania Thomas. "Depletion: The Social Cost of Reproduction." *International Feminist Journal of Politics* 16, no. 1 (2013): 86–105.

Raijman, Rebeca. "A Warm Welcome for Some: Israel Embraces Immigration of Jewish Diaspora, Sharply Restricts Labor Migrants and Asylum Seekers." Migration Policy Institute, June 5, 2020. https://www.migrationpolicy.org/article/israel-law-of-return-asylum-labor-migration.

Raijman, Rebeca, and Adriana Kemp. "Labor Migration in Israel: The Creation of a Non-free Workforce." *ProtoSociology* 27 (2011): 177–95.

Raijman, Rebeca, and Nonna Kushnirovich. *Labor Migrant Recruitment Practices in Israel*. Brussels: European Commission, 2012.

RavGil Nursing Services 2007 Ltd. "Looking for Caregivers? Looking for Caregivers Jobs? RavGil Nursing Services Is the Solution." Facebook, August 11, 2018. https://www.facebook.com/ybengera79/photos/a.932769343577015/932769463577003/.

Ravid, Barak. "Domestic Issues Again Cloud Netanyahu's Vision, but This Time Much Closer to Home." *Haaretz*, September 2, 2011. https://www.haaretz.com/2011-09-02/ty-article/domestic-issues-again-cloud-netanyahus-vision-but-this-time-much-closer-to-home/0000017f-df01-df7c-a5ff-df7b19c60000.

Ravid, Maayan. "Making Their Lives Miserable: Structural Violence and State Racism Towards Asylum Seekers from Sudan and Eritrea in Israel." *State Crime* 11, no. 1 (2022): 128–48.

Raz, Doron. "Every 55 Hours, the Body of a Helpless Elderly Man Is Discovered in Israel. Without Corona the Situation Would Have Been Worse." [In Hebrew.] *Walla*, February 20, 2021. https://news.walla.co.il/item/3418048.

Raz-Krakotzkin, Amnon. "Exile within Sovereignty: Critique of the 'Negation of Exile' in Israeli Culture." In *The Scaffolding of Sovereignty*, edited by Zvi B. Benite, Stefanos Geroulanos, and Nicole Jerr, 393–420. New York: Columbia University Press, 2017.

Reddy, Chandan. *Freedom with Violence*. Durham, NC: Duke University Press, 2011.

Regional Labor Court in Haifa. Molnar Atalka v. The Estate of the Late Zelucivar Penny, Mali Kesner, et al. (3549/06). [In Hebrew.] Accessed April 11, 2023. https://www.fridmanwork.com/LAWx-lawyer100227.html.

Rifkin, Mark. *Beyond Settler Time: Temporal Sovereignty and Indigenous Self-Determination*. Durham, NC: Duke University Press, 2017.

Rifkin, Mark. "Settler Common Sense." *Settler Colonial Studies* 3, no. 3–4 (2013): 322–40.

Rifkin, Mark. "Settler States of Feeling: National Belonging and the Erasure of Native American Presence." In *A Companion to American Literary Studies*, edited by Caroline F. Levander and Robert S. Levine, 342–55. Hoboken, NJ: Wiley, 2011.

Robinson, Shira. *Citizen Strangers: Palestinians and the Birth of Israel's Liberal Settler State*. Stanford, CA: Stanford University Press, 2013.

Rodriguez, Robyn M. "Migrant Heroes: Nationalism, Citizenship and the Politics of Filipino Migrant Labor." *Citizenship Studies* 6, no. 3 (2002): 341–56.

Rodriguez, Robyn M. *Migrants for Export: How the Philippine State Brokers Labor to the World*. Minneapolis: University of Minnesota Press, 2010.

Rodriguez, Robyn M. "Philippine Migrant Workers' Transnationalism in the Middle East." *International Labor and Working-Class History* 79 (2011): 48–61.

Rollins, Judith. *Between Women: Domestics and their Employers*. Philadelphia: Temple University Press, 1985.

Rom, Michael, and Orly Benjamin. *Feminism, Family, and Identity in Israel*. London: Palgrave Macmillan, 2011.

Romero, Mary. *Maid in the U.S.A*. New York: Routledge, 1992.

Rosenhek, Zeev. "The Political Dynamics of a Segmented Labour Market: Palestinian Citizens, Palestinians from the Occupied Territories and Migrant Workers in Israel." *Acta Sociologica* 46, no. 3 (2003): 151–69.

Rosenthal, Anat. "Terms of Endearment: Undocumented Domestic Workers and Their Israeli Employers." In *Transnational Migration to Israel in Global Comparative Perspective*, edited by Sarah Willen, 203–16. Lanham, MD: Lexington, 2007.

Roseware, Stuart. "The ILO's Domestic Worker Convention: Challenging the Gendered Disadvantage of Asia's Foreign Domestic Workers?" *Global Labour Journal* 4, no. 1 (2013): 1–25.

Rottenberg, Catherine. "The Rise of Neoliberal Feminism." *Cultural Studies* 28, no. 3 (2014): 418–37.

Rouhana, Nadim N. *Palestinian Citizens in an Ethnic Jewish State*. New Haven, CT: Yale University Press, 1997.

Rouhana, Nadim N., and Areej Sabbagh-Khoury. "Settler-Colonial Citizenship: Conceptualizing the Relationship between Israel and Its Palestinian Citizens." *Settler Colonial Studies* 5, no. 3 (2015): 205–25.

Rozen, Sigal. *Caregivers from Eastern Europe*. Tel Aviv: Hotline for Refugees and Migrants and Kav LaOved, 2017.

Rubin, Sarah. "Palestinian Kills 3 Israelis in Settlement Near Jerusalem." *USA Today*, September 26, 2017. https://www.usatoday.com/story/news/world/2017/09/26/palestinian-kills-israelis-near-jerusalem/702988001/.

Ruddick, Sara. *Maternal Thinking: Toward a Politics of Peace*. Boston: Beacon, 1989.

Sa'ar, Amalia. *Economic Citizenship: Neoliberal Paradoxes of Empowerment*. New York: Berghahn, 2016.

Sabbagh-Khoury, Areej. "Palestinian Predicaments: Jewish Immigration and Refugee Repatriation." In *Displaced at Home: Ethnicity and Gender among Palestinians in Israel*, edited by Rhoda A. Kanaaneh and Isis Nusair, 171–88. Albany: State University of New York Press, 2010.

Sabbagh-Khoury, Areej. "Tracing Settler Colonialism: A Genealogy of a Paradigm in the Sociology of Knowledge Production in Israel." *Politics and Society* 50, no. 1 (2022): 44–83.

Sabban, Rima. *Maids Crossing: Domestic Workers in the UAE*. Saarbrücken. Germany: Lambert Academic, 2012.

Sa'di, Ahmad H. "Modernization as an Explanatory Discourse of Zionist-Palestinian Relations." *British Journal of Middle Eastern Studies* 24, no. 1 (1997): 25–48.

Sa'di, Ahmad H. *Through Surveillance: The Genesis of Israeli Policies of Population Management, Surveillance and Political Control towards the Palestinian Minority*. Manchester, UK: Manchester University Press, 2014.

Sadowski, Yahya. "The New Orientalism and the Democracy Debate." *Middle East Report* 183 (July/August 1993): 14–21, 40.

Sagi, Doron. "Special Rights for Holocaust Survivors in Home Care Hours." Last updated December 1, 2021. https://www.reutheshel.org.il/en/special-rights-for-holocaust-survivors-in-home-care-hours/.

Said, Edward. *Covering Islam: How the Media and Experts Determine How We See the Rest of the World*. New York: Pantheon, 1981.

Said, Edward. *Orientalism*. New York: Vintage, 1979.

Saint James Vicariate for Hebrew-Speaking Catholics in Israel. "About Us." Accessed August 6, 2021. https://www.catholic.co.il/?cat=sjv&view=article&id=10171.

Salaita, Steven. "Beyond Orientalism and Islamophobia: 9/11, Anti-Arab Racism, and the Mythos of National Pride." *New Centennial Review* 6, no. 2 (2006): 245–66.

Salaita, Steven. *The Holy Land in Transit: Colonialism and the Quest for Canaan.* Syracuse, NY: Syracuse University Press, 2006.

Salaita, Steven. "Inter/Nationalism from the Holy Land to the New World: Encountering Palestine in American Indian Studies." *Native American and Indigenous Studies* 1, no. 2 (2014): 125–44.

Salamanca, Omar Jabary, Mezna Qato, Kareem Rabie, and Sobhi Samour. "Past Is Present: Settler Colonialism in Palestine." *Settler Colonial Studies* 2, no. 1 (2012): 1–8.

Sales, Joy. "Activism as Essential Work: Filipino Healthcare Workers and Human Rights in the Philippines." *Diplomatic History* 45, no. 3 (2021): 595–603.

Salt, John, and Jeremy Stein. "Migration as a Business: The Case of Trafficking." *International Migration* 35, no. 4 (1997): 467–94.

Samed, Amal. "The Proletarianization of Palestinian Women in Israel." *MERIP Reports* 50 (July/August 1976): 10–15.

Sampter, Jessie, ed. *A Guide to Zionism.* New York: Zionist Organization of America, 1920.

Sampter, Jessie, ed. *Modern Palestine: A Symposium.* New York: Hadassah, 1933.

Sanchez, Raf. "Tens of Thousands of Israeli Holocaust Survivors Are Living in Abject Poverty." *Telegraph*, January 27, 2016. https://www.telegraph.co.uk/news/worldnews/middleeast/israel/12122754/Tens-of-thousands-of-Israeli-Holocaust-survivors-are-living-in-abject-poverty.html.

Saranillo, Dean Itsuji. "Why Asian Settler Colonialism Matters." *Settler Colonial Studies* 3, no. 3–4 (2013), 280–94.

Sasson-Levy, Orna. "Contradictory Consequences of Mandatory Conscription: The Case of Women Secretaries in the Israeli Military." *Gender and Society* 21, no. 4 (2007): 481–507.

Sayegh, Fayez. "Zionist Colonialism in Palestine (1965)." *Settler Colonial Studies* 2, no. 1 (2012): 206–25.

Schotten, Heike. *Queer Terror: Life, Death, and Desire in the Settler Colony.* New York: Columbia University Press, 2018.

Scott, James C. *Domination and the Arts of Resistance.* New Haven, CT: Yale University Press, 1990.

Scott, James C. "Everyday Forms of Resistance." *Copenhagen Journal of Asian Studies* 4 (1989): 33–62.

Seikaly, Sherene. *Men of Capital: Scarcity and Economy in Mandate Palestine.* Stanford, CA: Stanford University Press, 2015.

Selby, Mark. "Israeli Longevity Industry 'Reaching Critical Mass'—Aging Analytics Agency." Innovation Warehouse, April 12, 2019. http://analytics.dkv.global/data/pdf/Longevity-in-Israel/Longevity_in_Israel_-_Press_Release.pdf.

Senor, Dan, and Saul Singer. *Start-Up Nation: The Story of Israel's Economic Miracle*. Toronto: McClelland and Stewart, 2009.

Shafir, Gershon. *Land, Labor and the Origins of the Israeli-Palestinian Conflict, 1882–1914*. Berkeley: University of California Press, 1989.

Shafir, Gershon, and Yoav Peled. *Being Israeli: The Dynamics of Multiple Citizenship*. Cambridge: Cambridge University Press, 2002.

Shalev, Michael. *Labour and the Political Economy in Israel*. Oxford: Oxford University Press, 1992.

Shalhoub-Kevorkian, Nadera. "The Biopolitics of Israeli Settler Colonialism: Palestinian Bedouin Children Theorize the Present." *Journal of Holy Land and Palestine Studies* 15, no. 1 (2016), 7–29.

Shalhoub-Kevorkian, Nadera. "The Gendered Nature of Education under Siege." *International Journal of Lifelong Education* 27, no. 2 (2008): 179–200.

Shalhoub-Kevorkian, Nadera. "Human Suffering in Colonial Contexts: Reflections from Palestine." *Settler Colonial Studies* 4, no. 3 (2014): 277–90.

Shalhoub-Kevorkian, Nadera. *Incarcerated Childhood and the Politics of Unchilding*. Cambridge: Cambridge University Press, 2019.

Shalhoub-Kevorkian, Nadera. "Infiltrated Intimacies: The Case of Palestinian Returnees." *Feminist Studies* 42, no. 1 (2016): 166–93.

Shalhoub-Kevorkian, Nadera. *Militarization and Violence against Women in Conflict Zones in the Middle East: A Palestinian Case Study*. Cambridge: Cambridge University Press, 2009.

Shalhoub-Kevorkian, Nadera. *Security Theology, Surveillance and the Politics of Fear*. Cambridge: Cambridge University Press, 2015.

Shalhoub-Kevorkian, Nadera. "Stolen Childhood: Palestinian Children and the Structure of Genocidal Dispossession." *Settler Colonial Studies* 6, no. 2 (2016): 141–52.

Shamir, Hila. "Migrant Care Workers in Israel: Between Family, Market, and State." *Israel Studies Review* 28, no. 2 (2013): 192–209.

Shani, Eli, Shira Ayal, Yonatan Berman, and Sigal Rozen. *No Safe Haven: Israeli Asylum Policy as Applied to Eritrean and Sudanese Refugees*. Tel Aviv: Hotline for Refugees and Migrants, 2014.

Shapiro, Faydra L. " 'Thank You Israel, for Supporting America': The Transnational Flow of Christian Zionist Resources." *Identities* 19, no. 5 (2012): 616–31.

Shapiro, Maya. "The Development of a 'Privileged Underclass,' Locating Undocumented Migrant Women and Their Children in the Political Economy of Tel Aviv, Israel." *Dialect Anthropol* 37, (2013): 423–41.

Shargel, Baila Round. "American Jewish Women in Palestine: Bessie Gotsfeld, Henrietta Szold, and Zionist Enterprise." *American Jewish History* 90, no. 2 (2002): 141–60.

Sharma, Nandita, and Cynthia Wright. "Decolonizing Resistance, Challenging Colonial States." *Social Justice* 35, no. 3 (2008): 120–38.

Sharon, Ariel. "Speech at Birkenau." Jewish Virtual Library, May 5, 2005. https://www.jewishvirtuallibrary.org/sharon-speech-at-birkenau.

Sharoni, Simona. *Gender and the Israeli-Palestinian Conflict: The Politics of Women's Resistance*. Syracuse, NY: Syracuse University Press, 1995.

Sherwood, Harriet. "Israeli Minister Inflames Racial Tensions with Attacks on 'Infiltrators.'" *Guardian*, May 31, 2012. https://www.theguardian.com/world/2012/may/31/israeli-minister-racial-tensions-infiltrators.

Shkolnik, Ido. "The Caregiver's Choice." Kav LaOved, July 20, 2015. https://www.kavlaoved.org.il/en/the-caregivers-choice/.

Shohat, Ella. "Sephardim in Israel: Zionism from the Standpoint of Its Jewish Victims." *Social Text*, no. 19/20 (1988): 1–35.

Shohat, Ella. "The Invention of the Mizrahim." *Journal of Palestine Studies* 29, no. 1 (1999): 5–20.

Silvey, Rachel, and Rhacel Salazar Parreñas. "Precarity Chains: Cycles of Domestic Worker Migration from Southeast Asia to the Middle East." *Journal of Ethnic and Migration Studies* 40, no. 16 (2020): 1–15.

Simpson, Audra. "On Ethnographic Refusal: Indigeneity, 'Voice' and Colonial Citizenship." *Junctures*, no. 9 (2007): 68–80.

Simpson, Gerry. *Make Their Lives Miserable: Israel's Coercion of Eritrean and Sudanese Asylum Seekers to Leave Israel*. Human Rights Watch, 2014. https://www.hrw.org/report/2014/09/09/make-their-lives-miserable/israels-coercion-eritrean-and-sudanese-asylum-seekers.

Smith, Matthew J. "Settler Colonialism and U.S. Home Missions." *Oxford Research Encyclopedia of Religion*. Oxford: Oxford University Press, 2018.

Smooha, Sammy. *Israel: Pluralism and Conflict*. Berkeley: University of California Press, 1978.

Spade, Dean. *Mutual Aid: Building Solidarity during This Crisis (and the Next)*. New York: Verso, 2020.

Sperling, Daniel. "Commanding the 'Be Fruitful and Multiply' Directive: Reproductive Ethics, Law and Policy in Israel." *Cambridge Quarterly of Healthcare Ethics* 19, no. 3 (2010): 363–71.

Spindler, "UNHCR Appeals to Israel over Forced Relocations Policy." UNHCR, January 9, 2018. https://www.unhcr.org/us/news/briefing-notes/unhcr-appeals-israel-over-forced-relocations-policy.

Staab, Silke, and Kristen Hill Maher. "The Dual Discourse about Peruvian Domestic Workers in Santiago de Chile: Class, Race, and a Nationalist Project." *Latin American Politics and Society* 48, no. 1 (2006): 87–116.

Standing, Guy. "Global Feminization through Flexible Labor." *World Development* 17, no. 7 (1989): 1077–95.

StandWithUs. "Dubbed 'Guards of Gold,' the Israel Defense Force will work with local authorities." Facebook, March 25, 2020. https://www.facebook.com/StandWithUs/photos/a.350931762688/10157288586547689/.

StandWithUs. LinkedIn page. Accessed November 27, 2022. https://www.linkedin.com/company/standwithus.

Stasiulis, Daiva, and Nira Yuval-Davis. "Introduction: Beyond Dichotomies—Gender, Race, Ethnicity and Class in Settler Societies." In *Unsettling Settler Societies: Articulations of Gender, Race, Ethnicity and Class*, 1–38. London: SAGE, 1995.

Steinberg, Gerald M. "Israel at Sixty: Asymmetry, Vulnerability, and the Search for Security." Jerusalem Center for Public Affairs, June 1, 2008. https://jcpa.org/article/israel-at-sixty-asymmetry-vulnerability-and-the-search-for-security/.

Summit Express. "POEA: Israel Hiring Filipino Caregivers with Monthly Salary of Around P75K." *Summit Express*, November 20, 2020. https://www.thesummitexpress.com/2020/11/poea-israel-hiring-caregivers-salary-p75k.html.

Svirsky, Marcelo. "The Reproduction of Settler Colonialism in Palestine." *Journal of Perpetrator Research* 4, no. 1 (2021): 71–107.

Swirski, Barbara, Hatim Kanaaneh, and Amy Avgar. "Health Care in Israel." *Israel Equality Monitor*. Tel Aviv: Adva Center, 1998.

Swirski, Shlomo, Ettie Konor-Attias, Barbara Swirski, and Yaron Yecheskel. *Women in the Labour Force of the Israeli Welfare State*. Tel Aviv: Adva Center, 2001.

Tabar, Linda, and Omar Jabary Salamanca. "After Oslo: Settler Colonialism, Neoliberal Development and Liberation." In *Critical Readings of Development under Colonialism: Towards a Political Economy for Liberation in the Occupied Palestinian Territories*. Palestine: Rosa Luxemburg Siftung Regional Office and Center for Development Studies, 2015.

Tadiar, Neferti X. M. "Uneven Times, Times of Inequity." *Scholar and Feminist Online* 11 no. 1–2 (2013).

Taha, Hebattalla. "Making Cheaper Labor: Domestic Outsourcing and Development in the Galilee." *Anthropology of Work* 41, no. 1 (2020): 24–35.

TallBear, Kim. "Caretaking Relations, Not American Dreaming." *Kalfou* 6, no. 1 (2019): 24–41.

Tamari, Salim. "Normalcy and Violence: The Yearning for the Ordinary in Discourse of the Palestinian-Israeli Conflict." *Journal of Palestine Studies* 42, no. 4 (2013): 48–60.

Tamir, Yossi, and Yossi Avraham. "Minimizing the Use of Foreign Workers: Alternative Approaches to Elderly Care in Israel." [In Hebrew.] *Social Security* 88 (2012): 65–96.

Tang, Eric. *Unsettled: Cambodian Refugees in the NYC Hyperghetto*. Philadelphia: Temple University Press, 2015.

Tatour, Lana. "Citizenship as Domination." *Arab Studies Journal* 27, no. 2 (2019): 8–39.

Telegraph. "Philippine Leader Duterte Eyes Arms Trade on Visit to Israel." September 2, 2018. https://www.telegraph.co.uk/news/2018/09/02/philippine-leader-duterte-eyes-arms-trade-visit-israel/.

Telesur. "Israel Urges Employers to Not Hire Asylum Seekers." April 5, 2016. https://www.telesurenglish.net/news/Israeli-Government-Urges-Employers-to-Not-Hire-Asylum-Seekers-20160405-0011.html.

Threadcraft, Shatema. *Intimate Justice*. Oxford: Oxford University Press, 2016.

Thrush, Coll. *Indigenous London: Native Travelers at the Heart of Empire*. New Haven, CT: Yale University Press, 2017.

Ticktin, Miriam. "Care beyond Innocence." Lecture given at McGill University, Montreal, Quebec, October 18, 2018.

Times of Israel. "52% of Israeli Jews Agree: African Migrants Are 'a Cancer.'" June 7, 2012. https://www.timesofisrael.com/most-israeli-jews-agree-africans-are-a-cancer/.

Tina, Inas. *Violence against the Elderly: Palestine*. New York: UNFPA, 2019.

Trask, Haunani-Kay. "Settlers of Color and 'Immigrant' Hegemony: 'Locals' in Hawai'i." *Amerasia Journal* 26, no. 2 (1996): 1–24.

Trimikliniotis, Nicos, and Mihaela Fulias-Souroulla. "Informalisation and Flexibilisation at Work: The Migrant Woman Precariat Speaks." In *Paradoxes of Integration: Female Migrants in Europe*, edited by Floya Anthias, 59–77. New York: Springer, 2013.

Tronto, Joan C. *Caring Democracy: Markets, Equality, and Justice*. New York: New York University Press, 2013.

Tronto, Joan C. "The 'Nanny' Question in Feminism." *Hypatia* 17, no. 2 (2002): 34–51.

Truong, Thanh-Dam, and Amara Quesada-Bondad. "Intersectionality, Structural Vulnerability, and Access to Sexual and Reproductive Health Services: Filipina Domestic Workers in Hong Kong, Singapore, and Qatar." In *Migration, Gender and Social Justice: Perspectives on Human Security*, edited by Thanh-Dam Truong, Des Gasper, Jeff Handmaker, and Sylvia I. Bergh, 227–39. Heidelberg, Germany: Springer, 2013.

Tuck, Eve, and K. Wayne Yang. "Decolonization Is Not a Metaphor." *Decolonization* 1, no. 1 (2012): 1–40.

Tuck, Eve, and K. Wayne Yang. "Unbecoming Claims: Pedagogies of Refusal in Qualitative Research." *Qualitative Inquiry* 20, no. 6 (2014): 811–18.

Tungohan, Ethel. "From the Politics of Everyday Resistance to the Politics from Below: Migrant Care Worker Activism in Canada." PhD diss., University of Toronto, 2014.

Tungohan, Ethel. "The 'Ideal' Female Migrant as Grateful and Uncomplaining: Gendered Colonial Ideologies, Pre-departure Orientation Sessions, and the

#Ungrateful Filipina." *Journal for Filipinx American and Diasporic Studies* 1, no. 1 (2021): 35–50.

Tungohan, Ethel. "Reconceptualizing Motherhood, Reconceptualizing Resistance: Migrant Domestic Workers, Transnational Hyper-maternalism and Activism." *International Feminist Journal of Politics* 15, no. 1 (2013): 39–57.

Tungohan, Ethel. "The Transformative and Radical Feminism of Grassroots Migrant Women's Movement(s) in Canada." *Canadian Journal of Political Science* 50, no. 2 (2017): 479–94.

Udell, Jacob. "Denied Basic Labor Rights, Migrant Caregivers Take to the Streets." *+972 Magazine*, January 5, 2014. https://www.972mag.com/deprived-of-labor-rights-migrant-caregivers-take-to-the-streets/.

Union of International Associations. "Asian Migrants Coordinating Body (AMCB)." Accessed September 23, 2022. https://uia.org/s/or/en/1100054563.

United Nations Department of Economic and Social Affairs (DESA). *World Population Ageing 2019*. New York: United Nations, 2020. https://www.un.org/en/development/desa/population/publications/pdf/ageing/WorldPopulationAgeing2019-Report.pdf.

Unsettling Minnesota. *Unsettling Ourselves: Reflections and Resources for Deconstructing Colonial Mentality*. Minneapolis: Unsettling Minnesota, 2009.

Vegh, Sandor. "Classifying Forms of Online Activism: The Case of Cyberprotests against the World Bank." In *Cyberactivism: Online Activism in Theory and Practice*, edited by Martha McCaughey and Michael D. Ayers, 71–96. New York: Routledge, 2003.

Veracini, Lorenzo. "Settler Collective, Founding Violence and Disavowal: The Settler Colonial Situation." *Journal of Intercultural Studies* 29, no. 4 (2008): 363–79.

Veracini, Lorenzo. *The Settler Colonial Present*. Basingstoke, UK: Palgrave, 2015.

Vimalassery, Manu, Juliana Hu Pegues, and Alyosha Goldstein. "Colonial Unknowing and Relations of Study." *Theory and Event* 20, no. 4 (2017): 1042–54.

Vinthagen, Stellan, and Anna Johansson. "'Everyday Resistance: Exploration of a Concept and Its Theories." *Resistance Studies Magazine* 1 (2013): 1–46.

Vizenor, Gerald. *Survivance: Narratives of Native Presence*. Lincoln: University of Nebraska Press, 2008.

Vora, Neha. *Impossible Citizens: Dubai's Indian Diaspora*. Durham, NC: Duke University Press, 2013.

Wedeen, Lisa. "Acting 'As If': Symbolic Politics and Social Control in Syria." *Comparative Studies in Society and History* 40, no. 3 (1998): 503–23.

Wedeen, Lisa. "Reflections on Ethnographic Work in Political Science." *Annual Review of Political Science* 13 (2010): 255–72.

Weeks, Kathi. *The Problem with Work: Feminism, Marxism, Antiwork Politics, and Postwork Imaginaries*. Durham, NC: Duke University Press, 2011.

Weinblum, Sharon. "Conflicting Imaginaries of the Border: The Construction of Asylum Seekers in the Israeli Political Discourse." *Journal of Borderlands Studies* 34, no. 5 (2018): 1–17.

Weinglass, Simona. "When Grandma's Caretaker Is a Debt Slave." *Times of Israel*, February 11, 2016. https://www.timesofisrael.com/when-grandmas-caretaker -is-a-debt-slave/.

Weiss, Meira. *The Chosen Body: The Politics of the Body in Israeli Society*. Stanford, CA: Stanford University Press, 2022.

Weissbrod, Rachel. "'Translated People' and the Receiving Culture: Filipino Caregivers in Israeli Literature." *Journal of English Studies and Comparative Literature* 16 (2017): 54–66.

Willen, Sarah. "Citizens, 'Real' Others, and 'Other' Others: The Biopolitics of Otherness and the Deportation of Unauthorized Migrant Workers from Tel Aviv, Israel." In *The Deportation Regime: Sovereignty, Space, and the Freedom of Movement*, edited by Nicholas De Genova and Nathalie Peutz, 262–94. Durham, NC: Duke University Press, 2010.

Willen, Sarah. *Fighting for Dignity: Migrant Lives at Israel's Margins*. Philadelphia: University of Pennsylvania Press, 2019.

Willen, Sarah. "'Flesh of Our Flesh'? Undocumented Migrant Workers' Search for Meaning in the Wake of a Suicide Bombing." In *Transnational Migration to Israel in Global Comparative Perspective*, 159–84. Lanham, MD: Lexington, 2007.

Williams, Fiona. "Care: Intersections of Scales, Inequalities and Crises." *Current Sociology* 66, no. 4 (2018): 547–61.

Williams, Fiona. "The Transnational Political Economy of Care." In *The Global Political Economy of Care: Integrating Ethical and Social Politics*, edited by Rianne Mahon and Fiona Robinson, 21–38. Vancouver: UBC Press, 2011.

Wise, Raúl Delgado, Humberto Márquez Covarrubias, and Ruben Puentes. "Reframing the Debate on Migration, Development and Human Rights." *Population, Space and Place* 19, no. 4 (2013): 430–43.

Wolfe, Patrick. "Settler Colonialism and the Elimination of the Native." *Journal of Genocide Research* 8, no. 4 (2006): 387–409.

Woodly, Deva. "Black Feminist Visions and the Politics of Healing in the Movement for Black Lives." In *Women Mobilizing Memory*, edited by Ayşe Gül Altınay, María José Contreras, Marianne Hirsch, Jean Howard, Banu Karaca, and Alisa Solomon, 219–37. New York: Columbia University Press, 2019.

Workforce Development Agency, Ministry of Labor (Taiwan). "Work Qualifications and Rules for Foreign Workers." August 7, 2017. https://www.wda.gov.tw/en /NewsFAQ.aspx?n=26470E539B6FA395&sms=0FCDB188C74F69A0.

Wuhrgaft, Nurit. "Our Challenge: To Break the Apathy." *Haaretz*, May 6, 2003. https://www.haaretz.com/2003-05-06/ty-article/our-challenge-to-break-the -apathy/0000017f-e3b0-d38f-a57f-e7f29e120000.

Wynter, Sylvia. "Unsettling the Coloniality of Being/Power/Truth/Freedom: Towards the Human, After Man, Its Overrepresentation—an Argument." *New Centennial Review* 3, no. 3 (2003): 257–337.

Yanay, Niza, and Tamar Rapoport. "Ritual Impurity and Religious Discourse on Women and Nationality." *Women's Studies International Forum* 20 (1997): 651–63.

Yiftachel, Oren. *Ethnocracy: Land and Identity Politics in Israel/Palestine*. Philadelphia: University of Pennsylvania Press, 2006.

Ynet. "Yishai: Foreigners Will Bring AIDS, Drugs." *Ynet*, October 31, 2009. https:// www.ynetnews.com/articles/0,7340,L-3798143,00.html.

Yuval-Davis, Nira. "Nationalism, Belonging, Globalization and the 'Ethics of Care.'" *Kvinder, Køn and Forskning* 2, no. 3 (2007): 91–100.

Yuval-Davis, Nira. "National Reproduction and 'the Demographic Race' in Israel." In *Woman-Nation-State*, edited by Nira Yuval-Davis and Floya Anthias, 92–109. New York: St. Martin's, 1989.

Yuval-Davis, Nira. "Women, Citizenship and Difference." *Feminist Review* 57 (1997): 4–27.

Zertal, Idith. *Israel's Holocaust and the Politics of Nationhood*. Cambridge: Cambridge University Press, 2006.

Zetter, Roger. "Refugees and Their Return Home: Unsettling Matters." *Journal of Refugee Studies* 34, no. 1 (2021): 7–22.

Zu'bi, Nahla. "The Development of Capitalism in Palestine: The Expropriation of the Palestinian Direct Producers." *Journal of Palestine Studies* 13, no. 4 (1984): 88–109.

Zureik, Elia. *Israel's Colonial Project in Palestine*. New York: Routledge, 2016.

Zureik, Elia T., and David Lyon. "Coronavirus Surveillance and Palestinians." *Jerusalem Quarterly* 89 (2022): 51–62.

INDEX

Abdo, Nahla, 41, 112

Abdulhadi, Rabab, 108–9, 221n3

Abu Sayyaf (Islamic separatist group), 166

abuse of caregivers: emotional closeness, surveillance, and abuse, 82–90;
physical and verbal, 89, 91–92; sexual,
88–89; spatial intimacy, affective automation, and abuse, 76–82

Abusneineh, Bayan, 33

adult children of employers, 26, 47, 56, 80,
112–13, 117; human shield trope, 7, 75;
"sandwich generation," 102, 107

advertising, 20, 32, 48–49, 101–2, 129–30;
recruitment of seniors to Israel,
61–62

affective automation, 64–66, 239n2; coping through, 77–78, 90–95; and death
of employer, 93; sacrifice, language of,
94–95; spatial intimacy, affective automation, and abuse, 76–82; "thinking
positive," 92–93. *See also* alienation;
emotional labor

"affective blackmail," 51

affective labor, 15, 65, 168, 232–33n24

Afula (northern district of Palestine/
Israel), 1–2

Agatha, Saint, 195–96

Agency for International Development
(MASHAV), 110–11

"aging crisis," 19, 30

aging-in-place, 20, 102, 130

Ahmad, Attiya, 8, 124, 156

Ahmed, Sara, 29, 65, 142

alienation, 2–3, 83, 128; "alienage," 64, 66,
87; disciplinary forms of, 80–81; in the
household, 75–95; and illness, 95–100;
intimacy, alienation, and the state,
66–75; public-private dichotomy,
discourse of, 87–88. *See also* affective
automation

"alien" labor force, 18, 37, 39, 233n24

Alsanah, Riya, 214

Alternative Information Center, 27

American Zion Commonwealth (AMZIC),
1–2

Anglo-American Jews, 126

anti-Blackness, 4, 29, 133, 201–9; caregiver
distancing from asylum seekers,
206–8; gendered forms of, 205–7;
"illegality" as dog whistle for, 207

anti-Zionists, 27, 121–22, 126–27, 134,
135–36

Aquino, Corazon, 22

"Arab," as term, 115

Arbel, Edna (Justice), 97–98, 130

Armon, Shmuel, 121

Ashkenazi, Gabi, 216

Ashkenazi Jews: colonization as entrée into
greater Europeanness, 28; as "natural"
managers of migrants, 37, 42–43, 55,

Commission for the Rights of Foreign
Workers, 73
commitment, collectivist language of,
33–34
"common destiny," myth of, 106, 245n30
"communities of care," 178, 182, 187–88;
online, 198–99. *See also* "backstage"
strategies
comparative racialization, 4, 20, 66; of
Mizrahi Jews, 24, 28, 104, 167; of Palestinians, 24, 28, 32, 68, 104, 136, 164,
166–67
Conference on Jewish Material Claims
against Germany (Claims Conference),
70, 107, 116
conjuncture, 19, 228n136
"conquest of labor," 18, 37–39, 217, 233n33,
234n44
Constable, Nicole, 50, 92
consumers, 4, 42, 49, 55, 132; "settler-
consumers," 111
contracts, 20, 48, 50, 52–54, 144, 188
Convention on the Elimination of All Forms
of Discrimination against Women
(CEDAW), 12
cosmopolitanism, 19, 104, 108–11, 132
Coulthard, Glen, 17, 35, 37
Couples for Christ, 193
COVID-19 pandemic, 30, 210–17; colonial-
capital accumulation during, 210–11;
and "founding generation," 213, 216;
isolation specific to in-home caregiving, 211–12; and lack of health insurance, 213; mutual aid for, 185–86; as
pretense for surveillance, 211, 215
criminalization, 4, 243n77; "blood
brothers" through, 69; criminality, accusations of, 64, 67, 75; of Eritrean and
Sudanese asylum seekers, 204, 206–7;
of migrant workers, 136, 162, 178–79,
197, 203–4; of Palestinians, 21, 69,
204; of political activity by migrants,
179, 181, 203
cuisine and food preparation, 106–7, 113–14,
123–24

Day, Iyko, 11, 18
debility/debilitation, 65, 96–97, 99, 239n11

debt: bondage, 10, 183, 201; and private
agencies, 23, 46–47, 185; relations, of
formerly colonized states, 22
decolonial approaches, 5–7
demographic control, Jewish Israeli, 10,
204; "facts on the ground" and land
expropriation, 9, 43, 66; and "gender
modernity," 127, 134–35; migrant challenges to, 6–7, 28, 33, 141, 150, 178;
mothers as demographic bearers of the
nation, 14
denaturalization, project of, 3, 7, 55, 219n1
deportation, 2–3, 223n55; "closed skies"
policy, 196; community protection
from, 196–97; employer assistance
with hiding from police, 128, 137;
human shield trope, 7, 75; increase
in, 74–75; "Oz Task Force," 196; for
political activity, 179, 203; threat of,
23, 67, 83, 86
deposit fund, 2–3, 145, 197
deservedness, tier of, 209, 214
"desire economy," 88
development tropes, 24, 29, 102–5, 108–11,
127–34; foreign donors in OPT governance, 130; "migration-development"
framework, 127; "mini-aid," 71, 132;
and Mizrahi and Yemenite Jews, 39,
41; and national love of caregivers,
167–68; "premodern," non-European
subjects categorized as, 109, 111
"diagnostic of power," 209
disability, 4, 96, 221n6
discipline, 62, 80–82; bodily, 10, 49–50,
79, 90–92; emotional, 49–50;
resistance to, 87–88
disinvestment, 5, 17–18, 21, 100; and affective automation, 66; contravened by
backstage strategies, 181, 183; in elderly Palestinians, 60
dispossession, 3, 17, 34–35, 37, 41–43, 213,
217; complicity in obscured by "settler
nativism," 105; "dispossessor, theory
of," 102; histories of, 42; justified by
"premodern" categorization, 109; of
migrant workers, 22; normalization of,
105, 110–11; ongoing, 6, 15; and proletarianization, 37; as recursive process,

114–15; regime of, 25; required for Jewish women's equality, 41; and settler self-indigenization, 114–15. *See also* land expropriation

Domestic Workers Convention (C189, 2011), 23

domination, discourse of, 143

Drori, Israel, 203

Duterte, Rodrigo, 68–69

earnings, migrant caregiver, 151; deposit fund requirement, 2–3, 145, 197; overtime pay denied, 48, 61, 72–73, 75; separation pay, 76, 87, 150; unpaid wages and wage theft, 185, 188, 190, 212, 240n19

economic reductionism, narrative of, 133–34

Eisenberg, Aharon, 39

eldercare: as "colonial-capital accumulation," 36–44; comparisons of Palestine/Israel with other countries, 224nn75–79; as "high-trust" work, 67, 72, 75, 77, 241n46; permits for, 10–11, 19–20, 221n20; as reproductive labor, 13–17; as specific kind of care work, 4, 14–15; as status symbol, 19–20, 53–54; in Zionist project, 14. *See also* care work; elderly Jewish Israelis

elderly Jewish Israelis: aging-in-place, 20, 102, 130; as "founding generation," 13–14, 31, 33, 55–56, 60, 137, 213; German benefits provided to, 70, 107, 116; as ideal image of state vulnerability, 5, 20, 36, 44, 161–62; in legal rulings about care workers, 60–61; as link between "Jewish past" and "Israeli present," 33; military care for during COVID-19, 215; from non-European countries, erasure of, 58, 104; Palestinians, fear of, 31–33, 115; popular perceptions of aging, 53; and poverty, 60, 213; social value of, 13; and state's rhetorical claims to fragility, 5, 55, 58, 60, 67, 164; as "symbolic type," 67; as term, 221n4. *See also* adult children of employers; eldercare; employers; Holocaust survivors; Jewish Israelis

elderly Palestinians, 20; disinvestment in, 60; impact of ongoing occupation on, 213–14; Nakba witnesses, 213

El-Haj, Nadia Abu, 33, 239n13

Elia, Nada, 109

emotional labor, 49–52; alleviating employer fears of mistrust, 83; moral claims on, 50–51, 69, 117; performance of required, 3, 51, 65, 75, 112, 117, 120. *See also* affective automation

employers: anti-Black racism of, 208; anti-Zionists, 27, 121–22, 126–27; caring attitude toward, 140–41, 144–45; employer-employee dyad, 32, 64; management of migrants, 37, 42–43, 55, 104, 127–28, 132–33; paternalism by, 15, 90, 188; as state agents of surveillance, 86. *See also* abuse of caregivers; elderly Jewish Israelis; indispensability, relationships of

Eng, David, 87, 221n18

Eretz Yisrael, 106, 114, 175, 225n81

Eritrean and Sudanese asylum seekers, 7, 29, 133, 178–79, 222n44, 255n62; 2014 protest and, 201–2, 204; characterized as "illegal," 206; criminalization of, 204, 206–7; imprisonment of, 201; racialization of, 204–5; referred to as "labor migrants," 205; single mothers, 185–86

ethnic cleansing, 30, 214

eugenics, 5, 14, 33, 42, 215

"everyday conversion," 156–57

"everyday resistance," 141–43, 174, 209, 250n5; mutual aid as, 177–78, 182, 187, 191–92; and national love, 142, 161; strategic avoidance as, 159; as "way of using a system," 142. *See also* national love

exceptionalism, Jewish Israeli, 12, 19, 29, 138, 225n81; and COVID-19 pandemic, 216; high-tech, 107; unsettled and reinforced by migrant caregivers, 142, 164–65

extracontractual work, 52–53, 79–81; refusal to do, 156; as "voluntary," 112–13, 117–19. *See also* labor extraction

"good" and "bad" caregivers, 22, 46, 152, 204, 209

Guards of Gold (IDF), 215

Gulf Cooperation Council (GCC) states, 10, 179, 180

Gutiérrez Rodríguez, Encarnación, 35

Hadassah (Zionist women's organization), 41, 61, 106

Haftom Zarhum, 206

Hall, Stuart, 19, 228n136

Har Adar settlement, 32

Hasso, Frances Susan, 5, 34

Hawara, attacks in, 11

Hazan, Haim, 67

health-care inequalities, 21, 95–100, 240n19; and COVID-19 pandemic, 210–17; mutual aid for, 183–86; normalization of settler health, 100. *See also* injury and illness

Held, Virginia, 15

Herzl, Theodor, 39, 106, 109, 245n34

High Court of Justice (HCJ), 72, 73, 97–98

Hilal, Jamil, 6, 39

Histadrut (Jewish labor union), 40, 135, 203

Hodes, Caroline, 122

Holocaust: invoked against targeting of migrants, 137–38; as justification for violence against Palestinians, 57–59; as key narrative of state, 33, 55–57, 161–62; Philippine government's support for Jewish refugees, 68

Holocaust Remembrance Day speeches, 58–60

Holocaust survivors, 13–14, 55–57, 237n115; German benefits provided to, 70, 107, 116; and Jewish Israeli solidarity with migrants, 137–38; survivors' rights, 69–70. *See also* elderly Jewish Israelis

Holocaust Survivors' Rights Authority, 69

home: contiguous with nation, 3, 13, 28, 36, 64–66; demolition of Palestinian, 5, 43; nationalistic ideologies generated and reinforced by, 66; as site for reproduction of public discourse, 87; as site of injury, resistance, unsettling, and care, 62; specific meaning of in Pales-

tine/Israel, 101–2; unsettling of by migrant care, 8; Zionist notions of, 8. *See also* homemaking, Jewish; household; kinship trope

homemaking, Jewish: based on surplus value from Palestinian and Yemenite women's labor, 40; as central goal of settler projects, 9; Palestinian villages, destruction of, 1–2, 26, 32, 38; as site of Palestinian home destruction, 38, 87. *See also* home; household

Home Work Convention (C177, 1996), 23

Hong Kong, 180

"host" countries, 22

household: apartments, 76; "everyday conversion" in, 156–57; expectation of being "always on," 77, 79, 81, 199; intimacy and alienation in, 75–95; lack of spatial boundaries in, 75; and naturalization of inequalities, 30; religious homes, 122–26; as site of "colonial-capital accumulation," 50–55; unsettling of, 86–87. *See also* home; homemaking, Jewish

humanitarianism, 70–71, 110, 133

human rights law and discourse, 12, 172, 204

human shield trope, 7, 75

Hurricane Yolanda, 71, 186

"imagined community," 9

(im)migrants, 6, 222n41, 37

immigration police, 3, 85–87, 166, 173, 202; employer assistance with hiding from, 128, 137; knowledge of, 160–61. *See also* securitization

imperialism, 4, 20–22, 116, 209; European, 21–22, 28, 35, 58, 64, 115. *See also* colonialism; coloniality; settler colonialism

imprisonment, 74–75; of anti-Zionists, 127; of asylum seekers, 201; and deportation, 196, 197; and "flying visa," 47; Israeli witness required for bailout, 188–89; without COVID-19 precautions, 211

Indian workers, 20, 50–51, 165; migrant-led organizations, 178–79; social media use, 189–90

mographic control, Jewish Israeli; exceptionalism, Jewish Israeli; Palestine/Israel; reproductive regime, Israeli

Israel Defense Forces (IDF), 56, 59, 123; Guards of Gold, 215; medical and disaster relief programs, 70–71, 110. *See also* military

"Israelisation," 123

Israel Ministry of Foreign Affairs, 111

Israel Studies scholarship, 41, 103

Jabotinksy, Zev, 109

Jaffa, 114–15

Jamal, Nimer, 32

Jerusalem Center for Public Affairs, 58

Jewish Israelis: "deproletarianization" of, 42; disavowal of collective violence against Palestinians, 4; elderly, 2; fear of Palestinians, 31–33, 83, 115, 126–27, 135, 172–73, 204–5; as outside settler category, 37–38; as rightful guardians of state, 136–38; territorial and temporal entitlement of, 2–3, 7–8, 66. *See also* elderly Jewish Israelis; Mizrahi Jews; Yemenite Jewish women; Yemenite Jewish workers

Jewish National Fund, 5, 61–62, 221n24

"Jewish state," 14, 39, 56, 59, 111, 135–37, 177, 195, 225n81; caregiver national love for, 141–42, 161, 197; caregiver unsettling of, 150. *See also* Israel; state

Jewish women: Ashkenazi women valorized as pioneers, 14, 17, 40–41, 106, 132, 217; as career women, 108, 117–18, 129–31; and food preparation, 106–7, 113–14, 123–24; matrilineal identity passed down by, 28, 106; as national reproducers, 14, 28, 104, 106–7, 113–14, 117–18. *See also* Mizrahi Jews; Shabbat; Yemenite Jewish women

Johansson, Anna, 142

"judaization," 5, 221n24

Kauanui, J. Kēhaulani, 6

Kav LaOved (Israeli advocacy organization), 45–46, 88–89, 159, 188, 190–91

Khalidi, Rashid, 109

kinship trope, 29, 82–84, 90, 111; kinship as mystification, 112–27; and masking of difference, 122–27; othering function of, 121, 124; and racial unity discourses, 103–4; and risk mitigation strategies, 147, 154; and "voluntary" labor, 112–22. *See also* family; home

Kumari, Tara (caregiver), 74

labor arbitration, privatization of, 48–49

labor extraction, 34; during COVID-19 pandemic, 211–12; enhanced by spatial intimacy, 75–76; land expropriation linked with, 35, 36–37, 43, 233n33. *See also* caregivers, migrant; extracontractual work; migrant workers; reproductive labor; reproductive regime, Israeli

labor markets: Palestinians excluded from, 18; racial/colonial organization of, 23, 34, 42, 170; utility of caregivers to, 128

"labor of care," 178, 182, 184, 198

labor relations: coloniality of, 7, 15; economic reductionism discourse, 133; indigeneity as part of, 6; mystification of, 24; as site of gendering and racialization, 34

Labor Zionism, 37–39, 131

land expropriation, 17–21, 28, 34, 225n84; 1967 occupation, 103; demographic "facts on the ground" generated by migrant labor, 9, 43, 66; "facts on the ground," 9, 43, 66; homemaking as self-justificatory evidence of, 9, 14, 17–18; labor extraction linked with, 35, 36–37, 43, 233n33; nineteenth century, 38; and Palestinian women's presence, 42; purchasing agreements, 1–2; and racial "strength to the land," 106–8, 245n34; settler self-indigenization, 11, 37–38, 105–11, 114–15. *See also* dispossession; settler colonialism

land redemption discourses, 56, 59, 106

Lashkar-e-Taiba (Islamist organization), 207

Lavie, Smadar, 40

Law of Return, 2, 5, 26–27, 74, 113, 132, 221n7; *aliyah*, 125–26, 135; Palestinian rejection of, 135

moral claims, 12, 84, 205–6, 215; differential normalization of, 100, 121; on emotional labor of migrant caregivers, 50–51, 69, 117; "life" as moral category, 216

Moro National Liberation Front (Philippines), 166

moshavot/moshavim (colony, rural Jewish settlements), 40, 42, 109

Mumbai attacks (2008), 207

Mundlak, Guy, 64, 67, 72, 240n19

Murphy, Michelle, 6

mutual aid, 160, 181; as "everyday resistance," 177–78, 182, 187, 191–92; as form of everyday resistance, 187; for health-care provision, 183–86; hybrid space of, 192; and migrant networks, 23–24, 42, 177–78. *See also* welfare provision by migrant caregivers

mystification, 7; kinship as, 112–27; of labor relations, 24, 117; of structural conditions, 116–18

Nadasen, Premilla, 198

Nakba, 41, 56, 213

Natan (recruitment agency), 129–30

National Alliance of Filipino Communities (NAFILCO), 181

National Association of International Manpower Companies, 121

national family, 104–7, 112–13, 116, 119, 121, 144; cultural and religious reproduction of, 124; "settler nativism" and the neoliberal family, 105–11

national helpers, migrant caregivers as, 28, 67–69, 75, 84, 174–75

nationalist discourse, 33, 167

national love, 9, 29, 161–72; of caregivers for "Jewish state," 141–42, 161, 197; and development tropes, 167–68; in relation to other "destination" countries, 170–71; secular, 166–67

Nation-State Bill (2018), 11

naturalization: of care work, 3, 15, 55, 74, 152, 198; of poverty, 30, 126; of settler state, 3, 5, 30, 65, 71, 219n1, 239n13

Nefesh B'Nefesh organization, 61–62

"neoliberal feminism," 108–9

neoliberal restructuring, 17–21; and contemporary "colonial-capital accumulation," 44–55; and contracts, 20; "enclosure and indirect rule" created by, 18–19; "market-based strategy of colonization," 45, 130; and Oslo Peace Accords, 11–12, 18, 104, 130; and settler colonialism, 9, 11; start-up discourse, 6, 10, 104, 109–10, 247n65; structural adjustment, 7, 21, 134. *See also* flexibilization/precaritization

Nepal earthquake (2015), 187

Nepalese workers, 20, 47, 93, 145, 172; assigned to Palestinian families, 170; and bilateral agreement, 49; migrant-led organizations, 178; mutual aid for, 184–85

Netanyahu, Benjamin, 68–69, 74, 133, 204–5; caregiver support for, 156

Netanyahu, Sara, 74

networks, migrant, 9, 16, 21, 29–30; mutual aid and service provision, 23–24, 42, 177–78; spiritual networks and community safety, 196–201; spiritual networks of support, 192–96

Neve Sha'anan, 192, 202, 206–9

"new Jew," 14, 123, 217

Nichols, Robert, 114–15

normalization: of dispossession, 105, 110–11; of precarity, 100; of settler emplacement, 3, 6, 100, 134–38, 142; of settler health, 100

"Nursing and Nursing Care" website, 134

Organization for Economic Co-operation and Development (OECD) countries, 10

organizations, migrant-led, 178, 202–3; preexisting communication structures, 184–85

orientalist tropes, 5, 109

Oslo Peace Accords, 11–12, 18, 104; and neoliberal restructuring, 11–12, 18, 104, 130; post-Oslo reserves of surplus labor, 11–12, 18, 45, 228n132

Other: migrant workers as "'Other' Others," 7; Palestinians as "'Real' Others," 7, 203

"Oz Task Force," 196

Palestine: global movement for liberation of, 143; historic land of, 219n1; Jewish state established in, 14; Nakba, 41, 56, 119, 213; "next year in Jerusalem" mandate, 119; "Palestinian occupied territories," as term, 6; Palestinian villages, destruction of, 1–2, 26, 32, 38; proletarianization of economy, 42. *See also* West Bank and Gaza Strip, Occupied

Palestine/Israel: aging population statistics, 11, 19–20, 103; as "Jewish state," 14, 39, 56, 59, 111, 135–37, 141–42, 150, 161, 177, 195, 225n81; jus sanguinis citizenship regime, 4, 10, 136; late entrance of migrant workers into labor market, 179–80; liability for migrant political activity in, 158–59, 179, 181, 203; migrant-led organizations in, 178; neoliberal restructuring in, 4, 18–19, 45; non-European subjects as "premodern," 109; normalized as Jewish homeland, 142; Palestinian citizens, 20, 104, 109–10; second intifada, 34, 162–63, 169; as second-tier destination country, 22–23, 144, 171–72; situating, 9–13; as term, 219n1; waves of settlement, 37–38. *See also* Eritrean and Sudanese asylum seekers; Israel; Palestine; settler colonialism; visas; West Bank and Gaza Strip, Occupied

Palestinians: agricultural labor, 41–43; as "available for injury," 67, 96; Christian, 166; and comparative racialization, 24, 28, 32, 68, 104, 136, 164, 166–67; debilitation of, 65, 96, 99; disavowal of collective violence against, 4; disinvestment in, 5, 18, 60; displacement of, 38; in domestic spaces, Jewish imaginary of, 31–33; European oppressors linked with, 57–58; expelled in 1948, 38; as "infiltrators," 12, 32, 38, 88, 133, 204, 255n60; internal displacement of, 232n21; Israeli citizens, 20, 104, 109–10; Jewish Israeli fear of, 31–33, 83, 115, 126–27, 135, 172–73, 204–5; as maids in Palestinian homes, 235–

36n70; ongoing killing of, 5, 219–20n1, 226n91; as "'Real' Others," 7; seen as untrustworthy, 31–32; "terrorist," Jewish Israeli imaginary of, 32, 68–69, 136, 167, 207; women's movement, 225n87

Pappé, Ilan, 58

paternalism, 15, 90, 188

Paul, Anju Mary, 171

"pedagogies of refusal," 160–61

permission, culture of, 90

permits for eldercare, 10–11, 19–20, 221n20

Philippines, 230n156; Abu Sayyaf, 166; bilateral agreements with Israel, 23, 45, 49, 230n160, 230n163; caregivers positioned as national helpers, 67–69, 174–75; corruption in, 175, 214; migrant-led organizations, 178; Moro National Liberation Front, 166; sex workers in South Korea, 67; support for Jewish refugees, 68; US and European imperialism in, 21–22; vote for State of Israel, 68. *See also* Filipinx workers

Philippines Overseas Employment Administration (POEA), 49

Physicians for Human Rights study, 97

Piastro, Claudia Pietro, 114, 123

Pioneer Women (Na'amat), 106

Pitchaimuthu, Jayaseelan, 165

Planters' Society, 39

poverty: and development discourse, 104, 127, 133–34; economic reductionist view, 133–34; of elderly Jewish Israelis, 60, 213; naturalization of, 30, 126. *See also* debility/debilitation; development tropes; dispossession

predeparture orientations (PDOs), 49, 123

pregnancy, 90, 193–94; policy against, 2, 9–10, 45, 99

"premodern"/"primitive," non-European subjects categorized as, 109, 111, 131

Prevention of Infiltration Law (1954), 204, 255n62

primitive accumulation, 17, 233n28

privatization, 7, 18–20, 44, 60, 132; coloniality of, 35–36, 55; of Israel's security industry, 45; of labor arbitration, 48–49

proletarianization, 37, 39–40, 233n28; of Palestinian economy, 41–42
pronatalism, 5, 14, 61, 175
Puar, Jasbir, 96–97, 239n11, 243n77
public-private dichotomy, discourse of, 87–88

Rabin, Yitzhak, 18, 32
"racial Fordist economy," 120, 128
racialization: "Arab" as term, 115; of asylum seekers, 204–5; of bodily discipline, 49–50; of care work, 22, 24, 36, 44–45, 49–50, 132, 241–42n47; colonialism and hierarchies of, 7, 11, 35, 40, 45, 109, 111; comparative, 4, 20, 28, 66, 68, 104, 136, 166–67; devaluation enabled by, 44, 54; and fee hierarchy, 32, 35–36, 45; gendered, 40–41, 44, 132, 214–15; of injury and illness, 67, 96; of intimacy, 66–68, 86–87, 221n18; of Palestinian and Yemenite women as less feminine, 40–41; "racial Fordist economy," 120, 128; recruitment agency stereotypes of caregivers, 22, 28, 32, 36, 50–51; of South and Southeast Asians as benign, 32; and "strength to the land," 106–8, 245n34
Ramallah, 166
Ramleh, 166
RavGil recruitment agency, 48–49
Raz, Doron, 213–14
recruitment agencies, 45–50; advertising, 20, 32, 48–49, 61–62, 101–2, 129–30; contestation of practices, 23, 158, 188–91, 217; economic reductionism employed by, 134; gendered and racialized stereotypes of caregivers, 22, 28, 32, 36, 50–51; hierarchical ladder of fees, 20, 32, 35–36, 45–48; illegal brokerage fees charged by, 22–23, 37, 45–46, 171, 181, 185, 217; secret "price-setting" processes, 47–48; as sites of "colonial-capital accumulation," 36, 45, 49
Recruitment Specification Form (POEA), 49
redemption discourses, 56, 59, 104, 106
refugees, 99, 111; Ashkenazi Jews positioned as, 12; "indigenous Pal-

estinians," 221n3; Jewish, during Holocaust, 68. *See also* Eritrean and Sudanese asylum seekers
regeneration discourse, 33, 43, 106
religion: Catholic Church, 163, 182, 193–95, 254n40; Christian Evangelism, 166; religious homes, 122–26; spiritual networks of support, 192–201; surveillance of migrant caregivers at events and churches, 195–97. *See also* Shabbat
remittances, 127, 175, 183, 197, 202, 230n156
reproductive labor: coloniality of, 39–43; eldercare as, 13–17; feminist valuation of, 6; and imperialism, 21–22; as land and labor relation, 35, 36–37; role in colonization, 9. *See also* caregivers, migrant; labor extraction
reproductive regime, Israeli, 174–75; "antilife" produced through, 177; coloniality of, 4–5, 28, 35, 232n17; differential provisioning and elimination of resources, 34; disinvestment in other lives, 5, 17–18, 60; Palestinian debility as condition for, 97; precarity produced by, 44; and vulnerability discourse, 34
resistance: caregivers' rights rally, Tel Aviv (2014), 176–77, 201; and criminalization of migrant worker, 178–79; deliberate slowness, 157; to employer surveillance, 87–88; "everyday," 141–43, 159, 161, 174, 177–78, 182, 187, 191–92, 209, 250n5; "hidden transcripts," 143; lack of political space for, 142–43, 202; to land expropriation, 42; liability for migrant political activity, 158–59, 179, 181, 203; May 2021 strike, 214; post-Oslo restructuring as attempt to suppress, 130; pressure from outside Israel, 218; recoded as irrational threat, 59, 69, 87; "resistance economy," 41; "tacit skills" as, 146. *See also* risk mitigation strategies of migrant caregivers
return, right of, 2, 12, 221n7
Rifkin, Mark, 102–3

South and Southeast Asians, 12, 32–33, 36, 126, 209
"spacio-cide," 106
Spade, Dean, 178
spiritual networks of support, 192–96; and community safety, 196–201
Sri Lankan caregivers, 160, 183–85, 188
StandWithUs public relations group, 215
start-up discourse, 6, 10, 104, 109–10, 247n65
Start-Up Nation (Senor and Singer), 110
state: care instrumentalized by, 16; decolonial critiques of, 5–6; fragility discourse, 5, 55, 58, 60, 67, 164; Holocaust as key narrative of, 33, 55–57, 161–62; intimacy and alienation in rhetoric of, 66–75; justification for depletion of Palestinian resources, 57–59; normalization of 1948 boundaries, 6, 103; retrenchment policies, 21, 44, 55; temporality as technology of, 8. *See also* Israel; "Jewish state"; Palestine; Palestine/Israel
state collectivist, 20, 33–34, 127
state of emergency, 4, 12, 226n91
structural conditions: as inevitable, 127; mystification of, 116–18
subjectivity, self-management of, 91
substitute caregivers, 152–53, 221n6
surplus labor reserves, 11–12, 18, 45, 55, 228n132
surrogacy of caregivers, 66, 70, 76–78, 80, 98
surveillance of migrant caregivers, 3, 9–10, 64, 171; camera installation, 83–85; COVID-19 as pretense for, 211, 215; emotional closeness, surveillance, and abuse, 82–90; employers as state agents, 86; in intimate spaces, 80–81; at religious events and churches, 195–97

Tabar, Linda, 104
"tacit skills," 51, 140, 142, 144, 151, 153, 155, 187; as resistance skills, 146
Taj Haroun, 208
Takhana Merkazit (Tel Aviv Central Bus Station), 71, 198, 202
Tal'at feminist movement, 214

Tatour, Lana, 136
Tel Aviv: built upon Palestinian villages, 26; caregivers' rights rally (2014), 176–77, 201; as "First Hebrew City," 114; as "migrant-worker capital of Israel," 108; Mizrahi Jews in, 202, 208; policing of migrants in, 85, 87; Takhana Merkazit (Tel Aviv Central Bus Station), 71, 198, 202
Telegraph article, 59
temporal imaginaries, 111
temporality: boundaries, 172–75; settler time, 6, 65, 102, 127, 178; and territorial entitlement, 2–3, 7–8, 178–79
territorial control: demographic management, 134–35
"terrorist," imaginary of, 32, 68–69, 136, 167, 207
topography of risk, 3–4, 64, 87, 90, 95, 209
trafficked migrant victims, 23
transnational context, migrant caregiver organizing in, 179–82
trauma: employers attuned to migrant vulnerability, 137; managed by caregivers, 56–57, 69–70; of Palestinians erased, 138; projected onto Israeli state, 136
Tronto, Joan, 17
trust, 72–75; eldercare as "high-trust" work, 67, 72, 75, 77, 241n46; emotional labor of alleviating employer fears, 83
Tuck, Eve, 105, 160
Tungohan, Ethel, 49, 192

undocumented caregivers, 3, 128; knowledge of immigration police, 160–61; live-out, 89, 126, 185
unions, 179–80, 203
United Nations Committee on the Status of Women, 111
United Nations conventions, 12
United Nations Relief and Works Agency (UNRWA), 27
United States, 9, 11; Black women's labors exploited in, 15–16
universalism, liberal tropes of, 7, 11, 136, 161

unsettling: by anti-Zionist citizens, 121–22, 126–27, 134, 135–36; "frontstage" and "backstage" strategies as, 29, 150; of household, 86–87, 90, 150, 155; in indigenous and migration studies, 65–66; of "Jewish state," 150; migrant caregiving as site of, 34–35; of settler-native binary, 4, 6, 8, 16; of temporal boundaries, 141; unsettled labors, 3, 5–10, 74

Uzan, Aharon, 42

Vinthagen, Stellan, 142

visas: for construction workers, 18; of dead people used by agencies, 48; deposit fund requirement, 2–3, 145, 197; extension of, 2, 7–8, 15; extension of, calls for, 69–70; "flying visa," 47, 145; and hierarchy of recruitment fees, 22–23, 45; "*shiva* rules," 145; short length of residency, 7–8, 87–88, 179; special visas, 2, 87, 94, 147–49, 154, 157, 221n6; "stretching" time allotted by, 2, 7–8, 64, 140, 141, 145–49, 153, 157, 192; for substitute caregivers, 221n6

vulnerability: of collective body, 28, 34, 36, 69; discourses of affixed to nation, 60, 67; divergent valuations of elderly and caregivers, 61–62; of elderly, 5, 13–14, 34; hierarchical ordering of, 36; Jewish national, 5, 14, 28, 106; of migrant labor force, 19–20, 67

Wedeen, Lisa, 24, 162
Weerawat Karunborirak, 203
Weinblum, Sharon, 204
Weizmann, Chaim, 109
welfare provision by migrant caregivers, 182–87; for hometown regions, 181, 183, 186–87; "voluntary care," 182, 187. *See also* mutual aid
West Bank and Gaza Strip, Occupied: 2023 attacks on Gaza, 219–20n1; "bantustanisation" of, 18, 228n132; caregiver visits to, 168–69; checkpoints, 18, 173; May 2021 strike, 207, 214; Palestinian domestic workers in, 42–43;

"Palestinian occupied territories," as term, 6; political economy and shifts in reproductive labor, 42–43; post-Oslo reserves of surplus labor, 11–12, 18, 45, 228n132; segmenting of workforce, 18, 43, 45, 130. *See also* Palestine

Willen, Sarah, 7, 69, 74
Work and Rest Hours Law, 188
"working-class settlers," 6, 119, 248n86
World Bank, 21
World Zionist Organization (WZO), 39

Yang, K. Wayne, 105, 160
Yavnieli, Shmuel, 38
Yemenite Jewish women: racialized as less feminine, 40–41; as "working-class settlers," 43, 119. *See also* Mizrahi Jews
Yemenite Jewish workers, 37–40, 234n44; as "alien" labor force, 39
Yishai, Eli, 74–75, 172, 206, 255n60
Yom Ha'atzmaut, Israeli Independence Day, 167

Zertal, Idith, 55–56
Zionism, 5–8, 33, 234n45; Ashkenazi women valorized as pioneers, 14, 17, 40–41, 106, 132, 217; Bible, historicization of, 72, 104, 105–6, 122–23, 166–67; "birthright" ideology, 7–8, 26–27, 105, 115, 225n81; as bodily revolution, 33; "common destiny," 106, 245n30; "conquest of labor" period, 18, 37–39, 217, 233n33, 234n44; displacement of indigenous populations as primary goal of, 39; disturbances in, 161; Labor Zionists, 37–39, 131; liberal, 104–5, 128, 135–37, 213–14; "new Jew," 14, 123, 217; non-Jewish reproductive labors required to uphold, 17–18, 40; as oppressor of Palestinian women, 109; pressure on migrant workers to express loyalty to, 12, 126; pronatalist policies, 5, 14, 61, 175; youthfulness, emphasis on, 14, 36, 44, 135, 231–32n11. *See also* Ashkenazi Jews; Christian Zionism; "founding generation"; Israel; Palestine/Israel

www.ingramcontent.com/pod-product-compliance
Lightning Source LLC
Chambersburg PA
CBHW030821290525
27270CB00016B/147